CONTENTS

The guide does not describe all the sights in New England. It presents, as do all Michelin Green Guides, a selection of the points of interest. The **stars** will assist the traveler whose time is limited in choosing the points of interest to visit.

***Worth a journey**
**Worth a detour*
Interesting

Other **Michelin Green Guides** available in English are:

Austria
Canada
England: The West Country
Germany
Greece
Italy
Portugal
Scotland
Spain
Switzerland

London
New York City
Paris
Rome

Brittany
Châteaux of the Loire
Dordogne
French Riviera
Normandy
Provence

NEW ENGLAND

Named in 1614 by Captain John Smith, New England includes the six northeastern states: Connecticut, Maine, Massachusetts, New Hampshire, Rhode Island and Vermont, and has traditionally had as its capital Boston.

The relatively small size of this corner of the country gives no hint of the important influence New England has exerted on the political, cultural, and economic development of the nation. For it was here that American independence was born, that the American culture was nurtured, that one of the best educational systems in the world developed, and that the American economy, turning from the sea to industrialization, came of age.

An Idyllic Region. – The region's unspoiled natural beauty is one of its foremost attractions. Along the rocky, indented coastline small fishing villages hug the shores of coves and bays, their quiet disturbed only by the sounds of the sea gulls and the waves calmly lapping on the shore. Against this coast, man can stand amidst the dunes of Cape Cod and in the words of Henry David Thoreau: "... put all America behind him."

Traveling inland, gentle hill-and-dale landscapes, blanketed with thick woodlands, are speckled with tiny white villages, their church spires rising above the trees and meadows. Narrow back roads wind through the countryside, passing over covered wooden bridges and beside quiet, crystal clear trout-filled streams. In the heart of the interior this serene setting is interrupted by the White Mountains, a looming mountain mass that includes Mount Washington, the highest point on the east coast.

Broad sandy beaches, the finest ski areas in the eastern United States, beautiful summer resorts, and a network of hiking trails that includes a major portion of the Appalachian Trail, have added to New England's image as a year-round vacation place.

Especially scenic are:

Acadia National Park★★★ (Me.) p 58
The Berkshires★★★ (Mass.) p 84
Blue Hill and Deer Isle ★★ (Me.) p 65

Cape Cod National Seashore ★★★ (Mass.) p 122
Northern Vermont★★ p 196
The White Mountains★★★ (N.H.) p 171

Cultural Offerings. – Culturally, the region is distinguished by its large number of museums and the high quality of the programs of music, dance and theater presented in the cities, at summer festivals and by universities and colleges.

Its wealth of architecture is varied, with splendid examples of the styles that have dominated from the colonial days to the present. The historical houses, rich in character, are restored with loving attention to detail and good taste, reflecting the reverence New Englanders have for the past.

These museums and museum villages are outstanding:

Museum of Fine Arts★★★ p 105
Isabella Stewart Gardner Museum★★★
   (Boston, Mass.) p 107
Clark Art Institute★★★
   (Williamstown, Mass.) p 158
Yale University Art Gallery★★
   (New Haven, Conn.) p 50
Hancock Shaker Village ★★★ (Mass.) p 129
Peabody Museum★★ (Salem, Mass.) p148
Mystic Seaport★★★ (Mystic, Conn.) p 45

Museum of Art, RISD★★
   (Providence, R.I.) p 190
Wadsworth Atheneum★★
   (Hartford, Conn.) p 42
Fruitlands Museums★★
   (Harvard, Mass.) p 129
Shelburne Museum★★★
   (Shelburne, Vt.) p 204
Maine Maritime Museum★★ (Bath, Me.) p 62
Old Sturbridge Village★★★
   (Sturbridge, Mass.) p 155

The Cities. – New England's cities developed first along the coast and are marked by their maritime past, with warehouses, custom houses and sea captains' homes huddled close to the waterfront. The decline that afflicted these and other major urban areas in the first half of the 20C as businesses and the population moved out to the suburbs, reversed itself in the 1960s and 1970s, as interest in revitalizing the cities led to the renovation of old warehouses and buildings into shops, restaurants and apartments. The lively new shopping malls and squares created as a result of these programs are delightful places to enjoy the flavor of the city's past, especially:

Massachusetts
Boston: Faneuil Hall Marketplace
Salem: Essex Street and Pickering Wharf
Newburyport: Market Square District
Nantucket: Main Street, Straight Wharf

New Hampshire
Portsmouth: Strawbery Banke

Rhode Island
Providence: South Main Street and Benefit Street
Newport: Bowen's Wharf, Easton's Point

Maine
Portland: Old Port Exchange

The Villages. – The small villages that dot the map of New England, are the heart of the region and typify the way of life of many of its people. Carefully planned and laid out, they are compact, picturesque units of white wooden houses dominated by the spire of the local church. In the center of the village is the **Green**, known also as the **Common**. This park-like space, formerly used as grazing land, a military training field, and a public meeting place, was originally owned in "common" by the members of the community. On the Green there may be a bandstand that is used for concerts in the summer.

Flanking the Green are the traditional elements of a New England village: the **Church** or **Meetinghouse**; the **Town Hall** – the site of town meetings, still the basis of local government in many New England villages; the **Country Store** – which often houses the post office as well; the **Inn** – a large comfortable dwelling that provides lodging and also serves as a restaurant; and the **Burial Ground** – generally enclosed by a low-lying stone wall.

For a selection of the picturesque villages in New England, see the Michelin tourist map accompanying this guide.

4

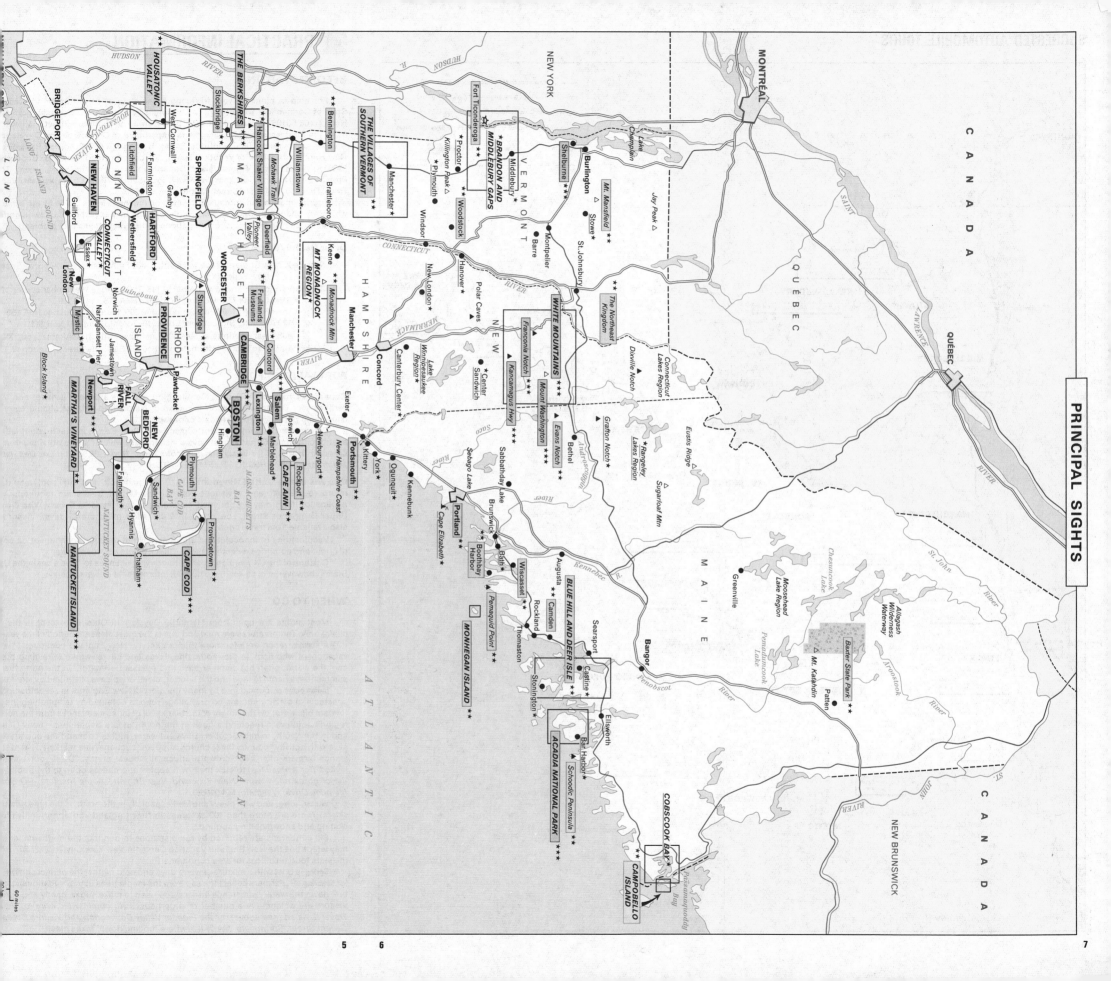

PRINCIPAL SIGHTS

SUGGESTED AUTOMOBILE TOURS

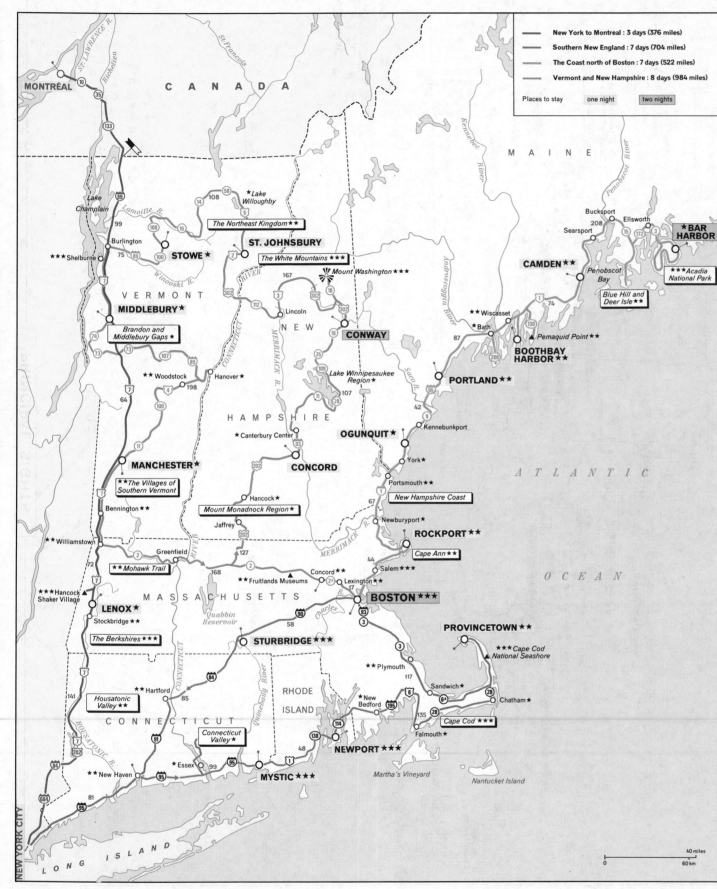

BEFORE STARTING

For help in planning your trip consult the state office of tourism in **Connec**... State of Connecticut Department of Economic Development, 210 Washington S... Hartford CT 06106; in **Maine:** Maine Publicity Bureau, 97 Winthrop Street, Hallowell 04347; in **Massachusetts:** Massachusetts Department of Commerce and Developm... Division of Tourism, 100 Cambridge Street, Boston MA 02202; in **New Hampshire.** New Hampshire Office of Vacation Travel, 105 Loudon Road, Box 856, Concord 03301; in **Rhode Island:** Rhode Island Department of Economic Development, To... Promotion Division, 7 Jackson Walkway, Providence, RI 02903; in **Vermont:** Ver... Travel Division, 134 State Street, Montpelier, VT 05602.

Tourist information bureaus (indicated on the maps in the guide by the symb... which will be found along the major highways and in many cities and towns gene... offer assistance in finding accommodations and solving other travel problems.

Other Useful Addresses

– in **New York** New England Vacation Center: 630 Fifth Avenue, Concourse Shop... 2, New York, NY 10111.
– in **Canada** Vermont Information Center: 1117 St Catherine West, near corner of ... Street, Suite 710, Montreal, Quebec H3A 1T6.
  Travel USA: 1405 Peel Street, Suite 300, Montreal, Quebec H3A 1S5.
  120 Adelaide Street West, Suite 916, Toronto, Ontario N5H 1T1.
  808 West Hootings, Suite 840, Vancouver, British Columbia, V6C 2X4.
– in **London** American Tourist Information Office: 22 Sackville Street, London W. I.

FORMALITIES FOR:

Canadian Citizens. – Proof of identification (such as a driver's license) and a ... certificate or Canadian passport is required. Naturalized citizens should carry ... citizenship papers, card, certificate or passport.

Permanent residents (except citizens of British Commonwealth countries) ... are not citizens of Canada must have a visitor's visa which may be obtained from ... **Consulate General of the United States,** *South Tower Room 28, Complexe Des Jar...* *Montreal, Quebec H5B 1G1* ℡ *(514) 281-1886.*

Citizens of the United Kingdom. – A 10 year passport valid until confirmed da... return to the UK, and a visitor's visa for the United States are required. A ... application form may be obtained by writing to the: **American Embassy Visa Bran...** Upper Grosvenor Street, London W 1A 2 JB (allow minimum 28 days). Visitor's ... also available from travel agents.

Vaccinations or innoculations are generally not required (contingent on co... of origin and countries recently visited). Check before your departure.

Citizens of the UK need only carry their driving licenses to drive a car in the U... States; however, it is advisable to hold an International Driver's License.

WHEN TO GO

Most sights are open from Memorial Day to mid-October (except in the ... cities) only. Temperatures are mild and this is the most pleasant period of the year ...

A **summer** resort area for more than a century, New England continues to at... vacationers who flock to the mountains, lakes and shore, where refreshing bre... cool the warm, often hot summer days and pleasant evenings. In the north the ... summer days begin to fade into the shorter, clear, crisp days of autumn by late Au...

Indian summer, considered by many the glory of New England, is accompanied ... spectacle of blazing autumn color. Foliage reports obtained by telephoning the ... tourism offices follow the height of the blanket of color as it advances from the nort... regions southward reaching a peak in the north, in late September – early Octo... and in the south, in mid-October. Days are warm, nights cool and the countrysi... alive with activity: country fairs, church suppers, auctions, flea markets... at road ... stands farmers offer fresh-grown produce at modest prices. "Do-it-yourselfers" ... invited *(for a small fee)* to pick their own apples at orchards open to the public ... *list of areas open write: New York and New England Apple Institute, PO Box ... Mainline Drive, Westfield, MA 01086).*

Winter, long, and with heavy snowfall especially in the north, is the time awaite... skiers. There are more than 100 ski areas in New England and opportunities fo... skating and snowmobiling abound.

Ski conditions are reported by radio stations throughout the northeast, or s... may telephone the New England Vacation Center in New York City ℡ *(212) 307-57...* the state tourism offices for area conditions.

Spring is brief with a mixture of warm days and cold nights, the perfect combina... for **sugaring off.** Farmers collect the sap from the maple trees in the "sugar bushes," ... boil down the watery substance into a syrup used to make sugar, candy and spre... Visitors are welcome at a number of sugarhouses *(to obtain a list write to: Ver...* *Travel Division (see above), or the Pioneer Valley Convention and Visitors Burea... Dwight Street, Springfield, MA 01103)* where "boiling down" takes place.

GETTING AROUND

By Air. – The principal airports are Logan International Airport (Boston), Bradley International Airport (Windsor Locks, Conn.), and Bangor International Airport (Bangor, Maine).

Airline service between New York City and Boston is offered by: Continental Airlines, Delta, Eastern, Pan Am and TWA. Consult the Yellow Pages for locations and telephone numbers.

By Train. – Amtrak Service:
– from New York City to major cities in New England (New York - Boston: 3 hours 55 min). Toll-free from New York and New England ℡ (800) 872-7245.
– from Montreal to Springfield, Mass. and to New Haven, Conn.

By Bus. – Most cities and towns in New England are accessible by one or more of the three major bus companies which operate in the region.

In New York City, buses depart from the Port Authority Terminal (8th Avenue and 41st Street). For information ℡: Greyhound (212) 635-0800
Trailways, Inc. (212) 730-7460
Bonanza (212) 635-0800

In Boston contact: Greyhound: 10 St. James Avenue ℡ (617) 423-5810
Trailways, Inc.: 555 Atlantic Avenue ℡ (617) 426-7838
Bonanza: 10 St. James Avenue ℡ (617) 423-5810

By Car. – This is the best way to travel around and see New England. Rental cars are available at car rental agencies, at most airports, and at rental offices in hotels, or check the yellow pages of the telephone directory.

Major companies have worldwide reservations systems and toll-free telephone numbers:

Avis	(800) 331-1212	Budget Rent-A-Car	(800) 527-0700
Hertz	(800) 654-3131	Thrifty Rent-A-Car	(800) 331-4200
National Car Rental	(800) 328-4567		

Driving in New England. – The speed limit on major highways is 55 mph and is strictly enforced. Speed limits on some highways and other roads range from 20 to 55 mph.

Most states have special regulations regarding trailers (speed limits, parking). Check with the state motor vehicle department.

Right hand turn on a red light is permitted throughout New England unless otherwise posted.

The "school bus" law is in effect in the six-state area: the motorist must bring his vehicle to a complete stop before reaching a school bus that has come to a halt to load or unload children. The motorist may not proceed until the warning signals on the school bus are deactivated, or until he is directed to do so by a police officer or other authorized person on duty.

SIGHTSEEING

During recent years many points of interest formerly open in the summer only, have extended their season from mid-April (or early May) through late October. Call ahead if you plan to visit on a holiday. A reduction in admission is generally available for senior citizens, students and children under 12. Inquire before purchasing tickets.

THE OUTDOORS

Camping. – There are many campsites in state and federal parks and forests and in private campgrounds. Reservation information and regulations regarding the use of public campgrounds vary and are available from state tourism bureaus *(p 10)*.

Hunting and Fishing. – Laws and licensing procedures vary. Contact state agencies for information regarding dates of open season and regulations.

Trails. – Many trail systems including the **Appalachian Trail,** a 2 035 mile footpath from Georgia to Maine, lace the region. The **Long Trail** in Vermont follows the ridge of the Green Mountains. Hikers are cautioned to be well equipped and advised regarding weather conditions when hiking in higher elevations in particular.

During the months of June and July insect repellant should be carried to counteract the large number of black flies. The bug season ends by late August. Hikers should carry good detailed trail guides and maps of the area in which they plan to hike *(see Books to Read p 210.)*

Useful Addresses:

Connecticut: Department of Environmental Protection, Information and Education, State Office Building, Hartford CT 06106 (camping, hunting, fishing).

Maine: Department of Inland Fisheries and Wildlife, 284 State Street, Augusta ME 04333.
Superintendent, Acadia National Park, PO Box 177, Bar Harbor, ME 04609.

Massachusetts: Division of Fisheries and Wildlife, 100 Cambridge Street, Boston, MA 02202 (fishing, hunting).

New Hampshire: Fish and Game Department, 34 Bridge Street, Concord, NH 03301.

Rhode Island: Division of Fish and Wildlife, Government Center, Tower Hill Road, Wakefield, RI 02879 (fishing, hunting).

Vermont: Department of Fish and Wildlife, 103 Main Street, 10 South Building, Waterbury, VT 05676 (fishing, hunting).

Green Mountain National Forest Supervisor, GMNF, PO Box 519, Rutland, VT 05701.

Agency of Environmental Conservation, Department of Forests and Parks, Division of Parks, Waterbury, VT 05676 (bicycle touring, camping).

Appalachian Trail Conference: PO Box 807, Harpers Ferry, West Virginia 25425.

Appalachian Mountain Club: 5 Joy Street, Boston, MA 02108 or Pinkham Notch Camp, Gorham, NH 03581.

The Green Mountain Club: 43 State Street, PO Box 889, Montpelier, VT 05602.

United States Forest Service: 719 Main Street, PO Box 638, Laconia, NH 03246.

United States Geological Survey. – Topographic maps are available from USGS, Map Distribution, Box 25286, Federal Center, Denver, CO 80225.

WHERE TO STAY

Accommodations range from modest to super deluxe and are usually found in clusters on the edge of a town or city where two or more highways intersect. In rural areas they line the roads that are frequently traveled by the tourist such as Route 16 in the White Mountains, and coastal Route 1. Major chains have toll-free reservation numbers.

Bed and Breakfast (B&B) accommodations in private homes are generally an economical alternative for the traveler, especially in urban areas. Rates range from $40-$85 for a double and include breakfast which can mean anything from a cup of coffee to an elaborate meal. For information contact the state offices of tourism *(p 10)*.

Inns. – For the tourist who wishes to enjoy the early American charm and hospitality of New England, a stay at one of the region's inns should be planned as part of the trip. The inns, many of which have been operating since colonial times, are often furnished with antiques, provide good home-cooked meals, and are found on or near the green of a small village. As rates vary, however, allow at least $50-$90 a day for a single room.

We suggest you consult the guides available on this subject for a selection of the inns throughout the region *(see Books to Read p 210)*.

Tips. – In season and holiday weekends reserve in advance.
– Low off-season rates may be in effect. Inquire when making your reservations.
– Advise of late arrival. Rooms, even though reserved, may not be held after 4 to 6 PM.

RESTAURANTS

The hearty, home-cooked meals served at New England's inns and multitude of restaurants are considered among the attractions of the region. Local specialties may often be traced back to the early settlers who, instructed by the Indians, learned quickly how to prepare the fish, shellfish, and unfamiliar fruits and vegetables (corn, squash, pumpkin, cranberries...) they found here in abundance.

Fish. – Fish is generally served filleted: broiled, baked or fried. Most common are haddock, pollack, trout, sole, flounder, cod, bass and "scrod" (the white fish that is the catch of the day). **Fish cakes,** crispy on the outside and smooth on the inside, and a variety of **fish chowders** are made from these fish.

Lobster. – A specialty along the coast of northern Massachusetts and Maine, lobster is most often boiled and served with a butter sauce. Piping hot **lobster chowder** or **bisque,** and lobster salad and **lobster roll** are also prepared fresh from the lobsterman's catch, at waterfront restaurants and fast food places.

Shellfish. – Clams (quahogs or "steamers" – according to the thickness of the shell), **mussels** and **scallops** are found everywhere along the coast. Clams are delicious in **New England clam chowder,** a fish chowder prepared with clams, corn and potatoes in a milk base.

The New England **clambake,** prepared on a sandy beach, originated with the Indians. A fire is lit in the sand with charcoal. Rocks are heated on the charcoal then covered with a layer of seaweed – topped with a layer of clams, corn and potatoes, and another layer of seaweed. Steamed in the salt water of the seaweed, the clams, potatoes and corn have a delectably rich, natural taste and aroma after they are cooked.

Desserts. – **Indian pudding,** made with molasses, cornmeal, milk and spices; and **Boston cream pie,** a cake filled with custard and topped with chocolate icing are the desserts most typical of the region, but pies topped with ice cream or whipped cream are also a favorite: **pumpkin, blueberry, pecan, apple** or **cranberry.**

Maple Syrup. – And who can imagine pancakes without golden maple syrup, a bottle of which will be found on breakfast tables across New England. A local product, varying in price according to its quality (determined by its consistency, color and aroma): Grade A light amber (fancy - the best), Grade A medium amber, Grade A dark amber, maple syrup goes well on ice cream, puddings, and is used in baking cookies, cakes and pies.

Other specialties you will want to try are:

New England boiled dinner – beef, potatoes and vegetables stewed together in a pot

Boston baked beans – brown beans prepared with salted pork and molasses

Johnny cake – cornmeal cake

Apple cider – a popular item at roadside stands in the fall

Blueberries – locally grown, are served with cream, or used to make muffins, sauces and cakes, and are a favorite topping for cereals and pancakes.

CALENDAR OF EVENTS

Listed below is a selection of the most popular events; for details contact the state offices of tourism *(p 10)*. Fold numbers refer to the Michelin tourist map.

DATE	PLACE and MAP FOLD No.		NATURE OF EVENT

SPRING

DATE	PLACE	FOLD	NATURE OF EVENT
Patriot's Day – third Monday in April	Boston (Mass.)	17	The Boston Marathon
	Lexington and Concord (Mass.)	16	Parades, reenactments of events of April 19, 1775
May-June	New Canaan (Conn.) . .	19	Art of the Northeast *(p 47)*.
Mid-May, July and September	Brimfield (Mass.)		Brimfield Antique Flea Market
Mid-May	Fairfield (Conn.)	20	Dogwood Festival
Late May-mid-June	Cranston and Warwick (R.I.)	22	Gaspee Days – Races, parades, contests, arts and crafts festival
Early June (even years) . .	Newport (R.I.)		Newport-Bermuda Race
Mid to late June	West Springfield (Mass.)	15	American Crafts Council Fair
Late June.	Gloucester (Mass.) . . .	17	St. Peter's Fiesta – Blessing of the Fleet *(p 118)*
	Block Island (R.I.)	22	Block Island Race Week

SUMMER

DATE	PLACE	FOLD	NATURE OF EVENT
Early July.	Boston (Mass.). . . .	17	Harborfest
	Newport (R.I.)	22	International Tennis Hall of Fame Grass Court Championships (Newport Casino)
Early July-late August . . .	The Berkshires (Mass.)	14	Jacob's Pillow Dance Festival
July 4	Hartford (Conn.)	14	The 4th of July River Festival – Races, concerts, fireworks
July to late August	Lenox (Mass.)	14	Tanglewood Music Festival *(p 86)*
Mid-July – mid-August. . . .	Marlboro (Vt.)		Marlboro Music Festival (Marlboro College)
First or second Friday in July	Rockland (Me.)	10	Great Schooner Race – Race, air show, parade of tall ships.
Mid-July	Litchfield (Conn.). . . .	14	Historic Homes Tour (one day)
	Boothbay Harbor (Me.)	10	Windjammer Days (Races)
	Newport (R.I.)	22	Newport Music Festival
Mid-July-early August	Burlington (Vt.)	7	Mozart Festival *(location varies: ☎ (802) 862-7352)*
Early July-mid-August	Burlington (Vt.)	7	Champlain Shakespeare Festival at the University of Vermont (Royal Tyler Theater)
Late July	Bath (Me.)	10	Friendship Sloop Days
	Galilee (R.I.)	22	Blessing of the Fleet
Early August	Rockland (Me.)	10	Maine Seafoods Festival
	Sunapee (N.H.)	8	Craftsmen's Fair at Sunapee State Park
Fridays in August	Plymouth (Mass.). . . .	17	Pilgrim Progress Procession *(p 143)*
Mid-August	Mystic (Conn.)	21	Mystic Outdoor Art Festival
	Castine (Me.)	11	Retired Skippers' Race

FALL

DATE	PLACE	FOLD	NATURE OF EVENT
September	Galilee (R.I.)	22	Rhode Island Tuna Tournament
Mid-September	West Springfield (Mass.)	15	Eastern States Exposition *(p 154)*
Mid-September-mid-October.	Stratton (Vt.)	7	Stratton Mountain Arts Festival
Late September	Craftsbury Common (Vt.)	2	Banjo Contest
Late September-early October	Vermont	8	Northeast Kingdom Fall Foliage Festival *(p 196)*
Mid-October	Warner (N.H.)		Fall Foliage Festival
Last Thursday in November	Plymouth (Mass.). . . .	17	Thanksgiving Day Celebration in Plymouth

WINTER

DATE	PLACE	FOLD	NATURE OF EVENT
Mid-January	Stowe (Vt.)	8	Annual Winter Carnival
February	Dartmouth College . . . . (Hanover, N.H.)	8	Dartmouth Winter Carnival
Early to mid-February	Laconia (N.H.)	9	World Championship Sled Dog Race

STATE SALES TAX

Connecticut 7.5 %
Maine 5 %
Massachusetts 5 %, 5. 7 % lodging

New Hampshire 7 % meals and lodging
Rhode Island 6 %
Vermont 4 %, 6 % meals and lodging

Outdoor attractions may not operate in inclement weather.
It is advisable to telephone ahead before starting out.

13

INTRODUCTION TO THE REGION

LANDSCAPE

Dominated by the White Mountains to the north and the Green Mountains and Taconic Range to the west, New England's gently rolling hills and valleys taper off to a coastline of sandy beaches in the south and a rockbound, irregular shoreline in the east. Add to this an extensive river and stream system, vast woodlands and thousands of ponds and lakes and the picture is complete.

New England's major mountain ranges are remnants of the uplands that were formed 300 million to 500 million years ago. In striking contrast is the relatively recent appearance of the many ponds, lakes, U-shaped valleys and winding ridges which owe their existence to the glaciers that covered North America until about 10 000 years ago.

Formation of New England. – During the first geologic era the earth's crust, composed of gneiss, was submerged beneath inland seas. Layers of sediment accumulated on the sea floor, until upheaval of the earth's crust caused the floor to buckle along the Canadian shield and rise above the water as a mountainous mass. The intense heat and pressure accompanying the uplift of these mountains (ancestors of the Green Mountains and the Taconics) transformed the sandstones and limestones into metamorphic rocks, primarily schists and marble. During the same era a mass of hot molten rock – granite – was thrust upward into another section of rock, resulting in the uplift of the Presidential Range *(p 171)*. These ancient mountains were probably as high as the Alps or the Himalayas today. During the geologic eras that followed, erosion wore the mountains down to a flat, vast plain that was repeatedly uplifted and eroded. It is this relief, subsequently carved and scoured by the glaciers, that one sees today.

A Glaciated Landscape. – The last of the four glacial stages that occurred during the Quaternary period ended 10 000 years ago. The glaciers began to form at the beginning of the Cenozoic era, about 65 million years ago, as the climate became increasingly colder and accumulations of snow continued to mount. The weight of these accumulations eventually compressed the lower layers of snow into ice, and when the ice reached a thickness of 150-200 ft the lower layer, no longer able to support the intense pressure, began to spread. Moving southeasterly from Canada to Long Island these enormous ice sheets spread across the northeastern part of the Appalachians, marking the region with signs of glacial activity which explains the bare, rocky mountain summits and multitude of lakes that characterize the landscape today.

The glaciers attacked the walls and floors of steep valleys, transforming them into U-shaped valleys known as *notches*, and the abrasive materials carried by the ice exposed, scoured and striated granite and other hard rocks. The boulders that will be found scattered across New England were plucked from mountain sides; valleys were dammed – creating ponds and waterfalls; and the large blocks of ice that were left behind, buried, and eventually melted, gave rise to the kettle lakes (named for their rounded shape) which dot the region. Near the coast, the glaciers left sticky clay deposits which form the low-lying oval-shaped hills (drumlins) such as Bunker Hill and World's End *(p 130)*. Finally, when the ice melted, it left behind enormous moraines. These prominent ridges of debris which remained above sea level when the ocean invaded the land, today form Cape Cod, Martha's Vineyard, Nantucket, Block Island and Long Island.

MAJOR FEATURES OF THE RELIEF

Appalachian Mountains. – The Appalachians, extending about 1 600 miles from the St. Lawrence Valley (in Canada) to Alabama, form the spine of New England. There are several mountain ranges in the northeastern Appalachian system:

- **The White Mountains.** – These heavily glaciated mountains, characterized by rocky, cone-shaped summits and U-shaped valleys, have the highest peak in the northeastern United States: Mount Washington (alt 6 288 ft).

- **The Green Mountains.** – These mountains are most prominent in Vermont where they form a north-south ridge through the center of the state. Composed of ancient metamorphic rocks which include Vermont's rich marble deposits, this mountain chain extends into Massachusetts where it is known as the Berkshires. Downhill and cross-country skiers flock to the many ski resorts in the Green Mountains.

- **The Taconics.** – Extending along the border between New York and New England, this range, comprised primarily of schists, includes Mount Equinox (Vt.) and Mount Greylock (Mass.).

- **The Monadnocks.** – Several isolated mountains, *monadnocks*, the remnants of ancient formations of erosion-resistant rocks, dominate the surrounding countryside. Mount Monadnock in New Hampshire is an example of this type of relief and its name has been adapted by geographers to designate all similar forms of relief. Mounts Katahdin and Blue in Maine, Mounts Cardigan and Kearsage in New Hampshire, and Mounts Wachusetts and Greylock in Massachusetts are other examples of this type of relief.

The Connecticut Valley. – New England is divided in two by this 400 mile long north-south corridor through which the Connecticut River flows. The valley is the result of a fault which caused the repeated uplift of the craggy basalt ridges that rise above the valley floor in Massachusetts (Mounts Sugarloaf, Holyoke) and in Connecticut (north of New Haven). The valley owes its abundance of fossils *(p 142)* to its rich geologic past.

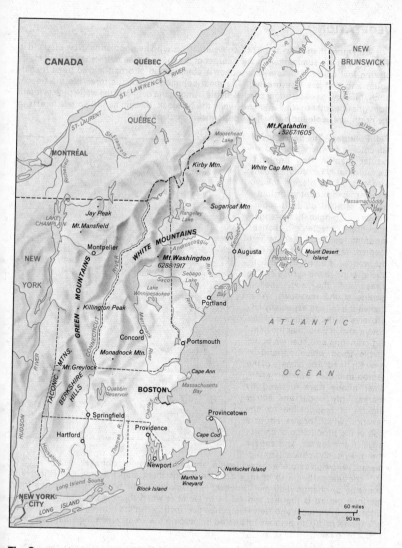

The Coast. – In the north, the coast is jagged and indented, with a series of peninsulas and bays oriented in a northwest-southeast direction. Melting glacial waters flooded the land, forming the bays and the hundreds of offshore islands. South of Portland, the coastal plain is broad, almost flat, giving way to sandy beaches. The estuaries and lagoons of quiet water, protected by barrier beaches, have given rise to vast salt marshes which provide food and resting grounds for birds and waterfowl in the Atlantic flyway. Further south, enormous accumulations of sand cover the glacial moraines that are Cape Cod and the islands, creating the landscape that is typical of the Cape.

Climate. – New England's varied climate results from the fact that the region lies in a zone where cool, dry air from Canada meets the warm, humid air from the southeast. Annual precipitation is considerable (42 inches) and the seasons are sharply defined:

– **Winter** is cold, particularly in the north where temperatures range from – 10° to 10 °F (– 23° to – 12 °C), and the annual snowfall in the mountain regions is 90-100 inches.

– **Spring,** a period of variable temperatures, is brief. In the north, the short 2-3 week interval between winter and summer during which the snow melts and the ground thaws, is known as Mud Season. Flooding can make driving on country roads hazardous during this time.

– **Summer,** warm and humid, is characterized by a pattern of cloudy, hazy or foggy days alternating with showers followed by clear weather. Daytime temperatures range from 70 °-90 °F (21°-32 °C), and evenings are cool along the coast, in the mountains and near the lakes.

– **Autumn,** with its sunny days and cool nights, is the season when "leaf watchers" travel to New England to view the brilliant coloration of the hard woods. A cool spell that may occur in late September, is followed by a milder period in October: **Indian summer,** during which the foliage reaches its peak.

Mean temperatures for northern and southern New England vary and are affected by differences in altitude and relief. Mean temperatures for Connecticut range from 27 °F – 3 °C) in January to 73 °F (23 °C) in July; while to the north, in Vermont, temperatures range from 16 °F (– 9 °C) in January to 70 °F (21 °C) in July. Mount Washington's *(p 172)* subpolar climate is exceptional for a summit of its altitude (6 288 ft).

Northeasters, coastal storms accompanied by high tides, heavy rain and gale force winds occur frequently, especially off the coast of Maine.

VEGETATION

With more than 80 % of the region's surface covered by woodlands, New England is appealing in the summer for its thick carpet of green, and even more so in the fall for its blazing leaf colors. The forests are often a combination of broad-leaved trees (deciduous) and conifers (evergreens). The most common deciduous trees are the beech, birch, hickory, oak and sugar or rock maple. Among the conifers, the white pine is found throughout southern New England, while the hemlock, balsam fir and spruce forests in the north, are exploited by the large papermaking companies.

Fall Foliage. – The pageantry of fall color is nowhere more spectacular than in New England. Extraordinarily beautiful and unforgettable, the blazing foliage transforms the countryside into a palette of vivid golds (birches, poplars, gingkos), oranges (mountain maples, hickories, mountain-ash) and scarlets (red maples, red oak, sassafras and dogwoods), framed by the dark background of the spruce and fir trees and the soft, mellow greens of the meadows. What makes the foliage especially impressive is the brilliance of the colors and in particular the flaming crimsons and scarlets of the maple trees which abound in New England. The climate of the region in Indian summer: crisp, clear sunny days followed by increasingly longer and colder nights, is responsible for the reaction which brings about a halt in the production of chlorophyll in the leaves, and causes the previously concealed pig-

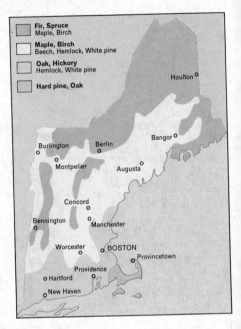

ments: yellowish carotene, brown tannin, and red anthocynin, to appear.

The leaves begin to change color in the northern states in mid-September and continue to change until mid-October, late October in the south. However, the most glorious period is the first two weeks in October when there is color all across New England. In Vermont and New Hampshire information centers provide foliage reports by telephone *(p 10),* to persons interested in learning the areas where the foliage has or is about to "peak."

The Sugar Maples. – Capable of adapting to a cold climate and rocky soil, the sugar or rock maple is found throughout Vermont and New Hampshire. The maples are appreciated in the fall for their foliage, and year round for the delectable syrup produced from maple sap. In early spring when the sap begins to rise in the tree, the farmer inserts a tube, from which a bucket is suspended, into the trunk to gather the sap. The sap that collects in the bucket is transferred to the evaporator in the sugarhouse (a wooden shed nearby) where the sap is boiled down into syrup: 30 gallons of sap produce one gallon of syrup. Modern improvements have simplified the harvesting of the sap by using plastic tubes which lead directly from the tree to the sugarhouse.

Marshes and Bogs. – Owing to its glacial origin, the soil in New England is often swampy. Along the coast there are vast marshlands – a kind of "no man's land" – where tall grasses and reedy plants grow. **Bogs,** swampy lands characterized by an acidic environment, support plants such as sedges, heaths, orchids, Labrador Tea, spagnum moss and, in low-lying sandy areas, cranberries *(p 21).* Dead matter which accumulates in the bog is prevented from decaying because of the acidic environment, and over a period of time is transformed into peat. Gradually the surface of the bog may be covered with a thick, soggy mat of spagnum moss, deposits of peat will support trees and shrubs, and eventually the bog, entirely filled in, will become dry, forested land.

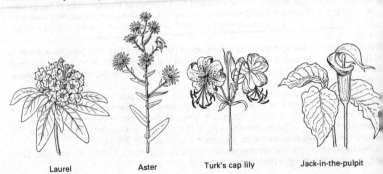

Laurel   Aster   Turk's cap lily   Jack-in-the-pulpit

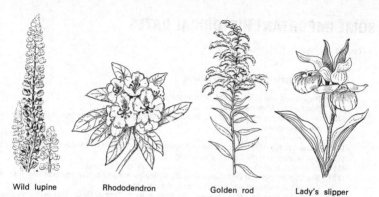

| Wild lupine | Rhododendron | Golden rod | Lady's slipper |

(By permission of Houghton Mifflin Company from "A Field Guide to Wild Flowers" by Roger Tory Peterson and Margaret McKenny.)

Wildflowers. – By late spring the mantle of snow has almost disappeared and the flowers in the woods, along the roadside, in the fields and in the mountains begin to burst into bloom. The magnificent **rhododendron** and **laurel** bushes add a bold stroke of pink to the dark, green woods. During the summer, the roadsides are alternately tinted with the orange of the flowering **turk's cap lily**, the yellow of the tall-stemmed and graceful **golden rod**, the pale blue of the multitude of tiny **asters** and the purplish hue of broad, swaying patches of **lupine**. Hundreds of species of more familiar wildflowers: buttercups, daisies, sunflowers, Queen Anne's Lace, lily of the valley... are scattered across the fields and grassy meadows. In moist, marshy areas look for the delicate **lady slipper**, a small pink or white member of the orchid family, and the greenish **Jack-in-the-pulpit**, so named because of the curved flap which gives the flower its appearance of a preacher in a pulpit. *The drawings on pp 16 and 17 will assist you in identifying some of New England's common species of wildflowers.*

WILDLIFE

There are virtually no forms of wildlife found uniquely in New England, however, several species of animals are typical to the region.

In the Woods. – The **white-tailed deer**, the favorite game of hunters, is found in many parts of New England. This species of deer, characterized by its white, bushy tail, inhabits the northern spruce-fir forests together with the **black bear** and the **moose**. The moose *(p 63)*, the region's largest mammal, boasts an enormous set of antlers and may be encountered in the middle of forest roads.

In pond and stream areas, colonies of **beavers** are hard at work, actively engaged in felling trees with their teeth, to build lodges and dams. Their structures often create deep ponds or cause flooding in low-lying areas, which results in swampy zones where trees cannot survive: thus the many bare and dead trunks that mark these ponds.

Among the other forest inhabitants are the **raccoons** with their beautiful striped fur, the **porcupines** with their protective bristly hairs, the **skunks** with their black and white fur, and the **red squirrel**. The **chipmunk**, a relative of the latter, is a small cuddly ball of striped fur that will be found in and near settled areas as well as in woodlands. Most of these animals leave their shelters only at night to work and forage for food and are difficult to observe.

(From a photo by Paul A. Knaut, Jr.)

White-tailed deer.

The Coast. – **Sea gulls** and **terns** are present everywhere along the coast, always searching for food: on boats, on the beaches, in inlets and marshes, and on the piers that line the waterfront. The **great cormorants** are larger in size and live principally on the rocky sea cliffs which they share with the **seals**.

The coastal marshes serve as the feeding and resting grounds for hundreds of species of birds. Located along the **Atlantic Flyway**, broad stretches of salt marshes such as those west of Barnstable Harbor on Cape Cod, are frequented by large numbers of birdwatchers during the spring and fall migrations. The **Canada goose**, its graceful V-formation a familiar sight in the New England sky during the migratory seasons, rests in these tranquil areas.

Raccoons.

SOME IMPORTANT HISTORICAL DATES

(in brown: European historical events)

The Period of Exploration

1000 The Vikings, led by **Eric the Red**, land on the coast of North America.
1492 Discovery of America by Christopher Columbus.
1497 **John Cabot** explores the coast of North America. English claims in the New World based on his explorations.
1509 Accession of Henry VIII.
1524 **Giovanni da Verrazano**, in the service of France, explores the coast of North America.
1534 Establishment of the Church of England.
1558 Accession of Elizabeth I.
1602 The English explorer **Bartholomew Gosnold**, sailing from Maine to Narragansett Bay, names Cape Cod, the Elizabeth Islands and Martha's Vineyard.
1604 The Frenchmen **Samuel de Champlain** and **Pierre de Guast, Sieur de Monts**, founders of Acadia (New France), establish a colony on St. Croix Island *(p 71)* and explore the Maine coast.
1605 Captain **George Weymouth** returns to England from Maine with five American Indians.
1607 Establishment of the Virginia Colony at Jamestown, the first permanent English settlement in North America.
 Sir John Popham and **Sir Ferdinando Gorges** finance an expedition to establish a colony on the coast of Maine *(p 63)*.
1608 The first settlement established at Quebec.
1613 The Jesuits establish a mission on Mount Desert Island (Me.).
1614 Captain **John Smith**, sailing for a group of London merchants, returns to England with a cargo of fish and furs. The term "New England" is used for the first time in his account of the voyage: *A Description of New England*.
 The Dutch navigator, Adrian Block, names Block Island.

The Period of Colonization

1620 Arrival of the Pilgrims on the **Mayflower**; establishment of the Plymouth Colony, the first permanent English settlement in New England.
1625 Accession of Charles I.
1626 Roger Conant leads a group of settlers to Cape Ann and establishes the Puritan colony, **Salem**.
 Peter Minuit purchases Manhattan Island from the Indians.
1630 **Boston** is founded by a group of Puritans led by **John Winthrop**.
1635 **Thomas Hooker** leads a group of settlers from Massachusetts Bay Colony to the Connecticut Valley and founds the Hartford Colony.
1636 **Harvard College** established.
 Roger Williams flees the intolerance of Massachusetts Bay Colony and establishes Providence (R.I.).
1638 **Anne Hutchinson** and John Coddington found Portsmouth (R.I.).
1638-39 Connecticut Valley towns: Hartford, Windsor and Wethersfield join to form the Connecticut Colony.
1653 Oliver Cromwell becomes Lord Protector.
1660 The Restoration; accession of Charles II.
1662 A royal charter unites the New Haven and Connecticut Colonies.
1688 Accession of William of Orange and his wife Mary.
1702 Accession of Anne.
1713 By the Treaty of Utrecht, France cedes Acadia, Newfoundland and the Hudson Bay territory to Britain.
1714 Accession of George I.
1763 The Treaty of Paris ends the French and Indian War (1756-1763); France cedes Canada and territories east of the Mississippi to Britain.

Independence

1765 Passage of the **Stamp Act**, a direct tax levied by England on the American colonies without the consent of the colonial legislature.
1766 Stamp Act repealed.
1767 Passage of the **Townshend Acts**, duties levied by Parliament on colonial imports of tea, paper, glass.
1770 The majority of the Townshend Acts are repealed; the tax on tea is retained.
 The Boston Massacre *(p 87)*.
1773 The Boston Tea Party *(p 87)*.
1774 Parliament passes the **Intolerable Acts**: five laws, four of which were directed against the citizens of Massachusetts in retaliation for the Boston Tea Party. In response to opposition to England's colonial policies, the **First Continental Congress** is held.
1775 The beginning of the **American Revolution**:
    April 18 – Ride of Paul Revere and William Dawes.
    April 19 – Battle of Lexington, Battle of Concord *(p 131)*.
    May 10 – Siege of Fort Ticonderoga *(p 196)* by Ethan Allen and the Green Mountain Boys and Benedict Arnold and his men.
    June 17 – Battle of Bunker Hill *(p 90)*.
    July 3 – George Washington is named commander in chief of the Continental Army
1776 March 17 – Evacuation of Boston by the British
    July 4 – **Declaration of Independence.**
1777 Battle of Bennington *(p 198)*.
 The Vermont Constitution; Vermont is declared an independent republic.
1780 Arrival of French forces led by Count de Rochambeau in Newport (R.I.).
1781 Defeat at Yorktown (Va.) of British troops led by General Cornwallis.
1783 End of the American Revolution. The **Treaty of Versailles**: Britain recognizes the independence of the United States.
1788 Ratification of the Constitution of the United States.
1789 **George Washington** chosen as the first President of the United States.
 The French Revolution.

1812	The war with England is ended by the Treaty of Ghent in 1814.
1815	The Battle of Waterloo. The end of Napoleon's reign in France.
1820	Maine enters the Union as the 23rd state.

To The Present

1837	Accession of Victoria.
1845	The famine in Ireland.
1851-52	Harriet Beecher Stowe's novel *Uncle Tom's Cabin* appears in serial form in the abolitionist paper *The National Era*.
1861-65	**Civil War.**
1865	Assassination of President Lincoln.
1905	Treaty of Portsmouth ending the Russo-Japanese War is signed at the Portsmouth Naval Base in Kittery, Maine.
1914-18	World War I.
1921	Trial of Nicola Sacco and Bartolomeo Vanzetti in Dedham (Mass.).
1929	Crash of the Stock Market – start of the Great Depression.
1932	Election of Franklin Delano Roosevelt to the presidency of the United States.
1933-1941	New Deal.
1939-45	World War II.
1944	Bretton Woods Conference held in New Hampshire *(p 175)*.
1954	Construction at Groton (Conn.) of the *USS Nautilus*, the world's first nuclear-powered submarine.
1960	John F. Kennedy elected President of the United States.
1963	Assassination of President John F. Kennedy.
1966	Massachusetts' State Attorney General Edward W. Brooke is the first black elected to the United States Senate since Reconstruction.
1976	The Liberian tanker *Argo Merchant* runs aground near Nantucket Island and spills 7.5 million gallons of crude oil into the North Atlantic, endangering the beaches and commercial fishing grounds in the region.
1980	Celebration of Jubilee 350, the 350th anniversary of Boston.
1983	*Australia II* wins the America's Cup by defeating the American yacht *Liberty* in the best of seven series at Newport, R.I.
1985	Vermont elects the first foreign-born woman governor in the nation, Madeleine M. Kunin.

POPULATION

New England's ethnically varied population of 12.5 million inhabitants is unequally distributed. Approximately 10 million people live in the southern half of the region where the largest cities are found: Boston, Providence, Hartford, New Haven, Worcester and Springfield. The large waves of immigrants who arrived in the 19C brought with them a diversity of cultures which are reflected in the ethnic character of the population today.

The Many Faces of New England. – The **Indians** of the Algonquin nation were the first to inhabit the region. They were woodland Indians who raised corn, hunted and during the summer fished and camped along the coast. Their numbers had already been greatly reduced by disease and tribal warfare when the European settlements were established in the 17C. The largest and most important tribe, the Narragansetts of Rhode Island, was virtually wiped out by the English colonists at the Battle of the Great Swamp (1676) during King Philip's War. Present-day descendants of the **Passamaquoddy** and **Penobscot** tribes live on reservations at Pleasant Point and Old Town in Maine. The weirs they have constructed offshore to trap fish *(illustration p 23)* are visible as you drive along this section of the coast. Members of the **Wampanoag** and **Mashpee** tribes make their home in Massachusetts on Cape Cod and Martha's Vineyard.

The **Yankees**, descendants of the 17 and 18C Puritan settlers, dominated the population until the mid-19C. Hard work, frugality and "Yankee ingenuity" – the talent for making the best of any situation – characterized these early New Englanders some of whom amassed great fortunes in trade and shipping, then in industry and finance.

The population remained basically homogeneous until the 1840s when the potato famine in Ireland caused thousands of **Irish** to emigrate to New England where they could find work in the mills. The **Italians** followed in the 1870s, and at the end of the 19C **French Canadians**, attracted as the Irish had been by job opportunities in the region's factories, began to settle in New England. Communities of **Portuguese** fishermen from the Azores developed in coastal ports: Gloucester, Provincetown, Quincy… while successive waves of immigrants brought **Swedes, Jews, Russians** and other **eastern Europeans** to settle in the cities and factory towns. As Boston's black community vacated the North End for Beacon Hill, the Irish, then the Jews and eventually the Italians made the North End their home. Each ethnic group tended to form its own cohesive neighborhood where the unity of language, culture and religion – the religion of the newcomers was often Catholic – was the bond that drew them together.

The descendants of these national groups now comprise the majority of the population. They are merchants, businessmen, white and blue collar workers, and are represented in the fields of medicine, law and education. The Irish are especially prominent in politics, while the Yankees continue to exert an important influence on finance, business and government.

The Irish, Italians and Jews tend to settle in or near the large cities while the Portuguese continue to reside in the coastal areas, maintaining their culinary and religious traditions such as the celebration of the blessing of the fleet which is held at several places along the coast during the summer *(see Calendar of Events p 13)*. French names are frequently encountered in New Hampshire, Maine and Vermont where French Canadians form a significant part of the population; and many Swedes, Russians and eastern Europeans have chosen Maine and the rural areas as their home. The black population lives primarily in southern New England, near or in large urban centers.

ECONOMY

The evolution of the economy of New England paralleled that of "Old" England. A period of intense agricultural activity was followed by maritime prosperity and then industrialization, which formed the backbone of the economy through the 19 and 20C.

After World War II the region suffered a recession owing to the migration of many factories to the South. New England turned to the new, diversified high-value manufactures such as electronics, and the economy, based primarily on manufacturing and the service industries, is now experiencing a rebirth.

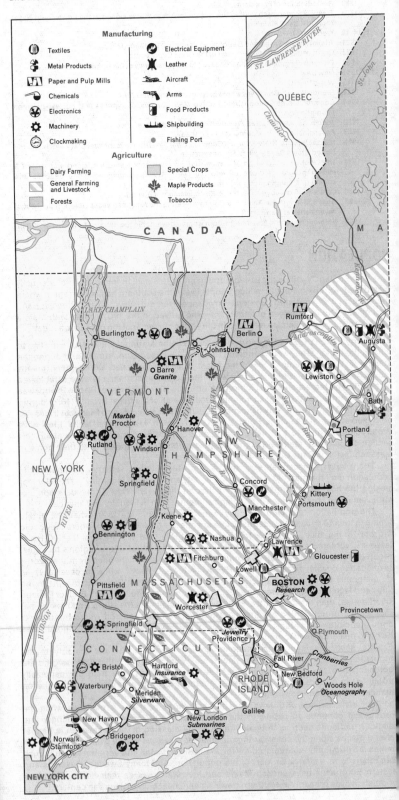

AGRICULTURE

Despite the poor soil and rocky, hilly terrain subsistence farming was an important activity until the mid-19C. In the spring, the settlers cleared the land to ready it for planting. The mounds of rock they removed from the soil were used to build the low stone walls which appear to ramble aimlessly through the woods. Farming reached a peak in New England between 1830 and 1880 with 60% of the region under cultivation. Then the opening of the fertile plains south of the Great Lakes drew farmers to migrate westward. They abandoned their farms and the land was gradually reclaimed by the forest.

Only 1% of the surface of New England continues to be devoted to agriculture, while 70% of the land (83% in Maine and New Hampshire) is covered with woodlands. However, certain areas have become widely known for their single crop specialties.

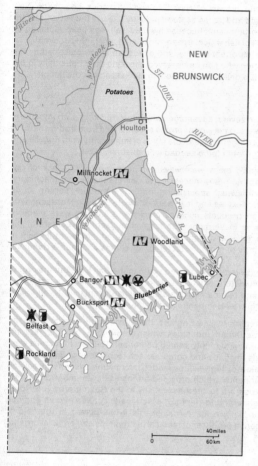

Dairy and Poultry Farming. – The major portion of income from agriculture (65%) is provided by dairy and poultry farming. The region's dairy farms are the chief suppliers of milk and milk products to the sprawling urban areas in southern New England. Dairy farms, well-suited to the terrain, predominate in Vermont where large red barns with their shiny aluminum silos are a prominent feature of the landscape.

Poultry farming is practiced throughout the region: Massachusetts specializes in the production of eggs, Connecticut in raising chickens, Rhode Island is especially known for the breed of chicken called the Rhode Island Red, and Vermont raises turkeys. Vermont's turkey farms, their buildings temperature controlled, well-lighted, and equipped with modern machinery, are busiest during the holiday seasons and in particular around Thanksgiving.

Specialty Crops. – Shade-grown **tobacco** is raised in the fertile Connecticut River valley. Firm and broad-leaved, this tobacco grown beneath a layer of netting, then hung in large sheds to dry, is used as the outer wrapping of cigars.

Fruit is cultivated in many areas: apple, peach and pear orchards extend along the banks of Lake Champlain and are found on the sunny slopes of New Hampshire, in the Connecticut and Nashua Valleys and in Rhode Island. The two crops for which New England is known are **blueberries**: Maine leads all other states in production (75% of the nation's total), and **cranberries**: the sandy bogs on Cape Cod and in nearby areas *(see Cranberry World p 144)* yield the nation's largest crop of this small, reddish berry used in making juice, jam, jelly and traditionally served as part of the Thanksgiving Day feast.

Maine's other specialty crop, **potatoes,** grown in the fertile soil of Aroostook County, ranks third in size after Idaho and Washington.

In the fall, **pumpkins,** colorful **gourds** and **Indian corn** raised by local farmers are sold at roadside stands.

Forests. – Despite the enormous area that they cover, New England's deciduous and coniferous forests *(p 16)* are not significant as sources of income due to the large-scale deforestation of the region throughout the 19C, and to the fact that vast tracts of land are now under the protection of the federal and state governments. Only the commercial timberlands owned by the large paper companies in northern Maine and New Hampshire constitute important sources of revenue. A major portion of the timber harvested is processed into wood pulp to be used by the paper and pulp mills in Maine (Millinocket, Bucksport, Woodland, Rumford) and New Hampshire (Berlin), with Maine ranking ahead of all but nine of the leading paper-producing countries in the world. Other plants and mills transform timber into a variety of wood products: lumber, veneer, furniture, bobbins, boxes, etc.

The production of **maple syrup** *(p 16)* in Vermont, New Hampshire and Maine, while not a major contributor to the overall economy, is a regional specialty.

FISHING

As early as the 15C European fishermen were drawn to the rich fishing grounds off the coast of New England. These shallow, sandy fishing banks (such as George's Bank) extending 1 500 miles east to west off of Cape Cod were teeming with fish. So vital to New England was the fishing industry that fishermen were exempt from military service, and the cod was adopted as the symbol of the Massachusetts Bay Colony.

Fishing continues to be an important activity in the ports of Gloucester, New Bedford, and Boston. Large diesel-powered trawlers return from the offshore banks, to these harbors, laden down with haddock, flounder and whiting. Modern techniques of filleting, freezing and packaging fish, and the construction of larger, more efficient vessels have contributed to the growth of New England's fisheries and made New England a leader in the packaged and frozen seafood industry (80% of the nation's total). Cod, at one time the most important catch because it salted well, has been replaced by whiting, pollack and other kinds of fish which, frozen and filleted, are highly desirable.

In Maine, lobstering is an important activity, and almost an art as practiced by the hundreds of downeast lobstermen who can be observed checking their traps daily in the offshore waters. Maine lobster is a delicacy that is sold in markets across the nation.

INDUSTRY

In the 19C New England had several advantages which fostered its growth into one of the leading manufacturing centers in the world: profits accumulated from trade, shipping and whaling; the spirit of Yankee ingenuity; and the influx of immigrants from Europe and Canada which provided the large labor force needed for industrialization.

The Mill Towns. – The region's many waterways compensated for the lack of raw materials and fuel by providing the power necessary to operate the factory machinery, and manufacturing towns: "mill towns," specializing in a single product, sprung up on the banks of rivers and streams. Textiles and leather goods were made in Massachusetts and New Hampshire, precision products such as clocks and firearms were made in Connecticut, and machine tools in Vermont. The large manufacturing centers in the Merrimack Valley: Lowell, Lawrence and Manchester – developed into world leaders in the production of textiles. Strings of red brick factories, dwellings and stores dominate these cities even today.

During the 20C most of these industries moved south to the Sun Belt, but the region remained a leader in the manufacture of woolen cloth (60% of the nation's total). The production of machine tools and fabricated metals has primarily replaced textiles, and the shoe industry is important in New Hampshire and Maine.

The New Industries. – The rebirth of New England after World War II was linked to the development of its research-oriented industries which could draw on the region's excellent educational institutions and highly trained personnel. The new industries were responsible for advances made in space and computer age technology and electronics, and gave rise to the production of high-value goods: information systems, precision instruments, electronic components, which provided an increasing number of jobs for the labor force. These industries are located essentially in the Boston area (on Route 128), in southern New Hampshire and in Hartford, which manufactures aircraft engines for Pratt and Whitney. Boston, known for the major role it has played in the field of medical research, is, in addition, a producer of medical instruments and artificial organs.

INSURANCE

Insurance has been an important business in New England since the 19C when investors offered to underwrite the risks involved in shipping. Every boat that sailed out of port represented a gamble; it could return with valuable cargo, or it could sink, eliminating forever all hopes of gain or profit. With the decline of sea trade, the insurance industry expanded to include losses due to fire and the center of the industry shifted inland, away from the ports. Hartford, a national insurance center, is the seat of 40 major companies. The modern office towers built in Boston to serve as headquarters of the John Hancock and Prudential insurance companies are the tallest structures in New England, symbolizing in their own way the importance of this industry to the economy.

EDUCATION

The concentration of preparatory schools, academies, and about 260 institutions of higher learning in the six-state area (8% of the nation's colleges and universities) makes education a significant contributor to the economy. Small businesses in cities (Worcester, New Haven, Providence), towns (Middlebury, Hanover, Brunswick, Amherst), and entire regions (Pioneer Valley, Greater Boston) depend on the revenue generated by the schools within their borders for their livelihood. In Massachusetts, where education is a major source of income, the 65 colleges and universities in the Greater Boston area alone generate about $1.5 billion in economic activity annually.

TOURISM

Tourism ranks second, only after manufacturing, in importance. Mountain and seaside resorts in New England have been welcoming visitors for over a century, and with the growing popularity of winter sports since the 1940s, the region has developed into a year-round vacation area. Handicrafts industries, depending to a great extent on the tourist, are a specialty of artisans working in New Hampshire, Vermont and along the coast, and their products will be found throughout New England.

NEW ENGLAND AND THE SEA

The development of New England has been closely related to the sea ever since the colonists turned from the rocky soil to the offshore waters, teeming with fish, for their food.

At first the colonists erected weirs (p 68), similar to those used to this day by the Indians in Maine, to snare fish near the shore. Not until the mid-17C did Yankee vessels sail in large numbers to the rich fishing grounds off Newfoundland where cod, haddock and pollack abounded. The Sacred Cod, hanging in the Massachusetts State House (p 101), is a symbol of the important role played by the cod fisheries in the history of

Weirs: An ancient method of catching fish.

Massachusetts. New England's fisheries became the backbone of the region's trade with Europe, and boatyards sprang up from Connecticut to Maine to build fishing and cargo vessels.

The fisheries, trade and shipbuilding prospered, reaching their zenith in the mid-19C, with each section of the coast having its own specialty: the south (Connecticut, Rhode Island and southeastern Massachusetts) was home to the Yankee whaling fleet; ports along the northern coast of Massachusetts and New Hampshire were leaders in the trade with the Orient (the China Trade) and shipbuilding; the Maine coast, with its protected inlets and thick forests, grew into a center of wooden shipbuilding. One-third of the boats constructed in the United States in 1885, and more than 80% of the nation's wooden ships turned out between 1862 and 1893, were built in Maine.

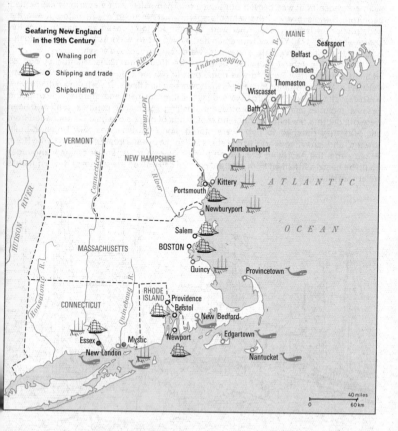

Small coastal villages grew into sophisticated urban centers as merchants, shipmasters, and sea captains accumulated great wealth and built the handsome Federal and Greek Revival style homes that still stand in Salem, Nantucket, Portsmouth, Providence, Newburyport, New Bedford and other seaport cities.

Several large museums are devoted to preserving New England's seafaring past: Mystic Seaport and the whaling museums in Nantucket, New Bedford and Sharon recall the Yankee whaling tradition; the Peabody Museum in Salem presents the story of New England's trade with the Orient; and the Maine Maritime Museum and the Penobscot Museum in Maine vividly portray the history of shipbuilding in that state.

23

WHALING

During the 19C whale oil was used to light the homes and streets of cities across America and Europe. New Bedford and Nantucket, leading whaling centers, were busy day and night with vessels arriving, departing or preparing for a whaling voyage. Herman Melville's novel *Moby Dick,* and Russell and Purrington's *Great Panorama (the New Bedford Whaling Museum p 139)* are odysseys of the whale hunt and the era of whaling.

A Few Words about Whales. – Ever since the beginning of recorded history man has been fascinated by the whale: by its size – no animal larger than the whale has ever been known to exist (the blue whale can weigh as much as 36 elephants and measure up to 100 ft); by the fact that the whale is a warm-blooded, air-breathing mammal that lives in the ocean; by the variety and value of products obtained from the whale – its blubber can be melted down into oil, its meat was and still is used as food, its baleen, the "plastic" of the 19C was used to make corset and umbrella stays, buggy whips and a variety of other products. Whales can be divided into two groups: toothed and toothless (baleen).

Toothed whales are predators that feed on fish. The **sperm whale**, a toothed whale, was hunted in large numbers because it was a source of rare and precious products: spermaceti (a solid waxy substance used in the manufacture of fine-smelling candles), sperm oil (pure oil obtained in liquid form from a cavity in the head of the whale) and ambergris (a substance found in the intestines of the whale and used commercially as a perfume fixative).

Baleen whales (such as the **blue whale** and the **right whale**) live on plankton sifted out of the sea by the long, fringed sheets of baleen (horny-like substance) hanging from the roof of the mouth. The blue whale, and the right whale – so called because it was the "right whale to hunt" since it floated when it was dead – were, together with the sperm whale, the common prey of Yankee whale ships.

Whaling in New England. – The Indians were hunting whales long before the first settlements were established. As soon as a whale was captured and brought ashore, the hunters cut up and distributed pieces of the animal to the members of the tribe. The colonists learned how to hunt inshore whales by observing the Indians. Tall watchtowers from which the whales could be sighted were built and large black cauldrons (tryworks) in which the whale fat was melted down were set up on the beaches. In the 18C a Nantucket seaman whose boat was carried out to sea returned safely with a sperm whale he had captured. His discovery of the valuable sperm whale in deep ocean waters led to the construction of larger vessels that were outfitted for long ocean voyages to hunt the sperm whale. By 1730 Yankee whalemen had moved the tryworks from the beaches to the decks of their whaling vessels, and whales were being processed at sea.

The whaling industry peaked between the 1820s and 1860s. Nantucket had 88 whaling vessels, New Bedford was home port to 339, and New London, Provincetown, Fairhaven, Mystic, Stonington, and Edgartown also had fleets. The whaling centers were beehives of activity. Shipyards were busy turning out new and sturdier ocean-going vessels, factories manufactured pleasant smelling spermaceti candles, tons of baleen were put out into the fields to dry, and thousands of barrels of whale oil, unloaded from ships as they returned to port, were stored along the wharves. New England-built, -owned, and -commandeered whale ships sailed the oceans from Greenland to the North Pacific, from the Azores to Brazil, and from Polynesia to Japan; and many languages could be heard as seamen from different ports of call walked the streets of New England's waterfront districts.

(From a photo the Whaling Museum, New Bedford.)

Oil stored in casks on the wharves of New Bedford.

As the number of whales diminished, longer voyages lasting up to three, four and five years were common. During these voyages, months could pass without a single whale being caught or even sighted. The captain was often accompanied by his wife and children on these trips, and the order was rarely given to turn toward home, until all the barrels on board were filled with oil.

The decline of the whaling industry in New England was brought about by the discovery of petroleum in Pennsylvania in 1859 and hastened by a series of Arctic disasters and the Civil War. About 35 whaling vessels were destroyed by the Confederate ship *Shenandoah* in 1865, and an additional several dozen whale ships were lost in the "Stone fleet" episode – vessels were loaded with stone and sunk to prevent blockade runners from entering Charleston harbor. New England sent out fewer and fewer whale ships, and in the following century whale hunting was outlawed in the United States.

The Whaling Adventure in the 19C. – Life aboard a whaler was rugged. Comforts were few, sleeping quarters overcrowded and the food poor. There were also the dangers of whaling. The entire crew of a whale boat could be lost if a whale attacked the boat or caused it to capsize. Yet, seamen anxious to share in the adventures and profits of the hunt signed on.

Whale ships were generally sturdy two- or three-masted wooden ships that carried a crew of 15 to 20 men. On the deck of a ship there were four to seven whale boats. The boats were lowered into the water as soon as the sailor on watch shouted the anxiously awaited signal, *Thar she blo-o-o-ws,* indicating a whale had been sighted. The signal referred to the tall misty spray (visible for miles) of warm moist air exhaled by the whale when he surfaced to breathe.

The chase began as soon as the boat carrying its crew of 6 to 8 men was lowered into the ocean. Rowing quickly so as to keep sight of their prey, the crew finally arrived close to the enormous animal.

The harpooner made the first strike against the whale, aiming his weapon at a spot behind the animal's eye. Reacting to the assault, the whale either sounded (dived below the sur-

(From a photo the Whaling Museum, New Bedford.)

Scrimshaw: A whaling scene.

face of the water), attacked the boat, or fled, pulling the boat at speeds of up to 20 mph – this was known to seamen as a Nantucket sleigh ride. The weary animal ultimately became the victim of the mate's skillfully aimed lances, certain to be fatal, and the hunt was over.

The processing of the salable products was carried on alongside the ship. Crew members working on platforms suspended high above the sea, *cut-in* to the whale, removing large sheets of blubber and depositing them on deck. The blubber was melted down in the tryworks on deck and the oil was stored in barrels. Smoke and heat from the fires, and the stench of melting fat and blood filled the air for hours and days on end until the whale was completely processed. After the cleanup, life aboard ship was once more calm, as the crew spent its time etching designs on whale teeth or bone, and awaiting the next shout of *Thar she blo-o-o-ws*!

MARITIME COMMERCE

New England's maritime commerce with Africa, Europe and the West Indies brought prosperity to many of its coastal ports during the early 18C, but not until after the Revolution when Americans were free to trade with the Orient, did Boston, Providence, Portsmouth, Salem and other cities develop into rich centers of the China Trade.

The China Trade. – Boats sailing to the Far East rounded Cape Horn, then generally made several detours to ports along the way to obtain returns (goods) that could be used in China to get silks, porcelains and tea. Furs were acquired along the northwest Pacific coast, sandalwood from the Sandwich Islands, and the delicacy beche-de-mer from the Polynesian islands.

Often, as the first outsiders to visit many of the islands, New England seamen were explorers as well. The collection of ethnological items owned by the Peabody Museum in Salem *(p 148)* was gathered by Salem mariners and sea captains. Later, when opium replaced furs and other goods as returns, boats stopped at ports in India and Turkey to barter for the illicit drug before continuing to China.

Until 1842 **Canton** was the only Chinese port open to foreign trade. Vessels dropped anchor at **Whampoa Reach** about 10 miles outside the city, and foreign merchants, who were prohibited from entering the city, continued upriver aboard smaller boats to the *hongs:* warehouses and living quarters built to house the outsiders. Several weeks or even months could be spent visiting shops, factories and negotiating with Chinese merchants before the foreign vessel, filled with a cargo of luxury items, set sail for home.

The museums and historical houses of New England exhibit countless examples of Chinese decorative arts and furnishings brought back to America from the Orient during the years of the China Trade. Pictures painted by Chinese artists commissioned by ship owners and merchants, illustrate the ports of Canton, Macao and Whampoa Reach and depict the Chinese trades and way of life.

Among other products obtained along the China Trade route were pepper from Sumatra, sugar and coffee from Java, cotton from Bombay and Madras, ivory from Zanzibar, spices from Makasar, gum arabic from Muscat.

Ice: A Unique New England Industry. – The ice trade developed in the 19C when ice was harvested north of Boston and in Maine, and shipped to the southern states, the West Indies and as far away as Calcutta to be used for refrigeration. The ice was harvested in the winter when the rivers, lakes and ponds were frozen over. The snow was removed from the ice by oxen or horsepower, then the ice field, marked off into squares, was cut into blocks weighing up to 200 lbs. The ice was packed in sawdust and stored in ice houses nearby until the first thaw, when boats arrived to transport the unique commodity to its warm-weather destination. Boats with specially constructed airtight hulks were used to prevent the ice from melting. The ice business continued to prosper until the introduction of mechanical refrigeration in the late 19C.

SHIPBUILDING

The wooden sailing vessel has been the basis of New England's boat building tradition ever since 1607, when the pinnace *Virginia* was built by the short-lived Popham colony on the banks of the Kennebec River in Maine.

The Early Days. – As quickly as the colonists established their first settlements, shipyards began to dot the coast. Small one-masted ketches and fishing sloops were built from the start, followed in the early 18C by two- and three-masted schooners capable of crossing the Atlantic.

The schooner had a long and glamorous career. When English dominance of American trade led to widespread smuggling by the colonists, it was the schooner, with its simple rigging, ease of handling, and ability to evade British revenue ships, that carried many an illicit cargo safely into port. During the Revolution armed, privately owned schooners (privateers) were authorized by the Continental Congress to capture enemy vessels. The schooner remained in service as a cargo carrier through the 19 and into the 20C, until the end of World War I.

The Age of the Clipper Ship. – The wooden sailing vessel and the era of sail reached their peak between 1820 and 1860 with the appearance of the beautiful and graceful clipper ship. These long, sleek three-masted square-rigged vessels with acres of canvas were famous for the great speeds they could achieve. The name *clipper* came from the expression "at a fast clip" and was applied to anything that went fast, be it a horse, carriage or ship. Clippers sailed the long ocean routes in the China Trade and during the California goldrush carried miners and supplies from the Atlantic coast, around Cape Horn, to San Francisco. Their names symbolized the importance of speed: the *Lightning, Flying Cloud, Eagle Wing*. The major boatyards working to turn out these ships were in Boston, New York and Bath and the master designer was **Donald McKay** of East Boston. Of the approximately 100 vessels that made the voyage around Cape Horn in less then 110 days,

(By permission of the Peabody Museum of Salem.)

An advertising poster for a voyage on a clipper ship.

19 were built by McKay including the first to make the journey in under 90 days – the *Flying Cloud:* 89 days on her maiden voyage in 1851, then again in 1854.

Last Sailing Ships. – In the last half of the 19 and beginning of the 20C, Maine specialized in the production of the commercial wooden sailing vessels: the **Down-Easter** and the **great schooner.** The Down-Easter, a three-masted square-rigger, had the long clean lines of, and could attain speeds almost equal to those of the clipper. Its advantage over the latter was a large, deep hull which offered greater carrying space and made the Down-Easter a more profitable means of transporting cargo.

The Down-Easters and two- and three-masted schooners were used in shipping until the 1880s when boat builders discovered that four-masted schooners, though larger, cost little more to operate. The construction of the great schooners: four-, five- and six-masted vessels, followed. These schooners hauled large bulk cargos – coal, lumber, granite, grain – from the East Coast, around Cape Horn, and up to the West Coast. Striving to compete with the steamboat, Maine shipyards turned to the production of a small fleet of steel four-, five- and six-masters; however, the days of sail were numbered. The efficient, regularly scheduled steamer triumphed, and with its victory an era in the maritime history of the United States came to a close.

Sailing vessels are distinguished

— by the type of sail they carry

square sail – rigged the width of the vessel

fore-and-aft sail – rigged parallel to the length of the vessel

— and the masts on which the sails are placed.

The following definitions will assist in identifying a ...

sloop: one-masted vessel, fore-and-aft rigged

schooner: two- (or more) masted vessel; all sails fore-and-aft rigged

ship: three- (or more) masted vessel, all sails square-rigged.

ART

ARCHITECTURE

European styles, imported via England, were the major source of inspiration for New England architecture during more than two centuries. From the first simple clapboarded structures to the ultramodern towers that define the skyline of Boston and other cities, regional trends in architecture have reflected the history of New England, and the interest of its people in constructing sturdy, attractive, and comfortable dwellings and public buildings.

Colonial

American Colonial. – By the late 17C the simple one-room wooden frame dwelling with an end chimney, built during the early colonial period, had evolved into a two-story structure. This larger clapboarded structure was dominated by medieval characteristics: tiny irregularly placed casement windows, an overhanging second story, long, steeply pitched roof line, and massive central chimney. Ornamentation was limited to the use of pendants that were suspended from the upper story. The main features of the interior were exposed beams, rough plaster walls and a steep stairway hugging the chimney. A one-story lean-to added to the rear of the dwelling resulted in the form commonly referred to as the **saltbox**, with its steep roof line resembling the outline of a box of salt (*illustration p 156*).

The **Cape Cod** dwelling, a small, timber framed cottage built during the colonial period and later to withstand the weather on the Cape, could be constructed quickly and easily enlarged, without destroying its original style.

Cape Cod

The Puritan **meetinghouse,** simple and unadorned, was a square wooden structure (Old Ship Church, Hingham, *p 130*) with a plain cupola or spire rising from the center of the roof. Usually the largest building in a village, the meetinghouse served as the town hall and as the center for religious services, reflecting the close ties between religion and politics in 17C New England.

Furniture: Elizabethan and Jacobean.

Georgian. – With prosperity came the desire for larger, more comfortable homes, and the colonial style gave way to the formal architecture in vogue in 18C England. This style, inspired by the Italian Renaissance, owes its name to the three Georges who succeeded to the English throne (1714-1820) during the period.

Georgian

In wood or brick, and topped with a low roof, the Georgian was distinguished from earlier styles by its harmonious proportions (doors were centered, windows were equidistant...), strict adherence to symmetry, and its embellished entranceway, sash windows, smaller fireplaces, wood paneled walls, broad stairway and deep central hall.

Meetinghouses ranged from the simple (Old South Church, Boston, *p 96*) to the elaborate (the Baptist Church, Providence, *p 190*) with the tower offset from the body of the church. Steeples, often inspired by the designs of London's Christopher Wren, were prominent features of the skyline.

Furniture: William and Mary, Queen Anne, Chippendale.

Architect: Peter Harrison in Newport and Boston.

Federal. – This light, delicate style was popular during the period of increased economic expansion that followed the American Revolution. Dwellings are large, four-square and constructed of wood or brick. The facade is plain, its only adornment being the treatment given to the main entranceway, with its columned porch, elliptical fanlight, and delicate leaded sidelights. In seaport communities the low, hipped roof is bordered by a balustrade, forming a "widow's walk", a high vantage point from which a wife could observe her husband's ship entering or leaving the harbor.

Inside, the use of small classical motifs (urns, rosettes, sheaves of wheat), the gracefully curved or free standing stairway, and a Palladian window above the entrance are common. In New England the influence of the London architects, the Adam brothers, was reflected in the use of slender pilasters and columns, and delicately adorned fireplace mantels contrasting with broad, plain wall surfaces.

Federal

The restrained ornamentation and subtle elegance characteristic of this style are reflected in the meetinghouses and **churches** of the period. The church tower, incorporated into the body of the building, is topped with a harmoniously detailed three-tiered steeple; the facade, surmounted by a triangular pediment, is adorned with pilasters or columns and begins to reveal the taste for the clean, vigorous lines of classicism.

Furniture: Chippendale, Sheraton, Hepplewhite.

Architects: Samuel McIntire in Salem, Charles Bulfinch in Boston.

Greek Revival. – The classical temples of ancient Greece served as models for the structures built in this majestic style. Columned building fronts, colossal in scale, are surmounted by a low unbroken pediment. The gable end is turned to the street, ceilings are high, windows tall, decorative motifs few, and public buildings are generally constructed of marble or granite.

The monumental scale of this style reflected the optimism of a rapidly growing America whose expanding commercial activities gave rise to such "temples of trade" as Quincy Market *(p 99)* and the Providence Arcade *(p 192)*.

Church towers rise from the body of the church and are squared off or topped with storied steeples (Church of the Presidents *p 147*).

Furniture: Empire, Sheraton, Hepplewhite.

Architects: Alexander Parris and Asher Benjamin.

Greek Revival

Victorian. – The architecture of this period (the second half of the 19C), is marked by an eclecticism inspired by the revivals of several styles: Gothic, Romanesque, Italian Renaissance ... . Gables, porches, turrets and balconies are used extensively creating the free, asymmetrical **Gothic Revival** (the Capitol, Hartford) and **Queen Anne** styles typified as Victorian. The polychromatic bands of tile, slate and brick (the Mark Twain House, Hartford), decorative wooden Gothic tracery "gingerbread" (the Gingerbread Cottages, Martha's Vineyard), and the shingle (Hammersmith Farm, Newport) and "stick" styles (the Art Association, Newport) added a picturesque quality to the burgeoning Victorian landscape.

Henry H. Richardson's masterpiece, Trinity Church (Boston; *p 103*), reveals the influence of the French and Spanish Romanesque on his work. The use of heavy stonework, arches and foliated ornamentation were traits of the **Richardsonian Romanesque** which inspired the designs of many of the libraries, city halls and court houses found across the nation.

The **Italian Renaissance** served as the inspiration for homes, mansions (the Breakers, Newport) and public buildings such as the Boston Public Library. The firm of **McKim, Mead and White** designed numerous buildings in this style and also worked in the shingle style. In Boston, the French influence was strong. The mansard roof, popular in Second Empire France, is a major feature of Boston's Old City Hall and rows of genteel townhouses in the Back Bay.

Contemporary. – Modern architecture is well represented by the works of Eero Saarinen, Alvar Aalto, Walter Gropius, Paul Rudolph, Philip Johnson, Louis Kahn and I. M. Pei. Extensive building programs of recent decades have led to the revitalization of blighted market and waterfront districts in Boston, Salem, Newburyport and other cities, and the construction of ultramodern buildings in Boston, Hartford, Portland and many other cities has provided additional office and living space and attracted new businesses to the region's major centers.

SCULPTURE

Sculpture was predominantly folk: shop and trade signs, weathervanes, figureheads, until the 19C when American sculptors, studying in Italy and at the Ecole des Beaux-Arts in Paris, were exposed to the grandeur and majesty of classical sculpture. **Daniel Chester French** (1850-1931) *(p 155)* and **Augustus Saint-Gaudens** (1848-1907) *(p 171)* trained abroad and exerted a strong influence on American sculpture from the period following the Civil War until the early 20C. Each obtained numerous public commissions for war memorials and statues during his lifetime. French became known early in his career for his statue of the *Minute Man* (Concord), while the monumental seated *Lincoln* (Washington, D. C.) is recognized as his most impressive achievement. Saint-Gaudens executed delicate low relief portrait plaques as well as such monumental sculptures as the Shaw Memorial in Boston *(p 101)*, for which he is best remembered.

The work of **John Rogers** (1829-1904), who studied for a while in Rome, differed from that of French and Saint-Gaudens. Influenced by the American scene, Rogers modeled small sculptured groups, in clay, depicting events of historical and topical interest *(The Slave Auction)* and everyday living *(Checkers at the Farm)*. His approximately 80 "Rogers groups" (as they became known), were reproduced by the thousands and gained immediate popularity and success. Their vivacious, anecdotal character and Roger's detailed presentation of his subject, make these groups, found in museums throughout the region, an interesting record of the times.

Visiting the house museums
and local historical societies in the area where you are staying
is an enjoyable way to spend time, especially on a day
when the weather is inclement.

FURNITURE

American furnishings were influenced from colonial days through the 19C by European and in particular English designs. Carpenters in rural villages copied the pieces the colonists had brought with them across the ocean, or reproduced from memory the furniture they had known in England. Cabinetmakers working in large cities and seaport towns turned to imported style manuals as a guide to contemporary furniture styles of the day.

The Styles

Pilgrim. – 1620-1690. The furniture of this period: tables, chairs, bible boxes, chests, is heavy and rectilinear, reflecting the medieval influences of the English Tudor and Jacobean styles. Oak is the principal wood. The Connecticut-made Hadley, Guilford and Sunflower chests ornamented with carved and painted floral designs or geometric motifs are native to New England.

William and Mary. – 1690-1720. This style was in vogue during the reign of William of Orange and his wife Mary. The Flemish influence and contact with the Orient introduced such decorative techniques as japanning (floral or scenic designs on lacquered wood surfaces), and turning (wooden pieces shaped on a lathe). Japanned highboys, chests with bold turnings, and chairs with caned or leather backs are characteristic.

Queen Anne. – 1720-1750. The curved line, represented by the gracefully shaped cabriole leg, is an important stylistic feature of the period. Wood is maple, walnut and cherry; decoration is minimal. The Queen Anne chair, with its cabriole leg and vase-shaped back splat, is typical.

The **Windsor chair,** unrelated to the Queen Anne style, was imported from England in the early 18C and remains popular, even today, in America. The Windsor is defined by its spindles inserted between a plank seat and curved upper railing. The comb back, bow back and writing table are variations of the original low-back Windsor.

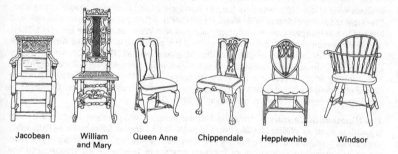

Jacobean   William and Mary   Queen Anne   Chippendale   Hepplewhite   Windsor

Chippendale. – 1750-1785. London cabinetmaker **Thomas Chippendale** borrowed elements of French rococo and Chinese art in creating the wide range of furniture forms illustrated in his design manuals. Pieces are generally of mahogany, legs are curved (ending in the ball and claw foot), and chair backs may be pierced with lacy fretwork. Adornment consists of rich carving, elaborate brasses and finials. The **Townsend and Goddard** families of Newport were among the most celebrated cabinetmakers working in this style. Their blockfront case pieces, deeply carved with the shell motif, are adaptations of Chippendale's designs.

Federal. – 1785-1815. Inspired by the English architect **Robert Adam,** and cabinetmakers **George Hepplewhite** and **Thomas Sheraton,** this style is defined by light, straight lines and refined decoration: veneers, inlay and marquetry in contrasting woods. The square, tapered leg, fluted, reeded or ending in a spade foot, is common. Chair backs in the Hepplewhite style are oval-, shield-, heart- or wheel-shaped; those of Sheraton are rectilinear. Cabinetmakers working in the Federal style include John and Thomas Seymour and John and Simeon Skillin of Boston. The eagle, adapted from the Great Seal of the United States, is a popular motif. Looking glasses with gold gilt frames surmounted by a flat cornice or delicate urn and floral sprays, and shelf and mantel clocks produced by New England clockmakers *(p 36)*, relieve the restrained classical interiors. The girandole mirror, ornamented with an eagle, is a favorite accessory.

Empire. – 1815-1840. Imported from Europe, this heavy, massive style was inspired by Greek and Egyptian antiquity. Bronze, gold gilt, winged and caryatid supports, lion's paw feet, rolled backs on chairs, and sofas with upswept ends help to identify this style.

Victorian. – 1840-late 19C. Inspired by a variety of styles: Gothic, Elizabethan, Renaissance, French Rococo, furniture of this period is heavy and overbearing. Upholstered chairs and sofas are overstuffed and velvet coverings are typical. Balloonback and fiddleback chairs, and tables with marble tops are popular.

Shaker Furniture. – 1800-1850s. Shaker chairs, tables and cupboards *(p 129),* simple and functional, are admired for their clean, pure lines and superb craftsmanship. Shaker chairs are recognized by their ladder backs, and seats made of rush, cane, splint or woven webbing.

For books on New England see Books to Read p 210.

PAINTING

From the beginning of the colonial period to the late 17C, painting was appreciated primarily for the practical uses it served: trade signs and portraiture. The artist often sketched only the face of his subject from life, then completed the remainder of the picture in a stylized manner. Highlighting this group of portraits appealing for their simplicity and charm, is the painting of *Mrs. Freake and Baby Mary* in the Worcester Art Museum.

Development of Painting in the 18C. – The arrival of the Scottish painter **John Smibert** (1688-1751) in America in 1729, opened the era of professional painting. At his studio in Boston, Smibert instructed his students in the art of portraiture as it was practiced in Europe. His works such as *Bishop Berkeley and his Entourage* (Yale University Art Gallery) served as models for the Americans who studied with him, including the Newport artist **Robert Feke** (1705-1750), and **John Singleton Copley** (1738-1815), America's first important portraitist. Copley painted the well-known persons of his day, rendering his subjects amazingly lifelike (*Paul Revere* – MFA, Boston) by his keen attention to detail and surface texture.

(From a photo, Worcester Art Museum, Worcester, Massachusetts.)

Mrs. Elizabeth Freake and Baby Mary.

Gilbert Stuart (1755-1828) was the most important painter of the period, although he is best remembered for his portraits of George Washington, the most famous being the *Athenaeum Portrait (p 106)*. While Stuart, in fact, painted only three portraits of George Washington from life, he used these as models for the replicas he executed.

In the late 18C many Americans traveled to London to study with their countryman **Benjamin West** (1738-1820) who was born in Springfield, and became a leader of the Neo-Classical movement. **Samuel F. B. Morse,** (1791-1872), a fine portraitist before he devoted himself to the invention of the telegraph, studied with West, as did **Ralph Earl** (1751-1801) who spent seven years in London, yet retained the simplicity of his native American folk style. It was also under the guidance of West that **John Trumbull** (1756-1843), the son of the governor of Connecticut, executed a series of historical paintings (*The Battle of Bunker Hill, Signing of the Declaration of Independence...* Yale University Art Gallery), which ultimately made Trumbull famous. Trumbull was later commissioned by the Congress to decorate the rotunda of the Capitol in Washington, D. C.

The Nineteenth Century. – Until the 19C the demand was primarily for portraits, with folk artists such as **William Matthew Prior** (1806-1873) and **Erastus Salisbury Field** (1805-1900) working well into the 1800s. Following the American Revolution, the opening of the West led to an increased awareness of the vast scale and beauty of the nation, and the American scene became a popular theme for artists. In the 1820s painters of the Hudson River school followed the lead of **Thomas Cole** and **Albert Bierstadt** by setting up their easels outdoors and painting directly from nature. Their favorite subjects in New England were the White Mountains and the Connecticut Valley.

The sea was a source of inspiration for other artists. **Fitz Hugh Lane** (1804-1865), living in Gloucester, illustrated in soft, glowing tones the serene beauty of the sea and the offshore islands; and New Bedford artist **William Bradford** (1823-1892), fascinated by the sea and the effects of the northern lights, depicted the rising and setting of the arctic sun, and whalers sailing among icebergs (New Bedford Whaling Museum).

Americans tended to live and study abroad for longer periods of time. **James McNeill Whistler** (1834-1903), a native of Lowell, became known in London for his delicate riverscapes of the Thames. **John Singer Sargent** (1856-1925), born in Italy, traveled extensively and won acclaim as the portraitist of the international social set. The grace and elegance he imparted to his subjects made him the most sought after artist of his day. **William Morris Hunt** (1824-1879), influenced by the French schools, opened a studio in Boston where he introduced artists to the principles of the Barbizon school.

The career of the brilliant watercolorist and master of the naturalist movement **Winslow Homer** (1836-1910) began during the Civil War when Homer served as an illustrator for *Harpers Weekly*. For many years he summered at Prout's Neck, Maine where he painted the large canvases of the sea for which he is known.

Twentieth Century. – During recent times several painters, each with his own distinctive style, have been identified with New England. **Grandma Moses** (1860-1961) *(p 198)*, who did not begin to paint until she was 75, illustrated themes associated with rural New England *(Sleigh Ride, Sugaring–Off)*. The vivid coloration and charm of her pictures are reminiscent of America's folk artists (collection – Bennington Museum).

Norman Rockwell (1894-1978), for many years an illustrator for the *Saturday Evening Post*, painted a chronicle of American life. Rockwell's vision of the persons and events he depicted was always tempered by his warmth, keen attention to detail, and sense of humor. His principal works can be viewed in the Old Corner House *(p 154)* in Stockbridge. **Andrew Wyeth**, born in 1917, summered in Maine where he painted his dramatic canvases which explore the relationship between man and nature. Wyeth's compositions, executed in a lucid, realistic style are simple and uncluttered as is his celebrated *Christina's World*. The Farnsworth Museum in Rockland *(p 79)* exhibits a group of his works.

FOLK ARTS

In rural New England, isolated from the mother country, the necessities for daily living were handmade by the farmer himself or by the tradesman who received a modest fee for his services. The tools, household utensils, cloth, weathervanes and furniture produced, revealed the tastes and flair of the persons who made them and were an expression of the loving attention the early craftsman gave to his work. These items are today admired for their unsophisticated charm, and for the picture they present of the way of life of rural America before the machine age.

Quilts. – Quilted bed coverings comprised of a top and bottom layer of cloth stitched together with a filling in between, were important during the long, cold winter. Finished in a geometric or floral motif, the quilt was one of the few decorative accessories in the rural household. Because of the scarcity of material, patchwork quilts, made from scraps of leftover cloth, were popular. Patchwork quilts were **pieced:** scraps were cut into geometric shapes and sewn together; or **appliquéd:** small pieces of cloth were sewn onto a broad layer of cloth to form a specific design.

Quilting had a pleasant social aspect as well: the **quilting bee.** When the top layer of a quilt was completed – perhaps it was a **wedding quilt** for a girl planning to be married, or a **freedom quilt** to be presented to a young man on his 21st birthday – the women gathered at one house to stitch the quilt together. The stitching could be the most difficult part of making the quilt, and after the quilting bee, there was a party to celebrate.

Stencils. – This early decorative technique which uses precut stencils and paint to embellish furniture, implements, cloth, floors and walls brightened the interiors of many homes. Wall stenciling added color and gaiety to the otherwise plain white plaster or wooden plank surfaces, and in the 19C was a low-cost alternative to the expensive imported wallpapers. The painter had a large selection of motifs from which to choose: geometric figures, flowers, baskets of fruit and the symbolic eagle (liberty), pineapple (hospitality), willow (immortality) and heart and bells (joy).

The popular "fancy" chair, produced by **Lambert Hitchcock** at his factory in Riverton (p 54), was decorated with hand painted stenciling.

A stenciled design.

Weathervanes. – When most New Englanders farmed or went to sea, weathervanes were important as indicators of changes in the weather. The simple profile of a weathervane, carved from wood or cut from metal, topped most buildings of any significant height. A weathervane made to top a church spire might be in the shape of a cockerel or fish, the early Christian symbols. In rural areas the silhouette of a cow, horse or sheep rose above farm buildings, while along the coast the whale, clipper ship and mermaid were popular. New England's famous grasshopper weathervane, atop the cupola of Faneuil Hall (p 96), has been the symbol of the port of Boston since the 17C. The **whirligig,** a carved three dimensional figure with paddle-like arms, was a variation of the weathervane. Large whirligigs indicated wind speed and direction, while smaller ones were used as children's toys.

Figureheads, Trade Signs and Shop Figures. – During the sailing era, carvers sculpted figureheads, sternboards and other accessories for new vessels. A small figure representing the wife or daughter of the ship's owner ordinarily adorned a whaling vessel, while figures (generally female) with windblown hair and clothing were carved as graceful extensions of the prows of clipper ships (see the collections of Mystic, New Bedford, Nantucket, Shelburne).

(By permission of the Peabody Museum of Salem.)

A ship figurehead.

Ship carvers also produced trade signs and shop figures as a sideline. These brightly painted hand carved signs and figures, an early form of advertising, illustrated the specialty of a shop: a mariner holding a sextant was associated with a nautical instrument maker; a sign bearing a large boot indicated a cobbler's shop ... The streets of the Old Port Exchange (p 75) are lined with similar eye-catching signs. Among the large group of **cigar store figures** (illustration p 206) produced in the 19C, the most familiar was the image of the Indian, a reminder that tobacco was a native product. The Indian, ranging from 2 to 7 ft in height, usually wore a headdress of tobacco leaves that was often mistaken for feathers.

Glass. – Until the mid-19C the bulk of the glass manufactured in New England was in the form of window glass and glass containers. Glassware was handmade and a luxury only a few could afford. Deming Jarves and his workmen at **Sandwich** (p 151) changed this situation forever when they made available, for the first time, attractive glassware that could be produced in large quantities and at a price the masses could afford. The factory at Sandwich became famous for its pressed glass that was "lacy" in appearance and manufactured in a variety of forms. Yet despite the large-scale production of pressed glass, the art of glassblowing continued to thrive. Of the numerous glass manufactories operating in New England during the 19C, those in Massachusetts: the New England Glass Company, the Boston and Sandwich Glass Company, and the Mount Washington Glass Works were unrivaled for the beauty of their glass. Production varied from tableware to the decorative blown art glass described below, and may be seen in museums at Sandwich (Sandwich Glass Museum *p 151*), New Bedford (New Bedford Glass Museum *p 140*), Bennington (Bennington Museum *p 198*) and Sturbridge (Old Sturbridge Village Glass Exhibit *p 156*).

Burmese Glass. – An opaque glass shaded from coral pink to yellow, made between 1885 and 1895 by the Mount Washington Glass Company. Shaded pink coloring was made possible by the gold in the glass mixture.

Peachblow. – Technique similar to the above, but coloring shades from opaque white to rose. Soft mat, satiny finish results from an acid bath. Peachblow was made in New England by the New England Glass Company (1886-1888) and known as Wild Rose.

Lava Glass. – Cobalt, metal and lava are used in the production of this glass.

Amberina. – This transparent glass shaded in color from pale amber to rich ruby was called Amberina by the New England Glass Company and Rose Amber by the Mount Washington Glass Company. The amber glass mix contained a small amount of gold which, upon reheating a portion of the glass, resulted in a ruby color.

(Courtesy of the Metropolitan Museum of Art.)

Sandwich lacy cake tray.

Pomona. – The designs and frosted appearance of this delicate, transparent glass manufactured by the New England Glass Company, were originally achieved by covering the piece with wax, scratching through the wax with an etching device, then applying acid which ate through the glass to create the frosted effect. Designs were stained, then the piece was fired. A less costly process was later developed.

Scrimshaw. – The art of carving and etching the surface of ivory, the tusk of the walrus, or the teeth or jawbone of the whale was perfected by New England sailors in the 19C. First, the tooth or other material was set out to dry. Then the surface was polished with shark skin and the picture or design to be etched: scenes of the whale hunt, port scenes, people... was incised onto the bone with a jackknife or needles. Ink, soot or tobacco juice were applied for color. The skill of the sailor was reflected by the intricately detailed ornamentation of the pie crimpers, bird cages, inlaid boxes and many other items he scrimshawed. Exceptional collections will be found at the Whaling Museums in New Bedford *(p 139)*, Nantucket *(p 138)* and Sharon *(p 112)*.

Decoys. – Wooden decoys sculpted and painted to resemble geese, ducks, shore birds and waterfowl have been used since colonial times to lure birds to within range of the hunter. The idea originated with the Indians who used heaps of mud, reeds, and skins filled with grass, to attract waterfowl, and by the 19C decoy making had developed into an art form. Regional characteristics became apparent as craftsmen portrayed the birds with increasing realism and attention to natural conditions. In Maine where the sea is rough and wind strong, decoys were large and heavy, and had a flat bottom and low head to ensure stability; in the Massachusetts Bay area where the waters are calmer, the decoys were lighter. Purely decorative decoys such as the shore birds and miniatures carved and painted by **A. Elmer Crowell** of Massachusetts *(Heritage Plantation p 152)* are among the more elegant forms this art has taken.

In our day it is still possible to observe craftsmen engaged in producing decoys along the coast from Cape Cod to Maine. The Shelburne Museum (Vt.) has a remarkably fine and comprehensive collection of approximately 2 000 decoys.

Gravestones. – The Puritans, who found little time during their lifetime for art, have left outstanding examples of the skill of the early stonecutters who carved and incised the gravestones that stand row after row, amidst the tall grass that has grown up around them in New England's old burial grounds.

The designs cut into the stones were at first symbolic and plain. In the 17C typical motifs were the hourglass, sun, scythe, winged skull, hearts and cherubim (symbols for life, death and resurrection). Throughout the 18C realistic portraits and detailed scenes illustrating the death of the deceased, became increasingly popular. The romantic tendencies of the 19C were interpreted in gravestone art by the extensive use of the weeping willow and the urn, classical symbols for death.

The old cemeteries in Lexington, Salem, Newport, Newburyport, Boston, New London and in numerous small villages have splendid examples of gravestone art.

Gravestones, Lexington, Massachusetts.

LITERATURE

The literature produced in the colonies in the 17 and 18C consisted primarily of histories and religious writings: sermons, pamphlets, diaries and journals. The *History of Plimoth Plantation* by William Bradford, Governor of Plimoth Plantation between 1621 and 1657; and a *Journal* account of life in the Massachusetts Bay Colony written by the Bay Colony's first governor, John Winthrop (1588-1649), are the principal records of this period. The churchman **Cotton Mather** (1669-1728) wrote hundreds of sermons, scientific tracts and treatises including his monumental *Ecclesiastical History of New England*.

The 18C is represented by **Benjamin Franklin** (1706-1790). Ben Franklin – inventor, statesman, philosopher and scientist was highly regarded at home and abroad for his satires of British policies in America. *Poor Richard's Almanac*, written and published by Franklin, contains his short, witty proverbs and was found in most New England homes.

Flowering of New England Literature. – In the 19C a literature distinctly American in theme, ideas, characters and setting emerged in New England. **Edgar Allen Poe** (1809-1849), a Bostonian whose sensitivities were deeply stirred by the mysterious, was the originator of a new genre, the modern detective story.

The Transcendental movement, based on the belief of the mystical union of all nature, gained popularity under the leadership of **Ralph Waldo Emerson** (1803-1882). Emerson's *Essays*, lectures he delivered across the United States, includes his essay on *Nature* (1836), a statement of the ideals and liberal principles of transcendentalism. **Henry David Thoreau** (1817-1862), a disciple of Emerson, put the tenets of transcendentalism into practice by living a solitary existence at Walden Pond for two years. *Walden* is a personal account of his experiences during this time. Transcendentalism inspired experiments in communal living: Brook Farm and Fruitlands, and had its own literary magazine, *The Dial*. Bronson Alcott was a contributor to *The Dial*. His daughter **Louisa May Alcott** (1832-1888) became famous as the authoress of the novel *Little Women*.

Attracted by transcendentalism, **Nathaniel Hawthorne** (1806-1864) lived at Brook Farm for a brief time. As a writer, he contributed toward establishing the short story and the psychological novel as significant American literary forms. Hawthorne's Puritan ancestry is reflected in the gloomy atmosphere and moralistic themes of his short stories and novels such as the *House of the Seven Gables (p 148)* and *The Scarlet Letter* – a symbolic study of the effects of sin on man's soul. **Herman Melville** (1819-1891) influenced by Hawthorne's technique wrote the classic epic of the whaling era *Moby Dick*.

Many writers supported the abolitionist movement. **William Lloyd Garrison** (1805-1879) published the anti-slavery newspaper *The Liberator* for more than three decades until the adoption of the 13th Amendment. **Harriet Beecher Stowe's** (1811-1896) best-selling novel *Uncle Tom's Cabin* exposed the brutality and cruelties of slavery.

With the expansion of the nation came a heightened awareness of regional differences, and the introduction of a literary genre depicting local color, scenery and speech. Hartford resident **Mark Twain** *(p 43)* was a master of the new regional literature. His popular works, *Tom Sawyer* and *Huckleberry Finn*, portrayed life on the Mississippi River. **Sarah Orne Jewett's** (1849-1909) novel *The Country of the Pointed Firs* is a poetic account, in prose, of the people, rural countryside and offshore islands of Maine.

History continued to be a favorite subject of New Englanders. **William Hickling Prescott** (1796-1859) wrote historical biographies and **George Bancroft's** (1800-1891) *History of the United States* was the first major history concerning the United States. **Francis Parkman's** (1823-1893) study of the conflict between England and France in the New World covers the period beginning with the *History of the Conspiracy of Pontiac* and ends four decades later with *A Half Century of Conflict*. **Henry Adams'** (1838-1918) *History of the United States of America* treats the factors responsible for shaping the nation's character.

In Amherst **Noah Webster** (1758-1843) published his *American Dictionary of the English Language* (1828) which, after many revisions, continues to be a major reference of the American language.

Twentieth Century. – In the 20C the American theater won international acclaim through the works of playwright **Eugene O'Neill** (1888-1953) whose close association with the Provincetown Players began in 1916 when his *Bound East for Cardiff* was produced in Provincetown. New England was the setting for a number of his plays: *Desire Under the Elms, Mourning Becomes Electra* and the Pulitzer prize winning *Beyond the Horizon*. New England born-and-bred authors: John P. Marquand, Kenneth Roberts, William Dean Howells, and writers who adopted New England as their second home: Edith Wharton, Pearl Buck, Norman Mailer, Alexander Solzhenitsyn are distinguished by the literary recognition they have earned during their lifetime.

Poetry. – **Henry Wadsworth Longfellow** (1807-1882) born in Portland, Maine was a professor of modern languages at Harvard. One of the most widely read poets of his day, Longfellow chose as the subjects of many of his poems American folk heroes: Hiawatha, Evangeline, Paul Revere, Miles Standish. His contemporary **John Greenleaf Whittier** 1807-1892) *(p 141)* was a spokesman for the abolitionist cause and wrote poetry that portrayed life in rural, pre-industrialized New England.

Emily Dickinson (1830-1886), an Amherst resident who remained a recluse throughout most of her life, wrote verses rich in lyricism and sensitivity. **Robert Frost** (1874-1963), a poet of nature, lived for a time (1901-1909) on a farm in New Hampshire, and later in life spent his summers in Vermont. His verse, inspired by the New England character and countryside, has a refreshing simplicity, as in his *Stopping by the Woods on a Snowy Evening*.

Amy Lowell (1874-1925), a leader of the Imagist movement, experimented with new rhythms and sharp images. **e.e. cummings,** (1894-1962), experimenting in a different way, used unusual punctuation and no capital letters in his verse.

LEGEND

★★★ **Worth a journey**

★★ **Worth a detour**

★ **Interesting**

Recommended sightseeing tour with departure point and direction indicated :

on the road   in town

The following symbols, when accompanied by a name in bold print, locate the sights described in this guide :

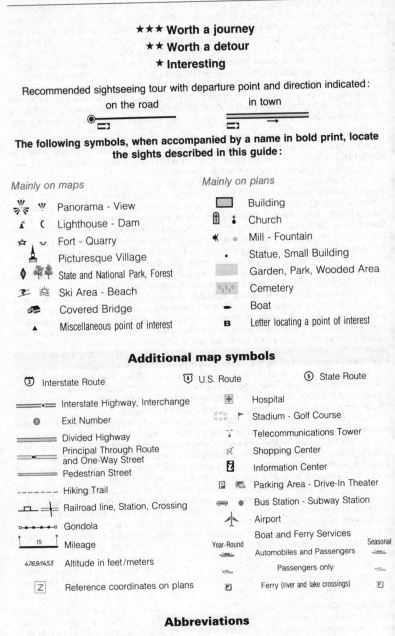

Mainly on maps		Mainly on plans	
☀ ☘	Panorama - View	⬚	Building
⌞ ⟨	Lighthouse - Dam	⬥ ✝	Church
☆ ⌄	Fort - Quarry	✶ ○	Mill - Fountain
⛪	Picturesque Village	▪	Statue, Small Building
◊ 🌳	State and National Park, Forest		Garden, Park, Wooded Area
🎿 ☀	Ski Area - Beach		Cemetery
🚐	Covered Bridge	⬤	Boat
▲	Miscellaneous point of interest	**B**	Letter locating a point of interest

Additional map symbols

③ Interstate Route	④ U.S. Route	⑤ State Route

	Interstate Highway, Interchange	➕	Hospital
❶	Exit Number	▶	Stadium - Golf Course
	Divided Highway	▔	Telecommunications Tower
	Principal Through Route and One-Way Street		Shopping Center
	Pedestrian Street	⊞	Information Center
- - - - -	Hiking Trail	🅿 🎦	Parking Area - Drive-In Theater
	Railroad line, Station, Crossing	🚌 ●	Bus Station - Subway Station
● ● ● ●	Gondola	✈	Airport
15	Mileage		Boat and Ferry Services
4769/1453	Altitude in feet/meters	Year-Round	Automobiles and Passengers	Seasonal
Z	Reference coordinates on plans		Passengers only	
		F	Ferry (river and lake crossings)	F

Abbreviations

c	Chamber of Commerce	L	Library	POL.	Police
H	City Hall, Town Hall	M	Museum	T	Theater
J	Courthouse	P.O.	Post Office		

PUBLIC HOLIDAYS

January 1: New Year's Day

The third Monday in February: George Washington's Birthday

The last Monday in May: Memorial Day

July 4: Independence Day

The first Monday in September: Labor Day

The second Monday in October: Columbus Day

November 11: Veteran's Day

The fourth Thursday in November: Thanksgiving Day

December 25: Christmas Day

The following special holidays are observed in some states:

January 15: Martin Luther King Day (Connecticut and Massachusetts)

February 12: Lincoln's Birthday (Vermont)

The last Monday in April: Fast Day (New Hampshire)

The Monday nearest April 19: Patriot's Day (Massachusetts)

The first Tuesday after the first Monday in Novembe Election Day (New Hampshire, Rhod Island, Vermont)

Connecticut

Area : 5 009 sq miles
Population : 3 154 217
Capital : Hartford
Nickname : Constitution State
State Flower : Mountain Laurel

This rectangle extending about 90 miles east to west and 55 miles north to south is named for the river that divides it almost in half : the *Connecticut* – an Indian name meaning "beside the long tidal river".

Small colonial villages are scattered throughout the state, offering a pleasing contrast to the densely populated industrialized centers in the Hartford region and on the south shore : Stamford, Bridgeport, Stratford, New Haven. The affluent communities in southwestern Connecticut's Fairfield County (New Canaan, Ridgefield, Greenwich) are suburbs of New York.

The state is predominantly rural with two-thirds of its woodlands included in the state park and forest system. To the south, on the shores of Long Island Sound – a long arm of the ocean protected by Long Island – long, sandy beaches separate the former whaling ports of New London, Mystic and Stonington. The idyllic Litchfield Hills, rising gently in the northern part of the state, are an extension of the Green Mountains and the Berkshire Hills.

The Constitution State. – Connecticut's first settlers were staunch Puritans who found the atmosphere in Boston too "liberal." They arrived from Massachusetts in 1633 by the Connecticut River, and within two years had founded the river towns of Hartford, Windsor and Wethersfield.

In 1639 these towns joined to form the Hartford Colony, later to become the Connecticut Colony. The Fundamental Orders of Connecticut, the document drawn up and adopted January 14, 1639 to serve as the basis of government in the Hartford Colony, is recognized by many as the world's first written constitution – thus the state's nickname, the Constitution State.

Economy. – Benefiting from the wide range of products developed by the state's innovators and inventors, Connecticut has traditionally been a prosperous manufacturing center and at present ranks second in the nation in per capita income. Mechanical innovations introduced by Connecticut clockmakers *(p 36)* made clockmaking one of the state's earliest major industries and put a clock in almost every home in America.

In the 19C, the production of firearms became an important business. The Colt .45 revolver, developed by Hartford entrepreneur **Samuel Colt,** and the Winchester rifle, were manufactured in Connecticut. During the same period Eli Whitney manufactured his revolutionary new cotton gin in New Haven and introduced the use of standardized parts at his firearms factory nearby. Danbury became known for its hats, Waterbury and Torrington for items made of brass, and Meriden for its fine silverware.

Connecticut continues to obtain a great part of its income from industry : electrical goods, tools, chemicals, plastics, jet engines, helicopters and nuclear submarines are its leading products. The Electric Boat Division of General Dynamics at Groton *(p 38)* builds submarines for the nation's submarine fleet. A number of major corporations (Xerox, General Electric, Union Carbide) and insurance companies maintain corporate headquarters in the state.

Agriculturally, poultry, fruit and dairy products, marketed locally, are major sources of income. Broadleaf tobacco *(p 21),* used for cigar wrapping, is shade grown in the Connecticut and Farmington Valleys. Picturesque tobacco sheds identify the flat valley regions where tobacco is grown.

Recreation. – On the south shore there are opportunities for swimming, boating (sailing is popular) and fishing in the calm waters of the Long Island Sound.

The streams and tributaries of the Connecticut River, and the Housatonic River (the Housatonic especially for trout) are favorites of fishermen.

Forest preserves and the state parks offer hiking, camping, picnicking and hunting. For reservations and information regarding camping at state campgrounds and hunting and fishing contact : *The Department of Environmental Protection, Information and Education, State Office Building, 165 Capitol Avenue, Hartford, CT 06106.* The *Connecticut Walk Book* is an outstanding guide to the blazed trails in the state *(see Books to Read p 210).*

The largest and most popular ski area in the state is Mohawk Mountain.

BRIDGEPORT

Michelin tourist map - fold 20 – Pop 142 140

This heavily industrialized and populated center on Long Island Sound was the home of **Phineas T. Barnum,** the colorful showman, promoter and former mayor of Bridgeport. Barnum's world famous three-ring circus toured America and Europe in the 19C and won acclaim as the Greatest Show on Earth. A statue of Barnum stands in Seaside Park at the end of Main Street, looking out on the harbor.

Manufacturing, government, service industries, and wholesale and retail activities are important to the local economy. Bridgeport's manufacturing plants produce machinery, transportation equipment and primary and fabricated metals.

Prominent among the city's educational institutions is the **University of Bridgeport.**

Barnum Museum. – *820 Main Street. Currently closed for renovation; scheduled reopening late 1988.* This ornate building planned by Barnum, and the circus memorabilia it houses, reflect his exuberant personality as a showman. Highlights include costumes and furnishings that belonged to Tom Thumb - Barnum's first major attraction, a model Alpine Village with 22 000 working parts, and the William Brinley Model Circus of more than 500 000 hand carved circus animals, performers and wagons.

Ferry to Port Jefferson, Long Island, NY. – *Union Square Dock. Car and passenger service year round (1 hour 20 min one way).* ☏ *(203) 334-5993.*

BRISTOL

Michelin tourist map - fold 20 – 18 miles west of Hartford – Pop 58 068

In the 19C, America's clockmaking industry was centered in the Bristol region where in one year alone – 1860 – more than 200 000 clocks were produced. The neighboring towns of Terryville and Thomaston were named for the Connecticut clockmakers **Eli Terry** and **Seth Thomas.** No longer a major producer of clocks, present-day Bristol earns its living by manufacturing electrical and electronic equipment and metal parts.

American Clock and Watch Museum★★. – *100 Maple Street. Open April through October 11 AM to 5 PM; $2.50. A slide show is presented on the history of clockmaking.*

Clocks were most often custom made until the early 19C when innovations introduced by Connecticut clockmakers revolutionized the industry. By using standardized wooden parts, Eli Terry made it possible to turn out a moderately priced timepiece most people could afford. His major innovation, the small and compact **shelf clock,** was easily carried by the Yankee peddlars who sold thousands of these lightweight timepieces in states east of the Mississippi. The clocks and watches in the museum's collection are of American and more specifically Connecticut production. There are numerous versions of Eli Terry's shelf clock. The Annex contains novelty clocks and timepieces easily identified by their shape: acorn, banjo and tall case clocks.

The CONNECTICUT VALLEY ★

Michelin tourist map - fold 21

Wide, shallow and bordered by unspoiled countryside, the Connecticut River sprawls into a multitude of coves and boat harbors as it ends its more than 400 mile journey downstream to the Long Island Sound. Villages such as Old Lyme and Old Saybrook have retained their early character because of a sandbar, at the mouth of the Connecticut River, which has always prevented deep-draft vessels from entering these waters.

There are several ways to explore the valley: by land – by following the itinerary below through small riverside towns; and from the river – by taking a cruise from East Haddam, Deep River or Essex, or a summer ferry ride *(3 hours)* from Haddam to Long Island.

From I-95 (Exit: Old Saybrook) to Moodus

20 miles – allow 4 hours – local map p 37

From I-95, Exit 69 (Old Saybrook) take Rte 9 to Exit 3 in the direction of Essex.

Essex★. – Pop 5 346. Established in 1645, Essex developed into an important shipbuilding center by the early 18C, and in 1775 produced America's first warship, the *Oliver Cromwell.* Today Essex attracts a sophisticated summer crowd whose yachts and cabin cruisers are berthed at local marinas. The town's main street has interesting shops, art galleries and the Old Griswold Inn, which has been operating since 1776. A former warehouse at Steamboat Dock houses the **Connecticut River Museum** *(open April through December 10 AM to 5 PM, closed Monday; $1.50),* with maritime exhibits including model of the *Oliver Cromwell.*

Valley Railroad. – *Essex Depot. Train rides from Essex to Chester with connecting river cruises from Deep River to East Haddam (2 hrs 10 min RT). Train ride only, 55 min RT. Daily mid-June to Labor Day; after Labor Day to late October Wednesday through Sunday and holidays; early May to mid-June Wednesday, Saturday and Sunday. Train rides on weekends in December except holidays. Train and cruise $9.95, 2 – 11 yrs $4.95; train ride only $6.95, 2 – 11 yrs $2.95. For additional information* ☏ *(203) 767-0103.*

Rides on the railroad's early 20C steam train afford views of the valley landscape and the Connecticut River.

From Essex take Rte 9 to Exit 6, then Rte 148 to the ferry that crosses the river.

Chester-Hadlyme Ferry. – *5 min. April through November 7 AM to 6:45 PM; car and driver 75¢.*

During the crossing there is a good view of Gillette Castle, perched high on a hilltop above the east bank.

Take Rte 148, then turn left following the signs for Gillette Castle.

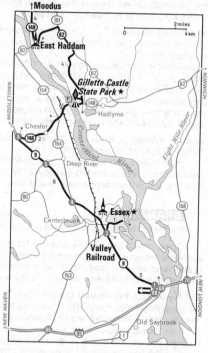

Gillette Castle State Park★. – *Open fourth Saturday in May to Columbus Day 10 AM to 5 PM; mid-October to third week in December weekends only 10 AM to 4 PM; $1.00. The castle may be visited.*

The castles of the Rhine Valley inspired the design of this bizarre stone castle built in 1919 by the actor **William Gillette**. Gillette drew up the plans for the castle and decorated each of the 24 rooms himself. Furniture that slides conveniently on metal tracks, and other devices in the castle were developed by Gillette who had a special fascination for gadgetry. The 190 acre estate offers splendid **vistas★** of the Connecticut River and valley below. *Picnicking and hiking trails.*

Take Rte 82 to East Haddam.

East Haddam. – Pop 6 068. This small town with beautiful old homes is proud of its little red **schoolhouse** where Nathan Hale once taught, and of being the site of the **Goodspeed Opera House,** a Victorian style opera house dating from the era when New York – Connecticut steamers called at East Haddam. Musicals are presented during the theater's season: April through December. *For ticket information ☏ (203) 873-8668.*

River cruises operate between Haddam and Long Island June through September (3 hours). For information ☏ New England Steamboat Line (203) 345-4507.

Follow Rte 149 which offers good views of the Connecticut River.

Moodus. – Facing the Moodus green is the **Amasa Day House** (1816) which contains well-preserved examples of the floor stenciling laid on more than a century ago. *Guided tours (1/2 hour) May 15 to October 15, 1 to 5 PM; closed Mondays, holidays and the rest of the year; $2.00.*

COVENTRY

Michelin tourist map - fold 15 – 20 miles east of Hartford – Pop 9 359

This small town in rural northeastern Connecticut was the birthplace of the American schoolteacher-patriot **Nathan Hale** (1755-1776). Hale was commissioned an officer in the Connecticut militia when the Revolution broke out. After participating in several military operations, he volunteered for the dangerous mission of obtaining information about the British troops on Long Island. Discovered by the British, and hanged as a spy September 22, 1776, the last words young Hale is said to have spoken: "I only regret that I have but one life to lose for my country," are among the most memorable in the annals of American history.

Nathan Hale Homestead. – *Open June 1 to October 15, 1 to 5 PM; closed the rest of the year; $2.00.*

This ten-room dwelling built in 1776 by Nathan Hale's father, was the family homestead until 1832. The house contains Hale family memorabilia and period furnishings.

*Other **Michelin Green Guides** available in English are:*

Austria		
Canada		
England: The West Country	*London*	*Brittany*
Germany	*New York City*	*Châteaux of the Loire*
Greece	*Paris*	*Dordogne*
Italy	*Rome*	*French Riviera*
Portugal		*Normandy*
Scotland		*Provence*
Spain		
Switzerland		

FARMINGTON ★
Michelin tourist map - folds 14 and 20 – 10 miles west of Hartford – Pop 17 005

Beautiful 18 and 19C residences line the streets of this elegant Hartford suburb on the Farmington River. Several of these early structures on Main Street are part of the well-known school for girls, **Miss Porter's School.**

Hill-Stead Museum★. – *671 Farmington Avenue. Guided tours (1 hour) Wednesday through Sunday 2 to 5 PM; closed Monday, Tuesday, January 15 to February 15 and holidays; $3.00.*

In 1900 the millionaire Alfred Atmore Pope had this residence designed by Stanford White *(p 184)*. Hill-Stead's attractive furnishings and European and Oriental objets d'art lend a pleasant, lived-in atmosphere to this mansion-museum. Pope's interest in the impressionists led him to purchase a large number of the works of art displayed, especially the fine paintings by Monet *(Haystacks)*, Manet *(The Guitar Lady)*, Degas *(The Tub, The Jockeys)*, and several canvases by Whistler and Mary Cassatt.

Stanley-Whitman House. – *37 High Street. Guided tours (1 hour) May through October 1 to 4 PM, closed Monday; $2.00.*

The influence of the Jacobean and Elizabethan building styles on American colonial architecture is seen in this 17C house, with its overhang, decorative pendants and central chimney. Inside there are furnishings and handcrafted items of the period.

GRANBY
Michelin tourist map - fold 14 – 16 miles north of Hartford – Pop 8 569

Open, netted fields of shade-grown tobacco lie outside of Granby, one of the major centers of tobacco production in the Farmington Valley. The tobacco raised in this region is dried and stored in the long, brown-weathered barns which dot the landscape, and is used commercially in sheet form as the outer wrapping of cigars.

Old New-Gate Prison and Copper Mine★. – *Take Rte 20 East then turn north onto Newgate Road. Open mid-May through October 10 AM to 4:30 PM, closed Monday and Tuesday; $1.75. Rubber-soled shoes advised.*

This former copper mine was worked until the mid-18C when financial setbacks induced the owners of the mine to sell the property to the colonial government. The government transformed the mine into a prison where robbers, counterfeiters, horse thieves and later Tories and British prisoners of war were held captive. Walking through the damp, cold mine tunnels buried deep within the earth, it is not difficult to imagine the despair of those prisoners who, as a precaution against escape, were forced to sleep in these subterranean passageways where sunlight never enters.

GROTON
Michelin tourist map - fold 21 – Pop 10 024

This small industrial city on the Thames River, opposite New London *(p 52)*, is the home port of the United States Atlantic submarine fleet. Sailing vessels, merchant ships, tugboats, sightseeing boats and submarines ply the waters of this busy deepwater harbor. Boatyards on the Thames turn out a variety of ships, but it is the Electric Boat Division of General Dynamics – builder of the *USS Nautilus (p 39)*, the world's first atomic-powered submarine – that is best known. On a hilltop above the river rises the **Groton Monument,** a stone obelisk which commemorates the battle fought at **Fort Griswold** in 1781 *(p 52)*.

Each year, in June, the Thames is the site of the colorful Yale-Harvard regatta.

■ **SIGHTS** *time: 4 hours*

River Boat Ride★. – *Thames Botel and Harbour Inn, 193 Thames Street. Boat rides (time: 1 hour) late May to mid-June and after Labor Day to Columbus Day weekends only 11:15 AM, 12:30, 1:45 and 3 PM; mid-June to Labor Day daily 10 and 11:15 AM, 12:30, 1:45 and 3 PM; $5.00. ☏ (203) 445-8111.*

The boat the *River Queen* travels upstream on the Thames to the U.S. Naval Submarine Base, before returning to the harbor. The following will be seen during the cruise:

On the Groton side of the river:

United States Naval Submarine Base. – *The Submarine Base is not open for general visiting.* The Submarine Base is a complex of more than 270 buildings: administrative offices, barracks, hospital and classrooms. Subs are berthed and repaired at the Lower Base beside the river. A 250 000 gallon Escape Training Tank, identifiable by its spiral stairway, is used for instruction on the methods of escape from a submarine.

Nautilus Memorial. – *Description p 39.*

Pfizer, Inc. – The buildings trimmed in blue are the laboratories of this world leading producer of antibiotics.

Electric Boat Division of General Dynamics. – Electric Boat produced the Navy's first submarine (the *Holland*) in 1900, and since then has gone on to build more than half of all the submarines for the U.S. Navy, including the first nuclear-powered sub, the *Nautilus (see p 39)*. At present General Dynamics Electric Boat Division is the sole producer of the Ohio Class submarine. Electric Boat is Groton's largest employer, with about 18 000 workers.

Groton Monument. – This obelisk is a memorial to the patriots who were killed when British troops captured Fort Griswold and set fire to New London *(p 52)*.

On the New London side of the river:

United States Coast Guard Academy. – *Description p 53.*

Submarines. – Near the Coast Guard Academy, submarines will be observed moored at the submarine tender *Fulton* where they are outfitted and repaired.

Connecticut College. – About 1 600 men and women attend this four-year liberal arts school.

Fort Trumbull and the Naval Underwater Systems Center. – The fort was the scene of a British victory in 1781 after which triumphant British troops, led by Benedict Arnold, set fire to New London.

Scientists and engineers working at the modern Underwater Systems Center on the grounds of the fort, are involved in developing technology related to undersea warfare.

Nautilus Memorial. – *Berthed at a pier adjacent to the Submarine Base. I-95 Exit 87 to Rte 12 North, then follow the signs. Open mid-April to mid-October 9 AM to 5 PM, the rest of the year 9 AM to 3:30 PM (5 PM Saturday and Sunday); closed Tuesday. During peak season the line to visit the Nautilus closes 3:30 PM. Schedule may vary ☎ (203) 449-3174.*

With the launching in 1954 of the *USS Nautilus*, the world's first nuclear-powered submarine, submarine technology entered the Atomic age. The *Nautilus* established new submerged records for speed, distance and length of time under water, and in 1958 became the first submarine to pass beneath the North Pole.

Decommissioned in 1980, the 320 ft vessel is now the principal attraction at the U.S. Naval Submarine Nautilus Memorial/Submarine Force Library and Museum complex. The torpedoe room, control room, and other sections of the ship may be viewed. At the **museum,** exhibits present the story of underwater navigation, the *Nautilus,* and life aboard a sub. Operational periscopes allow visitors to practice sighting.

A selection of the principal ski areas in New England is presented on the Michelin Tourist Map accompanying this guide.

Vermont ski areas described in the guide are:

Bromley Mountain	*Mount Mansfield*
Jay Peak	*Stratton Mountain*
Killington	

GUILFORD

Michelin tourist map - fold 20 – 14 miles east of New Haven – Pop 18 474

In 1639 the Vicar Henry Whitfield arrived at this place with twenty-five families and bought the land that became Guilford from the Menunketuck Indians. Fishing, commerce, mills, even a shipyard developed in this small town which grew rapidly because of its location on the main road between New York and Boston.

Guilford's lovely green and 18 and 19C homes reflect the town's early prosperity.

Henry Whitfield Museum. – *Old Whitfield Street. Open April through October 10 AM to 5 PM (4 PM the rest of the year); closed Monday and Tuesday, Thanksgiving Day and December 15 to January 14; $1.25.*

In a land where wood was plentiful the Vicar Whitfield, inspired by the dwellings of northern England, built his home of stone. It was the first dwelling (1639) built in Guilford, and also served as the village church, garrison and meeting hall. Restored to its 17C appearance, the house is the oldest stone dwelling in New England.

Hyland House. – *84 Boston Street. Guided tours (45 min) early June to mid-October 10 AM to 4:30 PM, closed Mondays and holidays; $1.50.*

This typical "saltbox" *(p 27)* built in 1660 is furnished with American antiques of the period. The parlor is noteworthy for its fine wood paneling.

HARTFORD ★★

Michelin tourist map - fold 14 – Pop 135 720

This Yankee city, the capital of Connecticut, is easily recognized from a distance by the tall office towers rising beside the Connecticut River. These modern buildings serve as the headquarters of numerous insurance companies – Hartford being a major national insurance center as well as the seat of the state government.

Manufacturing plays an important role in the city's economy. Pratt and Whitney Aircraft, the Colt Industries – the Colt revolver credited with "winning the West" was manufactured in Hartford during the 19C – and producers of typewriters, precision instruments and computers are located in the Greater Hartford region. The blue, star-speckled, onion shaped dome of the **Colt factory** is a landmark visible from I-91.

The extensive revitalization of Hartford's downtown area during recent decades has included the construction of two shopping and business complexes: Constitution Plaza and the Civic Center; the transformation of the Richardson-designed Cheney Building (1877) into the Richardson, a shopping mall and apartments; and striking examples of the architecture of the 1980s such as One Corporate Center.

HISTORICAL NOTES

From Good Hope to the Connecticut Colony. – Hartford's location on a waterway navigable to the sea led the Dutch to establish Fort Good Hope, a trading post, at this site in 1633. Because of the region's abundant supply of furs and timber, Puritans from the Massachusetts Bay Colony settled in the area two years later. Their village, Hartford, grew quickly and in 1638 Hartford joined with Wethersfield *(p 55)* and Windsor to form the Hartford Colony. The **Fundamental Orders of Connecticut,** the governing document drawn up by the members of the Hartford Colony in 1639, has been regarded by many as the world's first constitution. In 1662 the Hartford Colony became the Colony of Connecticut.

The Charter Oak. – The independence of the Hartford Colony was guaranteed by the Royal Charter of 1662. In 1687, however, the Royal Governor Edmond Andros demanded the return of the Charter. According to legend, during a meeting that took place one evening to discuss the matter, someone suddenly extinguished the candles and, in the darkness, fled with the Charter. The Charter was hidden in an oak tree where it remained until Sir Edmond returned to England a few years later. The tree, which became known as the Charter Oak, was felled during a storm in the 19C.

A variety of items made from the Charter Oak can be seen in the city's museums. The number of objects supposedly made from the tree is so large that it prompted Mark Twain to remark there is: "... a walking stick, dog collar, needle case, three–legged stool, bootjack, dinner table, tenpin alley, toothpick and enough Charter Oak to build a plank road from Hartford to Salt Lake City." The original Charter remains intact and is on display together with the Fundamental Orders of Connecticut and other documents at the State Library *(p 43).*

An Insurance Center. – Hartford's insurance industry originated in the 18C when a group of men agreed to cover a shipowner's losses if his vessel did not return home safely. As shipping began to decline in the 19C, the industry shifted from marine to fire insurance. The sound reputation of Hartford's insurance companies was established during this period after such incidents as the following occurred.

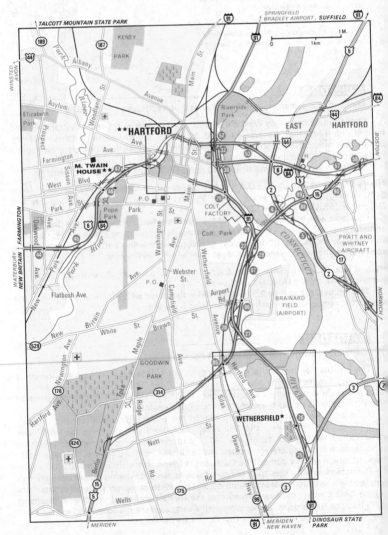

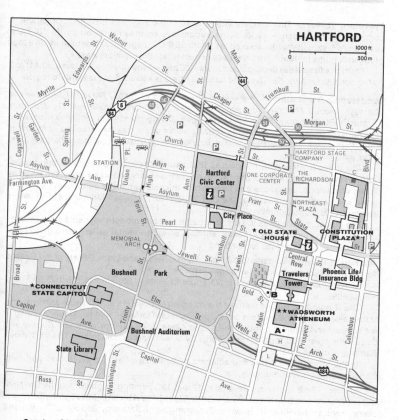

HARTFORD

October 31, 1835 more than 600 buildings were destroyed by fire in New York City. The enormous number of claims filed forced many New York insurance firms into bankruptcy, however, on a snowy winter night the President of the Hartford Fire Insurance Company traveled to New York to assure his policyholders that their claims would be honored. The Hartford Company promptly paid the claims and its business increased.

Hartford's continually fine record through the 19 and 20C following similar disasters in Boston and Chicago, earned for the city its title "Insurance Capital of the Nation." The approximately forty insurance companies located in Greater Hartford today employ more than 10 % of the labor force throughout the metropolitan region.

■ THE DOWNTOWN AREA *time: 4 hours*

Leave your car at the parking facility in the Civic Center.

CityPlace. – This is Connecticut's tallest building, a 39-story office-retail tower (1984) with setbacks and a granite and glass exterior that blends well with its surroundings. Designed by Skidmore, Owings & Merrill, CityPlace has an atrium where exhibits and concerts are offered year round. A pedestrian walkway links CityPlace to the Hartford Civic Center and shopping area.

Hartford Civic Center. – Completed in 1975, this concrete and glass structure is Connecticut's major convention center and the entertainment center of Hartford. Besides the 14 500 seat Coliseum, 10 000 sq ft of exhibition space, and Assembly Hall, the Center has an enclosed shopping mall, adjacent hotel, and underground parking facilities.

Diagonally across from the Civic Center, on Church Street, bold lettering identifies the simple elongated building mass (1977) with a smooth, patterned exterior as the home of the **Hartford Stage Company.** Performances are presented by the Company in its 489 seat theater October to June ☎ *(203) 527-5151.*

Old State House★. – *Open Monday through Saturday 10 AM (12 noon Sunday) to 5 PM. The Visitors Center on the lower level has brochures, maps and other information on Hartford and travel destinations throughout the state.*

This elegant Federal style building (1792) with its graceful staircases, arches, balustrades and classical pediments was designed by Charles Bulfinch, the architect of the capitol buildings of Massachusetts and Maine.

The legislative chambers on the second floor contain original furnishings.

Constitution Plaza★. – The modern 12 acre plaza completed in the 1960s provided Hartford with new office buildings, shops, an open mall, and added a striking landmark to the city's skyline: the **Phoenix Mutual Life Insurance Building** – an elliptical glass-sheathed tower referred to as "the Boat" because of its shape. The Plaza is the site of the annual Hartford Festival of Light, a colorful lighting display held every evening from late November to January 1.

Travelers Tower. – This building is the home of the Travelers Insurance Company, a company which began – as its name suggests – by insuring travelers. In 1864 the company's first policyholder insured his life for $5 000 "... against accident while on a four block walk home for lunch from his place of business;" the premium was 2¢.

From the **Observation Deck** *(guided tours – 20 min – June through August 8:30 AM to 3 PM; closed Saturdays, Sundays and holidays)* there is a **view★★** of the Hartford region.

Wadsworth Atheneum★★. – *600 Main Street. Open 11 AM to 7 PM (5 PM Saturday and Sunday); closed Mondays and major holidays; $3.00; free Thursdays. Guided tours (1 hour) 1 PM Thursday, Saturday and Sunday. During the current period of renovation and reinstallation of the collections specific works of art may be exhibited in locations other than those indicated below. For information regarding new installations inquire at the information desk.*

The present Atheneum building is the result of several additions to the original Gothic Revival structure erected in 1842 to house the library and art gallery established by Daniel Wadsworth. Donations and bequests to the museum made subsequent additions to the earlier structure possible: the Colt Wing (1907), Morgan Memorial (1910), Avery Memorial (1934) and Goodwin Wing.

The museum, an interesting blend of traditional and modern concepts in museography, has among its facilities a theater, studios, an experimental gallery and a gallery that offers aesthetic experiences for the blind.

Main Floor. – The modern galleries: Austin, Matrix, Avery, and Lions Gallery of the Senses (for the blind) are reserved for temporary exhibits.

In Avery Court there is an 8 ft tall figure of Venus, sculpted in the 16C by Pietro Francavilla.

The Huntington Gallery features the museum's collection of 19C **French paintings**, one of its major strengths. Canvases by Monet *(Beach at Trouville)*, Renoir *(Monet Painting in his Garden at Argenteuil)*, Toulouse-Lautrec *(Jane Avril Leaving the Moulin Rouge)* and Degas are presented together with works by Manet, Ingres, Delacroix *(Turkish Women Bathing)* and Cézanne.

In the Morgan Great Hall and adjacent galleries Egyptian, Greek, Roman and early Christian artifacts are on display.

Second Floor. – Four rooms are devoted to 17 and 18C painting. Highlighting the Spanish, Italian, French and Dutch masters are Goya *(Gossiping Women)*, Caravaggio *(Ecstacy of Saint Francis)*, Rembrandt, Rubens, Zurbarán *(Saint Serpion)*, Boucher, Chardin and Antony van Dyck.

The museum's comprehensive collection of **Meissen** is exhibited in the Morgan Wing. Collections of English silver and glass are also found on this floor.

Third Floor. – An airy, well-lit room *(G301)* contains contemporary painting and sculpture by artists such as Adolf Gottlieb, William de Kooning and Frank Stella. Note here, too, the delightfully realistic *Sunbather*, a creation in polyester and fiberglass by Duane Hanson.

American Collection. – Second and third floor galleries in the Avery Wing contain the museum's collection of American art spanning the early colonial period to the 20C.

Included are portraits by Copley *(Mrs. Seymour Fort)*, Ralph Earl *(Chief Justice Oliver Ellsworth and His Wife)*, Rembrandt Peale, Eakins; historic subjects and genre paintings by Benjamin West, Trumbull *(Signing of the Declaration of Independence)*, Homer *(The Nooning)*; a spectacular group of landscapes by painters of the **Hudson River school**: Cole *(Mount Etna From the Ruins of Taormina)*, Church, Bierstadt *(In the Mountains - Yosemite Valley)*, Durand; and more recent works by Avery, Davis, Hartley and Wyeth *(Chambered Nautilus)*.

Galleries A201 and A203 feature the distinguished collection of early colonial American furniture (note the elaborately carved chests), ironwork, and domestic implements and utensils gathered by **Wallace Nutting**. Nutting (1861-1941), a retired Congregationalist minister with great admiration for the furniture of the Pilgrim century acquired the items found in these galleries to serve as models for his furniture reproduction company. He authored more than twenty books on antique furniture and, in addition, restored half a dozen houses including the Wentworth-Gardner House *(p 170)*, the Saugus Ironworks *(p 111)* and the Webb House *(p 55)*.

Rounding out the American section is the Hammerslough collection of silver with its great variety of forms designed to serve many different purposes: porringers, salts, skewers, strainers, etc.

In Burr Mall outside the museum, between the Atheneum and the Municipal Building, is the giant red stabile **Stegosaurus (A)** by Alexander Calder; on the triangular open space diagonally across from the Atheneum note Carl Andre's controversial sculpture **Stone Field (B)**, a group of thirty-six boulders arranged in a geometrical pattern. The latter representative of Minimal Art, cost the foundation which commissioned the work, the "minimal" sum of $ 87 000.

Connecticut State Capitol★. – This Gothic Revival array of turrets, finials, gables, porches and towers, the work of Richard Upjohn, was a frequent topic of conversation when it was built in 1879. A golden dome rising above heavily sculpted walls, overlooks **Bushnell Park.**

The interior *(open to the public; currently being restored)* is no less restrained. Hand painted columns, elaborate stenciling, courtyards, stained glass windows, marble floors, balconies, all produce a startling and at times overwhelming effect.

The Capitol houses the legislative chambers and offices of state officials.

State Library. – *231 Capitol Avenue. Open 9 AM to 4:45 PM (1 PM Saturday); closed Sunday and major holidays.*

This building, across from the Capitol, houses the State Library (east wing), the Connecticut Supreme Court (west wing) and the State Museum (center wing). Museum exhibits include firearms from the Colt Collection, Connecticut clocks, coins, and historical items and documents including the Fundamental Orders of Connecticut.

Bushnell Memorial Auditorium. – *Trinity and Capitol Avenues.*

Concerts, opera, ballet, films and plays are presented in this brick colonial style building erected (1930) as a memorial to the Reverend Horace Bushnell (1802-1876).

■ MARK TWAIN HOUSE★★ *time: 2 hours – map of the Hartford region p 40*

The Mark Twain House, today a memorial to the well-known author, was one of the comfortable Victorian dwellings that stood on **Nook Farm,** a "nook" of woodland beside the north branch of the Park River. During the 19C a community of writers which included Mark Twain and Harriet Beecher Stowe lived in this pastoral setting. The homes of Mark Twain and Harriet Beecher Stowe have been restored and may be visited.

Visit. – *Open June through August 10 AM to 4:30 PM; the rest of the year 9:30 AM(1 PM Sunday) to 4 PM, closed Mondays and major holidays. Guided tours (1 hour each house) Mark Twain House $3.75; Harriet Beecher Stowe House $3.00; combination ticket $6.00.*

The Mark Twain House.

Mark Twain *(p 33)*, the pen name of Samuel Clemens (1835-1910), had this whimsical stick-style Victorian house built in 1874. A high-spirited and good-natured individualist, Mark Twain smoked forty cigars a day, slept backwards in his bed in order to face its elaborately carved headboard, did most of his best writing in the Billiard Room, and was intrigued by new inventions (his was the first private telephone in Hartford). His hospitality was legendary and he counted among his closest friends General Sherman and Rudyard Kipling. Mark Twain wrote seven of his most successful works including *The Adventures of Huckleberry Finn* and *The Adventures of Tom Sawyer* during the years he lived in this house.

Outside, decorative brick bands and a profusion of open porches, balconies, towers, brackets and steeply pitched roofs give the structure a free, irregular shape. Inside, the splendid decoration done in 1881 remains: the silver stenciling, elaborately carved woodwork, and exquisite wall coverings. Influenced by the years he spent as a pilot on a Mississippi riverboat, Mark Twain had such features as a dressing room that resembled the wheelhouse of a riverboat included in the design for the house. There is a special collection of Mark Twain memorabilia in the basement.

Nearby is the **Harriet Beecher Stowe House,** a simple Victorian cottage, which was the home of Harriet Beecher Stowe from 1873 until her death (1896). Mrs. Stowe, whose novel *Uncle Tom's Cabin* led to an unprecedented attack on slavery, was the authoress of several novels on New England.

Lacy, gingerbread motifs adorn the plain facade. The light, airy interior contains furnishings that belonged to Mrs. Stowe.

EXCURSIONS

Farmington★. – *10 miles west of Hartford. Leave the city on I-84. Description p 38.*

Wethersfield★. – *4 miles south of Hartford by I-91. Description p 55.*

Suffield. – *18 miles north of Hartford by I-91 North, Rte 20 West, then Rte 75 North. Description p 55.*

Dinosaur State Park★. – *West Street in Rocky Hill, 10 miles south of Hartford. Take I-91 to Exit 23, turn left at the light. Open 9 AM to 4:30 PM, closed Mondays and major holidays; $1.00, children 50¢.* The park offers a good opportunity to observe, intact and at its original site, an area covered with more than 500 dinosaur tracks *(p 142)*. The size of the impressions and the 4 ft pace suggest that the two-legged dinosaurs who made these tracks were probably 6 to 8 ft tall and about 15 ft in length. A full-scale model of Dilophosaurus, the dinosaur considered the best match for these tracks, and a model of Coelophysis, some skeletal remains of which have been found in the Connecticut Valley, are part of the exhibit. A geodesic dome constructed in 1977 protects the excavated site and accompanying displays. There is an area on the grounds where visitors may make plaster casts of actual tracks (bring 10 lbs of plaster of paris for each cast). *Casting area open April through November only.*

Talcott Mountain State Park. – *8 miles northwest of Hartford. Leave Hartford on Rte 189, then follow Rte 185 to the park entrance. Park open year round 8 AM to sunset; tower open early April to Labor Day Thursday to Sunday 10 AM to 5 PM; after Labor Day through October Sunday only.*

A 1 1/4 mile trail leads up to the Heublein Tower *(time: 1 1/2 hours RT)* which affords a sweeping **view**★ across the Farmington Valley to Hartford, and south to Long Island Sound.

New Britain Museum of American Art. – *56 Lexington Street in New Britain, 15 miles southwest of Hartford. Take I-84 to Exit 35. Follow the signs to downtown New Britain. Take Columbus Boulevard Exit, then turn left onto Lake Street, right onto West Main Street, left onto Lexington Street. Open 1 to 5 PM; closed Mondays and major holidays.*

The holdings of this small museum illustrate trends in American art from the colonial period to the present. The 18C portraitists (Trumbull, Stuart, Smibert), the Hudson River school, the Eight (including Sloan, Henri, Luks), and such greats as Homer, Whistler, Wyeth and Cassatt dominate the collection. Thomas Hart Benton's series of murals *Arts of Life in America* (1932), painted originally for the Whitney Museum of American Art in New York City, has been permanently installed in the New Britain Museum.

New England Air Museum. – *Bradley International Airport in Windsor Locks, 14 miles northeast of Hartford. Take I-91 North to Rte 20 West, then Rte 75 North. Open 10 AM to 5 PM, closed Thanksgiving Day and December 25; $5.00.*

Located in a spacious building on the west side of Bradley Airport, the museum displays approximately three dozen aircraft which trace the history of aviation.

Among the earliest exhibits is the 1909 Blériot XI, one of the first to be produced on a broad scale. Developments of later decades are highlighted by a large number of military aircraft. Helicopters are also on view: note the large Sikorsky Seabat, used for rescue missions in Antarctica.

The HOUSATONIC VALLEY ★★

Michelin tourist map - folds 13 and 19

The heart of the Housatonic Valley lies in the thickly wooded and hilly northwest corner of Connecticut, between the foothills of the Taconic Mountains and the Berkshire Hills. The valley is peaceful with no raucous entertainment districts, glaring neon signs or noisy highways; only quiet country roads that lead to small colonial villages, across covered bridges, and through parks and forests. Trails (including the Appalachian Trail) crisscrossing the region's parks and forests are used by skiers in the winter and hikers during the milder seasons. Alongside these trails, streams and falls mark the path of the Housatonic as it flows downstream to the Long Island Sound.

The beauty and proximity of this corner of the state to New York, has made the area a favorite of artists, writers and business people whose homes dot the countryside.

There was a brief period of prosperity in the 18C when iron ore was discovered in the Litchfield Hills. Forges were built and operated until coal fields were discovered in Pennsylvania. Ruins of the old furnaces still remain in several villages, although they are usually hidden by the woods that have grown up around them.

From Bulls Bridge to West Cornwall

19 miles – allow 3 hours – local map opposite

For the most part this itinerary follows Route 7, a major route linking Montreal and New York.

Begin at Bulls Bridge, 3 miles north of Gaylordsville, on Rte 7. Turn left onto Bulls Bridge Road which passes over a covered bridge that spans the Housatonic River. After crossing a second bridge, turn right onto Schaghticoke Road.

Schaghticoke Road. – *A section of this narrow road is unpaved. The road follows the river as it winds through wooded terrain that is offset by patches of gnarled ledges, and rock formations bordering the riverbed. After 3 miles you arrive at the*

Schaghticoke Indian Reservation and will pass an old Indian burial ground. The inscription on one of the stones reads simply: *Eunice-Mauwee – A Christian Indian Princess – 1756-1860.*

The road passes the buildings of **Kent School**, a prestigious private school, and continues on to Rte 341.

Macedonia Brook State Park. – *2 miles from Schaghticoke Road. Follow Rte 341 West 1 mile then turn right and follow the signs. Open 8 AM to sunset.*
    The park with its brook, streams and rocky gorge offers opportunities for camping, fishing and hiking.

Return to Kent.

Kent. – Pop. 2 365. Nestled among the hills bordering the Housatonic River, Kent is the home of artists and craftspeople whose works will be found in shops in the village center.

Follow Rte 7 North.

Sloane-Stanley Museum. – *Open mid-May through October Wednesday through Sunday 10 AM to 4:30 PM; closed Monday and Tuesday; $1.25.*
    This museum located near the ruins of the Old Kent Furnace (19C) contains an interesting collection of early American wooden and iron tools.

Kent Falls State Park. – Steps to the right of the falls lead to a point from which you can look down onto the cascades. From this point you can cross the bridge and descend to the parking lot by following a path *(time: 1/2 hour)* through the woods.

Rte 7 passes through **Cornwall Bridge** where the local General Store is a welcome sight to hikers on the Appalachian Trail.

The Housatonic Meadows State Park. – *Entrance on Rte 7. Open 8 AM to sunset. Camping, hiking and picnic tables.* The **Pine Knob Loop Trail** *(time: 2 hours RT from the parking lot on the west side of Rte 7)* leads to the summit of Pine Knob where there are views into the Housatonic Valley.

From Rte 7 turn right onto Rte 128.

West Cornwall★. – This tiny village with several shops and restaurants is known for its picturesque **covered bridge** built in 1837 and recently restored.

LITCHFIELD ★★
Michelin tourist map - fold 14 – Pop 7 649

A photographer's paradise in Indian summer when the trees are a blaze of color, Litchfield is a small, reserved New England village with broad streets and stately clapboard dwellings dating from the 18C. The nation's first law school *(see below)* and first institution of higher learning for women (Miss Pierce's School) were established in Litchfield during this early period. In the 19C the railroad and industrial development bypassed the center of town, a fact that accounts for Litchfield's having one of the loveliest and best-preserved ensembles of early American architecture in the nation today.

The Green. – North, South, East and West Streets meet at the green, dominated by Litchfield's **Congregational Meetinghouse**.
    The **Litchfield Historical Society** *(open mid-April to mid-November 11 AM to 4 PM; closed Sundays and Mondays)* nearby, has exhibits related to life in 17 and 18C Litchfield. Many handsome dwellings will be found along **North** and **South Streets**; most are privately owned and open to the public only on Open House Day *(see Calendar of Events p 13).*

Tapping Reeve House and Law School. – *South Street. Open mid-May to mid-October 12 noon to 4 PM; closed Tuesdays, Wednesdays and holidays; $1.00.*
    The home of Tapping Reeve, founder of the nation's first law school (1775), stands near the one-room schoolhouse in which he held classes.

White Memorial Foundation★. – *2 miles south of Litchfield by Rte 202 West. Open early April to late October 9 AM (11 AM Sunday) to 5 PM; the rest of the year 8:30 AM to 4:30 PM, Sunday 11 AM to 5 PM; closed Monday; $1.00.* There are many different types of vegetation and landscape on this 4 000 acre preserve which is owned and operated by the White Memorial Foundation. A map of the foundation's trails and wilderness areas may be purchased at the **White Memorial Conservation Center** *(on the grounds).*

MYSTIC ★★★
Michelin tourist map - fold 21 – Pop 3 216

The village of Mystic, on the Mystic River, has been building boats since the 17C. In the 1850s clipper ships reflecting the glory of America's maritime era were built in Mystic yards. At about the same time whaling became a major industry on the coast and Mystic's fleet grew to include more than 18 whaling ships. Many of the fine homes lining **Gravel, Clift** and **High Streets** were home to sea captains and sailors during this period. Local boatyards turned to the construction of pleasure craft in the early 20C and during World War II built ships for the Navy.

Today Mystic is above all known as the site of Mystic Seaport, a museum village which recreates the atmosphere and activities of an era out of America's maritime past.

■ MYSTIC SEAPORT★★★ *time: allow one day*

Mystic Seaport is a living replica of a 19C waterfront community during the days of sail. The tall sailing ships, the village center where the myriad of activities vital to a busy port are carried on, and the working shipyard add to the authenticity of the setting. Museum buildings house marvelous collections of marine art and artifacts. Originally a collection of nautical memorabilia displayed in a renovated mill, the project has since expanded into a complex of more than sixty buildings covering 17 acres.

How to get there: *from I-95 Exit 90, follow Rte 27 South.*

Visit. – *Open April through October 9 AM to 5 PM; (4 PM the rest of the year); exhibits open on a limited basis Thanksgiving and January 1; closed December 25; $10.00, under 15, $5.00. A schedule of daily events and map of the Seaport are distributed at the entrance.*

Begin your visit at the **Planetarium**. Daily programs *(location subject to change)* include a film of a whale hunt and offer a good introduction to the Seaport.

The 1908 steamboat **Sabino** makes trips *(1/2 hour)* on the river *(mid-May to mid-October, hourly 11 AM to 4 PM; $2.25 in addition to museum addition).*

The Village and Waterfront. – The heart of the village is the waterfront. Along the wharves and adjacent streets are the shops and businesses commonly found in a 19C seaport: the bank, printer, tavern, ship's chandlery, the shops of the craftsmen who worked to outfit the vessels, and the ropewalk – the incredibly long cordage company building where the miles of rope necessary for rigging the large sails were made.

Youngsters will particularly enjoy the **Children's Museum** *(on the green)* where they may participate in games and shipboard activities that were popular among the children who went to sea with their parents during the sailing era.

Two impressive, fully rigged sailing vessels are moored at the waterfront.

The Charles W. Morgan★★. – The *Morgan*, the sole survivor of America's 19C whaling fleet, has been declared a National Historic site. During eighty years of service the *Morgan* made 37 voyages, a number of which lasted from three to four years. Visitors may board the ship and examine the officers' cabin and gigantic tryworks *(p 25)*.

The Joseph Conrad. – This Danish-built training vessel (1882) has sailed under the Danish, British and American flags. As the property of Mystic Seaport, the *Conrad* is once again serving its original function as a training ship.

(From a photo by Kenneth E. Mahler,
Mystic Seaport Museum, Mystic, Conn.

The Charles W. Morgan.

Henry B. du Pont Preservation Shipyard. – All kinds of boats from the Seaport's vast collection are restored here. Visitors may observe craftsmen at work from a platform on the second level.

Fisheries Exhibit. – The exhibit features a diorama of Mystic as it appeared in 1853.

Berthed at a pier nearby is the *L.A. Dunton*, a Gloucester fishing schooner that sailed the fishing grounds of the Grand Banks in the 1920s and 1930s.

North Boat Shed. – Changing exhibits from the Seaport's small craft collection.

Stillman Building★★. – The three-story building contains an outstanding collection of ship's figureheads, nameboards, ship models and scrimshaw.

■ ADDITIONAL SIGHT

Mystic Marinelife Aquarium★★. – *Coogan Blvd. Open July 3 to Labor Day 9 AM to PM (4:45 PM the rest of the year); $6.25 under 18, $3.25.*

Living specimens of marine animals and plants are grouped in 45 major exhibi demonstrating aquatic communities, habitat and adaptation.

Seal Island, a 2.5 acre outdoor complex, features seals and sea lions in setting constructed to resemble their natural habitats: the New England coast, Pribilof Island and the coastline of California. *Dolphins and sea lions perform in demonstration presented hourly in the indoor theater.*

EXCURSION

Stonington★. – Pop 3 471. *4 miles east on Rte 1, then Rte 1A.*

This is one of the prettiest coastal villages in Connecticut. The early character of this former shipbuilding center is preserved by the lovely old homes lining Stonington's tree-shaded streets.

From the old stone lighthouse there is a view to **Fisher's Island,** a private island.

Old Lighthouse Museum. – *7 Water Street. Open May through October 11 AM to 4:30 PM, closed Monday; $1.00.*

Exhibits in the old lighthouse are nostalgic reminders of Stonington's days as a shipbuilding center and sealing and whaling port. Artifacts date from the 17-19C and include portraits, whaling tools and scrimshaw. Visitors may climb to the lighthouse tower where there is a view into three states and across the Sound.

NEW CANAAN

Michelin tourist map - fold 19 - 22 miles west of Bridgeport – Pop 17 791

This choice suburb in Connecticut's Fairfield County has been an art center since the early 20C when artists founded the **Silvermine Guild of Artists** here. The Guild maintains a complex of studios, galleries, classrooms, a library and photography lab on Silvermine Road, east of Route 123. Highlighting its program of events is the annual exhibition **The Art of the Northeast** *(see Calendar of Events p 13).*

NEW HAVEN ★★

Michelin tourist map - fold 20 – Pop 124 188

Seen from I-95 New Haven appears to be a city of factories and tall office towers (such as the unusual cylindrical-towered **Knights of Columbus Building – AX A)** framed by red basalt ridges – **East Rock and West Rock parks.** Only by leaving the interstate and driving toward the **green** will the serene residential streets: Whitney Avenue, Hillhouse Avenue, Prospect Street, and the ivy-covered buildings of Yale University be discovered.

HISTORICAL NOTES

Founded in 1638 by a group of Puritans under the leadership of Reverend John Davenport and Theophilus Eaton, New Haven was at first an independent colony. The efforts of its leaders to develop the economy of the settlement were unsuccessful and in 1662 New Haven was made a part of the Connecticut Colony.

In the 18C the dream of New Haven's founders was realized when the colony flourished because of its deepwater harbor. The War of 1812, however, brought an end to this period in New Haven, as it did in other ports throughout New England.

Then with the coming of the railroad in the 19C, the face of New Haven changed forever. Industry and manufacturing developed and immigrants by the thousands came to work in Connecticut's clock, firearms and carriage factories. One of the many innovative men working in New Haven was **Eli Whitney** *(p 35)* who is credited with being the father of mass production. Whitney introduced the use of standardized parts as the basis of the assembly line in his arms factory situated outside of the city.

By the mid-20C, burdened by the problems of unplanned industrial growth and increasing competition from the suburbs, the city was rapidly deteriorating. Projects focusing on the revitalization of the downtown area as well as the suburbs were undertaken in the 1960s, resulting in the rehabilitation and construction of schools, homes and parks. Today New Haven – a blend of both traditional and modern architectural styles – is recognized as one of the most interesting examples of urban renewal in the nation.

A Cultural Center. – The presence of Yale University, with its museums, libraries, programs of music, theater and dance has made New Haven a prominent cultural center. The wide range of fine shops and restaurants adds to the city's cosmopolitan flavor. The New Haven stage, once a proving ground for Broadway productions, has become well known in its own right.

Long Wharf Theater (**AX** T1). – 222 Sargent Drive. ☏ *(203) 787-4282.* Located in a former warehouse, this theater offers an interesting selection of plays each season.

Shubert Performing Arts Center (**CZ** T2). – *247 College Street.* ☏ *(203) 624-1825.* The Shubert's varied program of performances includes Broadway-bound productions, Broadway road shows and concerts.

Palace Performing Arts Center (**CZ** T5). – *246 College Street.* ☏ *(203) 789-2120.* Musicals and classical and popular concerts are presented at the 2 037 seat Palace, formerly the Roger Sherman Theater.

Yale Repertory Theater (**CZ** T3). – 1120 Chapel Street. ☏ *(203) 432-1234.* The "Rep" focuses on plays written by young playwrights, and modern interpretations of the classics.

New Haven Symphony Orchestra. – ☏ *(203) 776-1444.* One of the finest in the nation, performs at Woolsey Hall (**DZ** K).

Concerts are also presented at the **Yale School of Music** (**DZ** T4) ☏ *(203) 432-4157.*

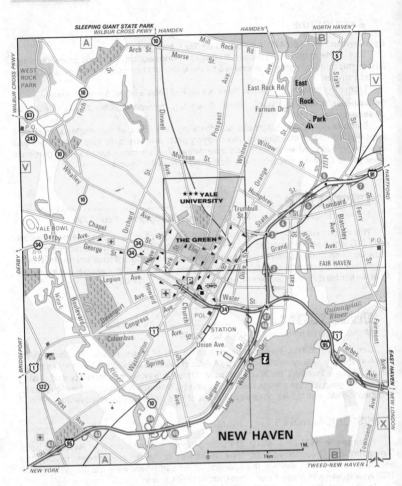

■ YALE UNIVERSITY★★★ *time: allow one day – plan p 50*

Leave your car near the green (p 51).

This Ivy League school is one of the oldest and most distinguished institutions of higher learning in the United States. Since 1789 almost 10 % of the nation's major diplomatic posts have been held by Yale men, and an average of fifteen congressmen a year are Yale graduates.

Yale was founded in 1701 by a group of Puritan clergymen who wished to provide Connecticut with an educational institution where young men could be trained to serve the church and state. The school they established, known at first as the Collegiate School, was located in Saybrook. In 1716 the school was moved to the New Haven green, and two years later the Collegiate School was renamed Yale for its benefactor, the wealthy merchant **Elihu Yale.**

Organization. – The University's 10 800 students, 2 270 faculty members and personnel staff represent a community of almost 19 000 persons. Yale's undergraduates are divided among twelve colleges, each of which has its own library, dining room, sleeping quarters, social activities and athletic programs. Graduate programs are offered by the university's graduate schools of Art, Architecture, Divinity, Drama, Forestry and Environmental Studies, Arts and Sciences, Law, Medicine, Music, and Nursing.

Yale gained university status in 1887 after its Medical School (1810) and Law School (1824) had already been established. The nation's first Ph. D's were awarded by Yale in 1861 and before the turn of the century women were admitted into the Ph. D. program. Women have been admitted to the undergraduate school since 1969.

Architecture. – The architectural diversity that characterizes the Yale campus is dominated by the **Gothic Revival** style with its medieval turrets, spires, massive towers, leaded stained glass and cathedral-like buildings in stone. The **Georgian** influence is also significant, although the facades of most of these handsome structures are visible only from their courtyards.

Since the 1950s Yale has turned to the leading architects of the day to design the university's most recent, modern structures: the Yale Art Gallery and the Yale Center for British Art – **Louis Kahn**, the School of Art and Architecture – **Paul Rudolph**, Morse and Ezra Stiles Colleges, the Yale Co-Op and the Ingalls Hockey Rink – **Eero Saarinen**, the Kline Biology Tower – **Philip Johnson**, and the Beinecke Rare Book and Manuscript Library – **Gordon Bunshaft.**

Walking tour of the University

Begin at **Phelps Gate (A)** on College Street. *Enter the Old Campus.*

Old Campus. – The site of Yale's earliest college buildings. **Connecticut Hall (B)** is the university's oldest structure. A statue of Nathan Hale, a Yale alumnus, stands in front of this simple Georgian hall where Hale lived as a student.

Cross the Old Campus and exit onto High Street.

Across High Street is **Harkness Tower (D)** (1920), a Neo-Gothic tower heavily ornamented with carved figures of famous Yale alumni: Noah Webster, Eli Whitney....

Turn left on High Street, pass under an arch, then turn right onto Chapel Street.

The **Yale University Art Gallery★★**. – Louis Kahn's first major work stands facing his last creation, the **Yale Center for British Art★★**. Both buildings present interesting conceptions of museum ar-

(From a photo, Office of Public Information, Yale University.)

Harkness Tower.

chitecture from the point of view of building materials, light and the use of space. *(For a description of museum collections see pp 50 and 51).*

Continue toward York Street. The former Gothic Revival style church on the left is the **Yale Repertory Theater (CZ T3)** *(p 47)*, home of the Yale Repertory Company, a professional company in residence at the university. Diagonally opposite rises Paul Rudolph's striking **School of Art and Architecture;** seemingly nine stories high, it has in fact thirty-six levels that are visible only from the inside of the building.

Turn right onto York Street and continue about halfway down the street.

Pierson and Davenport Colleges★. – These elegant Georgian buildings hidden beyond the colleges' Gothic street-side facades may be seen from the courtyards. On the opposite side of the street stands **Wrexham Tower (E)**, designed after the church in Wales where Elihu Yale is buried.

Cross Elm Street and continue on York Street. On the right is the **Sterling Memorial Library.** *At No. 306 York Street, walk through the narrow passageway on the left.*

Morse and Ezra Stiles Colleges★. – Saarinen's design for this ensemble of contemporary buildings was inspired by an Italian hill town. A continuous play of light and shadows is created throughout the day by the maze of stone passages with their vertical planes, geometric forms and sharp angular turns. Nearby is another of Saarinen's works, the **Yale Co-Op.**

On Tower Parkway, across the street from Morse and Ezra Stiles Colleges, is the **Payne Whitney Gymnasium,** one of Yale's cathedral-like structures. *Continue along Tower Parkway then turn right onto York Street.* This is a good point from which to view the skyline of Yale's towers. *Turn into the first street on the left (Wall Street).*

Sterling Law Buildings. – Law students live in this group of buildings similar in design to the English Inns of Court where students during the 16-18C studied law. Note the amusing portraits of the police and robbers carved in stone above the windows.

Cross High Street.

Beinecke Rare Book and Manuscript Library★. – The library's exterior walls are composed of a granite framework fitted with translucent marble panels. Enter the library and observe the unusual effect produced by the sunlight streaming in through the marble slabs. A Gutenberg Bible and changing exhibits are displayed on the mezzanine.

Facing the library are several buildings erected to celebrate Yale's bicentennial: **Woodbridge Hall (G)** offices, the **University Dining Hall (P),** and **Woolsey Hall (K)** auditorium. The rotunda, **Memorial Hall (N),** contains a large group of commemorative plaques.

Return to the corner of Wall and High Streets and turn left onto High Street. A number of small statues ornament the rooftops of buildings along this street.

Sterling Memorial Library. – This is Yale's main library, although at first glance its stained glass windows, frescoes and archways lead you to believe you have just stepped into a cathedral. The **Cross Campus Library,** located beneath the Cross Campus *(to the left),* was built underground to allow the Cross Campus green to remain intact.

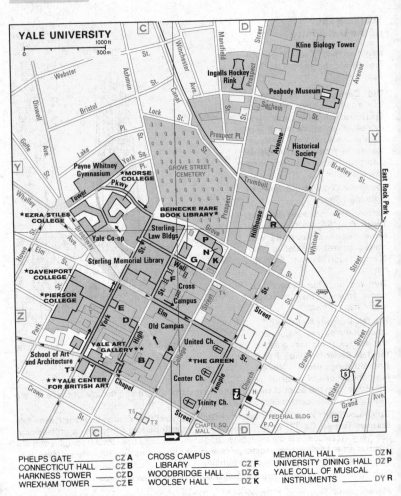

YALE UNIVERSITY

1000 ft
0   300 m

The Museums

Yale University Art Gallery★★ (CZ). – *1111 Chapel Street. Open 10 AM (2 PM Sunday) to 5 PM, October through April Thursday evening 6 to 8 PM; closed Mondays and holidays.*

This gallery was founded in 1832 with the gift of about 100 works of art by the patriot artist **John Trumbull**. The museum is comprised of two interconnected units, a 1928 building in the Italian Romanesque style, and the 1953 addition designed by Louis Kahn. The new gallery makes use of large spaces with movable partitions to display the collections.

Ground Floor. – The collection of ancient art features a Mithraic Shrine (Temple to the Sun God) with elaborate paintings and reliefs. Numerous artifacts excavated at Dura-Europos (an ancient Roman town), and a selection of Greek, Etruscan and Egyptian vases are on display. Teaching exhibits often include paintings and sculpture from the rich Société Anonyme collection of early modern art (Jacques Villon, Lipchitz, Mondrian, Schwitters).

First Floor. – Special exhibits and contemporary art.

Second Floor. – In addition to the Impressionist paintings, the 19C collection includes works by Manet *(Young Woman Reclining in Spanish Costume)*, Millet *(Starry Night)*, Courbet *(Hunter on Horseback)*, Van Gogh *(Night Café)*, Corot, Degas and Matisse.

In the section devoted to early 20C art will be found works by Marcel Duchamp *(Tu'm)*, Stella *(Brooklyn Bridge)*, Magritte (his haunting *Pandora's Box)* and canvases by Tanguy, Ernst, Klee and Kandinsky.

The new Ordway Gallery has changing exhibits of 20C art from the Ordway collection. Paintings by Picasso *(Coquillages sur un Piano, Femme Assise)*, Renoir *(Mount St. Victoire)*, Pollock *(No.4)*, Rothko *(No. 3, 1967)* and de Kooning are featured.

The collection of **African art** is comprised of carved masks and ceremonial and royal objects. Equally interesting are the stone, clay and jade artifacts in the **Pre-Columbian** collection. The group figurines provide glimpses into the daily life of the period.

Third Floor. – The **Jarves** collection of early Italian painting (13-16C) includes such jewels as da Fabriano's *Madonna and Child* and Ghirlandaio's Mona Lisa-like *Lady With a Rabbit.* The adjacent galleries devoted to European art contain the medieval collection; among the Flemish paintings are portraits by Holbein and Hals, an oil sketch by Rubens *Assumption of the Virgin*, and the *Allegory of Intemperance* attributed to Jerome Bosch.

The American collection is arranged didactically for the university's teaching purposes. Furniture, silver, pewter and ironware are used to illustrate the development of American art forms and their relationship to the society that produced them. The last gallery in this section displays many of the works of John Trumbull including the original *Bunker Hill* and *Declaration of Independence,* used as the models for copies later produced by Trumbull for the Capitol in Washington, D.C.

Fourth Floor. – The Oriental galleries have examples of Japanese sculpture and Chinese bronzes, ceramics and paintings spanning the period from 12BC – 20C AD.

Yale Center for British Art★★ (CZ). – *1080 Chapel Street. Open 10 AM (2 PM Sunday) to 5 PM; closed Mondays and major holidays.*

In 1966 **Paul Mellon** donated his collection of British art – 1 300 paintings, 10 000 drawings, 20 000 prints, 20 000 rare books – to Yale. Plans for a new building to house the collection were drawn by Louis Kahn. Kahn's design integrates the use of natural light and courtyards, allowing natural light to enter through numerous skylights and filter down through three- and four-story open courts to the display areas.

The Collection. – The collection, mirroring Paul Mellon's life-long interest in British art, includes sporting paintings, town and marine views, portraits, and "conversation pieces" (informal group portraits) dating primarily from 1700 to 1850.

The **fourth floor** houses paintings and sculpture which have been installed chronologically to provide a survey of British art from the late 16C through the early 19C. Several rooms on this floor are reserved for the works of **Gainsborough, Reynolds, Stubbs, Turner** and **Constable.** On the **second floor** is a selection of 19 and 20C paintings and sculpture.

Peabody Museum (DY). – *170 Whitney Avenue. Open 9 AM (1 PM Sunday) to 4:45 PM; closed major holidays; $2.00, free Tuesday.*

The Peabody is Yale's science museum. Among the museum's famous collection of **dinosaurs** will be found a horned dinosaur, the first stegosaurus ever mounted, and the full-scale fossil of a brontosaurus (67 ft long, 35 tons). The 10 ft archelon (75 million years old) is the largest turtle in the world. The Pulitzer prize-winning mural *Age of Reptiles* by Rudolph Zallinger depicts the dinosaurs and plant life of 70-350 million years ago.

In the Hall of Human Origins, skeletal mounts, videos and computerized displays are used to show the evolutionary trends in man and other primates.

Yale Collection of Musical Instruments (DY R). – *15 Hillhouse Avenue. Open Tuesday, Wednesday and Thursday 1 to 4 PM; Sunday also, 2 to 5 PM (except June and July); closed August and holidays. A series of concerts is held annually featuring restored instruments from the collection. ☎ (203) 432-0822.*

The collection consists of more than 800 instruments representative of the traditions of western European music from the 16-19C.

■ ADDITIONAL SIGHTS

The Green★ (DZ). – New Haven has been a good example of urban planning since its days as a Puritan colony, when the town was laid out as a giant square subdivided into nine smaller squares. The center square, the green, was reserved for the use of the entire community as pastureland, parade ground and burial ground. The green has remained the heart of the downtown district over the years. The three churches on the green were built between 1812 and 1815 and represent three different architectural styles: **Trinity Church** – Gothic Revival, **Center Church** – Georgian, **United Congregational Church** – Federal.

Hillhouse Avenue (DY). – Most of the beautiful mansions on this street were built in the 19C by wealthy industrialists and merchants, and are now owned by Yale University.

Ingalls Hockey Rink (DY). – *Prospect Street.* Saarinen's rhythmic design for the rink, a part of the Yale Campus, was inspired by the shape of a whale.

New Haven Colony Historical Society (DY). – *114 Whitney Avenue. Open 10 AM (2 PM Saturday and Sunday) to 5 PM; closed Mondays and holidays.* Antique pewter, china and toys dating from the period of the New Haven Colony are among the displays.

East Rock Park (BV). – *Follow Orange Street. Cross Mill River and turn left, then bear right. The road leads to the summit parking lot.* From the summit of this basalt ridge there is a **view★** of the entire New Haven area and, in the distance, the Long Island Sound.

EXCURSIONS

Shore Line Trolley Museum. – *5 miles from New Haven by I-95. 17 River Street, East Haven. Take Exit 51, turn right onto Hemingway Avenue, then left onto River Street. Open Memorial Day to Labor Day II AM to 5 PM; May, September and October Saturdays and Sundays only; April and November Sundays only; $3.50. 3 mile trolley excursions operate through the Connecticut shore area between the museum and Short Beach.*

The museum is primarily the work of volunteer trolley buffs who have restored a number of the more than 100 street, subway and elevated railway cars on the grounds.

Sleeping Giant State Park. – *6 miles from New Haven. Take Whitney Avenue (Rte 10) to Hamden and turn right on Mount Carmel Avenue. Trail maps and information available at Ranger Headquarters.* The park has picnic facilities and more than 25 miles of blazed trails around the Giant. **Tower Path** *(time: 1 1/2 hours RT)* leads to the highest point in the park where, from a stone tower, there are good **views★★** of the region.

NEW LONDON

Michelin tourist map - fold 21 – Pop 28 485

This city, located on a harbor at the mouth of the Thames River, has always depended on the sea for its livelihood. Its deepwater port was a haven for privateers during the Revolution, a fact which led to the British attack on New London and Groton in 1781 – during which **Forts Trumbull** and **Griswold** fell to the enemy and nearly all New London was destroyed by fire. In the mid-19C the city was a principal whaling port. Elegant homes built from the profits of whaling still stand in neighborhoods that have remained residential despite the development of onshore industries.

New London's ties with the sea continue even today. The city is home to the United States Coast Guard Academy, and the shipping industry and the U.S. Naval Submarine Base located on the other side of the Thames are major contributors to the economy.

Revitalization of the downtown area has included the renovation of the 19C Union Railroad station (designed by H.H. Richardson) into a multimodal transportation center.

■ **SIGHTS** *time: 4 hours*

Joshua Hempsted House★. – *11 Hempstead Street. Guided tours (45 min) May 15 to October 15, 1 to 5 PM; closed Monday; $2.00.*

Built in 1678, this house is a splendid example of 17C American architecture. The walls are insulated with seaweed and pierced with tiny leaded casement windows. Inside, the low-ceilinged rooms contain fine primitive American furnishings.

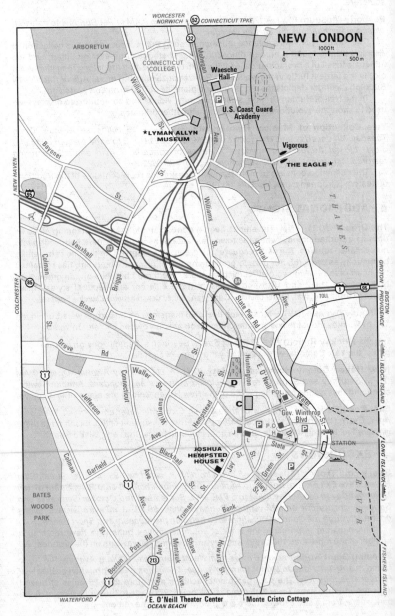

Lyman Allyn Museum★. - *625 Williams Street. Open 11 AM (1PM Sunday) to 5 PM; closed Mondays and holidays.*

This small museum established by a bequest of the Allyn family specializes in paintings by Connecticut artists and the decorative arts of Connecticut. Attractively arranged furnishings, paintings, sculpture, and decorative arts dating from classical civilizations to the present complement the American section. Of special interest to collectors and children is the group of dollhouses and dolls on the lower level.

United States Coast Guard Academy. - *Open 10 AM to sunset. A detailed map can be obtained at the entrance gate.* ☏ *(203) 444-8270 for special events and parade dates.*

The Coast Guard Academy, a four year military college that trains officers for the Coast Guard, had its beginnings in 1876 when the schooner *Dobbin* was chosen to serve as a floating training school, to prepare cadets for the Revenue Marine (which later evolved into the Coast Guard). The *Dobbin* was succeeded by several other ships until the early 20C when the Academy was

(By permission of The United States Coast Guard.)

The U.S.C.G.C. Eagle.

established at Fort Trumbull, then in 1932 moved to its present site beside the Thames.

Visitors Pavilion. - *Open May through October 9 AM to 5 PM daily.*

A brief multimedia presentation of the history of the Coast Guard, sailing on the *Eagle*, and various aspects of cadet life is shown.

Coast Guard Museum. - *In Waesche Hall. Open May through October, 9 AM to 5 PM; the rest of the year 9 AM to 4 PM, closed Saturday and Sunday.*

The museum's diversified exhibits deal with the history of the Coast Guard.

The Waterfront. - The Coast Guard cutter **Vigorous,** used to patrol the 220 mile fisheries boundary, and the **Eagle★**, the Academy's training vessel, are berthed at the waterfront. The German-built *Eagle* (1936) is a graceful three-masted square rigger used for cadet training cruises to Europe and the Caribbean in the summer. *When in port, the Eagle may be visited Saturdays, Sundays and holidays 1 to 5 PM.*

Ye Ancientist Burial Ground (D). - *Huntington Street.*

This old burial ground has many early New England slate tombstones carved with winged angels, skull and crossbones, geometric patterns and other designs.

Whale Oil Row (C). - *105-119 Huntington Street.*

These four white mansions with their imposing columns are typical of the Greek Revival residences constructed by wealthy merchants and seamen in the 19C.

The Monte Cristo Cottage. - *325 Pequot Avenue. South on Howard Street, then turn left on Pequot Avenue (in the direction of Ocean Beach). Guided tours (1 hour) weekdays 1:30 and 2:30 PM, closed Saturdays, Sundays and holidays; $2.00.*

The unpretentious two-story frame dwelling looking out on the Thames, was the summer home of playwright Eugene O'Neill during his boyhood years. The cottage *(under restoration)* was the setting for his two most autobiographical works: *Long Day's Journey Into Night* and *Ah, Wilderness!* A brief (18 min) film serves as an introduction to O'Neill, his family, and the years they spent at the cottage.

Ferry to Orient Point, Long Island, NY. - *Ferry Street. Car and passenger service daily year round except December 25. Time: 1 1/2 hours one way. Reservations advised. For information contact: Cross Sound Ferry Services, Inc., Box 33, New London, CT 06320.* ☏ *(203) 443-5281.*

EXCURSIONS

Ocean Beach. - *5 miles south of New London on Ocean Avenue.* This wide sandy beach offers swimming, bathhouses, an amusement arcade, rides, golf, archery and boating.

Eugene O'Neill Theater Center. - *6 miles south of New London. Take Bank Street then turn left at Ocean Avenue and continue to Rte 213 (Niles Hill Road). Follow the signs. Performances early July to early August. For schedule* ☏ *(203) 443-5378.*

Named in honor of the 20C playwright Eugene O'Neill *(p 33)*, the center is devoted to the development of new works for the American stage. Activities at the center's 100 acre grounds include the annual National Playwrights Conference and Opera/Music Theater Conference. Also housed here are The National Theater Institute and the National Critics Institute.

NORWICH

Michelin tourist map - fold 21 - 14 miles north of New London – Pop 38 405

Situated where the Yantic and Shetucket Rivers meet to form the Thames, Norwich has been an important industrial center since the 18C. The city's historic district, radiating out from a prim triangular **green**, has a fine group of early dwellings. Concerts, sporting events, exhibits and programs of live entertainment accompany the **Rose Arts Festival**, an eight day arts and crafts show held each year on the green.

Leffingwell Inn. – *Guided tours (1 1/2 hours) May 15 to October 15 10 AM to 12 noon and 2 to 4 PM (Sunday 2 to 4 PM only); closed Mondays ; $3.00.*

The tavern was the site of many political meetings during the Revolution. Restored and now a museum, the Inn contains furnishings, silver and other products made by Norwich craftsmen.

EXCURSION

Uncasville. – *5 miles south of Norwich by Rte 32.*

The names of two communities within the boundaries of the town of Montville – Mohegan and Uncasville – are reminders that Indians did and still do live in the area.

In the 17C the Mohegan sachem **Uncas** joined in an alliance with the colonists, who agreed to help him and his braves resist any attacks made by the powerful Narragansett Indians of Rhode Island. During the last major battle between the two tribes, in 1643, Uncas captured and killed the chief of the Narragansetts, Miantomono.

Fort Shantok State Park. – An old Indian burial ground, and remnants of the fort where the Mohegans were under siege by the Narragansetts, will be found in the park.

Tantaquidgeon Indian Museum. – *Open May through October 10 AM to 4 PM; closed Monday.*

This small museum was built by John Tantaquidgeon, a descendant of the Mohegan chief, Uncas. Items traditionally made and used by the Mohegans, and gifts from other Indian tribes are among the exhibits.

RIDGEFIELD

Michelin tourist map - fold 19 - 28 miles northwest of Bridgeport – Pop 21 084

Located a little more than an hour's drive from the hustle and bustle of Manhattan, Ridgefield's tree-shaded avenues, shops and mansions have, nevertheless, a distinctly New England character.

Keeler Tavern. – *132 Main Street. Guided tours (1/2 hour) Wednesday, Saturday and Sunday, and Monday holidays 1 to 4 PM, last tour 3:20 PM; closed January; $2.00.*

The Keeler Tavern operated as an inn from colonial days through the early 20C.

During the Battle of Ridgefield, April 17, 1777, a cannonball lodged in the wall post where it remains to this day – accounting for the tavern's nickname: the Cannonball House.

Aldrich Museum of Contemporary Art. – *258 Main Street. Open summer weekdays 2:30 to 4:30 PM Saturday and Sunday 1 to 5 PM, closed Monday; the rest of the year Friday, Saturday and Sunday only. Closed between exhibitions. $2.00. The Sculpture Garden is open dawn to dusk.*

Changing exhibits of contemporary art are presented in this handsome colonial dwelling.

RIVERTON

Michelin tourist map - fold 14 - 27 miles northwest of Hartford – Pop 315

During the 19C this small rural village was known as Hitchcocks-ville because of its Hitchcock chair factory. Too often confused with the town of Hotchkiss-ville, Hitchcocks-ville, situated on a branch of the Farmington River, was renamed Riverton.

Hitchcock Chair Factory. – *Factory showroom open 10 AM (12 noon Sunday) to 5 PM, closed holidays.*

Lambert Hitchcock's chair factory, established here in the early 19C, turned out thousands of rush-seated "fancy" decorated chairs *(p 31)* that were sold throughout the country. Restored in 1946, the factory is once again producing chairs, tables and chests in the Hitchcock tradition.

Museum. – *Open June through October 11 AM (1 PM Sunday) to 4 PM, closed Monday and Tuesday; April and May Saturday only 1 to 4 PM; closed the rest of the year. Film (15 min) "The Hitchcock Story" shown on request.* The museum, arranged in an old granite church nearby, contains hand painted and decorated furnishings made at the Hitchcock factory.

*Before planning your
trip to New England be sure to consult:*

– the Michelin Tourist Map accompanying the guide

– the Map of Principal Sights pp 5 to 7

– the suggested automobile tours presented on pp 8-9

Michelin tourist map - fold 14 – Pop 10 003

The Connecticut River forms the eastern boundary of this small countrified town established in 1670. Well-preserved houses border Main Street, together with the brick buildings of Suffield Academy, a private preparatory school.

Agriculture has always been the principal local activity. Tobacco growing was the major industry until World War II, and broadleaf tobacco continues to be raised here though much of the farmland today is given over to nurseries and dairying, or has been set aside for industrial parks.

The Hatheway House. – *55 South Main Street. Open May 15 to October 15, 1 to 5 PM; closed Mondays, Tuesdays and holidays; $2.00.*

The house, actually three structures in one, owes its present size to Oliver Phelps, a merchant and land speculator who acquired the property in 1788. Phelps enlarged the main section of the house (c. 1760) by adding a single-story structure to the south end, and about 1795 had the Federal style north wing built.

The earlier central section is simple and functional, furnished with William and Mary and Queen Anne pieces; the Federal wing, in contrast, is elegant, decorated with Adamesque ornamentation and fine Hepplewhite, Sheraton and Chippendale furnishings. A special feature of the house are the original 18C hand-blocked French wallpapers installed in the Federal wing.

WETHERSFIELD ★

Michelin tourist map - fold 20 – *map of the Hartford region p 40* – Pop 25 640

Established in 1634 on a harbor at the head of the Connecticut River, Wethersfield was an important center of trade until the 18C when floods changed the course of the river, leaving only a cove at the original harbor site. This change drastically affected the town's commercial activity which decreased rapidly until, by the late 18C, farming had replaced trade as the economic mainstay.

Unspoiled by industry throughout the 20C, Wethersfield is a pleasant Hartford suburb. Approximately 150 dwellings in the town's picturesque historic district, Old Wethersfield, date from before the mid-19C. A number of these 17 and 18C houses built by wealthy merchants and shipowners, have been restored.

■ OLD WETHERSFIELD★★

time: 3 hours

Main Street. – This wide street is lined with attractively restored houses. The 1760 brick **Congregational Meetinghouse (A)** adjoins an early burial ground which has tombstones dating from the 17C.

Webb - Deane - Stevens Museum★★. – *Guided tours (40 min each house) 10 AM (1 PM Sunday) to 4 PM; closed Monday year round, and Sunday October 16 to May 14; $2.00 each house, combination ticket for the three houses $5.00.*

These houses allow a comparison in architectural style and furnishings between the home of a wealthy merchant, a politician and a modest craftsman.

Webb House. – 1752. This elegant Georgian residence built by the prosperous merchant Joseph Webb, Sr. was the scene of a four day conference in May, 1781 between General Washington and the French Count Rochambeau. Plans for the Yorktown campaign which led ultimately to the defeat of the British in the American Revolution were discussed by the two military leaders during this time.

The house contains a choice collection of period furnishings and decorative arts. Highlights of the tour include the Council Room where the two men met, and the bedchamber that was specially decorated for General Washington, who was lodged at the Webb House during his stay in Wethersfield.

Deane House. – 1766. This house was built for Silas Deane, an American diplomat who traveled to France during the Revolution to negotiate for arms and equipment for the Continental Army. While abroad, Deane became involved in business deals that aroused suspicions regarding his loyalty, and he was accused of treason. He returned home and spent the rest of his life attempting, unsuccessfully, to clear his name.

The large spacious rooms and off-center stairway are unusual for a house of its day.

Stevens House. – 1788. Stevens was a leather worker who built this house for his bride. The modest furniture, woodwork, fabrics and decor offer a pleasing contrast to those of the more richly embellished Webb and Deane houses.

Buttolph-Williams House. – *Corner of Broad and Marsh Streets. Guided tours (45 min) July and August 12 noon to 4 PM, closed Monday; May 15 through June and September to October 15, Saturday and Sunday only; $2.00.*

The simple colonial house (1692) contrasts with the more elegant houses of a later date bordering the green.

Old Academy Museum. – *150 Main Street. Open 1 to 4 PM (Saturday 12 noon to 5 PM), closed Sunday and between exhibitions; $1.00.*

This handsome brick building (1804) has served as the Town Hall, library, armory, a female seminary and is the headquarters of the Wethersfield Historical Society. Changing exhibits depict the development of Wethersfield during the last 300 years.

Cove Warehouse. – *At the park overlooking the cove. To visit ☏ Old Academy Museum (203) 529-7656 for appointment.*

In the 17C, goods that arrived by sea were stored in Wethersfield's seven warehouses before they were transported inland. This is the only one of the seven which remains.

WOODSTOCK

Michelin tourist map - fold 15 – 47 miles northeast of Hartford – Pop 5 205

Woodstock's village green is set in the sparsely populated northeast section of the state. Facing the green is the summer residence known as Roseland Cottage.

Roseland Cottage. – *Guided tours (1 hour) Memorial Day weekend to September 15 Wednesday through Sunday 12 noon to 5 PM, closed Mondays, Tuesdays and holidays; September 16 to October 18 Friday, Saturday and Sunday only 12 noon to 5 PM; closed the rest of the year; $2.50.*

This handsomely landscaped and furnished board and batten cottage built by New York publisher Henry Bowen in 1846, became famous in the 19C for the spectacular July 4 celebrations held here by Mr. Bowen. The celebrations, accompanied by fireworks, dancing and parties, were attended by such distinguished guests as Presidents Grant, Hayes, Harrison and McKinley.

Maine

Area : 33 215 sq miles
Population : 1 156 536
Capital : Augusta
Nickname : Pine Tree State
State Flower : White pinecone
    and tassel

Equal in surface area to the other five New England states combined, Maine is a vast, thickly forested region fringed with a 3 500 mile coastline (228 miles from Kittery to Calais, the way the crow flies). The origin of the name Maine is uncertain. Attributed by some historians to the French province Maine, the name is believed by others to derive from the term "the main," used by fishermen to distinguish the mainland from the offshore islands. Maine is also referred to as **Downeast** because of the winds which carry sailing vessels eastward along this section of the coast.

The glaciers cut and sculpted the irregular, deeply indented coastline which comes to mind at any mention of Maine. Moving southeast across the land, then retreating northwest, the ice chiseled out the elongated peninsulas and headlands that are oriented in the same direction as the hundreds of offshore islands, the peaks of submerged mountains. Pine trees grow everywhere : on the islands, along the shore, and inland across the interior to the north − except for an occasional clearing formed by a lake − covering 83 % of the surface area and giving the state its nickname : the Pine Tree State.

History. − The Maine coast was one of the first regions explored in New England : by the Vikings in the 11C, and several centuries later by European fishermen. In 1604 Pierre de Guast, Sieur de Monts and Samuel de Champlain established a small colony on an island in the St. Croix River (p 71) from which they set out the following year to found the Acadian territory. An English settlement, the Popham Colony, was established at the mouth of the Kennebec River in 1607 ; then in 1635 the English monarch Charles I gave the region of Maine to Sir Ferdinando Gorges, appointing him "Lord of New England." From this time on, the coast was a constant scene of battle between the French and the English.

In 1677 the Massachusetts Colony bought Maine from the descendants of Sir Gorges and the region remained under the jurisdiction of Massachusetts until 1820, when Maine was granted statehood as a part of the Missouri Compromise.

Economy. − Maine has a vibrant, well diversified economy. In the early days the state's wealth depended upon its forests. Timber was harvested to supply masts for the Royal Navy during the colonial period, when all pine trees 24 inches or greater in diameter were the property of the Crown (p 76). In the 19C wooden **shipbuilding** peaked in Maine at Bath, Wiscasset and Searsport where boatyards turned out four-, five- and six-masted vessels. Today the forest supplies the important **paper** and **pulp mills** at Millinocket, Rumford, Bucksport and Woodland.

Fishing, especially **lobstering**, is a major industry, with approximately 75 % of the nation's lobster catch coming from Maine. The coast is dotted with small fishing ports where thousands of colorful buoys floating on the surface of the water, mark the location of traps set by lobstermen. The state is a leader in the sardine packing industry with plants at Rockland, Lubec and Prospect Harbor producing a total of about 100 million tins of sardines annually.

Textiles, shoes and boots are also Maine-made products. Agriculturally, state-o-Mainers raise one of the nation's five largest crops of potatoes, 95 % of the nation's blueberries, and peas, corn, apples, beans, poultry and eggs for local markets.

Recreation. − Many of the state parks have campgrounds with picturesque lakeshore sites. There are opportunities for sports, the most popular on the coast being boating, and in particular sailing. Along these lines those in search of adventure will find a sailing vacation aboard a **windjammer** − one of the tall-masted wooden sailing ships which operate out of Camden, Rockland, Belfast − a unique means of exploring the Maine coast and islands.

Canoeists can benefit from the abundance of lakes and rivers and the superb white waters of the **Allagash Wilderness Waterway** (p 74). Tour organizers based in Greenville operate raft trips on the Kennebec and West Branch of the Penobscot rivers.

Of the state's more than 40 ski areas **Sugarloaf** (p 78), with its extensive facilities, is the best known.

Fishing and Hunting. − Fishing for Atlantic salmon, or at the lakes in the north for trout. Surf and deep-sea fishing off the coast. Deer, moose, duck and raccoon may be hunted in season. For information see p 11.

ACADIA National Park ★★★

Michelin tourist map - fold 11

Acadia National Park is located primarily on **Mount Desert Island** with smaller sections on the island of **Isle au Haut** *(p 65)*, and on the **Schoodic Peninsula** *(p 61)* across Frenchman Bay.

Mount Desert Island, measuring 108 sq miles and cut almost in half by the fjord **Somes Sound**, is an unspoiled region of gentle pink granite mountains, dark forests and fresh-water lakes. Pointed evergreens emerging from rocky ledges that fall away from the shore, recall the description of Mount Desert as "... the place where the mountains meet the sea."

Bordering the temperate and subarctic zones, the park has a rich variety of plant and animal life. Approximately 500 species of flowers, shrubs, trees and nonflowering plants grow in the region and more than 300 species of birds have been sighted here over the years.

Practical Information. – Lodging: Motels will be found on Route 3 between Ellsworth and Bar Harbor. There are hotels and inns in Southwest Harbor, Northeast Harbor and Bass Harbor.

Camping. – There are two campgrounds in the park: Blackwoods Campground *(reservations necessary during the summer)* and Seawall Campground *(sites available on a first-come first-served basis)*. Camping within the park boundaries is limited to 14 days.

To Visit the Park. – The best way to visit the park is by car, or for the more athletic, by bicycle.

The more than 170 miles of trails, carriage and bridle paths make most sections of the park accessible to visitors.

Bus tours are conducted through the park by a commercial bus company: ☏ *(207) 288-5218.*

The park can also be viewed from the air by taking one of the Acadia Air, Inc. sightseeing planes *(Rte 3)*.

(From a photo by Hans Wendler.)

A Typical Fishing Village.

Mount Desert Island. – The island was once the summer fishing and campgrounds of the Penobscot and Passamaquoddy Indians. In September 1604, the French explorer **Samuel de Champlain, and De Monts,** the founder of Acadia (the French territory which extended from present-day Montreal to Philadelphia), anchored in what is now known as **Frenchman Bay.** Champlain's impression of the largest island in the bay as a line of seven or eight mountains with rocky, treeless summits led him to name the island *l'Isle des Monts Deserts*. Nine years later a group of Jesuits established a settlement on Mount Desert Island. Their colony had existed only a month, when it was destroyed by the British.

During the 150 years that followed, the Acadian territory was a constant battlefield between the English and the French. In the late 17C the governor of Canada gave Mount Desert Island to the Frenchman **Antoine de la Mothe Cadillac,** who spent only one summer on the island, before heading west where he founded the city of Detroit. Following the defeat of the French at Quebec in 1759, English colonists began to settle on the coast in increasingly large numbers. The island remained dominated by the English until after the Revolution, when the boundary between the United States and Canada was established by the Treaty of Versailles (1783).

In the mid-19C the region's beauty was discovered by artists. The enthusiasm expressed in their writings and paintings enticed the wealthy to vacation on Mount Desert Island. Elegant summer "cottages" were built and Bar Harbor *(p 61)* developed into a resort community similar to Newport, while Northeast and Southwest Harbors became popular yachting centers. It was among a group of Mount Desert's summer residents that the idea of protecting the island's natural environment first grew.

A National Park. – By 1913 more than 5 000 acres on Mount Desert Island had been set aside as a nature preserve. These lands, donated to the United States government in 1916, were declared a national park three years later and in 1929 the park was permanently named Acadia after the historic French territory of the same name.

More than one third of the park's 38 000 acres were donated by John D. Rockefeller Jr., who was also responsible for having fifty miles of carriage paths laid out in the eastern end of the island. Thirty-three thousand acres of the park are on Mount Desert Island. The park's main attraction, the Loop Road, parallels a spectacular section of open coast with expansive views, and climbs to the top of Cadillac Mountain.

■ **LOOP ROAD★★★** *Circle drive 30 miles – allow 4 hours – local map p 60*

The many scenic outlooks, turnoffs and parking areas along this coastal road afford vistas ranging from sweeping seascapes to panoramas of pink granite mountains and island-studded waters.

Begin at the Visitor Center on Rte 3.

Visitor Center. – *Open June 15 through August 8 AM to 8 PM (4:30 PM May and October 16 to November 1; 6 PM June 1 to 14, and September 1 to October 15). Introductory film to the park shown every half hour.*

Rangers are on duty to answer questions concerning special programs, park regulations, trail conditions and camping. Maps and literature related to the park and nature are available. A tape recorded tour of the park and cassette recorder may be rented. This modern building, rustic in appearance, faces Frenchman Bay.

Frenchman Bay Overlook★★. – From the overlook there is an unobstructed **view** to Schoodic Peninsula and across Frenchman Bay. An orientation table aids in identifying the many small, rounded islands in the bay.

The road passes through a forest, by an open meadow and skirts a marsh where you can see some beaver dams. In the early evening you may see the beavers at work. *Turn right for Sieur de Monts Spring.*

Sieur de Monts Spring. – The spring and surrounding area comprised one of the first parcels of land set aside as part of the nature preserve which became Acadia National Park. The spring was named for De Monts, leader of the 1604 expedition to North America.

The **Nature Center** nearby has exhibits related to the park. In the **Wild Gardens of Acadia** trees, flowers and shrubs of the region are arranged according to their natural habitat: marsh, bog, beach, mountain.

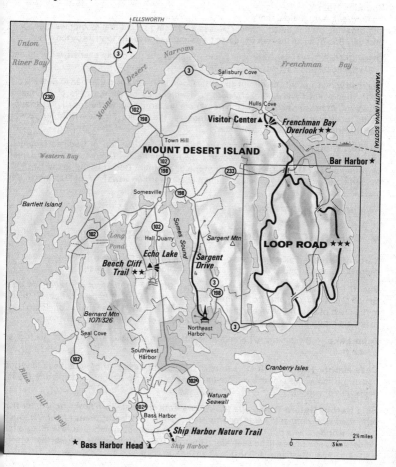

Abbe Museum of Stone Age Antiquities. – *Open May 16 through June and September to October 25, 10 AM to 4 PM, July and August 9 AM to 5 PM; $1.00.*

The dioramas and prehistoric artifacts (Stone Age tools, projectile points) in this small pavilion evoke the way of life of the Indians who inhabited the Frenchman Bay and Blue Hill Bay areas of Maine prior to the period of European colonization.

Return to the Loop Road which becomes Ocean Drive after you cross Rte 3.

Ocean Drive. – *It is one way for 11 miles.* To the left are the buildings of **Jackson Laboratory**, a research center internationally known for its role in cancer research. The cliffs of Champlain Mountain are to the right ahead. There are scenes typical to Acadia: pink granite mountains, rocky ledges, tall evergreens and natural roadside rock gardens.

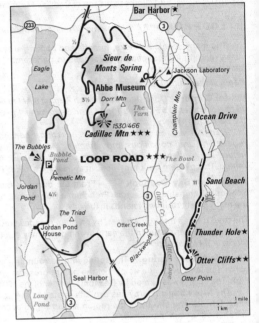

Sand Beach. – This is the only saltwater bathing beach in the park. The beach, composed of coarse sand and seashell particles, is a pleasant spot for sunbathing and swimming, for those who do not mind the cool water temperatures (50-55° F).

A **path** beginning at the upper parking level follows Ocean Drive to the end of Otter Point. This is an enjoyable walk along the top of the cliffs *(2 hours).*

Thunder Hole★. – *Parking on the right.* At high tide, the surf breaking on this narrow chasm causes a booming sound that resembles the roar of thunder. Sea gulls on the rocks seem to be as impressed as the tourists by the effect.

Otter Cliffs★★. – These sheer cliffs rising 110 ft above the ocean offer **views★★** up and down the coast and out to sea.

The road winds around Otter Point and Otter Cove, intersects with the road to Seal Harbor *(left)*, then follows the shore of **Jordan Pond** which lies below the cliffs of Penobscot Mountain. At the northern end of the pond note the large boulder balanced precariously on the top of one of the two rounded hills known as the **Bubbles**. From the Bubbles parking area there is a good view of the boulder.

Cadillac Mountain★★★. – Alt 1 530 ft. The ascent to the top of Cadillac Mountain affords views over **Eagle Lake**, Bar Harbor and the islands below. The mountain was named for Antoine de la Mothe Cadillac, the proprietor of Mount Desert Island in the late 17C. Guided trails on the rocky, treeless summit offer rewarding **views★★★** of Frenchman Bay and the park.

Return to the Park Loop Road, then turn right to complete the circle.

■ OTHER ATTRACTIONS ON MOUNT DESERT ISLAND

Sargent Drive. – *Passenger cars only. Begin at Northeast Harbor.* The road follows the shore of Somes Sound, a deep glacial valley now flooded by the ocean.

Beech Cliff Trail★★. – *From Somesville take Rte 102 South, turn right then left onto Beech Cliff Road. Continue to the end of the road.* This easy trail *(time: 1/2 hour RT)* leads to the crest of Beech Cliff where there are magnificent **views★★** reaching from Echo Lake to Acadia Mountain, rising above the opposite shore of Somes Sound.

Echo Lake. – Swimming is permitted at this freshwater lake which lies at the foot of Beech Cliff.

Bass Harbor Head★. – *At the end of Rte 102A.* The Bass Harbor lighthouse towering above the rocky shore of this remote headland is a scenic delight for camera or brush, especially at sunset.

Ship Harbor Nature Trail. – *Rte 102A. To walk the complete loop take a right at the first fork, then bear right at the sign for Ship Harbor Loop.* Two loops *(time: 1 hour RT).* Such natural wonders as a pot-bellied tree, and an exposed root system that resembles a tall modernistic sculpture will be seen along the trail. The trail follows the ledges, then enters a spruce forest. Best time is high tide when the surf is up.

■ OTHER AREAS IN THE PARK

Schoodic Peninsula★★. – This promontory jutting out from the mainland, across the bay from Mount Desert, is a colorama of tall stands of fir trees rimmed by pink granite ledges, and encircled by the blue waters of the bay. Two thousand acres of Acadia National Park are located on the peninsula. From **Schoodic Head** there are vistas across the bay to Mount Desert Island.

Isle au Haut★. – The park occupies two thirds of this small island south of Stonington. Isle au Haut is an ideal spot to explore on foot *(see How to get there p 65).*

AUGUSTA

Michelin tourist map - fold 10 – Pop 21 358

The capital of Maine is an attractive industrial and residential city on the banks of the Kennebec River. The Kennebec and its adjacent woodlands have been a source of wealth to Augusta ever since the 17C when the Pilgrims established a trading post on the east bank of the river. In the 18 and 19C, boat traffic on the Kennebec, ice cut from the river's surface during the winter *(p 26),* and the forests bordering the river were responsible for the region's prosperity. The Kennebec continues to be important as a vital resource of water power for local industry.

Government, industry and tourism are Augusta's major businesses. The Capital district, located essentially in the State Street area on the west bank of the Kennebec River, includes the State House and other public buildings.

State House. – *State and Capitol Streets. Open weekdays 8 AM to 4 PM; closed Saturdays, Sundays and holidays.*

The dome-topped capitol building is best viewed from a vantage point in the riverside park nearby. The major portion of the State House, constructed between 1829 and 1832 according to the designs of Charles Bulfinch, was later remodeled and enlarged, yet the columned facade and other Bulfinch characteristics were preserved. The House, Senate and Executive chambers and the offices of state agencies and departments are located in the State House.

Blaine House. – *State Street. Guided tours (20 min) weekdays 2 to 4 PM.*

Built for a Bath sea captain in the 1830s, this colonial mansion was the home of James G. Blaine (1830-1893) congressman, Secretary of State and candidate for the presidency of the United States in 1884. The house has served as the Governor's mansion since 1919. The public and family rooms on the main floor may be visited.

Maine State Museum. – *State Street. Open weekdays 9 AM to 5 PM, Saturday 10 AM (1 PM Sunday) to 4 PM; closed major holidays.* This modern building houses the State Library and Archives as well as the State Museum. Temporary and permanent exhibits in the museum treat the history, life and environment of Maine and its people.

Fort Western Museum. – *Bowman Street (on the east side of the river). Guided tours (40 min) mid-June to Labor Day 10 AM (1 PM Sunday) to 5 PM; $1.50.*

This was the site of the trading post built by the Plymouth Pilgrims in the 17C. In 1754 Fort Western was built at this riverside location as a defense against Indian raids. The reconstructed blockhouses and stockades, and the restored fourteen-room barracks furnished with antiques, appear as they did during the 18C. The fort was never attacked and for the most part acted as a supply depot for other forts further up the river.

BANGOR

Michelin tourist map - fold 5 – Pop 30 827

This tranquil city on the west bank of the Penobscot River faces the Maine woods in one direction and the sea in the other. Located at the terminus of the log drives from the north and near an outlet to the sea, Bangor developed into an international export center for timber in the 19C. Crews of lumberjacks felled the trees in the winter, drove them downriver in the spring, and spent the remainder of their time – and most of their pay! – during the off-season in Bangor. Rough, tough and the best at their job, these hearty outdoorsmen called themselves "the Bangor Tigers." When they were in town, the taverns, grog shops and brothels in the district nicknamed Devil's Half-Acre seldom had a quiet night or day. The mythical **Paul Bunyan** character, a legend created by a Michigan newspaperman, is an accurate portrayal of the typical Bangor Tiger. A gigantic **statue** of Paul Bunyan stands on lower Main Street in front of the Bangor Civic Center.

Bangor's International Airport is a refueling station for airlines flying the North American-Europe route and a port of entry for transatlantic flights arriving in the U. S.

BAR HARBOR ★

Michelin tourist map - fold 11 – *Local maps pp 59 and 60* – Pop 4 154

Located on **Mount Desert Island,** Bar Harbor is the major gateway to Acadia National Park *(p 58)* and a departure point for the passenger – auto ferry to Nova Scotia *(p 62).* Bar Harbor has been accustomed to a heavy influx of tourists ever since the late 19 and early 20C when the town developed into a fashionable summer resort for the wealthy.

The town's business-shopping district is approached by roads lined with hotels, motels and guest houses, and in the center of Bar Harbor there are many fine shops and restaurants. During the winter a number of the lodging places and shops close down and Bar Harbor is marked by quiet and an absence of visitors. A large part of the year-round population works in the Jackson Laboratories *(p 60)*.

A Gilded Past. – During the late 19 and early 20C Bar Harbor was second only to Newport as a playground of the wealthy. Summer residents arrived by rail and steamship and spacious Victorian style hotels provided them with comfortable lodging facing the sea. The affluent: the Rockefellers, Astors, Vanderbilts built cottages which became legendary for their magnificence – as in one mansion where the center of the dining room floor opened to allow the banquet table to descend, then reappear completely prepared for the next course! Only a handful of these residences still stand, the remainder having been destroyed by a fire that swept Bar Harbor in 1947.

Ferry to Yarmouth, Nova Scotia. – *CN Marine Terminal on Rte 3, 1 mile outside of Bar Harbor. The* BlueNose *makes the 6 hour crossing. Departures February 1 to October 15. Information* ☎ *CN Marine toll free in Maine: (800) 432-7344; from the remainder of the continental United States (800) 341-7981.*

BATH ★
Michelin tourist map - fold 10 – Pop 10 250

Bath has been a shipbuilding center since the 18C, when its favorable location on a channel to the sea provided the town with advantages over other boatbuilding centers in the region. The port, the fifth busiest in the nation in the 19C, had a fleet of merchant vessels that sailed regularly to the West Indies, California and the Far East. Boatyards along the Kennebec River turned out square-riggers, Down-Easters *(p 26)* and some of the largest schooners ever constructed.

The buildings of the **Maine Maritime Museum,** scattered throughout the city, and the graceful old homes on Washington Street date from this time.

The **Bath Iron Works,** on the west bank of the Kennebec River, has been building ships since 1893 and is Bath's major employer. The launching of a new tanker, container ship, frigate or cargo vessel is still a major event at the B.I.W.

■ MAINE MARITIME MUSEUM★★

The museum, devoted to preserving Maine's maritime heritage, maintains two exhibit sites in the city and offers boatbuilding programs which allow apprentices to study and apply the traditional skills of wooden boatbuilding.

Visit. – *Open mid-May to late October 10 AM to 5 PM; $4.50; the rest of the year Sewall House only 10 AM to 3 PM, Sundays and holidays 1 to 4 PM; $2.00. During the summer there are boat rides (1/2 hour) on the Kennebec River aboard the* Dirigo *($2.00 in addition to museum admission). A shuttle bus operates July and August between the Percy and Small Shipyard and the Seawall House (free to ticket holders). We suggest you begin at the shipyard where ample parking is available.*

Percy and Small Shipyard. – *263 Washington Street.*
Large wooden schooners were the specialty of the Percy and Small Shipyard (1894-1920). The six-masted, 3 720 ton *Wyoming,* the largest wooden sailing vessel ever to fly the United States flag, was built here.

The Buildings. – In the **Mold Loft** (1917) and **Mill and Joiner Shop** (1899) shipbuilding tools, power machinery, old photographs, and illustrated explanations of the building of a wooden ship tell the story of the Percy and Small Shipyard and the great wooden vessels turned out here.

The **Paint and Treenail Shop** (1897) where treenails (wooden pegs used in ship construction) and paints and stains used on the vessel were produced, contains exhibits on the trades related to shipbuilding: note the recreated 19C shipyard office, and the scale model of Donnell Cordage Company (1843) which – with its 1 000 ft long ropewalk – originally stood at the south end of Bath.

The **Shiphouse** surrounds the steam tug *Seguin* (1884) currently being restored.

Visitors are invited to observe apprentices constructing small wooden boats in the **Apprenticeshop**; on the floor below the boat-building area there are displays of small craft from the museum's collection.

The Waterfront. – The schooner *Sherman Zwicker* (1942), berthed along the riverbank, was used in the cod and haddock fisheries on the Grand Banks off of Newfoundland until 1968.

The *Dirigo* departs from a landing nearby. From the boat there is a good view of the Bath Iron Works and the B.I.W.'s 400 ft crane, capable of hoisting 220 tons.

Winter Street Center. – *880 Washington Street*. The Center is housed in a white 19C Gothic Revival church. Ship models, photographs, pictures, maps and dioramas focus on the people who built and sailed the ships, and how, where and why ships were constructed in Bath, the Kennebec region and on the Maine coast.

Sewall Mansion. – *963 Washington Street*. This was the home of the Sewall family, builders of approximately 150 Bath vessels between 1827 and 1902, including the only steel riggers ever produced in the United States. Furnishings, ships portraits, house flags, navigational instruments and other marine artifacts reflect the times and life of the Sewalls and other seafaring families of the Bath area. An extensive exhibit devoted to the origin and growth of the B.I.W. is displayed on the lower level.

EXCURSION

Popham Beach ★ . – *16 miles south of Bath on Rte 209.* Situated at the tip of a finger-like peninsula that reaches out into the ocean, this resort village lies between the Kennebec River and the sea. One of the earliest English settlements in the New World was established at Popham Beach in 1607. The colony lasted only one year but succeeded in building the first English ship constructed in America: the 30 ton pinnace *Virginia.*

Fort Popham, the granite fortress overlooking the point where the Kennebec and the Atlantic Ocean meet, was built during the Civil War to prevent Confederate vessels from sailing up the river to Bath.

Nearby, at **Popham Beach State Park** *(open May through September 9 AM to sunset; $1.00),* there is a broad sandy beach on the ocean side of the point.

BAXTER State Park ★★

Michelin tourist map - folds 4 and 5

Dominated by **Mount Katahdin** (alt 5 267 ft), the highest point in the state, Baxter State Park is a densely forested rectangular tract of land (200 000 acres) in the heart of the Maine wilderness. The park is named for **Perceval Proctor Baxter** (1876-1969), who devoted the greater part of his life and fortune to acquiring this land, which he ultimately deeded to the people of Maine, one of the major conditions of his bequest being the park be preserved "forever in its natural wild state."

In accordance with Baxter's wishes, the park has remained primarily a wildlife sanctuary for the deer, moose, bear and other animals of the north country. The roads through the park are narrow and unpaved *(speed limit 15-20 mph),* camping facilities are primitive, and there are no motels, shops or eating places within the park boundaries. While only a few scenic attractions can be observed from the road, the park's 160 mile trail system which includes the northern section of the Appalachian Trail, leads to points that afford spectacular views of this remote region.

Because of the unique circumstances underlying the establishment of Baxter State Park, the park is administered independently of other state parks. Headquarters are in Millinocket *(p 64).*

Mount Katahdin. – This giant granite monolith, its Indian name meaning "the greatest mountain," has always stirred the imagination of man. Mount Katahdin played an important role in the mythology of the Indians who inhabited the region, as in the Abnaki legend that tells of Pamola, a bird-like deity with the wings and claws of an eagle, the arms and torso of a man, and the enormous head of a moose. Pamola lived on the summit of Katahdin, and whenever he was angry, he cast violent rainstorms, lightning and thunder onto the lands below.

To visitors to the park today, Katahdin is especially of interest for the opportunities it offers for hiking and camping *(see p 64).*

Baxter Peak is the highest of Katahdin's four summits, the others being Hamlin Peak, Pamola Peak and South Peak. Observed from the east, the **Great Basin,** a bowl-shaped formation scoured out of the mountain by glacial ice, is Katahdin's most distinguished characteristic. Seen from the west, the **Knife Edge,** a narrow serrated granite wall that joins Pamola and South Peaks, cuts a jagged profile across the sky.

(From a photo by Paul A. Knaut Jr.)

Mount Katahdin.

VISIT *time: allow one day*

Open mid-May through November for picnicking and sightseeing; December to mid-May for day use in accordance with special regulations. Nonresident motor vehicle fee $5.00 per car. Park map available at entrance to the park. Pets or other domestic animals and motorcycles are not permitted in the park. Campgrounds are open mid-May to mid-October; reservations are necessary. Mail all requests for reservations to Reservation Clerk, Baxter Park Headquarters, 64 Balsam Drive, Millinocket 04462.

The main entrances to the park lead to the Park Road, the only route through the park; it is not a sightseeing route but does pass several scenic points of interest such as **Abols Falls** and the **Slide Dam**. *It is necessary to hike to see the other sights and views in the park.*

Some Hiking Trails. – *Most trails are in the south section of the park. Before starting out, hikers should register and check with the ranger in the area regarding weather and trail conditions.* Stephen Clark's *Baxter Park and Katahdin* is a comprehensive guide to the park trails. Park trails are blazed blue (white for the AT - Appalachian Trail).

Sandy Stream Pond Trail. – *Southeast section of the park. Length: 1 1/2 miles. Begin at Roaring Brook Campground.* After 1/2 mile a short spur left leads to Big Rock which affords a good view of Katahdin (the Great Basin and Hamlin Peak).

South Turner Mountain Trail. – *2 miles from Sandy Stream Pond Trail.* After 1/2 mile, where a fork leads left to Russell Pond Trail, take the right fork and follow the blue blazes to the summit. The trail becomes difficult as it ascends the steep boulder-covered slope of the mountain. Impressive view of Katahdin and the region from the summit.

Chimney Pond Trail. – *Ascent 3 1/2 miles (time: 2 3/4 hours). Begin at Roaring Brook Campground.* Chimney Pond, located on the floor of the Great Basin, is the site of one of the park campgrounds.

Appalachian Trail. – *Southwest section of the park. From Daicey Pond to Big Niagara Falls.* Follow the white blazed trail. After 1 mile you will see **Little Niagara Falls**. Continue a short distance for **Big Niagara Falls**.

Hunt Trail. – *10 1/2 miles RT. Begin at Katahdin Stream Campground. White blazed.* This is one of the popular trails to the top of Katahdin. Allow a full day for the climb and descent. Only those in good physical condition should attempt this long demanding hike.

A pleasant, much shorter hike *(1 mile)* on this trail leads to **Katahdin Stream Falls**.

EXCURSION

Patten. – Pop 1 280. *8 miles east of the park by the Park Road, then Rte 159.* This small agricultural community straddles the border between the rich potato fields of Aroostook County and the forests of northern Maine. High-powered diesel trucks hauling wood pulp and logs are a familiar sight on local roads, since lumbering is an important business in Patten even though the era of lumber camps and river drives has come to an end.

At the **Lumberman's Museum** *(1/2 mile west of Patten on Rte 159)* models, dioramas, exhibits ranging from crooked knives to steam log haulers, a sawmill and reconstructed lumber camps tell the story of the life of the lumberjack. The museum's life-size 1820 lumber camp is a replica of the type of shanty that was shared by about a dozen woodsmen during the lumbering season *(open Memorial Day through September 9 AM (11 AM Sunday) to 4 PM; closed Monday; October 1 to Columbus Day weekends only; $2.00).*

BETHEL

Michelin tourist map - fold 9 – Pop 2 327

Bethel's distinguished inn, prep school and carefully preserved homes situated near the green, are enhanced by the village's magnificent White Mountain setting. Bethel offers opportunities for hunting, fishing, golf, rock hounding in nearby abandoned mines and excursions into the White Mountains.

EXCURSIONS

Grafton Notch State Park★. – *25 miles northwest of Bethel by Rte 26. Open May 15 to October 15, 9 AM to sunset.* The road heads through the Bear River valley and into Grafton Notch State Park, an unspoiled area in the White Mountains. The drive through the park offers views of the notch dominated by **Old Speck Mountain** (alt 4 180 ft) to the west and **Baldpate Mountain** to the east. Several points of interest near the road have been designated as picnic areas.

Screw Auger Falls. – The falls tumble over water-worn slabs of rock and into shallow pools.

Mother Walker Falls. – *1 mile north of Screw Auger Falls.* Old Speck can be seen from these small falls.

Evans Notch★★. – *16 miles southwest of Bethel. Follow Rte 2 West for 10 miles, then turn left onto Rte 113.* The drive through Evans Notch *(Gilead to North Chatham)* in the White Mountain National Forest offers **views★★** of the Cold River valley, one of the most beautiful valleys in the White Mountains.

The key on p 34 explains the symbols used on the maps.

BLUE HILL and DEER ISLE ★★
Michelin tourist map - fold 11

The quiet, breeze-swept peninsula that reaches from Route 3 down to Stonington seems to have been overlooked by modern civilization. Small, secluded villages, and cozy inlets harboring lobster boats, are tucked into woodlands that grow close to the water's edge. There are views of Penobscot Bay and Mount Desert Island which are especially striking on a clear day, with the dark green spruces framed by the blue sky.

Round trip from Bucksport – *87 miles – allow 1 day*

Leave Bucksport (p 67) on Rte 1/3 North, then turn right onto Rte 175 South. Continue straight to Rte 166, then Rte 166A.

Castine★. – *Description p 69.*

Take Rte 166, then Rte 199 to the junction with Rte 175 and follow Rte 175 South.

Reversing Falls. – 5 miles south of South Penobscot there is a picnic area from which an unusual phenomenon can be observed, a "reversing falls." At this point the waterway is very narrow. When the tide changes, the narrow passage creates a bottleneck causing the water to rush in (or out, depending upon whether the tide is rising or falling) with such great force that a series of falls is formed. The best view of the reversing falls is from the bridge on Route 175.

Continuing on through North Brooksville and Brooksville, the road is hilly and begins to climb. Blue Hill is visible to the left. From the **Caterpillar Rest Area** there is a spectacular **panorama★★** of Deer Isle, Penobscot Bay, the Camden Hills and the bay islands.

At the jct of Rtes 175 and 15 follow Rte 15. Cross the bridge to Little Deer Isle, then continue to Deer Isle. Rte 15 passes through the village of Deer Isle and follows the eastern shore to Stonington.

Stonington★. – Pop 1 289. This tranquil fishing village at the tip of the peninsula facing the bay, is typical of the picturesque villages along the coast. The arrival of a boat or the coming and going of workers at the sardine packing factory, are the main activities along the waterfront.

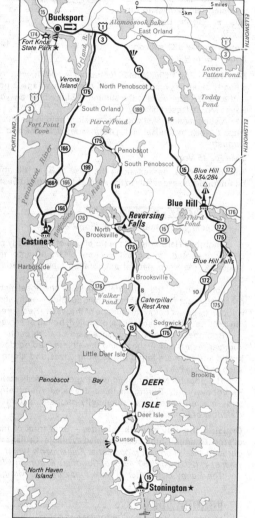

Stonington's granite quarries were formerly worked for stone used in the construction of public buildings and monuments throughout the country; however, today, the quarries for the most part lay abandoned. The hoisting machinery can be seen on the offshore islands. Boats to Isle au Haut, a part of Acadia National Park *(p 58)*, leave from Stonington.

Isle au Haut★. – *The mail boat makes several round trips daily except Sundays and holidays between Stonington and Isle au Haut. During the summer one special round-trip each day for day hikers and campers; this boat stops at Duck Harbor where there is access to the trail system of the National Park. $5.00 one way; time: 40 min. For schedule information ☎ (207) 367-5193.*

The boat stops at Isle au Haut Harbor, an anchorage for pleasure craft, and one of the morning boats *(summer only)* continues on to Duck Harbor. The best way to explore the island is by taking the hiking trails in the National Park.

From Stonington continue through the village and along the western shore of the island. A beautiful view unfolds as you approach Sunset. *After Sunset take Rte 15. Cross the bridge, and follow Rte 175 east. In Sedgewick turn onto Rte 172 which a little further on junctions with Rte 175. Turn right onto Rte 175.* Cross two bridges to **Blue Hill Falls**, a reversing falls similar to the falls at North Brooksville (p 65).

Return to Rte 172 and continue to Blue Hill.

Isle au Haut.

Blue Hill. – Pop 1 690. Named for the hill (alt 940 ft) which dominates the town and yields a hearty blueberry harvest annually, this pretty village is home to many craftsmen, writers and artists. A trail leads to the summit of Blue Hill where you can look out across Blue Hill Bay to Mount Desert Island.

A summer school of chamber music is held in the village and concerts are presented twice a week at Kneisel Hall *(Wednesday 8:15 PM and Sunday 4 PM during July and August).*

Take Rte 15 North.

The road climbs, passes along the base of Blue Hill, then descends to Rte 3 offering beautiful views, especially to the rear, as it leads on to East Orland.

BOOTHBAY HARBOR ★★

Michelin tourist map - fold 10 – Pop 2 231

Boothbay Harbor lies at the tip of one of the craggy peninsulas that extend from the deeply indented, mid-coast section of Maine into the sea. Protected headlands sheltering the deep natural anchorages make the Boothbay region a major boating center.

Lobstering is the principal activity of the local fishermen who can be observed practically year round gathering their catches – shiny, green-brown lobsters – from the wooden traps set below the surface of the water. Restaurants and lobster wharves feature the fresh caught delicacy: broiled, stuffed, boiled or served up as lobster salad.

Boothbay Harbor's importance as a boating center has made the town a popular summer resort. Small shops line the streets leading down to the wharves, and motels, hotels and inns are found in the snug coves and along the rugged stretches of shore such as **Ocean Point**.

The popular New England boating event, **Windjammer Days**, takes place at Boothbay Harbor every July. During the three-day celebration there is a harbor parade of two- and three-masted schooners, community suppers, a pageant and a street parade *(see Calendar of Events p 13).*

Cruising the Bay and its Islands. – Boat trips of the Boothbay Harbor region are offered. Charter fishing boats are also available. Cruises vary from one to several hours in duration. *For information contact at Fisherman's Wharf: Boothbay Navigation Co., Ltd. (Pier 6) ☏ (207) 633-5090/4925, or Goodtime Excursions (Pier 1) ☏ (207) 633-3244.*

The Balmy Days (Pier 8) makes day trips to Monhegan Island in summer (p 73).

BRUNSWICK

Michelin tourist map - fold 10 – Pop 17 539

This attractive community, with wide avenues and streets such as Maine Street, is the site of Bowdoin College. The Bowdoin campus, in the heart of Brunswick, radiates outward from the town's pleasant green laid out by citizens in the early 18C. Shade trees and handsome mansions line Federal Street and other streets nearby.

Construction of a hydroelectric dam was begun in 1979 in the vicinity of the Androscoggin River falls, the major power source in the 19C for the town's lumbering and textile industries. Small manufacturing plants and the United States Naval Air Station are the chief contributors to the local economy today.

Bowdoin College. – Established in 1794, this fine small college counts among its alumni: authors Nathaniel Hawthorne and Henry Wadsworth Longfellow, explorers Admiral Robert Peary and Admiral Donald Mac Millan, and the nation's 14th president Franklin Pierce. Harriet Beecher Stowe wrote *Uncle Tom's Cabin* while she and her husband, a professor at Bowdoin, lived in Brunswick.

The college is named for James Bowdoin, a former governor of Massachusetts (1785-1787). The Bowdoins were a French family who arrived in Maine in the 17C and rose to prominence during the colonial period. Grateful to their new country, they endowed the college with land, money, and paintings from their personal art collection.

Museum of Art ★. – *Walker Art Building. Open September through May 10 AM (2 PM Sunday) to 4 PM (5 PM Saturday and Sunday); the rest of the year 10 AM (2 PM Sunday) to 8 PM (5 PM Sunday); closed Mondays and holidays.*

On the main floor, selections from the museum's group of early American portraits include Gilbert Stuart's painting of *Thomas Jefferson* and Robert Feke's life-size canvas of *General Samuel Waldo.* Bowdoin family portraits by Smibert, Blackburn, Stuart and Feke are also on display.

The lower level has galleries with Greek and Roman antiquities: red and black figure vases, statues, tanagra figures. A group of drawings and watercolors by Winslow Homer will be found nearby.

Peary-Mac Millan Arctic Museum. – *Same hours as the Museum of Art above.*

This museum dedicated to Admirals Robert Peary and Donald Mac Millan presents the history of polar exploration from the voyage of Pythias in 4C BC through the Arctic expeditions made by Peary, the first man to reach the North Pole (1909), and his assistant Mac Millan.

The major part of the collection consists of clothing, instruments, tools and record books of the Peary and Mac Millan expeditions. In the last room there are interesting photos and artifacts related to the Eskimos of Greenland and Labrador.

BUCKSPORT

Michelin tourist map - folds 5 and 11 – *Local map p 65* – Pop 4 466

This small town lies on the east bank of the Penobscot River at the point where the river is divided by **Verona Island.** Bucksport's main street, lined with shops and the **Jed Prouty Tavern,** runs parallel to the river. At the northern end of Bucksport, a large paper company employs an innovative technique which prevents the noxious odors generally associated with papermaking from being released into the air.

Across the river Fort Knox, a massive granite structure, guards the entrance to the Penobscot.

Fort Knox State Park ★. – *Open May through October 9 AM to sunset; $1.00.*

The tense political situation which arose between the United States and Great Britain in 1840 as a result of the New England-Canada boundary dispute, led to a decision by the American military to build a fort at this site. Although the dispute was settled before work on the fort had been started, construction was nevertheless initiated. The fort, never completed, served as a military training ground during the Civil War.

The fort is named for General Henry Knox *(p 80),* the chief of artillery under General Washington during the Revolution.

The enormous stone fortress with its archways, buttresses and winding staircases is a model of 19C American military architecture. From the top of the fort there is a **view** of Bucksport and the Penobscot River.

CAMDEN ★★

Michelin tourist map - folds 10 and 11 – Pop 4 509

Camden's setting at the foot of the Camden Hills, looking out onto the island-speckled waters of Penobscot Bay, is one of the loveliest on the New England coast. The pleasant living-style of Camden's residents is evident throughout the attractive village center and waterfront. Restaurants, galleries, and shops decorated with flower-filled window boxes abound in the business district, and nearby the streets are lined with comfortable large homes. In the harbor, sleek yachts are anchored amidst the tall two-masted windjammers, sailing vessels that offer vacationers desirous of spending several days or longer at sea, the opportunity to "sign on" as part of the ship's crew.

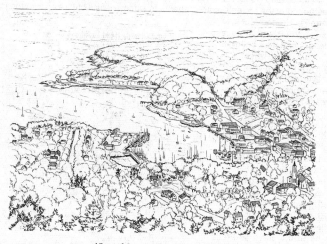

View of Camden from Mount Battie.

Beyond the pastoral setting of the **Camden Public Library** is the **Bok Amphitheatre** where concerts, and plays performed by the Camden Shakespeare Company are presented outdoors with the harbor and bay as the backdrop. The waterfront park, close by, is an ideal place from which to watch the activity in the harbor.

Camden Hills State Park★★. – *Rte 1 north of Camden. Open May 15 to October 15, 9 AM to sunset; $1.00; camping $7.00 per site per night.*

A road leads to the top of **Mount Battie** (alt 800 ft) where there is a **view★★★** *(illustration p 67)* of the harbor, Penobscot Bay and the bay islands. The view inspired Maine-born poet Edna St. Vincent Millay to write her first volume of verse *Renascence*, in 1917.

Returning to the center of Camden on Rte 52, you will have another good view of the Camden Hills as they slope down to Megunticook Lake.

Old Conway House. *From Camden take Rte 1 South 1 mile then turn right onto Conway Road. Open July and August Tuesday through Friday 10 AM to 4 PM; $1.50.*

This small group of buildings: an old barn, farmhouse, blacksmith shop and museum, houses historical artifacts and memorabilia of Camden and Rockport.

EXCURSION

Rockport. – Pop 2 913. *7 miles south of Camden by Rte 1.* This seaside hamlet formerly known for its lime industry, is a picturesque, relaxing spot. Ruins of the lime kilns can be viewed in Marine Park near the harbor.

At the **Apprenticeshop** (near Walker Park) overlooking the harbor, skills used for centuries in building wooden boats are practiced. The smell of fresh cedar shavings fills the loft and visitors may observe apprentices as they construct dories, peapods, skiffs and other small craft ranging from 8 ft to 38 ft in length. *(Open June through October 10 AM to 5 PM).*

CAMPOBELLO Island ★★

Michelin tourist map - fold 6 – *Local map below*

Campobello Island is part of New Brunswick, Canada. *United States citizens need only present some personal form of identification (such as a driver's license) at the border; it is, however, advisable to carry some proof of citizenship with you.* This Canadian time zone is one hour later than Maine.

Campobello Island, at the mouth of the Bay of Fundy, is linked to Lubec, Maine by the Franklin Delano Roosevelt Memorial Bridge. An international agreement signed by the United States and Canada in 1964 established an international park dedicated to Franklin Delano Roosevelt on Campobello Island.

A Summer Retreat. – Discovered in the 17C by Samuel de Champlain and De Monts the island was named in 1767 for the governor of Nova Scotia, William Campbell – *Campo bello* calling to mind the island's beautiful scenery. In the late 19C the island was again discovered – this time by wealthy Bostonians and New Yorkers such as the Roosevelts who built summer cottages here. Land developers were quick to use the island's frequent thick fogs to their advantage, and advertised: "basking in the fog was as healthy for the body as basking in the sun."

Easily accessible from the mainland, Campobello Island receives many visitors attracted by the international park and the island's wild, unspoiled beauty. A prominent feature in the offshore waters are the circular **weirs** *(see illustration p 23)* an ancient Indian method that uses nets strung on stakes to trap fish.

Roosevelt Campobello International Park★★. – *Open the Saturday before Memorial Day and remains open 20 weeks, 9 AM to 5 PM EST.*

Franklin Delano Roosevelt whose four terms as President of the United States were unprecedented in the nation's history, spent his summers as a child and a young man at Campobello. He continued to summer on the island with his wife Eleanor and their children until August 1921 when, following a swim in the icy waters of the Bay of Fundy, he was suddenly struck with polio. Seriously ill, FDR began a long period of convalescence during which he gradually regained his health and strength; however, he remained partially paralyzed for the rest of his life.

Turning his energies toward politics, Franklin was elected governor of New York in 1929 and within four years was elected to the first of four terms he would serve as President. FDR did not re-

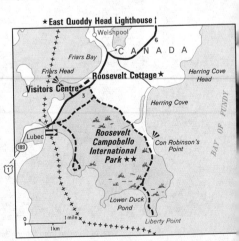

★ East Quoddy Head Lighthouse

Welshpool

CANADA

Friars Bay

Friars Head

Roosevelt Cottage ★

Herring Cove Head

Visitors Centre ●

Herring Cove

Lubec

Roosevelt Campobello International Park ★★

Con Robinson's Point

BAY OF FUNDY

189

Lower Duck Pond

Liberty Point

0   1 mile

1 km

turn to the island until 1933, twelve years after his tragic illness. Then, as on the several other occasions during which he visited the island before his death (1945), he stayed for a brief time only. The Roosevelt cottage and property were donated to the government in 1963 by the Hammer family, to serve as a park in memory of FDR.

Visitors Centre. – Films are shown as an introduction to Campobello and Franklin Delano Roosevelt's life on the island.

Roosevelt Cottage★. – The 34 room house facing Eastport across the bay is modestly furnished. Many personal mementoes: FDR's hat, fishing rod, family photos and letters recall the vacations spent by the Roosevelts at Campobello.

Drives in the Park★★. – The vast 2 600 acre park has a variety of magnificent landscapes: forests, bogs, cliffs, lakes and beaches. The humid, seaside climate favors a dense, very rich growth of vegetation. From **Friars Head** *(south of the Visitors Centre turn right at the sign marked Picnic Area)* there is a view west of Lubec and the Maine coast.

A sweeping view along the shore of **Herring Cove** to **Herring Cove Head** is offered from **Con Robinson's Point** *(follow Glensevern Road east to the end)*.

At **Lower Duck Pond**, a pebble beach borders the rocky shore. The island's woodlands are so often enveloped in a thick fog, they have come to be known as "fog" forests.

Tour of the Island. – *Begin at the Visitors Centre. 7 1/2 miles.* Follow the paved road along the west side of the island past Friars Bay to Harbour de Loutre. At Welshpool, one of the three villages on the island, there are several gift shops.

East Quoddy Head Lighthouse★. – *A short distance north of Wilson's Beach, take the gravel road.* The lighthouse and its picturesque surroundings look out on Head Harbor Island.

CASTINE ★

Michelin tourist map - fold 11 – *Local map p 65* – Pop 1 328

The first and lasting impression one has of Castine is of beautiful tree-lined streets and stately white homes. A stroll along Main Street leads you past small shops and down to the waterfront. The large brick buildings in the village are the Maine Maritime Academy, owned and operated by the state of Maine.

Each year Castine is the site of the **Retired Skippers Race** *(see Calendar of Events p 13).* To participate in the regatta skippers must be at least 65 years of age and Maine born.

Forts George and Madison and the historical markers found along Castine's streets recount the tumultuous history of this now quiet, peaceful town.

A Stormy History. – For more than 200 years after Castine was established as a trading post by the Plymouth Pilgrims (1629), this vulnerable port on the Penobscot peninsula was constantly the scene of turmoil. Known first as Bagaduce, then as Fort Pentagoet, the town remained in British hands until the French Baron de St. Castine gained control in 1667. Conditions continued to be stormy and Castine, renamed for the Baron, subsequently fell to the Dutch and then to the British.

The English were granted control of Castine by the Treaty of the Peace of Paris (1763), however, within thirteen years England was once again at war – this time with her rebellious colonies in America. A second treaty signed in Paris in 1783 established the St. Croix River as the eastern boundary between the United States and Canada and determined Castine's future as an American settlement.

Fort George, built by the British in the 18C, and Fort Madison, an American fortification (1811), were occupied by the British during the War of 1812.

Maine Maritime Academy. – Founded in 1941, the Academy trains men and women to serve as officers in the United States Merchant Marine, Navy Reserves and Coast Guard. Cadets receive a B.S. degree, Merchant Marine Officers license, and a commission in the United States Naval Reserve upon completion of the Academy's four year program.

A tour of the **State of Maine** *(8 AM to 4 PM July and August),* the Academy's training vessel berthed at the waterfront, is possible when the ship is in port. Designed originally as a passenger and cargo ship, the *State of Maine* was converted into a troop transport vessel during the Korean conflict and has since served in the Cuban crisis, during the tensions in Lebanon, and in the Vietnam War.

COBSCOOK BAY ★

Michelin tourist map - fold 6

Emptying into **Passamaquoddy Bay,** Cobscook Bay is an almost entirely landlocked natural basin. The coastal fishing towns of Eastport and Lubec, separated by less than 3 miles of water but nearly 40 miles apart by land, stand sentinel over the channels linking the two bay areas and witness the exceptionally high tides (18-24 ft) for which *Cobscook* (Indian for "boiling waters") Bay and its neighboring shores are known.

During the 1930s the United States and Canada entered into a joint effort: the Passamaquoddy Tidal Power Project, to provide power for local farms and industry by harnessing the energy released by the tides of Passamaquoddy and Cobscook bays. The project called for the construction of a dam or series of dams that would link several of the islands to the mainland. Construction began in 1935 but after only a short time was abandoned, leaving several thousand workers unemployed and the city of Eastport bankrupt. The energy crisis of the 1970s and 1980s has brought renewed interest in the Passamaquoddy Tidal Power Project.

69

From Lubec to Saint Croix Island National Monument

64 miles – allow 1/2 day

Lubec. – Pop 1 977. During the 17 and 18C this small fishing port was a center for goods smuggled into the United States from Canada. Ships authorized to sail to Europe set out from Lubec and returned in several days with cargoes of rum, sugar and other staples. The record-breaking time of these highly profitable round-trip "transatlantic" voyages – in fact only short trips to Canada where goods were available at low prices – was never questioned. By the late 1800s twenty sardine packing factories had been established in Lubec, forming the basis of the town's economy. Only two of these factories still remain.

From Lubec the Franklin Delano Roosevelt International Bridge provides access to the International Park on Campobello Island (p 68).

Quoddy Head State Park★. – *6 miles south of Lubec. Follow Rte 189 4 miles to the gas station and turn left at the sign. Open May 30 to October 15, 9 AM to sunset.*

The red and white striped **Quoddy Head Lighthouse,** marking the easternmost point of the United States, is in the park. From this spot there is a view of the island of Grand Manan in New Brunswick, Canada.

A coastal **footpath** *(time: 1 hour 15 min RT)* beginning at the parking lot *(to the right of the lighthouse, arriving from Rte 189)* affords a superb **panorama** of the sea and the granite ledges.

Leave Lubec on Rte 189 heading west. Outside Lubec the road climbs to a point which offers a view of Passamaquoddy Bay and the harbor. At Whiting take Rte 1 North.

Cobscook Bay State Park. – *Open May 15 to October 30, 9 AM to sunset; $1.00.* The park has campsites located on the shores of Cobscook Bay. Here tall stands of evergreens growing out of crevices in the coastal ledges, dominate the island-speckled waters of the bay.

Continue on Rte 1. At West Pembroke take an unmarked road on the right (opposite Rte 214) and follow signs for Reversing Falls Park.

Reversing Falls Park★. – This is one of the best places from which to admire the pine-covered islands and secluded coves of Cobscook Bay. Twice daily, with the change of tides, the current is so strong in a certain area that the rushing waters form an approximately 1/2 mile long falls. *Picnic tables.*

Return to Rte 1. Continue through Perry, then take Rte 190 South.

Pleasant Point Federal Indian Reservation. – Homes of the Passamaquoddy Indian tribe dot the landscape of this small community. The Passamaquoddys, one of the dozen tribes that originally inhabited Maine, at present number about 2 400 throughout the state. They depend primarily on fishing for their livelihood and have constructed a network of weirs *(p 23)* to trap fish in the offshore waters.

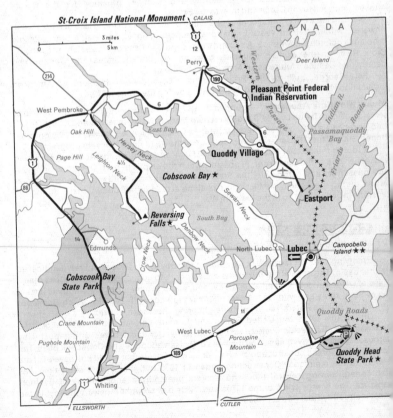

Most of the Indians at Pleasant Point are Catholic, and the celebration of special occasions combines Christian religious rituals with the traditional ceremonies and native costumes of the Passamaquoddy tribe.

Between Pleasant Point and Quoddy Village Route 190 passes over one of the dams constructed as part of the Passamaquoddy Tidal Power Project.

Quoddy Village. – Enhanced by the absence of industry, crowds and pollution, the village's spacious dwellings built in the 1930s to house workers on the Tidal Project, are currently being remodeled to provide comfortable, modern living space.

Eastport. – Pop 1 881. This small community, the easternmost city in the United States, is located on Moose Island between the entrances to Cobscook and Passamaquoddy bays. Exceptionally high tides invade the shore at Eastport making it necessary for the city's wharves to be built on unusually tall piles.

The sardine canning industry flourished in the region between 1875 and the 1920s, together with the production of fish meal and pearl essence (a liquid derived from herring scales and used to add an iridescence to artificial pearls). Today the manufacture of textiles which employs about 250 people, and the newly established aquaculture industry are the important activities. A recent project to develop cargo facilities along the waterfront has once again made Eastport an operational deepwater port and promises to bring new life to the economy.

Return to Rte 1, and turn right at Perry.

St. Croix Island National Monument. – This island off the reddish-colored shores of the mainland, was the site of a colony established in 1604 by a group of about 75 men led by Samuel de Champlain and De Monts. The winter was severe resulting in the death of a number of the members of the group, and the following year the colony moved across the Bay of Fundy to Nova Scotia. The island was later significant in setting the St. Croix River as the boundary line separating the United States and Canada in this eastern region.

*For your trip to Canada – use the **Michelin Green Guide Canada**.*

ELLSWORTH

Michelin tourist map - fold 11 – 26 miles southeast of Bangor – Pop 5 301

Ellsworth, at the same time a traditional coastal village and small modern city, is graced with the attractive First Congregational Church and Scandinavian-inspired City Hall. The business district, destroyed by fire in 1937, has been rebuilt while older dwellings will still be found in the residential areas close by.

Black Mansion. – *West Main Street. Guided tours (30 min) June to October 15 10 AM to 5 PM; closed Sunday; $2.00.*

The Georgian elegance of this brick mansion is reflected in its harmoniously proportioned columns and balustrades, its tall chimneys and symmetrical single-story wings. There is no entranceway on the street side of the house. The interior contains period furnishings and personal possessions of the Black family.

FREEPORT

Michelin tourist map - fold 10 – 17 miles northeast of Portland – Pop 6 205

This small town is the home of **L.L. Bean** the famous sporting goods mail-order enterprise. The L.L. Bean factory store in the center of Freeport, features a complete line of clothing, foot gear and equipment for hunting, camping, fishing, hiking and canoeing. It is not unusual to see the company's parking lot crowded at 3 or 4 AM as the store is open 24 hours a day, year round. The popularity of L.L. Bean and the many brand-name factory outlets and stores established in Freeport in the past several years, make the town a favored shopping spot during the summer and other periods throughout the year.

Desert of Maine. – *From I-95 take Desert Road 2 1/2 miles. Open late May through August 9 AM to 7 PM; September to October 15, 9 AM to 5 PM ; $3.50.*

Once a densely wooded area, these 500 acres are now covered with sand dunes which began to appear in the 18C, after a farmer made a large clearing in the woods to provide his animals with grazing land. As the wind and rain caused the soil to wear away, the sandbed which had lain hidden beneath the earth was gradually revealed. Over the years, the wind has shaped and reshaped the sandy expanse into dunes which now spread across the formerly wooded landscape.

Wolf Neck Woods State Park ★. – *5 miles from the center of Freeport. From Rte 1 turn right onto Bow Street, then right onto Wolfs Neck Road. Open 9 AM to sunset (5 PM after Labor Day to May 29); $1.00.*

The beauty and calm of the park's wooded picnic sites and trails looking out on Casco Bay, offer a pleasant diversion from the shop-lined streets of Freeport village. The Casco Bay Trail is especially scenic with views close up of Googins Island, where ospreys nest in a tree directly opposite the trail.

The KENNEBUNKS

Michelin tourist map - fold 9 – 26 miles south of Portland – Pop 12 589

The popular resort villages of the Kennebunk region: **Kennebunk, Kennebunkport, Kennebunk Beach, Goose Rocks, Arundel** and **Cape Porpoise** are frequented by many artists and writers. Kennebunkport is said to be the setting of *Arundel*, a novel by Kenneth Roberts, a native of the region.

The magnificent elm trees and white houses and churches in Kennebunk and Kennebunkport are from the prosperous shipping and shipbuilding days of the 19C. Kennebunk contains many year-round homes and businesses. An architectural tour of the historical district is an interesting introduction to the buildings in this village *(see below)*.

Kennebunkport's shopping area, Dock Square, has a variety of small shops.

Wedding Cake House. – *In Kennebunk on Rte 9A. The art studio located on the property is the only area open to the public.*

According to legend, the captain who lived in this house was about to be married, when he was unexpectedly called to sea. Although the wedding took place, there was not enough time to bake and decorate a traditional wedding cake, and to console his wife, the captain promised he would have the house "frosted" like a wedding cake as soon as he returned ... . The lacy gingerbread trim ornamenting the house and barn was the result.

The Wedding Cake House.

Brick Store Museum. – *117 Main Street in Kennebunk. Open 10 AM to 4:30 PM; closed Sundays, Mondays, holidays and December 20 to January 10; closed Saturdays also January through April; $1.00.*

Formerly a general store, this brick structure has been renovated into a museum of local history that features the region's seafaring past.

An architectural walking tour (time: 1 1/2 hours) of the Kennebunk historical district is conducted by guides of the Brick Store Museum May to September, Friday at 2 PM; $2.00; ☎ (207) 985-4802.

Seashore Trolley Museum. – *In Kennebunkport. From Kennebunk take Rte 1 North 3 miles to Log Cabin Road (blinking light), then turn right and continue east about 2 miles. Open late April to mid-June and after Labor Day through late October 1:30 to 3:30 PM; mid-June to Labor Day 10 AM to 5:30 PM; $3.50. For schedule of trolley rides and additional information ☎ (207) 967-2712.*

The two mile ride on an open trolley car will be a new experience for some and a bit of nostalgia for others. Antique trolley cars which have been restored are on display.

Cape Porpoise. – The indented shores of Cape Porpoise shelter a fishing village that is a pleasant resort during the summer months.

Goose Rocks Beach. – *Motels provide guests with a beach sticker required for parking.* This inviting 2 mile sandy beach is framed by the grasses of the salt marshes.

Clusters of motels will generally be found near the intersection of several major highways.

KITTERY

Michelin tourist map - fold 9 – Pop 9 666

Shipbuilding, fishing and tourism are the mainstays of this village located just north of the New Hampshire line. Kittery has been associated with shipbuilding ever since its earliest days. In 1775 Admiral John Paul Jones' ship, the *Ranger,* built in Kittery, carried the news to France of the surrender of General Burgoyne and received the first salute ever given an American ship by a foreign power. The **Portsmouth Naval Base and Shipyard**, established on several islands in the Piscataqua River in 1806, has been the most important business in Kittery since the 19C. Private boatyards on the Piscataqua turn out pleasure craft, adding to the town's role as a shipbuilding center.

A drive along the tree-shaded road leading to Kittery Point affords glimpses of the river and attractive homes dating from the 18 and 19C.

Whatever your destination in Maine, plan a stop at the Information Center (open daily) on Route 95/1 north of the New Hampshire line.

Fort McClary Memorial. – *On Rte 103 east of Kittery in Kittery Point. Open May 30 to October 1, 9 AM to sunset; 50¢.*

A hexagonal-shaped blockhouse is all that remains of the 17C fort, known first as Fort William, and afterward renamed for Major Andrew McClary who was killed at the Battle of Bunker Hill. The blockhouse is situated in a calm, waterfront park setting.

EXCURSIONS

Jonathan Hamilton House★. – *9 miles from Kittery by Rte 236 West to South Berwick, turn left opposite the junction with Rte 91 and continue to the end of the road. Bear left, then take the first right onto Vaughan Lane. Guided tours (45 min) June 1 to October 15 Tuesday, Thursday, Saturday and Sunday 12 noon to 5 PM; $2.00.*

This Georgian mansion and its riverside gardens were the setting for much of Sarah Orne Jewett's novel *The Tory Lover*. The house, built (1785) for the merchant Jonathan Hamilton, has hand carved archways, cornices and molding. Japanned and painted furnishings, and murals of the local countryside adorn the first floor.

Sarah Orne Jewett House. – *In South Berwick, 10 miles north of Kittery on Rte 236. Same hours and admission as the Jonathan Hamilton House above. Guided tours 45 min.* This was the home of 19C novelist **Sarah Orne Jewett** (1849-1909). Miss Jewett's novels *Country of the Pointed Firs* (1896), an expression of her admiration for Maine and its people, and *The Tory Lover*, set in Berwick during the Revolution, are American classics. The house is arranged as it was when Miss Jewett lived here.

MONHEGAN Island ★★

Michelin tourist map - fold 10 – Pop 92

This rocky island 10 miles off the mainland, appears from the distance like a large whale floating on the surface of the ocean. Seen from a closer point, Monhegan's steep, picturesque cliffs dropping sharply down to the sea, are visible.

Ledge markings discovered on Manana, the islet across the harbor from Monhegan, are considered, by some, as evidence that the Vikings landed here in the 11C. Several centuries later Monhegan served as a fishing station for European fishermen.

The island's small year-round population earns its living from fishing and lobstering. A law prohibiting fishermen from trapping lobsters in Monhegan waters between June 25 and January 1, allows Monhegan lobsters to grow bigger and bring a better price.

In the summer Monhegan is a haven for artists and a popular day trip for tourists. The island's magical beauty and 17 miles of trails attract many hikers and photographers.

Accommodations are available at the island hotels and a few guest houses. Reservations required. Cars are not permitted on the island.

How to Get There. – From Port Clyde (at the end of Rte 131): *there is round-trip service (3 1/2 hours RT) on the mail boat* Laura B. *May through October Monday to Saturday (daily mid-June through September); three times weekly the rest of the year weather permitting; $17.00. Reservations and deposit required.* ☎ *(207) 372-8848.*

From Boothbay Harbor (Chimney Pier, Pier 8): *The Balmy Days early June to late September makes one round trip daily (3 hours RT) with a 4 hour stopover on Monhegan; $20.00; trolley shuttle operates between parking area on Rte 27 (1 1/2 miles from the pier) and town. For reservations and information* ☎ *(207) 633-2284.*

■ SIGHTS *time: 4 hours*

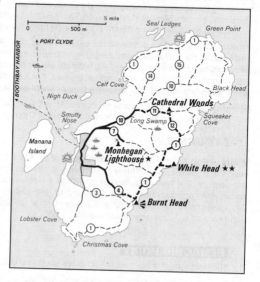

The main sights on the island are Monhegan's sheer cliffs, boulder-strewn shores, rough surf and the sea. Trails are numbered and can be identified by tiny wooden blocks placed on tree trunks wherever two or more trails meet.

Burnt Head. – Trail No. 4. Burnt Head affords a view★★ of the cliffs of White Head.

White Head★★. – From Burnt Head follow Trail No. 1 which straddles the ledges and an evergreen forest. White Head's 150 ft cliffs are generally covered with sea gulls.

Cathedral Woods. – Trail No. 12 runs alongside Long Swamp to Cathedral Woods, an inland forest of evergreens towering above lush growths of fern and moss.

Monhegan Lighthouse★. – From the top of Lighthouse Hill there is a **panorama** of Monhegan, the harbor and Manana.

The lighthouse keeper's house has been transformed into a **museum** *(open July to September 15, 11:30 AM to 3:30 PM)* which displays artifacts, photographs and prints related to the inhabitants and bird and plant life of the island; and to Ray Phillips (1897-1975) – the hermit of Manana (his house still stands on the hillside on Manana).

The MOOSEHEAD LAKE Region

Michelin tourist map - fold 4

This vast, remotely situated inland body of water, New England's largest lake (120 sq miles), is dotted with hundreds of islands and surrounded by timberlands that reach as far as the Canadian border. Numerous bays and coves indent the lake's 350 mile shoreline, making it appear from the air like a wide set of antlers.

The region has been a paradise for sportsmen since the 19C. There is fishing and hunting at easy-to-reach ponds and lakes, as well as at isolated lakeshore sporting camps accessible only by plane. Canoe and raft trips including the Allagash Wilderness Waterway *(see below)* begin on the shores of Moosehead Lake.

Greenville. – Pop 1 956. Situated at the southern end of Moosehead Lake, Greenville is a resort center, headquarters for two large paper companies, and a major outfitting center for sportsmen heading into the north country. *Guides and seaplane services for sightseeing, hunting and fishing parties are based near and on the lake. Tour operators in Greenville arrange rafting and canoe trips on the Kennebec River and West Branch of the Penobscot. Information available at sporting goods stores or the Chamber of Commerce ☏ (207) 695-2702.* In the winter there is skiing at the **Squaw Mountain Ski Area** outside of Greenville. **Lily Bay State Park,** north of town, has a beach and facilities for camping, boating and picnicking. The State Park Road, north of Greenville, provides access to Baxter State Park *(p 63).*

Mount Kineo. – Rising abruptly from the waters of Moosehead Lake, Mount Kineo is the lake's most impressive feature. There is a good view of Kineo from Route 6/15 just north of Rockwood. Kineo was well known among the many tribes who journeyed to this mountain – composed primarily of flint – to obtain the hard, durable stone needed to make weapons, tools and other implements.

Allagash Wilderness Waterway. – *74 miles north of Greenville.* The 92 mile Allagash Wilderness Waterway offers experienced canoeists a magnificent stretch of white water in the heart of a wilderness area. Facilities for camping are primitive, and there is no public transportation or telephone in the area. Everyone entering the Allagash Waterway must register at the Telos-Chamberlain entrance, or at the Churchill Dam, Umsaskis Lake or Michaud Farm check points. *For additional information contact the Maine Bureau of Parks and Recreation, State House Station 22, Augusta, ME 04333.*

OGUNQUIT ★

Michelin tourist map - fold 9 – 36 miles south of Portland – Pop 1 487

In the Algonquin language *Ogunquit* means "beautiful place by the sea." The artists who discovered this coastal fishing village undoubtedly agreed with the description, for by the turn of the century many painters and writers had come to live and work close to Ogunquit's rocky shores and long sandy beach. Works by members of Ogunquit's present-day artists' colony are exhibited in the galleries scattered throughout the village, including the **Ogunquit Art Center** on Hoyt's Lane, and the rustic **Barn Gallery** on Shore Road. The small, modern **Museum of Art,** also on Shore Road, overlooks the sea.

During the summer a different play is presented every week at the **Ogunquit Playhouse.**

Perkins Cove ★ . – This picturesque boat haven has charming boutiques and craft shops and several good seafood restaurants. A footbridge across the entrance to the cove can be raised to allow boats to pass. *Party boats are for hire for deep-sea fishing; there are also breakfast, lobstering, and cocktail cruises. For a modest fee tourists are welcome to join local lobstermen as they set out in their boats to gather the day's catch.*

Marginal Way ★ . – *Cherry Lane to Lookout Motel. Turn right, continue to parking area.* This scenic coastal footpath from the center of Ogunquit leads to Perkins Cove.

EXCURSION

Wells. – Pop 7 988. *5 miles north of Ogunquit on Rte 1.* Located on the stretch of sandy beach that extends from Kittery to Portland, Wells has been a summer resort since the last century. The **Wells Auto Museum** on Route 1 displays antique automobiles as well as motorcycles and bicycles *(open mid-June to mid-September 10 AM to 6 PM; Memorial Day weekend to mid-June and mid-September to Columbus Day weekend Saturdays, Sundays and holidays only 10 AM to 5 PM; $3.00.*

PEMAQUID POINT ★★

Michelin tourist map - fold 10 – 31 miles southeast of Bath

Carved by the glaciers centuries ago, the gnarled ledges at Pemaquid Point are especially spectacular for their pegmatite formations – long, narrow bands of black and white rock, that extend sharply into the sea. The lighthouse rising on the bluff above stands guardian over this dramatic section of coastline and is reflected in the shallow pools left by the surf as it rolls back into the ocean: the site is a photographer's dream!

Located south of Damariscotta *(p 82),* this peninsula was one of the first regions of the coast to be settled. The artifacts excavated at the site of Colonial Pemaquid, are evidence that the area was colonized in the 17C. The Point was most likely a fishing station for European fishermen in the 15 and 16C as well.

Pemaquid Point Light★★★.
– *Open Memorial Day to Columbus Day 10 AM to 5 PM; parking 50¢ per person.*

From the lighthouse *(closed to the public)* there is a magnificent view of the rocky, splintered coastline.

Fishermen's Museum. –
Open Memorial Day to Columbus Day 10 AM (11 AM Sunday) to 5 PM.

This small museum located in the former lighthouse keeper's house contains photographs, fishing gear and other items related to the life of the fisherman.

Pemaquid Point Lighthouse.

Pemaquid Beach. – *From the lighthouse take Rte 130, then turn left.* It is unusual to find such a beautiful sandy beach along this rugged section of the coast.

Colonial Pemaquid★. – *Continue past Pemaquid Beach on Rte 130.* Excavations have been conducted in the area near **Fort William Henry Memorial,** a replica of a 17C fort that stood on this site. There is an archaeological museum *(open Memorial Day to Labor Day 9 AM to 5 PM; $1.50),* nearby.

Christmas Cove. – *13 miles west. From Colonial Pemaquid take Rte 130 to Pemaquid Falls, then turn left onto Rte 129.* Rocky headlands and offshore islands shelter this waterfront settlement. Christmas Cove was named by Captain John Smith who spent Christmas Eve in 1614 here during his expedition along the New England coast.

PORTLAND ★★
Michelin tourist map - folds 9 and 10 – Pop 61 803

The largest city in Maine, Portland is located on Casco Bay, known for its picturesque Calendar Islands. The city is the financial and commercial center of northern New England's major metropolitan area, and an important oil port. It is also the departure point for the Prince of Fundy Line (BX) ferry to Nova Scotia ☏ *(207) 775-5616.*

After having experienced a period of decay during the early 20C, Portland is at present undergoing a major economic rebirth.

Resurgam: "I shall rise again." – True to its motto *Resurgam,* Portland has risen Phoenix-like from its ashes after being almost entirely destroyed on three different occasions. During the early 17C a trading post was established here by the English and by 1658 the village of Falmouth had grown up on the site. Abandoned in the 1670s after Indian raids caused the inhabitants to flee, the village was resettled in 1716 and prospered, the mast trade with England being its most important activity. Falmouth's strong anti-Loyalist sentiments led the British to bomb the town prior to the outbreak of the Revolution, as an example to the other colonies. Following the war Falmouth was reborn and in 1786, ten years after the birth of the nation, was renamed Portland.

The city was the capital of Maine between 1820 and 1832. Mansions lined High and State Streets and the railroad linking Montreal and Portland was completed in the mid-19C. Portland had grown into a prosperous shipping center by July 4, 1866, when a fire swept through the downtown area, leveling most of the buildings in the business district. From these ashes rose the city's rich group of Victorian structures.

During recent decades Portland has experienced an economic revival. The city is responsible for shipping petroleum products to Canada via the Portland pipeline. Renewal of areas such as the Old Port Exchange generated new interest in Portland as a business center in the 1970s, and this interest promises to continue sparked by the construction of projects such as One City Center, the expansion of the Bath Iron Works into Portland, and the development of an 18 acre fish pier complex on the waterfront.

■ **SIGHTS** *time: 1 day*

Old Port Exchange★★ (DY). – The warehouses, offices and shops in this old waterfront district were rundown and deteriorating rapidly when in the early 1970s several persons decided to open a few small restaurants and shops in the area. Their immediate success encouraged other merchants to move into the district and renovate neighboring buildings into attractive specialty shops, professional offices and living space. A stroll along Middle, Exchange and Fore Streets will allow you to admire the window displays, art galleries and craft shops and to try one or more of the dozens of restaurants.

The 19C architecture is interesting for its diversity of styles and decorative brickwork: keystones, cornices, coursing, etc.

Exchange Street: Nos. 103-107 (A). – This block is inspired by the Italianate style; the building on the corner of Middle and Exchange Streets (B) has a *trompe l'œil* mural – several of the windows, though they appear to be a part of the mural, are actually real.

Middle Street: Nos. 133-141 (**D**). – The mansard roof reveals the French influence on this elaborately arched and arcaded block.

Fore Street: No. 373. – The **Seaman's Club** (**E**), a restaurant, is in the Neo-Gothic style; Nos. 336-376, the **Mariner's Church** (**F**), with its tall windows and triangular pediment, is in the Greek Revival style. No. 312, the **Custom House** (**DY**), a good example of the French Second Empire style, reflects the maritime wealth of 19C Portland.

Old Port Exchange – Shop sign.

Victoria Mansion – Morse-Libby House (CZ). – *109 Danforth Street. Guided tours (50 min) June through August 10 AM to 4 PM, September 10 AM to 1 PM; closed Sundays, Mondays and holidays; $3.00.*

Built by the architect Henry Austin, this brownstone mansion (1859) reflects the sumptuous design, decor and furnishings characteristic of the high-style Victorian dwelling. The structure's asymmetrical form with its triangular pediments, arched windows and central tower is inspired by ancient Greek and Roman architecture.

Inside, the lavish decoration includes frescoes, elaborately carved woodwork and stained glass.

Tate House★ (AX). – *1270 Westbrook Street. Guided tours (1 hour) June 15 to September 15, 11 AM (1:30 PM Sunday) to 5 PM; closed Monday.*

This unusual gambrel-roofed dwelling (1755) located in Stroudwater beside the Fore River, was the home of George Tate, the mast agent for the King. Tate's duties included arranging for the shipment to England, of the trees selected to be used as masts for the Royal Navy. All trees higher than 74 ft and at least 24 inches at the base were marked with the King's Arrow, a symbol which identified the tree as royal property and prohibited the colonists from cutting it down. The trees were transported from the forest by 38 to 40 yoke of oxen, and then transferred to ships built especially to carry the masts to England.

The attractively furnished interior contains very fine paneling, cornices, doorways and furniture similar to those in an 18C London townhouse.

Wadsworth-Longfellow House (CY). – *487 Congress Street. Guided tours (45 min) June through September 10 AM to 4 PM; closed Sundays, Mondays and holidays; $2.50.*

This brick dwelling built in 1785 was the childhood home of Henry Wadsworth Longfellow *(p 33)*. Longfellow's simple, narrative poems recounting legends from America's past won him fame across the nation and abroad, and after his death, he was the first American to be memorialized in the Poet's Corner in Westminster Abbey.

Furnishings and memorabilia of the poet and his family are on display.

Portland Museum of Art★ (CZ). – *7 Congress Square. Open 10 AM (12 noon Sunday) to 5 PM (9 PM Thursday), closed Mondays and holidays; $3.00. The McLellan–Sweat House and L. D. M. Sweat Memorial are currently closed for renovation.*

The museum is the largest and oldest public museum in Maine. Founded in 1882, its original quarters were the McLellan-Sweat House, to which an extension, the L. D. M. Sweat Memorial, was added in 1911. The most recent addition to the complex is the brick and granite **Charles Shipman Payson Building** (designed by Henry N. Cobb of I.M. Pei and Partners – 1983) which adjoins the earlier structures and triples the previous amount of exhibition space. A facade that is an arresting blend of circles, rectangles and other forms, and an interior boasting gallery spaces illuminated by domed clerestories are features of the building.

The Collections. – The museum's strength is its collection of 19 and 20C American art and in particular the **State of Maine** collection of paintings, sculpture and prints by artists associated with Maine. Winslow Homer *(Weatherbeaten)*, Andrew Wyeth *(Broad Cove Farm, Cushing, Maine)*, Edward Hopper *(Pemaquid Light)* and John Marin *(Deer Isle Series: Mark Island Lighthouse)* are among the artists represented who drew their inspiration from the Maine landscape. The collection, which began in 1888 with Benjamin Akers's sculpture, *Dead Pearl Diver*, has grown steadily over the years and within the past decade has been enriched by the gifts of 17 canvases by Homer and more than fifty works by early 20C artists associated with the Ogunquit art colony.

Several galleries contain sections devoted to American glass, American and English ceramics and the decorative arts. Highlighting the displays are cases of Portland glass, Federal period paintings and furniture, and the Pepperrell collection of silver presented to Maine-born Sir William Pepperrell, leader of the successful siege of the French fortress of Louisbourg in 1745.

Portland Observatory (BX). – *138 Congress Street. Open July and August 1 to 5 PM, Thursday evening 7 to 9 PM, closed Monday and Tuesday; Memorial Day through June, September and October Saturday and Sunday only 1 to 5 PM; $1.00.*

Prior to the days of the telephone and telegraph, the observatory was used to advise Portlanders of the ships entering the harbor.

From the upper deck there is a beautiful view of Portland and Casco Bay.

PORTLAND and Vicinity

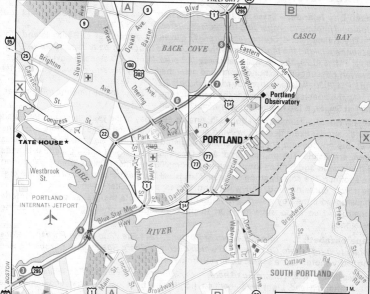

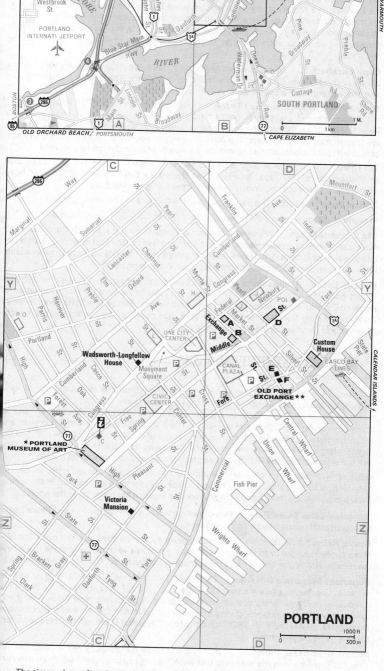

*The times given after the distance for drives and excursions,
allow the traveler to see and enjoy the scenery.*

MAINE

★★PORTLAND

EXCURSIONS

Casco Bay Islands. – Casco Bay Lines (DY) *Custom House Wharf. For reservations and additional information regarding the cruises offered* ☎ *(207) 774-7871.*

The Bailey Island Cruise *(4 hours RT)* allows for a stopover at Bailey Island *(for passengers taking the morning cruise). Late June to Labor Day daily departures at 10 AM and 2 PM; $10.75.* The US Mail Boat Cruise *(2 hours 45 min RT)* stops at several islands, however, passengers are not permitted to disembark. *Daily departures year round 10 AM and 2 PM (2:30 PM after Labor Day to mid-June); $7.25.*

As the boat leaves the harbor the large storage tanks for the oil pipeline to Montreal, and **Fort Gorges,** a 19C granite structure, can be seen.

Calendar Islands. – Numbering about 365, one for each day of the year, these tiny tree-clad islands appear like a fleet of low-lying ships all moving in the same direction. From the boat, the houses and shops on heavily populated **Peaks Island,** and the beaches of **Long Island,** are visible. The population of **Great Chebeaque,** the largest of the Calendar Islands (3 miles wide and 5 miles long) increases from 400 in winter to more than 3 000 during the summer. The solitary stone tower on **Mark Island** is a memorial to shipwrecked sailors; the tower contains food and water and serves as a shelter in the event anyone is shipwrecked in nearby waters. Arriving at **Bailey Island,** note the granite cribwork bridge constructed so as to allow the surf to pass through the openings without meeting resistance.

Cape Elizabeth★. – *10 miles south of Portland. Take Rte 77 to South Portland, at the library turn right onto Cottage Road which becomes Shore Road.* Cape Elizabeth's wild and rocky shoreline is a scenic excursion from Portland.

Portland Head Light★. – *Shore Road north to the lighthouse; located at Fort Williams.*

Portland Head Light was the first lighthouse built on the east coast after the Revolution. Materials from the local shores and fields were used in constructing the tower to reduce building costs. The 300 000 candlepower electric light is visible 16 miles offshore. From the deck of the tower there is a **view★** of Casco Bay and the islands.

Two Lights. – This tiny community is named for the two lighthouses standing side by side on this section of the Cape. Nearby is **Two Lights State Park★**; picnic tables have been arranged on a bluff overlooking this stretch of the surf-pounded coast.

Crescent Beach State Park. – The park has one of the finest sandy beaches in Maine.

Freeport. – *20 miles north of Portland by Rte 1 or Rte 295 (I-95). Description p 71.*

Old Orchard Beach. – *12 miles southwest of Portland by Rte 1.* French Canadians and Americans have been summering at Old Orchard Beach, the first stretch of salt-water beach south of Montreal, for more than a hundred years. Motels, cottages, trailer parks, restaurants and fast food places front the broad, 7 mile long beach.

Sebago Lake. – *20 miles north of Portland by Rte 302.* Sebago Lake, the second largest inland body of water in Maine after Moosehead Lake *(p 74),* is a favorite destination of Portlanders who enjoy swimming, boating and fishing. **Sebago Lake State Park** *(25 miles from Portland by Rte 302)* bordering the lake, has picnic and campsites and a beach. *Open May to October 15, 9 AM to sunset; $1.00.*

The RANGELEY LAKES Region ★

Michelin tourist map - fold 3

Nestled in the mountains of western Maine, the region has an abundance of lakes and ponds, the largest being the lakes of the Rangeley chain.

Spectacular mountain and lake panoramas unfold along Routes 4 and 17, and for those who prefer the solitude of the woods there are trails leading to quiet brooks and mountain tops. Scenic turnoffs on Route 17, south of Oquossoc, afford **views★★★** of the region's largest lakes. There are also rewarding views from Route 4 between Oquossoc and the village of **Rangeley.** Rangeley has small shops, and motels with lake views.

Activities. – Possibilities for warm-weather activities include tennis, golf, swimming, canoeing, mountain climbing and fishing – especially for trout and salmon in the spring. Ski areas have been developed at **Saddleback** and **Sugarloaf Mountains** for winter sports.

Rangeley Lake State Park. – This park on the shores of Rangeley Lake has a beach area, with boat ramps, docks and campsites.

Eustis Ridge★★. – *26 miles north of Rangeley by Rte 16, then turn left onto Rte 27. __ miles further turn left onto the unmarked road.* From this vantage point there is a **view** of the region. Rte 27 continues on to the Canadian border through unspoiled countryside.

Sugarloaf Mountain Ski Area. – *On Rte 27.* This is Maine's largest and most popular ski area. Located in a heavy snowbelt, Sugarloaf (alt 4 237 ft) is known for its fine skiing conditions which generally prevail until late spring. A panoramic **view** *(about 100 ft walk up from the gondola station – during foliage season gondola operates mid-September to October 11, 10 AM to 5 PM; $5.00)* from the top of **Sugarloaf Mountain★★** includes Mounts Katahdin and Washington.

Mount Blue State Park★. – *31 miles southeast of Rangeley by Rte 4, then Rte 14.* This 1 273 acre park on the shores of **Lake Webb★** offers boating, camping, picnicking and swimming in a picturesque setting. From the **State Park Beach Road** there are mountain and lake vistas. *Park open May 15 to October 15, 9 AM to sunset; $1.00.*

78

ROCKLAND

Michelin tourist map - fold 10 – 60 miles south of Bangor – Pop 7 923

Visitors heading north on Route 1 to the towns and islands of Penobscot Bay, frequently pass through Rockland, a busy modern seaport and one of the leading exporters of lobsters in the world today. Light industry including sardine packing, and tourism are also major activities.

During the summer, Rockland is the home port of a small fleet of windjammers *(p 57)*. The **Maine Seafoods Festival** *(see Calendar of Events p 13)*, held the first weekend in August, offers a good opportunity to savor fresh seafood caught along this area of the coast.

William A. Farnsworth Library and Art Museum. – *19 Elm Street. Open 10 AM (1 PM Sunday) to 5 PM; closed Mondays October through May and holidays; $2.00.*

Highlights of the museum's collection of 19 and 20C American oil paintings and watercolors, include works by Homer and Eakins and a large group of Wyeth family paintings. The bleak New England landscape is the setting for many of the works by Andrew Wyeth who summers in Maine. His father, N.C. Wyeth, and son, James Wyeth, are also represented in the collection.

EXCURSIONS

Owl's Head. – *4 miles south of Rockland*. This tiny community is known for its lighthouse: **Owl's Head Lighthouse,** perched atop a 100 ft cliff.

Owls Head Transportation Museum. – *2 miles south of Rockland by Rte 73. On the grounds of Knox County Airport. Open May through October daily 10 AM to 5 PM; weekdays only the rest of the year; $3.50. Off season:* ☎ *(207) 594-4418.*

The museum's collection of working antique airplanes, automobiles and bicycles dates from the early 20C. *Demonstrations of automobiles and airplanes from the collection are held every Sunday on the museum grounds.*

Vinalhaven and North Haven. – *Automobile and passenger ferries operate daily between Rockland and the islands of Vinalhaven (time: 1 hour 15 min) and North Haven (time: 1 hour 10 min). For information* ☎ *Maine State Ferry Service (207) 594-5543.*

The boat cruises among the serene tree-clad islands in Penobscot Bay, the region that is the setting of Sarah Orne Jewett's novel, *Country of the Pointed Firs (p 73)*.

Residents of **Vinalhaven** earn their living from lobstering. Lobster boats are anchored in quiet inlets, and fishing sheds, with their stacks of lobster traps and brightly painted buoys, are found throughout the island. Several of the island's abandoned granite quarries are used for swimming in the summer. From the northern end of the island there is a view across the water to the island of **North Haven.**

North Haven, a small quiet island, has many summer residents.

SABBATHDAY LAKE

Michelin tourist map - fold 9 – 29 miles north of Portland

This hilly lakeside property is the site of the Sabbathday Lake Shaker Village, the last active Shaker community in America. Founded in the 18C by Shaker missionaries, the Sabbathday Lake settlement continued to exist throughout the 19 and 20C, a period when most other Shaker villages became extinct. Although there are less than a dozen Shakers now living at Sabbathday Lake, the principles of Shakerism: "hands to work and hearts to God," and a strong devotion to the Shaker religion continue to guide their lives.

Shaker Village and Museum. – *Take I-95 to Exit 11, then Rte 26 North 8 miles. Guided tours Memorial Day to mid-October 10 AM to 4:30 PM; closed Sunday. 1 hour tour (Meeting House, Ministry, Boys' shop) $3.00; 1 1/2 hours tour (in addition includes the Laundry and Brick Dwelling House) $4.50.*

The Shakers occupy a number of these buildings, most of which can be viewed from the outside only. The **Brick Dwelling House** with its granite trim and delicate wooden porch appears elegant when contrasted with the simple white clapboarded structures found throughout the village.

The museum in the **Meeting House** (1794) contains examples of Shaker furniture, clothing, fancy goods and other Shaker industries and inventions *(p 129)*.

EXCURSION

Poland Spring. – *3 miles north of Sabbathday Lake by Rte 26.*

This mountain and lake hamlet became famous in the 19C after a man who had been violently ill drank from the spring on Ricker's Hill, and quickly regained his health. A small factory was established to bottle the water, and a lavish hotel complex including the Poland Spring House developed near the spring, to cater to the businessmen and dignitaries who came "to take the waters." Poland Spring water is still bottled at a factory on Ricker's Hill and sold in stores and supermarkets around the world. From the hill it is possible to look out onto the mountains in the southern part of the state.

Business Hours — Banks: 9 AM to 3 PM
Shops: 10 AM to 5 PM (or 6 PM)
Shopping Centers: 9 AM (or 10 AM) to 9 PM (or 10 PM)
Post Office: 8 AM to 5 PM (12 noon Saturday)

SEARSPORT

Michelin tourist map - fold 11 – 32 miles south of Bangor – Pop 2 321

Located near the head of Penobscot Bay, this seafaring town was a boatbuilding center and the home of more than 10 % of the nation's deepwater shipmasters in the 19C. Searsport captains sailed the trade routes to the other side of the world, making the name of their hometown one of the most familiar along the waterfronts of the Orient, Africa, Europe and the Carribean. The beautiful dwellings built for these seamen still line the streets of Searsport near the waterfront.

The second busiest harbor in the state, Searsport is also a major export center for the important potato crop raised to the north in Aroostook County.

Penobscot Marine Museum★. – *Church Street off of Rte 1. Open Memorial Day weekend to October 15, 9:30 AM (1 PM Sunday) to 5 PM; $3.00.*

The museum's rich collection of marine paintings, models and artifacts illustrating the era of sail and trade is arranged in a group of buildings that includes several restored sea captain's homes, the former Town Hall and the new Phillips Memorial Library.

In the **Fowler-True-Ross House** (1820) are wall hangings, furniture, tableware and paintings that were brought back to New England by Searsport captains and their families. Products of the Chinese artisan were highly admired for their fine craftsmanship and decorative quality and very often adorned almost every room in a sea captain's home. Fine paintings and furniture will be found in the **Nickels-Colcord-Duncan House** (c 1880); the barn attached to the house has an exhibit on Penobscot Bay fisheries and a display of small craft. The old **Town Hall** contains shipbuilding tools, half-models, ship models, Oriental trade objects, and a permanent exhibit on "The Challenge of the Down-Easters," the large wooden ships built in Maine in the 19C *(p 26)*.

In the **Captain Merithew House** (c. 1850) there is an extensive display of nautical instruments, charts and maps. On the first floor note the collection of photographs of Searsport captains dating from the late 18-20C. Rooms on the second floor contain paintings by Thomas and James Butterworth, as well as a variety of items ranging from ship models and watercolors to, in the Whaling Room, ostrich eggs skillfully etched with whaling scenes and a map of the world!

THOMASTON

Michelin tourist map - fold 10 – Pop 3 000

This yachting center, a village of attractive old homes and churches, is the site of the Maine State Prison. Adjacent to the prison, on Route 1, is a showroom where furniture and other woodenware made by the inmates is sold. Thomaston's major employer is a large modern cement plant located outside the village center.

Montpelier. – *Rte 1. Guided tours (1 hour) May 30 to Labor Day 9 AM to 5:30 PM; closed Monday and Tuesday; $1.50.*

This stately white mansion is a replica of the original residence built in 1794 by **General Henry Knox,** an aid to General Washington during the Revolution. In the winter of 1775-1776 General Knox was the leader of an expedition which carried cannon and supplies from Fort Ticonderoga to Boston, to be used against the British the following spring *(p 90)*. He later served as the nation's first Secretary of War and was a wealthy landowner, when he resigned his government position and settled in Thomaston.

Special features of the Federalist mansion are its graceful oval rooms, a freestanding staircase flanking an arched doorway, and antique furnishings which include Knox family pieces and a mirrored bookcase said to have belonged to Marie Antoinette.

WISCASSET ★★

Michelin tourist map - fold 10 – Pop 3 222

An appealing town with broad tree-lined streets, Georgian mansions, antique shops and restaurants, Wiscasset now appears to spend its days quietly recalling the era when it was the home of wealthy merchants and shipmasters and the busiest international port north of Boston. Wiscasset's shipyards, built on the banks of the Sheepscot River, turned out clipper ships that carried lumber and ice to the West Indies and returned laden down with the staples necessary for daily living.

The deteriorating hulks of two schooners once active along the Atlantic coast: the **Hesperus** and the **Luther Little,** lie on the west bank of the river.

The Maine Yankee atomic power plant situated midway between Wiscasset and the mouth of the Sheepscot River has been in operation since 1972.

Musical Wonder House★★. – *18 High Street. Guided tours Memorial Day to October 15, 10 AM to 5 PM; single floor tour (1/2 hour) $5.50; two floor tour (1 1/2 hours) $9.50. Demonstrations of the instruments on request. Candlelight concerts July and August feature performances by antique musical boxes; $20.00. For tickets and information ☎ (207) 882-7163.*

This Georgian dwelling contains a superb collection of approximately 400 19 and 20C phonographs, instruments, and mechanical and automatic music boxes, almost all of which are in working order. Constructed primarily to reproduce musical melodies and voices by means of metal discs or cylinders, these machines, enclosed in handcrafted boxes or cabinets, were highly treasured by their owners as works of art.

The Regina Orchestral Corona which changes discs automatically, the Harpe Aeolienne music box, the Emerald polyphon with its hand tuned silver bells, and the Regina Sublima drum table – a Louis XV style table decorated with hand painted scenes, all play tunes as rich as their names imply.

Lincoln County Museum and Old Jail. – *Federal Street. Guided tours (1/2 hour) July and August 10 AM to 4 PM; closed Monday; $1.50.*

This grim, stone-walled jail was built (1809) when the whipping post and other forms of public punishment were no longer effective in dealing with the many problems that were arising in the rapidly growing villages on the coast. About forty prisoners could be contained in the cells, while the third floor was set aside for debtors, the insane and women.

Nickels-Sortwell House. – *Corner of Main and Federal Streets. Guided tours (45 min) June through September, 12 noon to 5 PM; closed Mondays, Tuesdays and holidays; $2.00.*

This Federal style mansion (1807) with its beautifully proportioned facade and entranceway fronts Main Street. The house, built by a Wiscasset shipmaster, contains period furnishings.

EXCURSION

Fort Edgecomb. – *1 mile southeast of Wiscasset. Take Rte 1 across the Sheepscot River, then turn right. Open Memorial Day to Labor Day 9 AM to 6 PM; 50¢.*

This small fort was built during the War of 1812 to protect Wiscasset. The wooden octagonal-shaped blockhouse commands a view of the river and Westport Island.

Picnic area on the grounds.

Fort Edgecomb.

YORK ★
Michelin tourist map - fold 9 – 8 miles north of Portsmouth – Pop 9 643

The town of York includes several communities: historic **York Village** – dating from colonial times; **York Harbor** – a fashionable resort at the mouth of York River, **York Beach** – a beachfront amusement and swimming area, and **Cape Neddick.**

HISTORICAL NOTES

In 1624 the Pilgrims established a trading post at Agamenticus, the present-day site of York. The small settlement that grew up around the trading post was chosen by **Sir Ferdinando Gorges,** the proprietor of Maine, as the capital of his vast New World territory. In 1641 the village was given a city charter by sir Gorges and renamed Gorgeana in his honor. Sir Gorge's dreams of developing "the main" (later Maine) were never realized and when the Massachusetts Bay Company assumed control of this section of the coast in 1652, Gorgeana was reorganized as the town of York.

Although York was completely destroyed by a raiding party during the French and Indian wars, the town had developed into a busy port and the county seat by the dawn of the Revolution.

The continued interest of residents since the 19C in protecting the character of their community has preserved the early colonial charm of York.

■ COLONIAL YORK★★
time: 1/2 day

A group of early structures flanks the green: to one side is the 18C **church** with its cock weathervane, and the **Town Hall** which served for a time as the York County courthouse; nearby are the Emerson-Wilcox House, an 18C schoolhouse, the old cemetery, Jefferd's Tavern, and rising from the top of a small hill, the Old Gaol, an 18C jail.

A combination ticket ($6.00) for the sights described below can be purchased at Jefferd's Tavern; rates also available for individual buildings.

Old Gaol Museum★. – *Guided tours (30 min) mid-June through September 10 AM to 3 PM; closed the rest of the year; $2.00.*

Originally a stone dungeon built in 1720 to serve the entire province of Maine, this jail was enlarged soon after to include several cells and provide living quarters for the jailer and his family. Small openings cut in the thick stone walls allow slithers of sunlight to enter the cool, damp cells.

Emerson-Wilcox House. – *Same hours and admission as Old Gaol Museum.*

Built (1740) as a private dwelling, this large house variously served over the years as a tailorshop, tavern and post office. The tavern catered to travelers on the Post Road, as well as local residents and the occupants of the Old Gaol.

The interior contains some interesting period furnishings.

Old Burying Ground★. – Surrounded by a low stone wall, this cemetery is interesting for its many tombstones dating from the 17C. Note the **Witch's Tomb,** the grave covered with a large horizontal stone flanked by two low vertical slabs. The large stone was placed over the grave to prevent the witch's body from escaping from its final resting place.

Jefferd's Tavern★. – *Same hours and admission as Old Gaol Museum.*
This tavern built in Wells *(p 74)* in 1750, was a wayside station on the York – Kennebunk stage route. The large cozy tap room has plank floors and a wooden bar. Rooms on the floor above were set aside for women and children who ordinarily did not congregate downstairs with the men. A mural in the upstairs Keeping Room portrays the early York village and countryside.

Return to your car and follow Lindsay Road to Sewall's Bridge beside the York River. Nearby are the John Hancock Warehouse, the George Marshall Store (a craft shop), and fishermen's sheds covered with lobster buoys. The inviting red colonial dwelling beside the river was the home of **Elizabeth Perkins** (1879-1952) one of York's prominent residents. *Same hours and admission as Old Gaol Museum.*

John Hancock Warehouse. – *Same hours and admission as Old Gaol Museum.*
John Hancock, the Revolutionary War patriot and signer of the Declaration of Independence, was a very rich and successful merchant. This was one of a string of warehouses he owned along the coast.

■ ADDITIONAL SIGHTS

York Harbor. – This landlocked boating center is a haven for small craft. Beautiful homes are tucked among the harbor's tree-covered shores.
The coastal road leads to **Long Beach,** a two-mile stretch of beach bordered by summer cottages.

Nubble Light★. – *Leave Rte 1A and take Nubble Road on the right to the tip of Cape Neddick.* From the shore there is a magnificent view of Nubble Lighthouse and the island it is on; the Isles of Shoals can be seen beyond.

York Beach. – This summer resort on the shores of Short Sands Beach has an assortment of busy concession stands, eating places and souvenir shops. Several hotels built during the last century stand near the beach like a group of distinguished dowagers proudly surveying their waterfront domain.

OTHER PLACES OF INTEREST

COLUMBIA FALLS. – Michelin tourist map - fold 6 – Pop 540 – 64 miles east of Bangor.
Columbia Falls was one of the numerous shipbuilding and lumbering centers on the coast in the 19C. The **Ruggles House** *(Rte 1 to sign for Columbia Falls turn onto this road 1/4 mile; guided tours June 1 to October 15, 9:30 AM (11 AM Sunday) to 4:30 PM; 50¢)* built (1818) during this period, was one of the finest dwellings in the village. Though modest in size, the house has a handsome exterior and bright, comfortable rooms; the hand carved wainscoting, fireplaces and cornices were, according to legend, executed by an Englishman whose hand was guided by an angel.

DAMARISCOTTA. – Michelin tourist map - fold 10 – Pop 1 655 – 19 miles northeast of Bath.
Situated across the river from Newcastle is Damariscotta, a pretty seafaring town which offers vacationers a selection of restaurants, shops and motels.
The rustic **Chapman-Hall House** (1754), lived in until the 1950s, is a good example of an early Cape Cod dwelling. Antique furnishings and historical exhibits reflect the way of life of the period 1750-1820 *(on Rte 1; guided tours – 30 min – June 15 to September 15, 1 to 5 PM; closed Mondays and holidays; $1.00).*

FARMINGTON. – Michelin tourist map - fold 4 – Pop 6 980 – 37 miles northwest of Augusta.
This farming community is the shopping center for the vacation areas of the Belgrade Lakes to the south, the Rangeley Lakes *(p 78)* to the west and the Sugarloaf and Saddleback Mountain ski areas.
Farmington became known for its famous resident, **Lillian Norton** (1857-1914), the celebrated opera star. Miss Norton's home has been transformed into a museum, the **Nordica Homestead,** which has exhibits on her life and career. *(From Farmington Center take Rte 4 north and turn right onto Holley Road; guided tours – 1 hour – June 1 to Labor Day 10 AM to 5 PM; closed Monday; $1.00).*

Massachusetts

Area : 8 093 sq miles
Population : 5 797 582
Capital : Boston
Nickname : Bay State
State Flower : Mayflower

Extending across the width of New England, Massachusetts provides a cross section of the region's varied topography : the tree-covered Berkshire Hills in the west, slope gradually down to the fertile meadows of the Connecticut Valley in the center of the state ; miles of sandy beach lie south of Boston, while to the north the coast is irregular and rockbound. The state is rectangular in shape, except for the bulbous southeast section which extends into the ocean, adding hundreds of miles to the Massachusetts coastline.

The Birthplace of American Independence. – New England's earliest permanent settlements were in Massachusetts. The Pilgrims, in search of religious freedom, established the Plymouth Colony in 1620, followed within ten years by the Puritans who founded Boston. Colonization continued and as the population expanded and prospered, Parliament's taxation policies placed an increasing financial burden on the colonists. The latter, angered by England's policy of "taxation without representation," and inspired by the oratory of **Samuel Adams, James Otis** and **John Hancock,** turned to open hostility : the riots following the passage of the **Stamp Act,** the **Boston Tea Party** and the **Boston Massacre.** These events proved to be merely the prelude to the confrontations at Lexington and Concord, and the battle for American independence.

Economy. – For two centuries Massachusetts earned its living from the sea – fishing, whaling and trade. Great fortunes were made in trade, especially the China Trade, and when in the 19C maritime commerce declined, these fortunes provided the capital investment needed for the shift to industrialization.

With the advantages of an abundance of waterpower and the increasing waves of immigration which provided a large labor force, the Berkshires, the southern section of the coast, and the Merrimack Valley were soon dotted with many small industrial centers – "mill towns." Massachusetts developed into a prominent manufacturer of textiles and leather goods, and by 1850 **Lowell** *(p 132),* the first planned industrial city in the nation, was the leading producer of textiles in the world. In the 20C these industries migrated south and were supplanted by the manufacture of electronics, machine tools and electrical equipment. Today the state's most important source of revenue is its **"brain power,"** as represented by its excellent educational institutions and research industries : aerospace, information systems, etc.

Massachusetts continues to lead all the New England states in commercial fishing, with Boston, Gloucester and New Bedford ranking among the nation's major ports. **Agriculturally,** the Bay State is known principally for its specialized crops : **tobacco** shade-grown in the Connecticut Valley ; and **cranberries,** cultivated in the region of Cape Cod.

Recreation. – The state abounds in cultural opportunities year round. **Boston** *(p 87)* is especially rich, with programs offered by the Boston Symphony Orchestra, the Boston Pops, the Opera Company of Boston and the Boston Ballet Company.

In the **summer,** theaters along the coast : Beverly, Dennis, Hyannis, Provincetown... and inland : Stockbridge, Williamstown... offer dramas, light comedies and musicals. Concerts are held at many locations (Ipswich : Castle Hill ; Cape Ann : Hammond Castle), the highlight of the season being the Tanglewood Music Festival *(p 86).*

Cape Cod and the islands of Martha's Vineyard and Nantucket, with their windswept beauty, sandy beaches and fine boating waters, are favored destinations of vacationers. The activity minded, in addition, enjoy the fishing trips, and opportunities to hunt in the inlets and marshes of the Cape.

"Whale watching," a unique new adventure (remember to take along a pair of binoculars !), is offered by whale-watch cruises departing from several ports (Provincetown, Boston, Gloucester). Day-long excursions operate spring through fall in the ocean waters off the coast where whale sightings are likely to occur. For **hikers** there are the trails of the Appalachian Trail, and footpaths that run through the cool, green Berkshire Hills. The Berkshires are a year-round resort, with skiing at **Butternut Basin** (Great Barrington), **Brodie Mountain** (New Ashford), and several smaller areas.

Deep-sea game fish include marlin and tuna. Inland streams and lakes are stocked with trout, bass, pickerel, perch and pike.

The BERKSHIRES ★★★

Michelin tourist map - folds 13 and 14

In westernmost Massachusetts lies a valley watered by the streams of the Housatonic and bordered by the foothills of the Taconic and Hoosac ranges. This region, the Berkshires, is a mixture of small industrial towns: 19C "mill towns," and comfortable residential communities which blend gracefully with their surroundings.

The Berkshires is a popular year-round resort where many New Yorkers and Bostonians have country homes. Of special interest in the summer for its refreshing climate and cultural offerings, in the fall for its splendid foliage, and in the winter for skiing, the region in addition offers hiking, fishing, golf and other sports.

The Mohegans. – The Mohegans once lived on the banks of the Hudson River and journeyed to the Housatonic Valley "the place beyond the mountains" to hunt. In time, reduced in number by disease and warfare, they abandoned the lowlands for the thickly wooded hills where they lived peacefully until the arrival of the colonists in the 18C. The colonists were devoted to Christianizing the Indians, and in 1734 Stockbridge *(p 154)* was established as an Indian mission on land granted for this purpose by the General Court.

To the north lived the **Mohawks,** enemies of the Mohegans and the French, and allies of the British. One of the major routes traveled by pioneers migrating to the midwest from the seaboard colonies and the Berkshires, followed an old Indian trail blazed by the Mohawks through the Appalachian Mountains to the Great Lakes.

From Agriculture to Industry. – The early settlers farmed the land, but after the Revolution, many farms were abandoned as their owners migrated westward to the fertile plains region. In New England, the migration westward was accompanied by a transition from farming to industry. The Berkshires developed into a major manufacturing center, and **mill towns,** small factory towns comprised of monotone stacks of red brick mill buildings: North Adams, Pittsfield, Dalton, Lee sprang up throughout the region. The railroad followed, linking the valley towns to the rest of the state, especially after the construction of the Hoosac Tunnel in 1873 *(p 136).*

The Grand Estates. – Favorable descriptions of the Berkshires, written in the mid-19C by Nathaniel Hawthorne, Henry Ward Beecher and others attracted wealthy families to summer here. These families built the handsome residences that still dot the countryside outside Great Barrington, Lee, Lenox and Stockbridge. At the beginning of the 20C Lenox alone could count 75 of these magnificent properties including **Tanglewood** *(p 86)* and the estate of Andrew Carnegie, the richest man in the Berkshires.

Increased taxes, spiraling costs and the Depression brought an end to the luxuries of the era, and most of the estates were abandoned or sold, to be converted into schools or resorts. A growing number of former estates are now operated as year-round inns.

TOURING THE BERKSHIRES

Allow several days to follow the excursions described below and to attend at least one of the music or dance festivals held in the summer. Included among these events are the **Tanglewood Music Festival** *(p 86)* ☎ *(413) 637-1600, (617) 266-1492,* and the **South Mountain Concert Festival** ☎ *(413) 442-2106.* The **Jacob's Pillow Dance Festival** brings together international performers of ballet, modern dance and mime ☎ *(413) 243-0745 (February to Labor Day).* See *Calendar of Events p 13.*

Summer theater is offered at the **Berkshire Playhouse** in Stockbridge and at the **Williamstown Theater** in Williamstown. Classical Shakespearian theater is presented in Lenox at **The Mount,** once the summer home of novelist Edith Wharton (1862-1937).

In the winter there is skiing at **Butternut Basin, Brodie Mountain** and **Otis Ridge.**

The map on *p 85* includes the southern part of the Berkshires. For attractions in the northern part of the region: see **Mount Greylock** *(p 136)* and **Williamstown** *(p 158).*

For information on festivals and lodging in the Berkshires ☎ *(413) 443-9186,* or toll free in the northeast except Massachusetts *(800) 237-5747.*

Program for one day in the Berkshires. – From the south take Route 7, stop in **Stockbridge**(*p 154*), follow the itinerary below between Stockbridge and Lenox, visit the **Hancock Shaker Village** *(p 129)* outside of Pittsfield, then the **Clark Institute** in Williamstown *(p 158).*

■ GREAT BARRINGTON AND THE SURROUNDING REGION★★

Great Barrington. – Pop 7 314. Great Barrington is the commercial center for the many vacation homes in the outskirts of this pleasant town. The Geat Barrington Rapids, once the site of Mohegan camps, was the major power source for local mills in the 18C. It was here, on the banks of the Housatonic, that the inventor William Stanley demonstrated for the first time the use of alternating current, and on March 20, 1886 Great Barrington became one of the first cities in the world to have its streets and homes lit by electricity.

Bartholomew's Cobble. – *11 miles south of Great Barrington. Take Rte 7 South, then Rte 7A to Ashley Falls; there take Rannpo Road then Weatogue Road. Open 9 AM to sunset; $2.50.* This natural rock garden covered with a variety of trees, wildflowers and ferns, rises above the Housatonic River. The **Ledges Trail** through the Cobble *(time: 45 min RT)* follows the river. At station 17 cross the road and continue on Hulburt's Hill Trail *(insect repellent necessary summer and fall)* to an open pasture on Miles Mountain (alt 1 050 ft). View into the Housatonic Valley.

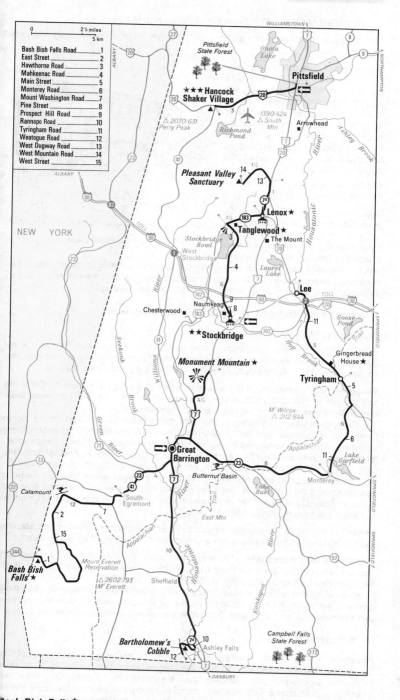

Bash Bish Falls Road _____ 1
East Street _____ 2
Hawthorne Road _____ 3
Mahkeenac Road _____ 4
Main Street _____ 5
Monterey Road _____ 6
Mount Washington Road ____ 7
Pine Street _____ 8
Prospect Hill Road _____ 9
Rannapo Road _____ 10
Tyringham Road _____ 11
Weatogue Road _____ 12
West Dugway Road _____ 13
West Mountain Road ____ 14
West Street _____ 15

ash Bish Falls★. – *16 miles southwest of Great Barrington. Follow Rte 23/41 West to
gremont, then Mount Washington Road, East Street, West Street and Bash Bish Falls
Road. From the parking area a steep trail marked with blue triangles and white blazes
eads to the falls. Continuing on the same road one mile there is another parking area;
rom there a longer but easier path leads to the falls. Bash Bish brook flows over a 275 ft
creating a 50 ft waterfall and natural pool in this forest setting.*

Monument Mountain★. – *4 1/2 miles north of Great Barrington on Rte 7. From the
arking area on the west side of Rte 7 two trails lead to the summit. The easier trail, the
dian Monument Trail (time: ascent 1 hour), begins to the left, 600 yds south along the
ghway, and enters the woods where a sign points right to Indian Monument (a cairn
bout 100 yds off the trail). Turn right and continue, always selecting the right spur. The
econd, more difficult trail (time: ascent 45 min) begins to the right of the parking area
d is blazed with round white markers. From the rocky summit, named Squaw Peak for
 Indian maiden who leaped to her death from this point, there is a* **panorama★** *of the
erkshires. A cairn at the base of the mountain is said to mark the grave of the Indian
aiden.*

TYRINGHAM VALLEY★ From Great Barrington to Lee

Take Rte 23 to Monterey, then turn left onto Tyringham Road which becomes Monterey Road.

Tyringham. – Pop 365. This charming valley town was the site of a community of Shakers in the 19C. The valley's scenic landscape attracted many artists (including Henry Kitson, sculptor of the *Minuteman*) at the beginning of the century. Kitson's former studio, the picturesque **Gingerbread House★**, is the home of the Tyringham Art Galleries.

Continue along Main Street, then Tyringham Road to Rte 102.

(By permission of the Tyringham Galleries, Massachusetts.)

The Gingerbread House

Lee. – Pop 6 093. In the mid-19C there were five paper factories operating in this mill town. At about the same time, rich marble deposits were discovered beneath a section of land which, until then, had been considered worthless because it was too poor to farm. Lee marble was quarried and used in the construction of the Capitol in Washington, D.C. and other public buildings, making the name of this small town famous.

FROM STOCKBRIDGE TO LENOX★★★ via Tanglewood

Stockbridge★★. – *Description p 154.*

In Stockbridge take Pine Street opposite the Red Lion Inn. Turn left onto Prospect Street (Mahkeenac Road), and drive along the lakeshore of Stockbridge Bowl; then continue on Hawthorne Road. At the junction with Rte 183 there is a good view of the lake.

Tanglewood★. – Tanglewood is the summer home of the Boston Symphony Orchestra and the site of one of the nation's most famous music festivals, the **Tanglewood Music Festival.** More than 300 000 music lovers attend every year.

The festival was inaugurated in 1934 with concerts by the New York Philharmonic Symphony. In 1936 the New York Philharmonic was replaced by the Boston Symphony Orchestra, which has presented the summer series of concerts ever since. Tanglewood, formerly the residence of the Tappan family, was given to the Berkshire Festival Society in 1937 to serve as the festival's permanent home. Buildings on the 210 acres include the 6 000 seat Music Shed designed by Eliel Saarinen, a theater where chamber music is performed, and the main house. From the gardens there is a **view** of **Stockbridge Bowl** and **Hawthorne Cottage,** a replica of the dwelling where Nathaniel Hawthorne lived for 18 months and wrote *House of the Seven Gables (p 148).*

Lenox★. – Pop 6 528. Surrounded by estates which have been transformed into schools and resorts Lenox, with its inviting inns and restaurants, is a delightful place to stay.

Pleasant Valley Sanctuary. – *3 miles from Lenox. Take Rte 7 North and turn left opposite the Quality Inn onto West Dugway Road; then bear left at the fork, West Mountain Road. Open 9 AM to 5 PM; office closed Monday; $2.00.*

The refuge has trails that lead through fields and woodlands revealing vegetation typical of the region. A beaver colony occupies the string of ponds in the valley and their dams and cuttings are easily seen. To observe the beavers at work, visit the area at dusk.

PITTSFIELD

Pittsfield. – Pop 50 340. Pittsfield is a commercial center and the capital of the Berkshires. The GE Company is the city's largest employer, providing more than 8 000 jobs for residents. The **Berkshire Museum** exhibits fine European and American paintings and sculpture, and displays related to history and science *(39 South Street. Open 10 AM (1 PM Sunday) to 5 PM; closed Mondays September through June, and major holidays).* **Pittsfield State Forest** *(entrance on Cascade Street, 2 miles from the rotary at Park Square; take West Street, turn right onto Churchill Street, then left on Cascade Street)* offers opportunities year round for horseback riding, camping, skiing and other activities.

Arrowhead. – *780 Holmes Road. From Park Square, east on East Street; turn right onto Elm Street, then right onto Holmes Road. Open Memorial Day weekend through October 1 AM (11 AM Sunday) to 4:30 PM (3:30 PM Sunday); $3.00.*

Arrowhead, the home of Herman Melville between 1850 and 1863, has been restored to reflect the atmosphere of the era when he lived here. Melville wrote a number of his most important works at Arrowhead including his masterpiece, *Moby Dick.* The kitchen with its huge fireplace bearing an inscription from Melville's *I and My Chimney,* the upstairs study with its view of Mount Greylock, and the remaining rooms contain furnishings owned by the Berkshire County Historical Society which maintains the house as a memorial to Herman Melville, and as the Society's headquarters.

Hancock Shaker Village★★★. – *3 miles west of Pittsfield by Rte 20. Description p 12?*

BOSTON ★★★

Michelin tourist map - fold 17 – Pop 570 719

Boston, the capital of New England, is one of the most livable cities in the United States. Rich in culture and history, the cradle of American independence, and the administrative and financial hub of New England, Boston offers the advantages of a large urban center, yet is a city of neighborhoods: the Back Bay, Beacon Hill, the North End impregnated with the charm of an earlier era. Its population of almost 600 000 inhabitants is ethnically mixed and rises to a total of about 3 million when the combined population of the 92 towns and cities in the metropolitan area are considered.

The city benefits from the museums, libraries and concert halls (p 91) associated with the many colleges in the metropolitan area, and its proximity to the university city of Cambridge has contributed to Boston's role as a leading center of culture.

HISTORICAL NOTES

Birth of Boston. – In 1630, 1 000 Puritans led by John Winthrop arrived on the coast of Massachusetts to establish a settlement for the Massachusetts Bay Company. Having tried Salem where they found that living conditions were poor, and Charlestown, where the situation was no better, they then set their sights on the peninsula called Shawmut, where the hermit Reverend William Blackstone lived. The Reverend welcomed the Puritans, who in return for his hospitality, made him a member of their church, then proceeded to appropriate all but 50 acres of his land for the site of their new settlement. The hermit, displeased by the invasion of his privacy, sold his 50 acres to the Puritans and left in search of more peaceful surroundings.

The new colony known at first as Trimountain because of its hilly topography, was a short time later named Boston after the English town. Organized under the stern guidance of Governor John Winthrop, the settlement developed as a theocratic society: the church and state were one, and religion and government were inseparable. A rigid moral code was strictly enforced and a pillory was built on the Common to punish offenders, its first victim being the carpenter whose price for constructing the pillory was considered too high! Economically, Boston grew rapidly owing to its maritime commerce and shipbuilding, and quickly became one of the most important cities in the American colonies.

Boston, the Cradle of American Independence. – In the 18C Parliament's efforts to enforce high taxes and harsh trade regulations against the American colonies enraged the colonists, who claimed their rights as British citizens to representation were being denied. Following the passage of the Stamp Act (1765), a tax on publications and official documents in Massachusetts, public reaction was violent. Mobs roamed the streets, the governor's mansion was burned, and a boycott was organized. Parliament repealed the Stamp Act the next year, however, renewed demonstrations broke out in 1767 when the Townshend Acts, regulating customs duties, were passed. England's response to the crowds of protesters was to send troops to Boston immediately to enforce British law. The colonists, especially those who were forced to lodge and feed the soldiers, grew increasingly hostile each day, and steadily mounting tensions eventually exploded into a series of clashes between the people of Boston and the British.

The Boston Massacre was the first. March 5, 1770 a group of Bostonians gathered near the State House to protest recent events. When a British officer answered the insults of a member of the crowd with the butt of his musket, the crowd became abusive and the guard was called out. Several Redcoats, provoked by the civilians, loaded their weapons and fired, killing five men. Sam Adams seized on the incident to rally growing numbers of citizens to his cause.

The Boston Tea Party, three years later, aggravated the situation further. By 1773 Parliament had repealed all the Townshend Acts except the tax on tea which gave the East India Company a monopoly to sell tea in the colonies. The tax on tea so angered the colonists that in November, 1773 when three ships of the East India Company carrying tea arrived in Boston harbor, the people refused to allow the captains to unload their cargo. At a meeting held December 16, 1773 in Old South Meeting House, an attempt was made to resolve the issue; however, when at the end of the evening Sam Adams concluded that nothing more could be done, ninety Bostonians disguised as Indians made their way to the waterfront, boarded the ships, and dumped the tea into the harbor. In retaliation, England closed the port of Boston and invoked punitive measures which served only further to unite the colonists against the British. The colonial militia was organized and groups of minutemen began to train on village greens.

The Ride of Paul Revere. – April 1775 General Gage, aware that the colonial militia had hidden arms and ammunition in Concord, ordered a force of 700 British soldiers to seize the weapons. The Americans, forewarned by their spies, were prepared. According to a prearranged plan, the night the British began to march to Concord the sexton of Old North Church signaled the direction they took by hanging two lanterns in the church steeple. In the meantime, Paul Revere safely crossed the river to Charlestown, and from there set out on horseback to warn John Hancock and Sam Adams, who were at Lexington, that the British were on the march.

Because of the legendary ride made by Paul Revere and the other riders that night, the militia was ready and waiting when the British arrived at Lexington, and a short time later at Concord (see Concord p 125, Lexington p 131).

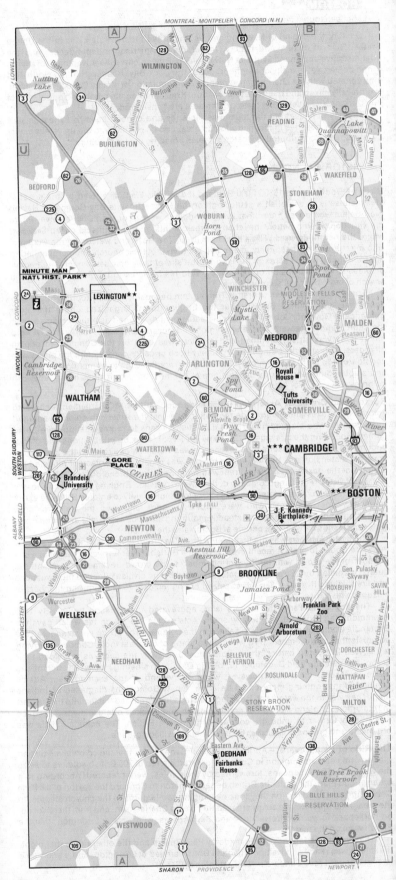

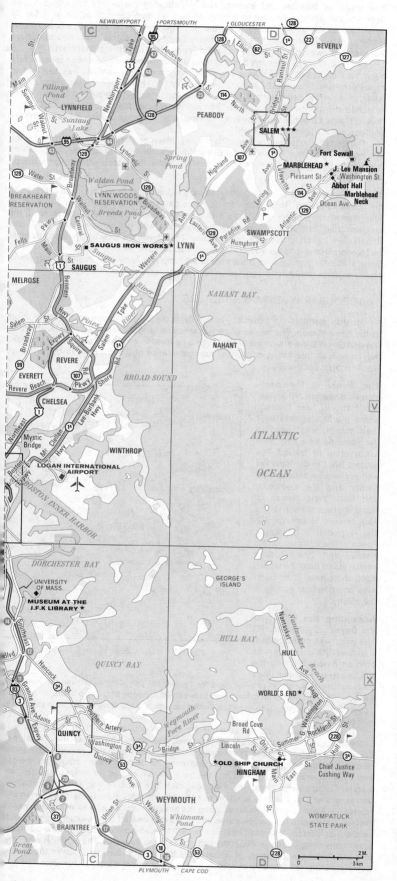

The Siege of Boston and Bunker Hill. – Following the events at Lexington and Concord, the British retreated to Boston where they were surrounded on all sides by rebel forces. While the British eyed the strategic heights around Boston, colonial leaders, informed of the British plan to fortify Dorchester Heights, hastened to occupy Bunker Hill (however, instead they occupied Breed's Hill) as a diversionary tactic.

On June 17, 1775 when the British awoke and discovered an American redoubt had been built on Breed's Hill during the night, a force of 5 000 soldiers was sent out to capture the site. The redoubt was manned by only 1 500 militiamen, however, the British failed in their first two attempts to secure the fort; they set fire to Charlestown, then launched the third, and final attack against the rebels. The colonial leader Colonel Prescott, aware that his men were low on ammunition, commanded the militia: "Don't fire until you see the white of their eyes!"

The British succeeded in capturing the fort; however, they paid a high price for the victory. For more than 10% of all the British officers killed during the Revolution fell on Breed's Hill that day, and at the conclusion of the battle, the morale of the colonial troops was never better.

The Evacuation of Boston. – During the early months of 1776, the supplies captured by the colonists at Fort Ticonderoga *(p 196)* were hauled across New England to Boston. American artillery began to bombard Boston on March 2, and when by March 5 the colonists had fortified the Dorchester Heights area with the cannon from Fort Ti, the British were forced to accept a compromise. The Americans peacefully retook Boston, and General Howe and his troops were permitted to leave the city unharmed. Soon after, General Washington and his troops made a triumphant entry into Boston, a city where enemy soldiers would never again enter for the duration of the Revolution.

TOPOGRAPHY AND ARCHITECTURE

Boston, perhaps more than any other city, is the product of changes brought about by the hand of man. The names of certain areas no longer seem appropriate: the Back Bay and South Cove are dry land, and there is no beacon on top of Beacon Hill; however, they furnish an interesting account of the appearance of Boston prior to the extensive landfill projects of the 19C.

The Pear. – The pear-shaped Shawmut peninsula, later known as Boston, where the first settlers built their homes, was linked to the mainland by a long, thin sandy stem or "neck." The settlers lived in the **North End** and in the area between the harbor and the Common, and built their homes of wood, homes similar to the Paul Revere House *(p 97)*. The public buildings: Faneuil Hall, the State House and the Custom House stood near the waterfront, the center of all business and financial activity in the colony.

Assaulting the Hills and the Bays. – By the late 18C "the pear" was overcrowded. The new State House was built on **Beacon Hill,** and the Hill, a steep mountain, was

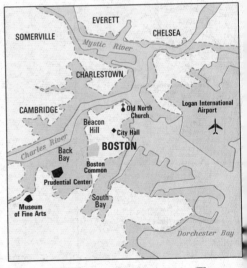

: Land reclaimed from the sea since 1775

soon reduced in size to provide land for residential use. The earth hauled away from Beacon Hill was used to fill in **North Cove** between Beacon Hill and Copp's Hill.

In 1833 developers turned to the **South Cove** which, once it was filled in, was covered with railroad tracks.

The appearance of Boston continued to change until after 1870. In 1819 a dam buil between Beacon Hill and Brookline enclosed 580 acres of the **Back Bay.** Developer dreamed of the windmills, airy factories and gracious mansions, refreshed by sweet smelling sea breezes, that they would build along the dam. However, once built, the dar was a menace. Sewage emptied into the Back Bay which had no outlet to the sea, an stagnant odors were carried by the "delightful" sea breezes into the residential an business districts. The only solution was to fill in the Back Bay. Rows of Victorian styl homes were built on the new land, along the straight avenues and streets which were striking contrast to the narrow paths and lanes that twisted their way through the olde sections of Boston. After the Great Fire of 1872 leveled a major section of the downtow area, many congregations rebuilt their churches in the Back Bay. The Gothic Revival sty and the Romanesque style, of which **Henry Hobson Richardson** *(p 28)* was the maste dominated this 19C church architecture and became part of the city's character.

The New Boston. – By the early 20C Boston was deteriorating. The steadily decreasing population, rising property taxes, and the exodus of businesses to the suburbs or out of state had taken their toll. Faced with the problems of urban blight, the city reacted by establishing the **Boston Redevelopment Authority** (BRA) in 1957. Under the leadership of **Edward Logue,** the BRA inaugurated a program aimed at revitalizing 25% of Boston.

The architect **Ieoh Ming Pei** who had studied at MIT, was called upon with his associates, to draw up the renewal plans for the city. Guided by the commitment of the BRA to preserve the historic monuments in the downtown area, Pei made these early structures an essential part of the New Boston. The keystone of his plan was the new City Hall, set in a plaza surrounded by the towers of **Government Center** *(p 98)*. Another major project, the **Prudential Center** *(p 104),* with its shops, apartments and office towers joined the South End and Back Bay to the heart of the downtown district.

Throughout the 1960s and 1970s I.M. Pei and his associates continued to play a leading role in the renewal of Boston. Their design plans changed the face of a quarter of the city, and were responsible for such major architectural achievements in Boston as the John Hancock Tower and the West Wing of the Museum of Fine Arts.

In the 1980s the transformation of yet another section of old Boston, Dewey Square, is being brought about as banks and other institutions of the Financial District expand eastward into the area of the square. A transportation crossroads, Dewey Square was formerly dominated by the curved classical facade of South Station (1899). Today two new office towers: the **Federal Reserve Bank of Boston** (FZ) (33 stories) and **One Financial Center** (FZ) (46 stories) are redefining the square in modern terms.

BOSTON TODAY

Economy. – Ever since the early days of the Bay Colony, shipping and trade have been the mainstay of Boston's economy. Following a period of decline in the early 20C, modernization of the port's services and 25 miles of docking space in the 1950s and 1960s stimulated a sharp increase in the amount of cargo handled by the port of Boston. A similar surge of growth was experienced in the business sector by businessmen, investors and the insurance industry. Boston financiers, guardians of the Yankee fortunes made in shipping and industry, continue to generate a large share of New England's financial activity from their offices in the commercial area and the Back Bay.

Industrially, a new era was born in the 1950s with the construction of Route 128 and the emergence along this highway of about 700 firms specializing in research and development. Boston is a recognized world leader in these fields and its universities are training grounds for the industry's scientists and research specialists.

Boston is also a world leader in the field of health. Boston hospitals, notably **Massachusetts General Hospital,** are international centers of medical research and innovation.

A Cultural Center. – By the 19C Boston had been nicknamed the "Athens of America." The city was a gathering place for intellectuals and writers, and Bostonians, devotees of the arts, traveled extensively, returning home with art treasures that served as the foundation of the collections of the Museum of Fine Arts, the Isabella Stewart Gardner Museum and the museums of Harvard. The philanthropist Henry Lee Higginson founded the **Boston Symphony Orchestra.** Today the BSO and the **Boston Pops,** with its repertoire of lighter music, perform alternately in **Symphony Hall.** In the summer, the Boston Pops presents concerts at the **Hatch Memorial Shell** on the Charles River Esplanade.

Opera enthusiasts enjoy attending performances of the **Opera Company of Boston** which are held in the Opera House, the former Savoy Theater. The heart of the theater district is located in the area near the Boylston Street station. Boston is a testing center for Broadway productions. The Colonial Theater, the Shubert Theater and the Wilbur Theater present musicals and comedies primarily; the Next Move Theatre concentrates on original plays and plays new to Boston. Dramas are presented at the Charles Playhouse and at numerous university theaters. There are performances by the **Boston Ballet Company** late winter and spring at the Wang Center, and in summer on the Esplanade. *(See p 95).*

Education. – One of the principal concerns of the Puritans who founded Boston was the establishment of a sound educational system. Ever since the founding of Boston Public Latin School (1635), the first public school in America, and Harvard College (1636), the first college in the colonies, Boston has remained a leader in the field of education. The metropolitan area's roster of approximately 50 colleges and universities includes Harvard, Radcliffe, Boston University (EZ), New England Conservatory of Music (EZ), Boston College (EZ), Brandeis University (AV), Tufts University (BV) and Wellesley College.

The "Emerald Necklace" and Sports. – The city's system of public parks, parkways and tree-shaded malls, designed in the 19C by **Frederick Law Olmsted,** encircles the city with an emerald necklace of green spaces: the Public Garden, Commonwealth Avenue, the Charles River Esplanade (FY), the Arnold Arboretum. Linking the downtown area to the Arborway, Jamaica Pond, the Fenway and other parts of Boston, these green spaces contrast with the built-up areas and offer opportunities for in-city recreation.

And Bostonians are avid sports fans. Staunchly loyal, they support the Celtics (basketball) and the Bruins (hockey) who play at the Boston Garden, and the New England Patriots (football) and the Red Sox (baseball). **Fenway Park** (EZ), in the Back Bay, is familiar to every baseball fan as the home of the Red Sox. The 26 mile **Boston Marathon,** run every year from Hopkinton to the Back Bay, is held on Patriot's Day *(see Calendar of Events p 13).*

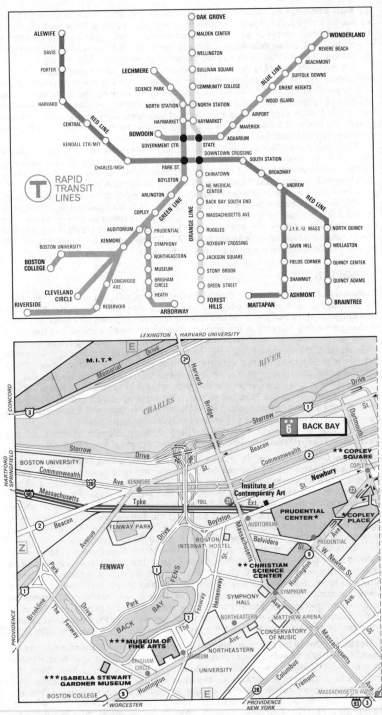

TRANSPORTATION

Getting to Boston. – *See map above and pp 88-89; and practical information p 95.*

By Air. – Logan International Airport (**CV**) is serviced by domestic and foreign carriers. A shuttle service operates between Boston and New York. Airport limousine service *($7.00)* operates between Logan and major hotels, the Park Street subway station and Greyhound and Trailways terminals. Direct service to Logan Airport on the MBTA's Blue Line.

By Train. – AMTRAK trains arrive at South Station (**FZ**). Suburban trains arrive at North Station (**FY**).

By Bus. – Trailways, Inc. (**FZ**) and Greyhound bus companies (**FZ**).

By Car. – Principal access routes to the downtown area are the major highways. Within the city, the major arteries are **Storrow Drive, Memorial Drive** and the **Central Artery** (the Fitzgerald Expressway).

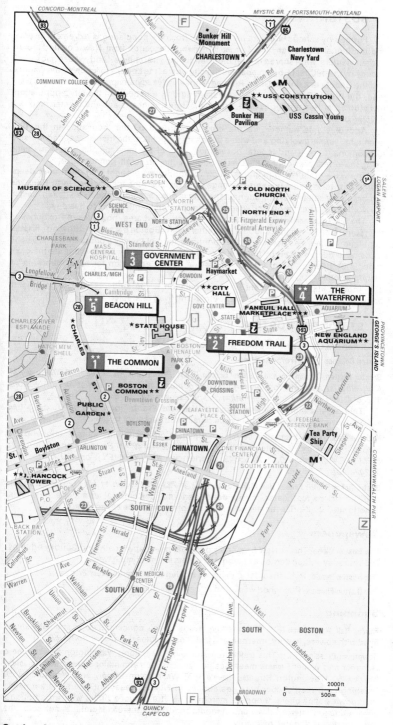

Getting Around. – It is advisable to walk or use public transportation, as the heavy traffic, limited parking and many one-way streets make it difficult to drive in Boston.

The Subway and Buses. – The Massachusetts Bay Transportation Authority (MBTA) operates underground and surface transportation in the Boston area. Stations are indicated by a circled "T" at street level. Maps of the bus and subway lines may be purchased at the Park Street station entrance newsstand. *For route information ☎ 722-3200 weekdays 6:30 AM to 11 PM, weekends 9 AM to 6 PM.*

A Few Tips. – *Most trains operate from 5:20 AM to 12 midnight.* Rapid transit trains run on subway surface or elevated lines; streetcars run underground in central Boston.

– Subway fare is 60¢, 75¢ if your ride begins as a surface fare; bus fare is 50¢. Fares for travel to outlying areas may be higher. *Exact fare required.*

– Most entrances lead to trains going in one direction only: inbound – *to* Park Street/ Government Center stations; or outbound – *from* Park Street/ Government Center.

BOSTONIANS

Formed by various waves of immigration, Boston's population is extremely diverse. The traditional Bostonian, the "proper Bostonian," descends from New England's early Puritan settlers who shared a common language and culture, and whose close-knit society by the 19C, set Boston apart as the city where "the Lowells talk only to the Cabots, and the Cabots talk only to God." Refined, conservative, dynamic, well-traveled and well-read, the proper Bostonian, today representing only a minority of the city's population, has studied at Harvard if possible, attends lectures, concerts and the theater, and is a devotee of the arts.

Added to this number are the **Irish**, who arrived by the thousands in the 19C. Penniless, yet hardworking and with a penchant for politics, the Irish succeeded in rising to positions in local and federal government, one of the most famous Irish-Americans being the former president of the United States, John Fitzgerald Kennedy.

The wave of Italian immigrants followed. The **Italians** brought with them their deep-rooted old world traditions and language, and replaced the Irish in the North End. The celebration of saints' days throughout the year is often accompanied by an Italian feast in the North End, a neighborhood which remains predominantly Italian to this day.

The **black community**, once centered in the downtown area, now lives in Roxbury and the surrounding neighborhoods. Together with Boston's rapidly growing **Hispanic** population, minorities now comprise about one-third of the city's people. The 1970s and 1980s have been marked by the efforts of the Federal Government to integrate the city's schools by busing, in an attempt to provide quality education for all students, in all neighborhoods.

Another important element in the population is the students. The large student population in Boston gives the city a youthful and lively character.

STAYING IN BOSTON

Information Centers. – *see map pp 92-93 (area code: 617)*

Boston Common (FZ): Tremont Street.

Greater Boston Convention and Visitors Bureau (EZ): *Prudential Plaza West. 9 AM to 5 PM. Multi-lingual staff and foreign language brochures available to assist foreign visitors.* ℡ 536-4100. *For recorded information on special events* ℡ 267-6446.

This organization publishes *Boston Weekend Events and Package Guide*, a free seasonal events calendar which may be obtained in person or by mail.

National Park Service Information Centers: Information on Boston and all the national parks across the country. 15 State Street (FY): *open 8:30 AM (9 AM Saturday and Sunday) to 5 PM (6 PM in summer),* ℡ 242-5642; Charlestown Navy Yard (FY): *open 9 AM to 5 PM,* ℡ 242-5601.

Bostix Ticket Booth: Faneuil Hall Marketplace (FY) ℡ 723-5181; *open 11 AM (12 noon Sunday) to 6 PM.* Tickets for theater, music, dance performances, special attractions, museums, historic sites, half-price theater tickets on day of performance are sold here.

Newspapers

The **Boston Globe:** This is New England's principal newspaper; daily and Sunday editions. The Thursday edition carries a calendar of events for the coming week.

The **Boston Herald:** Published daily; includes a calendar of events every Friday.

The **Boston Phoenix:** Published weekly on Friday; available at newsstands.

Shopping

Faneuil Hall Marketplace (FY): The marketplace is a lively concentration of specialty shops filled with flowers, jewelry, international fashions, candles ... *(description p 99).*

Downtown Crossing (FZ): This traffic-free shopping area along Washington Street, where Summer and Winter Streets meet, has numerous shops and major stores such as **Jordan Marsh** (450 Washington Street), **Filene's** (426 Washington Street) and **Woolworths** (350 Washington Street). Super bargains abound in Filene's basement where the automatic markdown policy offers shoppers merchandise at a reduced price, with an additional 25% reduction after 12 days and periodic reductions thereafter until, if not sold, the merchandise is donated to charity.

Lafayette Place (FZ), an indoor mall with dozens of shops, a hotel, restaurants, food stands and an ice skating rink is a recent major addition to Downtown Crossing.

Copley Place (EZ), a two-level shopping galleria with dozens of boutiques, stores, restaurants, a department store: Neiman-Marcus, and more inspired by the shops of Newbury and Boylston Streets. *Description p 103.*

Prudential Center (EZ): Specialty shops, men's, women's and children's apparel, gifts, and two department stores: **Lord and Taylor** and **Saks Fifth Avenue.** *Description p 104.*

Newbury (EZ), **Boylston** and **Charles Streets** (FZ): Antique shops, galleries and boutiques.

Haymarket (FY): Blackstone Street. This colorful outdoor market featuring fresh produce, is held by the Italians from the North End every Friday and Saturday from dawn to dusk *(p 97).*

Cambridge: See map p 113. Droves of bookstores, and youth-oriented clothing and record shops and home decorating centers.

Entertainment

Colonial Theater (FZ T): 106 Boylston Street ☎ 426-9366.

Shubert Theater (FZ T1): 265 Tremont Street ☎ 426-4520.

Wilbur Theater (FZ T2): 246 Tremont Street ☎ 423-4008.

Charles Playhouse (FZ T3): 76 Warrenton Street ☎ 426-6912.

Next Move Theatre (FZ T6): 1 Boylston Place ☎ 423-7588.

Wang Center for Performing Arts (FZ T5): 270 Tremont Street ☎ 482-9393.

Opera House (FZ T4): 539 Washington Street ☎ 426-5300.

Symphony Hall (EZ): 301 Massachusetts Avenue ☎ 266-1492.

New England Conservatory of Music (EZ): 290 Huntington Avenue ☎ 536-2412.

Hatch Memorial Shell (FZ) – **Charles River Esplanade:** Summer performances by the Boston Pops *(July)* and the Boston Ballet Company *(August)*.

Boston at Night. – The lively areas are the **Back Bay, Faneuil Hall Marketplace,** and the **North End.** Harvard Square (Cambridge) with its many coffee houses and restaurants attracts the young primarily.

Transportation

South Station (FZ): Atlantic Avenue and Summer Street ☎ (800) 872-7245.

Back Bay Station (FZ): 145 Dartmouth Street ☎ (800) 872-7245.

Trailways, Inc. (FZ): 555 Atlantic Avenue ☎ 426-7838.

Greyhound (FZ): 10 St. James Avenue ☎ 423-5810.

Miscellaneous

Boston Garden (FY): 150 Causeway Street ☎ 227-3200.

Boston International Hostel (EZ): 12 Hemenway Street ☎ 536-9455.

Fenway Park (EZ): 24 Yawkey Way ☎ 267-8661.

Massachusetts General Hospital (FY): Fruit Street ☎ 726-2000.

Travelers Aid: ☎ 542-7286.

WALKING TOURS

The best way to visit Boston is on foot. The itineraries presented below *(pp 95-104)* will allow you to discover the unique character of the different sections of the city.

The **Freedom Trail,** leading through the business district and into the **North End** takes you past many pre-Revolutionary War monuments; the **Waterfront,** on the other hand, invites a leisurely stroll. The beautiful tree-lined streets and mansions of the staid **Beacon Hill** neighborhood will transport you back into the 19C, as will the Victorian town houses and broad avenues of the livelier **Back Bay** district, with its shops and art galleries.

1 THE COMMON ★★
time: 1 hour – see plan p 101

The Common is the heart of Boston. Its walkways link Beacon Hill and the Back Bay to the downtown shopping and theater areas, and underground is the Park Street Station, the hub of the city's rapid transit system. The Common has belonged to the people of Boston since 1634 when Reverend Blackstone sold this 50 acre parcel of land to the Puritans. Early settlers used this spacious green as a pasture and military training field, and in the 17C the cage for Sabbath Day offenders, and the pillory and stocks were constructed here. In 1638 a gallows was erected on the green for the execution of Quakers, pirates and other "malefactors." At about the same time smoking, in general frowned upon, was permitted outdoors, but only in a specified area on the Common.

The Common was and still is a public meeting place and rallying ground. In 1851, a woman dressed in a strange kind of wearing apparel resembling men's trousers, stood on the Common and defended the right of all women to dress in a similar fashion. Her name was Anita Bloomer and her scandalous attire, with minor changes, now bears her name.

In the summer concerts are held on the Common. On the Boylston Street side is the Central Burying Ground (1756) where the portraitist Gilbert Stuart *(p 30)* is buried.

Public Garden★. – Across from the Common, on Charles Street, is the Public Garden, America's first botanical garden. Neat lawns with formal flower gardens, and a man-made lake cover this area which until the 19C was swampy marshland of the Charles River. The **swan boats,** carrying their passengers on the lake, are one of the sights most often associated with Boston.

The Public Garden – The Swan Boats.

2 **THE FREEDOM TRAIL**★★★ *time: 4 hours – see plan pp 98-99*

This walk includes most of the historical monuments found along Boston's official Freedom Trail, an itinerary of the major sites in the city related to the Revolution. The itinerary is indicated by a red line painted on the sidewalk, and easy-to-read signs. Begin at the **Information Center** on Tremont Street.

Park Street Church★. – 1809. The graceful steeple of Park Street Church, rising above the Common, is one of Boston's loveliest landmarks. The church carillon chimes the melodies of familiar hymns several times daily *(8:40 AM, 12 noon and 4:50 PM)*. William Lloyd Garrison delivered his first antislavery speech in this church in 1829, and *America* was sung for the first time here on July 4, 1831.

Old Granary Burying Ground. – This burial ground was named for the 17C granary which stood nearby. An obelisk in the center of the cemetery honors Benjamin Franklin's parents. The great Revolutionary War orators James Otis and Samuel Adams as well as Paul Revere and Robert Treat Paine are buried here. A tombstone in memory of Mary Goose is believed to mark the grave of "Mother Goose."

King's Chapel★. – *Open 10 AM to 4 PM; closed Sundays, Mondays and major holidays. Services Sunday 11 AM and Wednesday 12:15 PM. Recitals Tuesday 12:15 PM.*

This granite church designed by Peter Harrison in 1754, was the first Anglican church established in New England. Protected by the Crown during its early days, the church fell into disuse for a while following the Revolution, and was referred to as the "Stone Chapel." In 1785 King's Chapel became the first Unitarian Church in America. The Georgian interior is extremely elegant.

The obelisk to the left of the chapel pays tribute to a French soldier who aided the patriots during the Revolution. An ominous curse inscribed on the monument threatens anyone who attempts to destroy the friendship between France and the United States.

Adjoining the chapel is an old cemetery that was for several years the only burial ground in Boston. The colony's first governor, John Winthrop, John Alden (the son of Priscilla and John), and Elizabeth Pain, a woman accused of adultery in the 17C, whose story is thought to have inspired Hawthorne's novel *The Scarlet Letter,* are buried here.

Old Corner Bookstore. – *Corner of Washington and School Streets.* In the 19C this bookshop was the meeting place of the well-known writers Longfellow, Emerson and Hawthorne. The building contains offices of the *Boston Globe.*

Old South Meeting House★★. – *Washington and Milk Streets. Open April through October 9:30 AM to 5 PM; the rest of the year 10 AM to 4 PM (5 PM Saturday and Sunday); closed major holidays; $1.25.* The great orators Sam Adams, James Otis and John Hancock led many of the protest meetings held at Old South prior to the Revolution. The best remembered of these meetings took place on the evening of December 16, 1773 and gave rise to the **Boston Tea Party** *(p 87)*.

The Meeting House, with its plain brick facade and tower and wooden steeple, resembles the churches of Christopher Wren. Inside, the galleries and much of the woodwork are original, except for the box pews which were used as firewood by the British who transformed Old South into a riding school during the siege of Boston *(p 90)*.

A lasting symbol of America's struggle for Independence, Old South Meeting House is a **museum** devoted to the Revolution.

Old State House★★. – *206 Washington Street. Open April through October 9:30 AM to 5 PM; the rest of the year Monday to Friday 10 AM to 4 PM, Saturday 9:30 AM to 5 PM, Sunday 11 AM to 4 PM; closed major holidays; $1.25.*

The brick building (1713) adorned with the symbols of the English Crown, the lion and the unicorn, is easily recognized amidst the maze of office towers that crowd the streets of the business district. The emblems of the lion and unicorn are copies of the originals which were burned when the colonies declared their independence on July 4, 1776.

In 1761 James Otis delivered his fiery speech against the Writs of Assistance here and in 1770 the **Boston Massacre** *(p 87)* took place beneath the windows of the State House (a plaque near the State House indicates the site of the Massacre). The Massachusetts government met in this building until the new State House was completed in 1798, after which the Old State House was converted into shops and a Masonic temple. In 1881 the Bostonian Society was founded to maintain the site. Inside, a spiral staircase leads to the second floor where museum galleries feature the maritime history of Boston.

Faneuil Hall★★. – *Open 9 AM to 5 PM. Brief interpretive talks by Rangers of the National Park Service (meet in the hall).*

Faneuil Hall has been a public forum for speakers from colonial times through the present. Among the noted American leaders who have at one time or another addressed groups assembled here are Samuel Adams, Wendell Phillips, Susan B. Anthony and John F. Kennedy. The Hall was nicknamed the "Cradle of Liberty" by Sam Adams because of the many important pre-Revolutionary War meetings that were held here to protest England's colonial policies and to urge the citizens to rebel. A statue of Sam Adams, the Great Orator, stands in front of the building.

Faneuil Hall was given to Boston in 1742 by Peter Faneuil and served as the principal marketplace and the town meeting hall of the colony through the Revolutionary period. Damaged by fire in 1762, the building was reconstructed according to the original plan drawn by John Smibert, and in 1806 a third story was added by Charles Bulfinch.

Faneuil Hall's cupola is topped with the famous grasshopper weathervane, made by Deacon Shem Drowne in 1742. Modeled after the gilded bronze weathervane atop the Royal Exchange in London, the grasshopper has reigned as the symbol of the Port of Boston since the 18C.

A staircase leads up to the large meeting hall where Healey's painting *Daniel Webster Speaking to the Senate* covers the front wall. The **Ancient and Honorable Artillery Company,** America's oldest military organization, maintains a museum of historical arms and paintings on the floor above *(open 10 AM to 4 PM, closed Saturday and Sunday).*

Union Street. – During the late 18C this street was lined with taverns and pubs. The Duke of Orleans, later King Louis Philippe of France, lived on the second floor of **Ye Olde Union Oyster House** (No. 41 – still a restaurant) for several months, where he gave French lessons to earn his keep.

Cross Blackstone Street where the **Haymarket** *(p 94)* is held every weekend and continue through the pedestrian tunnel and into the North End.

North End ★. – The North End, separated from the rest of the city by the Central Artery, is Boston's predominantly Italian neighborhood. The Irish and eastern European immigrants who settled here in the 19C eventually moved on, and were replaced by the Italians who have stayed. Rooftop gardens, shops bulging with fresh meats, poultry and vegetables, and restaurants that serve up home-cooked pasta, pizza and pastry crowd Hanover and Salem Streets, the main thoroughfares.

The historic sites in this part of the city date from the 17 and 18C when the North End was Boston's most fashionable neighborhood.

Paul Revere House ★. – *19 North Square. Open 9:30 AM to 5:15 PM (4:15 PM November to mid-April); closed major holidays; $1.50.*

This two-storied wooden clapboard dwelling is the only 17C structure in Boston today. The house was already a hundred years old when the patriot-silversmith Paul Revere bought it in 1770. It was from here that he departed April 18, 1775 on his historic ride *(p 87)* to Lexington. Furnishings include items owned by the Revere family.

St. Stephens Church. – 1806. The former Congregational meetinghouse was renamed in 1862, after it was sold to the Catholic diocese of Boston to serve as a church for the immigrants in the North End. Of the twelve churches designed by Bulfinch in Boston this is the only one which is still standing.

Paul Revere Mall.

Paul Revere Mall. – Beyond the equestrian statue of Paul Revere, the work of Cyrus Dallin, is Old North Church. On days when the weather is pleasant the mall is a meeting place for the older residents in the area whose lively discussions in Italian add to the charm of the square. A series of bronze plaques set into the side walls traces the role played by the people of the North End in the history of Boston.

Old North Church or **Christ Church ★★★.** – *Open 9 AM to 5 PM (4:30 PM December 22 through January); Sunday services at 9:30 AM, 11 AM and 4 PM.*

As Americans we cherish this beautiful church, for it was here, on the evening of April 18, 1775 that the sexton hung two lanterns in the church steeple to signal the departure of the British from Boston by boat, on their way to Concord. A century later Old North and the ride made by Paul Revere that night were immortalized by Henry Wadsworth Longfellow in his poem, *Paul Revere's Ride.*

Built in 1723, Old North was inspired by the designs of the English architect Christopher Wren, and surmounted by a spire that was destroyed and replaced on several occasions following violent storms. The present steeple dates from 1954.

Inside, the box pews, the large windows – that allow an abundance of natural light to filter into the church – and the pulpit – from which President Ford initiated the celebration of the nation's Bicentennial – are characteristic features of New England's colonial churches. The four wooden cherubims near the organ were part of the bounty captured from a French vessel.

Replicas of the famous lanterns are in the museum (**M**) adjacent to the church.

Copp's Hill Burying Ground. – *Open year round.*

The burial ground contains the graves of noted Bostonians including members of the prominent Mather family of educators and churchmen: Increase Mather (1639-1723), minister and Harvard president; Cotton Mather (1663-1728), churchman and writer; and Samuel Mather (1706-1785).

From Copp's Hill terrace there is a good view across the river to Charlestown, the Bunker Hill Monument and the *USS Constitution.*

To reach the nearest "T" station: Haymarket, follow Salem Street, pass through the tunnel, and return to Blackstone Street.

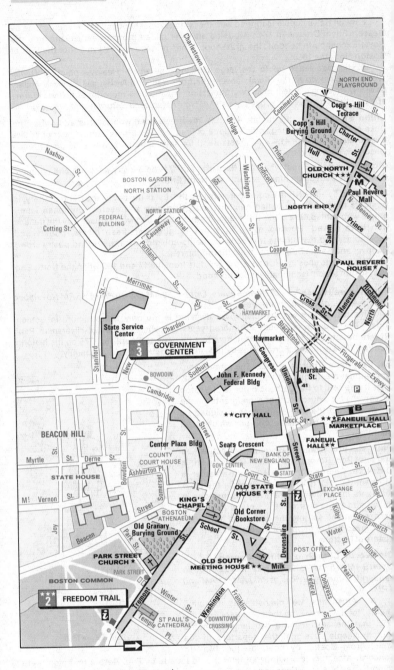

③ **GOVERNMENT CENTER**★

time: 1/2 hour

Government Center, the symbol of the New Boston, was the focal point of th
renewal programs of the 1960s and 1970s. Admiring this plaza with its streamlined offic
towers, who is able to visualize the deteriorating **Scollay Square** district – with its clutter of
retail stores and bawdy entertainment establishments – which stood on this site a littl
more than two decades ago?

The enormous steaming kettle, suspended from a building on the corner of th
square, has been delighting Bostonians for over a century, and is a reminder that th
largest tea store in Boston was at one time located on this spot.

The New Boston. – Built on the 60 acres that were formerly Scollay Square, the $26
million Government Center is the administrative center of the city and state governmen
Pedestrian walkways and the spacious plaza are paved with brick, harmonizing with th
elaborate use of brick in the city's older buildings. Bordering the plaza are: the tw
towers of the **John F. Kennedy Federal Office Building**, the **Center Plaza Office Building** that curve
to the contour of Beacon Hill, the **Sears Crescent** the only 19C building retained as part of
this modern complex and, northwest of the plaza, the **State Service Center**, with its clea
sharp lines, the work of architect Paul Rudolph. In the center of the plaza is the City Ha

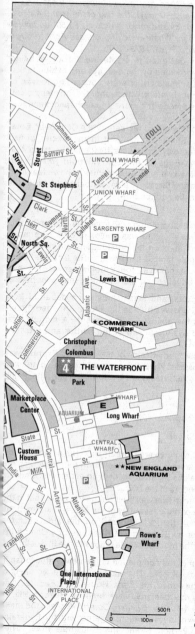

City Hall★★. – The architecturally striking City Hall is considered one of the major achievements of contemporary architecture. Designed by three young architects working together on the project: Kallman, McKinnell and Knowles, the City Hall resembles an inverted pyramid rising from a foundation of brick. Lower sections of the building contain the offices most often visited by the public.

Visitors are welcome to observe city council meetings from the galleries on the fifth floor.

④ THE WATERFRONT★★

time: 2 hours

During Boston's era of maritime prosperity, sailing ships filled with exotic cargoes arrived and departed daily from the harbor. The appearance of the waterfront was altered gradually over the years, at first owing to deterioration and neglect, then later to the construction of major highways that separated it from the rest of the city. More recently, changes in this historic area have been the result of renewal and restoration programs, the most exciting being the renovation of the Faneuil Hall Markets by Benjamin Thompson Associates.

The waterfront is one of the most delightful places in Boston, despite the elevated expressway that runs above its streets. Numerous warehouses have been transformed into attractive living and office space, streets have been converted into pedestrian walkways and **Christopher Columbus Park**, a large harborside park between Long and Commercial Wharves *(see below)*, joins the waterfront to Faneuil Hall Marketplace.

Faneuil Hall Marketplace★★★. – This lively commercial center is one of the leading examples in the nation of the successful revitalization of a formerly blighted urban area. Run-down market buildings and warehouses have been restored and the renewed Faneuil Hall Marketplace has grown into one of the most popular sections of the city. Bostonians and tourists are attracted day and night to its numerous restaurants, outdoor cafés, specialty and craft shops, and the never-ending holiday spirit that animates the area round-the-clock.

The heart of the marketplace is the group of three granite buildings built in 1825 by **Alexander Parris**. The central building, **Quincy Market,** is a long arcade in the Greek Revival style; the sides of the building are glass enclosed and contain dozens of small shops and eating places. The North and South Street buildings flanking Quincy Market, house more elegant stores. In **North Market** is the large, very popular family style restaurant **Durgin Park (B)**.

At the harbor end of the markets is **Marketplace Center** (1986), a low-rise granite structure that curves around and is a terminus for the busy marketplace. The Center houses retail shops and adjoins 200 State Street, a 26-story office building.

Commercial Wharf★ and **Lewis Wharf.** – The granite blocks on these wharves have been renovated into modern harborfront offices and luxury apartments.

Long Wharf. – This "long" wharf, at one time 800 ft in length, extended from the Old State House into the deepest part of the harbor.

The simple, low-scale profile of the **Long Wharf Hotel** (designed by Cossutta and Associates – 1982) **(E)** constructed of red brick, harmonizes well with the traditional architecture of the waterfront. Installed in the lobby is a fresco by the 19C itinerant painter Rufus Porter, depicting the Boston Harbor scene.

Excursion boats and sightseeing cruises of the harbor and harbor islands leave from Long Wharf *(p 109)*.

New England Aquarium★★. – *Central Wharf. Open July to September 10, 9 AM to 6 PM (9 PM Wednesday and Friday; 7 PM Saturday and Sunday); the rest of the year 9 AM to 5 PM (9 PM Friday, 6 PM Saturday and Sunday); closed major holidays; $5.50, under 15, $3.25, admission slightly lower Friday evenings. Whale-watching cruises April through October; schedule and prices subject to change ☎ (617) 973-5277.*

The semi-dark interior of the Aquarium, designed to create the illusion of being underwater, is illuminated solely by the light provided by the displays and exhibit tanks.

The more than 70 exhibits of fishes and animals are arranged according to type of environment: temperate, fresh, cold, and tropical waters, with seahorses, an electric eel, primitive fishes, flashlight fish and penguins among the more unusual specimens that will be seen.

A four-story 187 000 gallon ocean tank containing a recreation of a Caribbean Coral reef dominates the center of the aquarium. Sharks, turtles and many species of fish inhabit the tank and watch every step of the way as visitors descend the ramp that encircles their glass-enclosed world. In the Edge of the Sea Tidepool *(third level)* youngsters are invited to pick up and examine crabs, turtles, starfish. Shows featuring the dolphins and sea lions are presented in the **Discovery,** a vessel berthed next to the aquarium. Special programs are presented in the auditorium.

Custom House. – *State and India Streets.*

The Custom House (1847) became the tallest building (29 stories) in Boston in 1915 when the dome of the original Greek Revival structure was enclosed by a pyramidal-topped tower. The massive 42 ton granite columns on the outside, and the rich marble and granite work within enhance the building's temple-like design. The Custom House has been a Boston landmark since it was built, however, today looking down on a rejuvenated waterfront, it seems to stand just a bit taller and more proudly than ever before.

Rowe's Wharf. – Merchant vessels, packets, and steamships once departed from Rowe's Wharf, formerly Rowe's and Foster's wharves built in the 1760s. A modern hotel-residential-office development now covers the almost 5 1/2 acre site. A monumental entrance arch offers passersby on Atlantic Avenue a view of the harbor and provides access to the waterfront areas.

As you leave Rowe's Wharf, note on the opposite side of the elevated Express-way the distinctive cylindrical tower of **One International Place**, the centerpiece in a complex of five intersecting structures 11 to 46 stories tall, designed by John Burgee and Philip Johnson (1987).

⑤ **BEACON HILL**★★ *time: 3 hours – see plan p 101*

Begin at the State House. "T" Station: Park Street.

Despite its location in the heart of the downtown area, the Beacon Hill neighborhood has a serene, small town atmosphere. Its streets, lit by gas lamps and lined with shade trees and elegant brick town houses, have a charm reminiscent of an earlier era. Only the automobiles passing in the streets are reminders of the 20C.

The neighborhood is named for the beacon that was built on the top of this hill in the 17C. In the 18C a group of investors, aware of the desirability of the site, transformed the Hill's slopes into a fashionable residential district. Bordered on the side near the Common by Beacon Street, along the river by Embankment Road, and by Cambridge and Bowdoin Streets, Beacon Hill is one of the most desirable places to live in Boston.

Architecture on Beacon Hill. – Shortly after the completion of the new State House in 1798, the remainder of the hill fell prey to developers. The most sought after architect of the day was Charles Bulfinch who had designed the State House. His Federal style mansions, and residences modeled after his designs, were built on Beacon Hill for wealthy Boston families. Asher Benjamin's *American Builders Companion* was the major inspiration for the elegant Greek Revival town houses, which, together with the Federalist mansions, lined Beacon Street, Mount Vernon Street and Chestnut Street. Their handsome brick facades, pitched and dormered rooflines, swelled and flat bays, lacy wrought iron balconies, and beautiful entranceways lent a graceful rhythm to the entire area. In back of the main streets, intimate lanes and courts were lined with modest dwellings, the living quarters of the servants.

Between 1818 and 1824 window glass from England was installed in some of the houses on the Hill. The reaction of sunlight on impurities in the glass caused it to turn lavender color. This purple glass that attracted quite a bit of attention in its day, may be seen on Chestnut Street (No. 29A) and Beacon Street (No. 63).

State House★. – *Open weekdays 10 AM to 4 PM. Guided tours (30 min) 10 AM to 3:. PM leave from Doric Hall.* This is the seat of the Massachusetts State Government. The golden dome of the State House dominates Beacon Hill and is visible from many parts the city. The central part of the building, completed in 1798, was the work of Charle Bulfinch. The size of the building has since been increased tenfold by extensions adde in 1895 and 1916. The Doric Hall, Senate Chamber, Senate Reception Room ar Governor's Office are in the section of the building that was designed by Bulfinch. Most the original ornamentation and design of these rooms remain intact.

Statues on the front lawn are of Anne Hutchinson *(west wing),* banished from the 17 colony for her theological views; Mary Dyer *(east wing),* hanged because she was Quaker; Daniel Webster, the orator *(left),* and Horace Mann, a pioneer of American public school system *(right).* Opposite the State House, on Beacon Street, is th

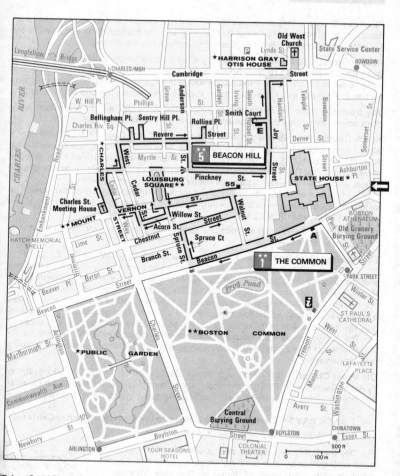

Robert Gould Shaw Civil War Monument (A), a bronze bas-relief by Augustus Saint-Gaudens. The monument honors Colonel Shaw and the 54th Regiment, the first regiment of Negro volunteers, organized during the Civil War.

Enter the State House. The main entrance leads into **Doric Hall,** named for its rows of Doric columns. In the 19C addition the **Senate Staircase Hall,** with its marble walls and floors, has paintings illustrating Paul Revere's ride, James Otis arguing against the Writs of Assistance, and the Boston Tea Party. The **Hall of Flags,** built to house the collection of Civil War battle flags, has paintings that portray the Pilgrims on the *Mayflower,* John Eliot preaching to the Indians, and the scene at Concord Bridge April 19, 1775.

The main staircase leads to the **Third Floor Hall,** dominated by Daniel Chester French's statue of Governor R. Wolcott. The Senate Chamber, Senate Reception Room, Governor's Office and House Chamber are on this floor. Before leaving note in the House Chamber the **Sacred Cod,** the symbol of Massachusetts' early cod fishery.

Walking along Beacon Street, opposite the Common note **No. 45** designed by Bulfinch.

Turning right onto Spruce Street, you will have a glimpse of the gardens and houses of **Spruce Court** and **Branch Street** where the servants of the Hill's wealthy families once lived.

Chestnut Street. – An ensemble of architectural styles dating from 1800 to 1830 lines this street. From the corner of Spruce and Chestnut you will notice the purple glass of **No. 9A** Chestnut Street, another Bulfinch-designed structure.

Mount Vernon Street★★. – This is the most beautiful street on Beacon Hill. No. 85 with its gracefully rounded brick arches, iron railings and tall first-story windows was designed by Bulfinch. Across Mount Vernon Street and to the right is No. 55, the **Nichols House Museum** *(guided tours – 30 min – schedule varies* ℡ *(617) 227-6993; $2.00).* The house, formerly the home of Rose Standish Nichols (1872-1960), offers the public an opportunity to view the tastefully furnished interior of a Beacon Hill dwelling.

Louisburg Square★★. – Louisburg Square is one of the most select residential enclaves in Boston. The elegant Greek Revival rowhouses and small private park on the square epitomise the decorum and refined living-style for which the Beacon Hill district is known. Caroling on Christmas Eve at Louisburg Square is a holiday tradition in Boston.

Acorn Street. – This is one of the quaint cobblestone passages found on the Hill.

Charles Street★. – Antique shops, art galleries and coffee shops will be found on Charles Street, the Hill's commercial center. The **Charles Street Meeting House** (No. 70) provided a forum for 19C abolitionists William Lloyd Garrison, Wendell Phillips and Sojourner Truth.

Pinckney Street. – This street was the dividing line between the aristocratic neighborhood on the sunny south slope of Beacon Hill, and the modest north slope where the servants lived. Note the difference in architecture between the two sections.

Revere Street. – To the left on this street are the intimate private courts: **Bellingham Place,** **Sentry Hill Place** and **Rollins Place.** At Rollins Place the white "house" at the end of the court is not a house at all, but rather a decorative wall at the head of a 40 ft drop. From the intersection of Pinckney and Anderson Streets there is a **view** across the Charles River to MIT.

Joy Street. – The street descends the north slope of the Hill, the site of Boston's early black community. Many of its members worked in the homes on the south slope.

Smith Court. – A group of wooden houses stands in Smith Court, the heart of Boston's black community following the Revolution. The large brick building, the **African Meeting House (E)**, was built (1806) by members of the community who refused to sit in the galleries of white churches. The Meeting House is the oldest black church building standing in the nation, and in the 19C served as a major center of the antislavery movement.

The Museum of Afro American History, a center for the exhibition of African-American history in New England, owns the building which is open to the public. *For schedule and exhibition information ℡ (617) 742-1854.*

At the foot of Joy Street, on the opposite side of Cambridge Street, are the Harrison Gray Otis House and Old West Church.

The Harrison Gray Otis House★. – *Guided tours weekdays 9 AM to 5 PM; $2.50.*

The house (1796) was the creation of two men who permanently influenced Boston's architecture and topography: Charles Bulfinch and the lawyer-speculator-politician Harrison Gray Otis. Designed by Bulfinch for Otis, it reflects the refined Federalist taste of the upper classes during the early years of the Republic. Exquisite hand-blocked borders, skillfully draped window hangings and a freestanding staircase adorn the interior. The severe facade is lightened by the Palladian window and graceful entranceway.

The house serves as a house museum and headquarters of the Society for the Preservation of New England Antiquities, a regional organization dedicated to architectural preservation.

Old West Church. – *131 Cambridge Street.* The present building (1805) was designed by Asher Benjamin. In 1775 British troops razed the original meetinghouse that stood on this site when they suspected the patriots of using its steeple to signal American troops.

⑥ **BACK BAY★★ From the Public Garden to the Christian Science Center**
time: 1/2 day – see plan below. "T" Station: Arlington

The Back Bay, a beautiful and successful 19C land development project, was built on land reclaimed from the sea. Following a simple plan, rows of four-and five-story Victorian town houses were built along the straight grid-style streets that were laid out parallel to Commonwealth Avenue, a broad avenue inspired by the wide boulevards of Paris.

The area is essentially residential, with a lively commercial character dominating Boylston and Newbury Streets where a concentration of art galleries and boutiques will be found.

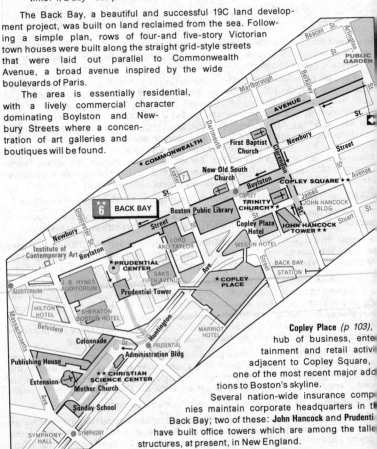

Copley Place (p 103), hub of business, entertainment and retail activi adjacent to Copley Square, one of the most recent major add tions to Boston's skyline.

Several nation-wide insurance comp nies maintain corporate headquarters in th Back Bay; two of these: **John Hancock** and **Prudenti** have built office towers which are among the talle structures, at present, in New England.

Begin at the Arlington Street entrance to the Public Garden. Walking along the tree-shaded mall in the center of **Commonwealth Avenue★**, you will arrive at rows of Victorian town houses and several colleges and churches. Pause at Clarendon Street across from the **First Baptist Church**; the church tower is the work of sculptor Frédéric-Auguste Bartholdi (1843-1904) who used well-known figures of the day: Henry Wadsworth Longfellow, Ralph Waldo Emerson and Nathaniel Hawthorne as his models. Turn into Clarendon Street, then cross **Newbury** and **Boylston Streets** to arrive at Copley Square.

Copley Square★★. – This busy square named for the colonial painter John Singleton Copley is a microcosm of 19 and 20C Boston architecture. The Italian Renaissance facade of the library faces the Gothic-inspired **New Old South Church** across the Square; the image of the Romanesque style **Trinity Church** is reflected in the mirrored sheet of the John Hancock Tower, and at the base of the Tower is the classically-inspired **Copley Plaza Hotel**, designed by Henry J. Hardenbergh, architect of the Plaza Hotel in New York City; rising between the library and the Copley Plaza Hotel is **Copley Place** *(see below)*, one of Boston's newest landmarks.

Trinity Church★★. – *Open 8 AM to 6 PM; closed holidays.*
Trinity Church (1877), recognized as the masterpiece of architect **Henry Hobson Richardson**, initiated the Romanesque Revival in America. Richardson studied at the Ecole des Beaux Arts in Paris, where he was influenced by the power and richness of the Romanesque style. His successful designs for Trinity Church reveal this influence: a massive central tower inspired by one of the towers of the Old Cathedral in Salamanca, Spain, dominates the church; the West Porch (influenced by that of a church in Arles, France) is carved with statues and friezes representing biblical figures and events.

Inside, Richardson chose John La Farge to oversee the decoration. Trinity's lavishly painted walls, murals and paneled ceilings, as well as the small lunettes above the high, tower windows, are among the best works executed by La Farge. Intricately carved scenes depicting the life of Christ, and the figures of past preachers adorn the pulpit, dedicated in 1916. The richly decorated chancel, designed in 1938, appears to be illuminated solely by light reflecting from the metal leaf covering the ceiling.

John Hancock Tower★★. – This innovative 60 story skyscraper sheathed in 10 344 units of 1/2 inch thick tempered glass was designed by **I.M. Pei and Partners**. The tower's unusual rhomboid shape creates a variety of profiles, depending upon the point from which the building is viewed. From a vantage point on the opposite side of Boylston Street, the tower appears one dimensional; from other angles it is a gigantic mirror reflecting the sky and buildings of Boston.

The Observatory. – *Open Monday through Saturday 9 AM to 11 PM, Sunday 10 AM (12 noon November through April) to 11 PM; closed Thanksgiving Day and December 25; $2.75, children $2.00.*
High-speed elevators travel the distance (740 ft) from street level to the 60th floor observatory in 30 seconds. The glass-walled observatory offers a panoramic **view★★★** of the Boston region: the downtown, Cambridge, the harbor islands, the North and South Shores, and the mountains of southern New Hampshire.

A topographic map of Boston in 1775, a taped tour of Boston narrated by historian Walter Muir Whitehill, and a 5 minute film presenting a portrait of the city as it is today provide an interesting orientation to the view.

Boston Public Library. – *Open Monday through Thursday 9 AM to 9 PM (5 PM Friday and Saturday), Sunday 2 to 6 PM. Closed legal holidays and Sundays June through September.*
The facade of this handsome Renaissance Revival structure (1895), designed by McKim, Mead and White, is ornamented with wrought iron lanterns and two bronze statues by Bela Pratt which represent Art and Science. The new wing (1972 – designed by Philip Johnson), the General Library, is a smooth-surfaced granite unit that complements the earlier structure, the Research Library.

Inside, the high styling of the original building is apparent as you stand in the elaborate entrance hall; the doorways are copies from a temple in Athens and the main staircase, faced with variegated yellow Siena marble, is a gem. Mural paintings by Puvis de Chavannes *(The Muses)*, Edwin Abbey *(Quest of the Holy Grail)* and John Singer Sargent *(Judaism and Christianity)* decorate the upper floors.

Before leaving the library visit the **courtyard** *(main floor)*, a delightful place to spend some time before returning to the hustle and bustle of the city streets.

Copley Place★. – Boston's largest and most expensive private development project ever is a 9.5 acre, $500 million multi-use complex (1984) constructed on the air rights of, and over, the Massachusetts Turnpike. Below street level and hidden from view, the turnpike and rail and rapid transit lines continue to operate; above, in a pocket that formerly separated the Back Bay from the South End, rise two luxury hotels, four office buildings, a galleria with more than 100 shops, pricey boutiques and restaurants, a department store (Neiman-Marcus), apartment residences, and a 1 500 car garage. Glass-enclosed pedestrian bridges spanning Stuart Street and Huntington Avenue join the **Westin Hotel** and the Prudential Center to the entire Copley Place complex.

Despite its great size Copley Place (designed by The Architects Collaborative, Inc., the Marriott Hotel designed by The Stubbins Associates, Inc.) with its simple lines, neutral coloration and plain surfaces, blends well with and is sensitive to the scale and style of its historic neighbors. The interior is a visual delight of bay-windowed shop fronts, and a pleasant place to browse, shop, dine or simply enjoy the 60 ft travertine and granite **waterfall sculpture**★ by Dimitri Hadzi in the central atrium.

At USA Cinemas Copley Place, the audio-visual presentation **Where's Boston** portrays the many faces and the spirit of the people of Boston (10 AM – 1 PM Sundays and holidays – to 5 PM; $3.50).

Continue along Boylston Street to the Prudential Center.

Prudential Center★. – The Prudential Center was one of Boston's first major urban renewal projects in the 1960s. Designed by Charles Luckman Associates, the "Pru" was built primarily on and over the air rights of the railroad yards which divided the Back Bay district from the South End. The Center's modern towers and shopping mall now join these neighborhoods and link them to the uptown area.

The 32 acre, $150 million complex contains apartment towers, an ice-skating rink, underground parking for 3 000 cars, specialty shops, major department stores such as Lord and Taylor and Saks Fifth Avenue, banks and restaurants. Nearby are the Sheraton-Boston Hotel, the Back Bay Hilton Hotel, the **John B. Hynes Veterans Auditorium** which hosts major national conventions and the opera, and Boston's second tallest skyscraper, the Prudential Tower.

Prudential Tower. – *The Observatory, on the 50th floor, is open 10 AM (12 noon Sunday) to 10 PM. Closed major holidays. $2.00.*

From the observatory there is a panoramic **view**★★★ of the Boston region: to the west – the suburbs of Brookline and Roxbury, Fenway Park; to the north – the Back Bay, Cambridge; to the east – Beacon Hill, Government Center, Logan Airport; to the south – the South End, the Boston Islands, and in the distance the Blue Hills Reservation.

Cross the Prudential Center to Huntington Avenue, then turn right.

Christian Science Center★★. – This harmonious group of buildings situated around a large reflecting pool, is the world headquarters of the Christian Science religion, founded in the 19C by **Mary Baker Eddy.**

Christian Science Religion. – The Christian Science religion was founded in 1866 by Mary Baker Eddy following a serious injury from which she quickly recovered after meditating on a Gospel account of one of Jesus' healings. Mrs. Eddy believed she had discovered the science of man's true relation with God and that through the practice of Christian Science the individual could learn to overcome the ills and evils that challenge mankind. After a decade of studying the Bible she published *Science and Health with Key to the Scriptures,* the textbook of Christian Science, and in 1879 Mrs. Eddy and her students established the Church of Christ Scientist, which was reorganized as the First Church of Christ Scientist (The Mother Church) in 1892. The Christian Science Publishing Society was later founded to help carry the word of Christian Science around the globe.

Today members of the Christian Science Church gather weekly at their churches to attend services during which passages from the Bible, and texts written by Mary Baker Eddy are read. The *Christian Science Monitor,* a newspaper published by the Church of Christ Scientist since 1908, has correspondants around the globe and is highly respected for its objective manner of reporting the news and avoiding sensationalism.

The Architectural Ensemble. – Until the early 1970s the Christian Science Center consisted solely of the **Mother Church** built in 1894, the **Mother Church Extension** (1904), and the **Publishing Society** (1933). In 1972 plans were made to enlarge the Center and the firms of I.M. Pei and Partners and Cossutta and Ponte were called in to design the complex. Their creation, the modern and expanded Christian Science Center, is a successful blend of the old and the new. The three original buildings and the more recent additions: a 26 story office tower (open 10 AM – 12 noon Sunday) (the **Administration Building**), the **Colonnade Building**, housing a permanent Bible Exhibit *(open 10 AM – 12 noon Sunday – to 5 PM, closed Tuesday; film and slide show on the hour)* and radio and film facilities, and the semi-circular **Sunday School** are arranged around a vast pool which unifies the entire ensemble.

Tours of the Mother Church May through October 9 AM to 4 PM, Sunday 12 noon to 4:45 PM; the rest of the year 10 AM (11:15 AM Sunday) to 3:45 PM; closed January 1 and December 25.

Mother Church. – 1894. This Romanesque structure at the heart of the Center is easily recognized by its square belltower and rough granite facade. The interior is decorated with Italian mosaics, and stenciled designs frescoed on the ceiling.

The Mother Church Extension. – This basilica-like structure inspired by the Byzantine and Italian Renaissance styles, has a spacious freestanding square area surrounded on three sides by tiered galleries. The central dome (92 ft high) rises 108 ft from the floor.

Massachusetts Avenue is a good place from which to admire the portico which was added to the building in 1975; ten limestone columns are topped by 6 ton capitals which were carved to match the earlier parts of the building.

Publishing Society. – All Christian Science literature including textbooks, magazines, periodicals and *The Monitor* are published here. The classical interior is richly decorated with Italian travertines, English and French woodwork and German mosaics. The **Mapparium** *(guided tours May through October 8 AM - 9AM Saturday – to 4 PM – 4:45 PM Sunday; the rest of the year 8 AM - 10 AM Saturday, 11:15 AM Sunday – to 3:45 PM; meet at the Publishing Society)* located in the Publishing Society building, is a walk-through globe which illustrates the worldwide scope of the Christian Science Church. The glass-paneled construction of the globe causes unusual sound effects.

■ THE MUSEUMS

Museum of Fine Arts★★★ (EZ). – *465 Huntington Avenue, "T" Station: Ruggles-Museum, Arborway/Huntington Avenue on the Green Line. Open 10 AM to 5 PM (10 PM Wednesday); closed Mondays and major holidays; $5.00, free Saturday 10 AM to 12 noon. Free introductory tours Tuesday to Friday 11 AM and 2 PM, Saturday 11 AM and 1:30 PM.*

In the 19C Bostonians traveled abroad extensively and returned with art treasures for their private collections. These collections ultimately formed the core of the holdings of the Museum of Fine Arts when it opened in 1876 in Copley Square. By the turn of the century, the need for more spacious quarters led to the construction of the present classical style building (1909 – designed by Guy Lowell) with its impressive portal, columns and domes, in the Back Bay Fens.

More recently, the need for new space was met by the addition of the West Wing, in 1981, to the original museum building. High-tech in character, the sleek three-story granite structure designed by I.M. Pei and Partners, has as its most striking feature a 225 ft galleria capped by a barrel-vaulted glass roof. The new facility provides gallery space for traveling exhibitions and 20C art, and offers expanded visitor services.

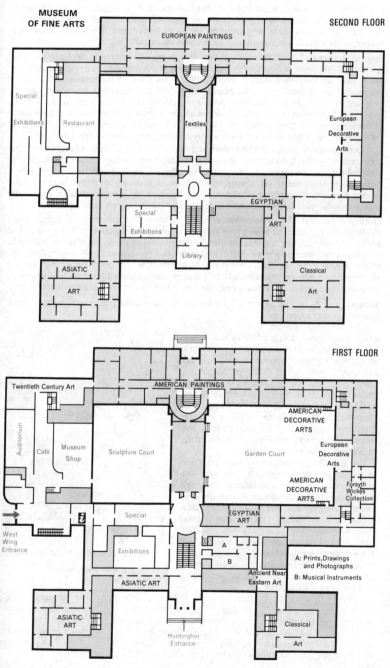

The museum has eight distinct departments: Asiatic Art, Egyptian Art, Classical Art, European Decorative Arts and Sculpture, American Decorative Arts and Sculpture, Paintings, Prints, Drawings and Photographs, Textiles and Costumes, 20C Art.

Asiatic Department★★★. – The Japanese and Chinese collections are exceptional. The works gathered by **Edward Morse, Ernest Fenollosa** and **Sturgis Bigelow** during their travels across Japan in the late 19C form the basis of this department.

Japanese art began to develop in the 6C, when Buddhism arrived in Japan through Korea. Painting was one of its favorite means of expression and the MFA has examples of Japanese painting which date from the 13C: a series of handscrolls *The Burning of the Sanjo Palace* (Heiji Monogatari Emaki) portraying the violence of the Civil Wars in Japan; to the 18C: the decorative and colorful screen *The Gay Quarters of Kyoto* – a detailed record of the dress and activities of the times. Buddhism dominated sculpture as well: the wooden statue of the *Miroku Bosatsu* (12C) and *Sogyo Hachiman* (14C), representations of the Buddha, are remarkable for the strength implied by their simplicity.

Highlighting the section on Chinese art is the extensive collection of ceramics from different periods. Two statues are interesting for their contrasting styles: a graceful limestone **Bodhisattva** (6C), and the magnificent polychromed wooden statue of **Kuan Yin** (12C), with its relaxed, casual pose.

Displays include selections from the **Hoyt collection** distinguished, in particular, for its lovely and rare **Korean celadons**. A series of paintings representing the Kings of **Shambala**, a mystical Tibetan Kingdom, and beautiful works of Indian and Islamic art: paintings, sculpture, metalwork will, in addition, be found in these galleries.

Egyptian Department★★. – The bulk of the MFA's superb collection of Egyptian arts, spanning 4 000 years of Egyptian civilization, came to the museum as a result of a 40 year (1905-1945) MFA-Harvard expedition to Egypt and the Sudan. Excavations conducted by the expedition at Giza yielded **Old Kingdom** (2778-2360 BC) treasures rivaled only by the museum in Cairo. Among the many pieces of sculpture excavated from the tombs and temples of the Fourth Dynasty **King Mycerinus** and his queen Chamerernebti, is a **pair statue** of the king and his queen that is one of the oldest statues extant portraying a couple. Dating from the same period is the incredibly realistic portrait bust of **Prince Ankh-haf.**

The expedition's digs at El Bersheh and in the Sudan produced treasures from the more recent Twelfth Dynasty: the well-preserved paintings on the coffins of **Prince Djehuty-nekht and his wife,** the black granite statue of **Lady Senuwy,** painted wooden servant models designed to serve the dead in eternity, and Meroitic jewelry from Meroë, capital of the former Kushite (Ethiopia) civilization. The collection of cylindrical **seals** carved by Mesopotamian seal cutters reflects a degree of skill that has rarely been equaled.

Classical Department★★. – The cameos, coins, bronzes and collection of Greek vases (5C BC) were gathered by **Edward Perry Warren,** curator of the department in the late 19 and early 20C. It was under his guidance that the department acquired the major portion of its holdings which include a three-sided marble bas-relief discovered in Rome in 5C BC, the Head of Aphrodite (4C BC) named the **Bartlett Head** for its donor, a golden earring representing a winged charioteer (4C BC) that probably adorned a statue, and finally the ivory and gold statue of the **Snake Goddess,** dating from the Minoan civilization (1500 BC).

American Art★★. – The American collection is represented primarily by paintings, furnishings and silver.

In American **painting** it was portraiture which predominated in the 17C as is illustrated by the portrait of *Robert Gibbs*, painted by an unknown artist. Prominent among the 18C portraitists were Gilbert Stuart *(p 30)*, whose paintings of George and Martha Washington (the *Athenaeum Portraits*) are exhibited alternately at the Smithsonian Institution in Washington, D.C. and the MFA; and John Singleton Copley *(p 30)*, who painted the wealthy and noted Bostonians of his day, such as *Samuel Adams* and *Paul Revere*.

In the 19C painters turned their attention to nature and in particular to the sea. The adventure, excitement and beauty of the sea was portrayed on canvas by Fitz Hugh Lane *(Boston Harbor; Owl'sHead, Penobscot Bay, Maine)*, Albert Ryder, and Winslow Homer *(Fog Warning; The Lookout – «All's Well»)*. During the same era John Singer Sargent and Mary Cassatt *(At the Opera)* – who was influenced by the Impressionists – lived abroad. Sargent's *Daughters of Boit* was inspired by *The Meninas* of Velázquez.

(By permission of the Boston Athenaeum.)

Athenaeum Portrait.

Works by Jackson Pollock, Georgia O'Keefe *(White Rose with Larkspur No.2)*, Joseph Stella *(Old Brooklyn Bridge)*, and a number of canvases by Morris Louis a leader of the pure abstract art movement, have brought the museum's collection up to date.

Among the MFA's collection of **American Decorative Arts** is a large and representative group of furniture made by the early American craftsmen of Boston, New York, Newport and Philadelphia. Many pieces are from the rich **M. and M. Karolik collection.**

The museum's extensive collection of early American silver includes the historic **Liberty Bowl** (1768), dedicated to the members of the Massachusetts legislature who refused to rescind a letter to the colonies protesting against the Crown.

European Decorative Arts. – Period rooms, including an English Tudor paneled room (15C), an English Georgian room and the Hamilton Palace Room will be found in these galleries. Noteworthy are the medieval statues carved from wood and ivory, and the enamels.

On the first floor, in a special suite of rooms, is the **Forsyth-Wickes Collection** of 18C French furnishings, porcelain, paintings, watercolors and sculpture. The graceful red and gold laquered writing desk was made for Marie Antoinette.

European Painting★★. – Most of the European schools from the Middle Ages to the present are represented. A Catalonian chapel with 12C wall and ceiling frescoes is interesting for its Romanesque decoration. From the Flemish school you will admire *St. Luke Painting the Virgin* (15C) by Rogier Van der Weyden. Displayed in a nearby gallery is Tiepolo's *Time Unveiling Truth*, a powerful and symbolic analogy. The section given over to the Spanish school contains paintings by Goya, El Greco *(Fray Felix)*, Velázquez and Zurbarán *(Saint Francis)*.

The preference of Bostonians for the Romantics (Delacroix, Géricault), realists (Courbet), the Barbizon school (Corot), impressionists and postimpressionists brought a distinguished group of 19C French paintings to the MFA. Among the masters represented are: Renoir *(Bal à Bougival)*, Monet *(La Japonaise, Haystacks, Rouen Cathedral)*, Degas *(Carriage at the Races)*, Manet *(Execution of Maximillian, The Street Singer)*, Van Gogh *(Postman Joseph Roulin)*, Cézanne *(Madame Cézanne in a Red Armchair)*. Gauguin's *D'où venons-nous? Que sommes-nous? Où allons-nous?* (Where do we come from? Who are we? Where are we going?) treats the eternal questions regarding man's life and destiny. Millet's sympathic rendering of the peasant is illustrated in *The Sower* and his many other works owned by the museum.

More recent paintings by Gris, Kandinsky, Miró, Munch and Picasso are exhibited in a gallery on the first floor. Picasso's strong anti-war sentiments are expressed in his bold, vibrantly colored *Rape of the Sabine Women*.

Isabella Stewart Gardner Museum★★★ (EZ: p 92). – 280 The Fenway. Open 12 noon to 5 PM (9 PM Tuesday September through June); closed Mondays and major holidays; $3.00. Guided tour (1 hour) Thursday at 2:30 PM meet in the Spanish Cloister. Concerts Labor Day through June Tuesday 6 PM, Thursday 12:15 PM, and Sunday 3 PM.

Isabella Stewart Gardner, born in New York in 1840, became a Bostonian when she married the financier Jack Lowell Gardner. Daring and vivacious, Mrs. Gardner was a free spirit whose actions were often frowned upon by other members of Boston's staid and proper society. Art and music were her life-long delights, and in 1899 she initiated the construction of Fenway Court to house her art collection, part of which was gathered in Europe, and part of which was acquired by her agents, in the United States.

The galleries of **Fenway Court**, permanently arranged by Mrs. Gardner herself, contain furnishings, textiles, paintings and sculpture from her collections. Nothing has been changed since her death and the galleries, opening onto flower gardens in an intimate courtyard, give the impression that it is summer year round.

Ground Floor. – In the **Spanish Cloister** the walls are covered with ceramic tiles from a 17C Mexican church, enhancing John Singer Sargent's dramatic painting, *El Jaleo*.

The **Courtyard** with its refreshing gardens and Venetian window frames and balconies decorated with fresh flowers and plants, is a graceful haven from city life. Classical sculptures surround an ancient Roman mosaic pavement (2C) from the town of Livia.

In the **small galleries** off the court are the 19 and 20C French and American paintings, including portraits by Degas and Manet, and land-

(From a photo Isabella Stewart Gardner Museum, Boston.)

The Courtyard.

scapes by Whistler, Matisse and Sargent. In the Yellow Room you will find *The Terrace of St. Tropez*, the first canvas by Henry Matisse to enter an American museum.

Second Floor. – The room of **early Italian paintings** contains Simone Martini's altarpiece *Madonna and Child with Four Saints*, two allegorical panels by Pesellino, Fra Angelico's *Death and Assumption of the Virgin*, and Gentile Bellini's delicately executed *Turkish Artist*. The fresco of Hercules is the only fresco by Piero della Francesca outside of Italy.

The **Raphael Room,** named for the Italian painter, has two of his works on exhibit: a portrait of *Count Tommaso Inghirami* and a *Pietà*. The *Annunciation* exemplifies the technique of linear perspective as developed in the 15C. Other works in the room include Botticelli's *Tragedy of Lucretia* and Giovanni Bellini's *Madonna and Child*.

Adjacent to the Raphael Room, in the **Short Gallery,** is Anders Zorn's spirited painting of Mrs. Gardner at the Palazzo Barbaros in Venice. Continue through the **Little Salon,** decorated with 18C Venetian paneling and 17C tapestries, to the Tapestry Room.

The **Tapestry Room** is the setting for the concerts held at Fenway Court. On an easel is the *Santa Engracia* by Bermejo, (15C-Spain). There are lovely 16C tapestries.

The **Dutch Room** is especially rich with Rubens' masterful portrayal of *Thomas Howard, Earl of Arundel; The Concert*, one of only 36 paintings known to exist by the 17C artist Jan Vermeer; and works by Hans Holbeïn and Anthony van Dyck *(Lady with a Rose)*. Look for Rembrandt's *Self-Portrait* and only known seascape: *Storm on the Sea of Galilee*.

Third Floor. – From the **Veronese Room** with its Spanish and Venetian tooled and painted leather wall coverings, enter the **Titian Room** which contains one of Titian's masterpieces, the sensual *Rape of Europa*, painted for Philip II of Spain.

In the **Long Gallery,** the life-size terra cotta statue of the *Virgin Adoring the Child*, attributed to Matteo Civitali, is a beautiful example of Renaissance sculpture.

On the wall above a large sideboard is Botticelli's *Madonna and Child of the Eucharist* (1410 – the "Chigi Madonna") which hung in the Chigi palace until the 19C. *A Lady of Fashion*, by Uccello, is characteristic of portrait art of the 15C in Florence.

The **Gothic Room** contains a full length portrait of *Mrs. Gardner* (1888) painted by her friend John Singer Sargent. Nearby is a small panel *The Presentation of the Infant Jesus in the Temple* attributed to Giotto, the master of the 14C Florentine school.

Children's Museum★★ (FZ M1: *p 93*). – *Museum Wharf. Open 10 AM to 5 PM (9 PM Friday); closed Mondays after Labor Day to mid-June; $4.50, under 16, $3.50; free Friday 5 to 9 PM.*

This museum, conceived exclusively for children, will delight adults as well. There are games to play with computers, an automobile to service in the Garage, and for aspiring young commentators, a newsroom equipped with television monitors. City Slice (a cross-section of a city street and house), the Indian Wigwam and an authentic two-story Japanese House also encourage children to participate in a variety of "hands-on" activities. Young adults will enjoy Clubhouse, an exhibit area with activities designed for preteens and teens.

Museum of Science and the Charles Hayden Planetarium★★ (FY: *p 93*). –"T" Station: Science Park. *Open 9 AM to 5 PM (9 PM Friday), closed Monday except Monday holidays, and major holidays; $5.00, under 14 $3.00. Science films (45 min) shown in the giant-screen Omni Theater; $5.00, museum and Omni $7.50. Planetarium admission is an additional $1.50*

Located in a modern building beside the Charles River, the museum invites children and adults to explore the world of science and technology. The kaleidoscopic array of push-button displays and life-size models allows visitors to push a series of buttons to play games with a computer, speak into a telephone then hear your voice as it sounds to others on the telephone, test your responses to an energy quiz; or simply observe the motion of waves in the 90 ft wave tank, how brain cells communicate with each other, the earth as it moves beneath a Foucault pendulum, and a hot air balloon rising and falling as the air temperature within the balloon varies.

Full-size models of American spacecraft, animal and physical science demonstrations, a 20 ft model of Tyrannosaurus Rex, the largest carnivorous dinosaur ever known to exist, the spectacular visual effects – including man-made lightning – produced by the world's largest Van de Graaff generator, and the "Talking Transparent Woman" are features of the museum's program.

In the **Charles Hayden Planetarium** programs are presented that explore the world of stars, galaxies, pulsars, clusters, quasars and other phenomena of outer space. There are generally two or more programs daily.

Computer Museum (FZ M1: *p 93*). – *Museum Wharf. Open 10 AM to 6 PM (9 PM Friday); closed Mondays September through June and major holidays; $4.00.*

Computer-literate or not, visitors to the museum will marvel at the incredible advances made in computer technology since the 1950s. These advances are explored in a series of exhibits tracing the history of computers from the abacus to the fifth generation artificial intelligence computers programmed to imitate human reasoning. The displays include examples of equipment which represent key developments in the evolution of the computer: the **Whirlwind** – the first vacuum tube computer with core memory, the **Q7** – which substituted codes for machine language thereby making computers more accessible to businesses and large numbers of people, and **SAGE** – a sophisticated system (only about three hours downtime per year!) used for more than three decades by the U.S. Air Defense.

In the Personal-Computer Gallery and the Computer and the Image Gallery observers may interact with computers: here you will even find a computer that "talks" and with which you are encouraged to carry on a "conversation."

Institute of Contemporary Art (*EZ: p 92*). – *955 Boylston Street. Open 11 AM to 5 PM (8 PM Thursday and Friday); closed Mondays and Tuesdays, major holidays and between exhibitions; $3.50; free Friday 5 to 8 PM.* This Romanesque style building which once housed a police station has been renovated into modern brightly-lit gallery space. The Institute presents a multi-media program of exhibitions, CURRENTS, which explores the trends and themes in American and international contemporary art. Changing selections of video art complementing the exhibitions are shown in the ICA theater.

The Museum at the John Fitzgerald Kennedy Library★ (*CX: p 89*). – *Columbia Point in Dorchester, near the University of Massachusetts. "T" Station: Columbia Station, 1/2 mile from the Museum. Open 9 AM to 5 PM; closed major holidays; $2.50.*

This sleek, white concrete and glass structure, a monument to the late President John F. Kennedy, was designed by the architect I.M. Pei. The building's neat sharp lines seem to point across the harbor to the impressive view of the Boston skyline opposite. Approximately one third of the library building is reserved for the **contemplation pavilion,** an eight-story grey glass pavilion that contains simply an American flag, a bench and a quotation from President Kennedy, on the wall.

A 35 minute film on the life of John Kennedy is part of the tour. In the exhibit area, backlit photographs, texts, letters and documents related to the family and administration of John Kennedy, are arranged in sequential order around a special display that features his desk and personal memorabilia. Major events of the Kennedy administration are replayed on TV monitors. The archives on the upper floors have thousands of photos, tapes and taped interviews with people who knew John Kennedy.

■ ADDITIONAL SIGHTS

Tea Party Ship (*FZ: p 93*). – *Congress Street Bridge. Open 9 AM to dusk; closed January 1, Thanksgiving Day and December 25; $3.25.*

A full-size replica of the brig *Beaver II,* one of the original tea ships that was boarded by marauding "Indians" December 16, 1773 is berthed at the pier on Congress Street. The museum alongside the *Beaver* has pictures, documents, slides and a model of 18C Boston which illustrate the Boston Tea Party and the events leading to the Revolution.

Cruises. – *Plan pp 98-99.* Sightseeing cruises and excursion boats (Provincetown, Nantasket) that depart from the Boston waterfront, are a wonderful way to see the harbor and view the Boston skyline.

George's Island. – *Boats depart from Long Wharf and Rowe's Wharf; time: 1 1/2 hour RT; tickets may be purchased at the ticket office on Long Wharf, or on Rowe's Wharf; $3.00. For further information contact Bay State–Spray and Provincetown Steamship Co.℡ (617) 723-7800 or Massachusetts Bay Lines ℡ (617) 749-4500. The early boats allow you to interrupt your cruise for a visit of the island and to return to Boston on a later boat.*

George's Island, inhabited during colonial times and later fortified because of its strategic location, is now a public recreation site. Picnic areas slope down to the water's edge, and Fort Warren, the military post where high-ranking confederates James Mason and John Slidell were imprisoned during the Civil War, may be visited.

Of the legendary tales of shipwrecks, buried treasure and ghosts associated with the island, the most popular is the story of Fort Warren's Lady in Black who is said to have appeared at the fort several times since the 19C. The black-clad figure is thought to be the ghost of a southern woman who was captured and hanged by Union soldiers, when she attempted to help her husband escape from Fort Warren.

A circular granite stairway at the end of the parade ground in the fort, leads to an observation tower which offers a view of the island, its ledges and the harbor.

Music Cruises. – *Music cruises aboard the Cabaret Jazzboat Friday evenings (7:30 PM and 9:30 PM) late June to early September. Departures from Long Wharf. Tickets available by mail: Water Music Inc., 12 Arrow Street, Cambridge, MA 02138; or at Water Music Bay State Cruises ticket office on Long Wharf 45 min prior to first sailing on the day of cruise only; $13.50 and $11.50. ℡ 876-7777.*

Whale-Watching Cruises. – *Cruises to Stellwagon Bank between Provincetown and Gloucester depart from Commonwealth Pier early May to mid-June Saturday and Sunday 9 AM; mid-June to Labor Day Sunday only; time: 6 hours; $18.00.*

Black Heritage Trail. – *A trail guide and map may be obtained at the National Park Visitor Center, 15 State Street, or by writing: the Museum of Afro-American History, Abiel Smith School, 46 Joy Street Boston, MA 02114 ℡ (617) 742-1854.*

The Black Heritage Trail traces the history of the black community in Boston beginning with the settlement on Beacon Hill. Major trail sites include Copp's Hill Burying Ground (where more than 1 000 colonial blacks are buried), the Abiel Smith School on Smith Court (the first public school for black children), the site of the Boston Massacre, the African Meeting House *(p 102)* and the Charles Street Meeting House *(p 101)*.

The first black Bostonians in the colony arrived from Barbados, West Indies in 1638 and by the 18C Boston's first free black settlement was established in the North End. Its members were active in the Revolution and later prospered as barbers, sailors, laborers and coachmen. In the 19C, with the dedication of the African Meeting House on Beacon Hill and in search of better living quarters, the black community moved to the north slope of the Hill. Better housing, job opportunities and schools led the blacks to gradually move out to Cambridge, the Back Bay and the South End. Since World War II increased migration from the south has led to the growth of black neighborhoods in Roxbury, North Dorchester and parts of Mattapan as well.

Chinatown (FZ: *p 93*). – Alive with its own language, culture and traditions, Boston's Chinatown is the regional center of New England's more than 32 000 (1984) Chinese and Chinese-Americans. Street signs written in oriental characters, pagoda-roofed telephone booths, markets filled with exotic-sounding foods, shops stocked with jades, porcelain and brocades, and an abundance of fine restaurants line the streets of this district, east of Washington Street and a 10 minute walk from the Common.

The celebration of the Chinese New Year in January or February (depending on the calendar), is Chinatown's major annual festival. During the two-week period red signs, red streamers and red decorations fill the bleak, grey streets of winter. A parade is traditionally held the first Sunday of the New Year, as a grotesque ceremonial lion avoiding firecrackers meant to scare him away, devours the offerings left by proprietors in front of their shops.

Arnold Arboretum (BX: *p 88*). – *Arborway. Open sunrise to sunset. The elderly or handicapped may obtain a permit to drive through the arboretum (weekdays only); apply at the Hunnewell Visitor Center (Jamaica Plain Gate). Limited parking is available at the Jamaica Plain Gate.*

This 265 acre arboretum is an outdoor research-educational facility administered by Harvard University and the Department of Parks. Inaugurated as a tree farm in 1872, the arboretum has evolved into a living museum of approximately 7 000 species of ornamental trees, flowers and shrubs. It is especially beautiful in May and June when the delicate scents of blooming lilacs, azaleas, rhododendrons and magnolias fill the air.

Suggested walk: Jamaica Plain Gate to pond area *(time: 15 min);* pond area to Bonsai House *(time: 10 min);* Bonsai House to Bussey Hill – panoramic view – *(time: 15 min).*

Franklin Park Zoo (BX: *p 88*). – *The end of Blue Hill and Columbia Road. From Boston take Rte 1 South to Rte 203 then follow the signs. Open 9 AM to 5 PM (4 PM November through March). Admission free; Children's Zoo $1.00.*

Franklin Park is part of Boston's emerald necklace of parks laid out by Frederick Olmsted in the 19C *(p 91).* Principal attractions are A Birds World housing naturalistic bird environments, a free flight outdoor Aviary *(open summers only)* through which visitors may walk, the Children's Zoo with contact area and informal animal demonstrations, and the Range, featuring antelope, horses and other hoofed animals.

EXCURSIONS

CAMBRIDGE★★★. – *Description p 113.*

CHARLESTOWN★ (FY: *p 93*).

Located on a hill across from Boston, on the other side of the Charles River, Charlestown is easily recognized by its tall stone obelisk, the Bunker Hill Monument. The *USS Constitution* – Old Ironsides – permanently berthed at a wharf in the Navy Yard, is the pride of this quiet community. Charlestown's colonial dwellings were destroyed by the British during the battle of Bunker Hill and replaced, following the Revolution, by the rows of Federal style houses that line the streets leading to the monument.

A project currently underway to rebuild the Charlestown Navy Yard includes the addition of luxury apartments, offices, shops and marinas to the waterfront area.

Bunker Hill Monument. – *Open 9 AM to 5 PM; closed major holidays.*

This 221 ft granite obelisk designed by Solomon Willard, marks the site of the American redoubt during the battle of Bunker Hill *(p 90).* The observatory, reached by a 294 step winding stairway, offers a **view**★ of Charlestown, Boston and the harbor.

Bunker Hill Pavilion. – *Open June through August 9:30 AM to 6 PM (4 PM the rest of the year); closed major holidays; $1.50, under 17, 75¢.*

The battle of Bunker Hill, as seen through the eyes of a militiaman and a British soldier, is presented in a dramatic 30 minute mixed-media program: *"Whites of their Eyes."*

Charlestown Navy Yard. – Construction of the United States Naval Shipyard at Charlestown in 1800 made this city a shipbuilding center. Thirty of the yard's 43 acres, including the site of the *USS Constitution* and the USS Constitution Museum, were designated a part of the Boston National Historical Park after the yard was closed in 1974.

Visitor Information Center. – *Open 9 AM to 5 PM.*

Information on the Navy Yard, the Freedom Trail, and the Boston National Historical Park is available here. Park Rangers conduct walks along the Freedom Trail from mid-spring to late fall *(April through October weekends, daily in summer; free).*

The USS Constitution★★. – *Open 9:30 AM to 3:50 PM (1 to 5 PM July 4).*

The *USS Constitution*, the pride of the American fleet, is the oldest commissioned warship afloat. Authorized by Congress in 1794, this 44-gun frigate designed by Joshua Humphreys and Josiah Fox was constructed from timbers provided by states from Georgia to Maine. Within four years after being built, the *Constitution* sailed to the Mediterranean at the head of the American Fleet, to participate in the Tripolitan War which ended the payment of tribute by American shipping to the Barbary pirates.

Distinguished for the role she played in the war against the Barbary States, the *Constitution* nevertheless won her greatest victories during the War of 1812 against the British: in 1812 by capturing the *HMS Guerrière* and the *Java*, and in 1815 by capturing simultaneously the *Cyane* and the *Levante*. It was during the battle with the *Guerrière*, when enemy fire seemed to bounce off her planking without causing damage, that the

Constitution was given her nickname "Old Ironsides." By 1830, after having survived 40 military engagements, the *Constitution* was declared unseaworthy and destined for the scrap heap, when Oliver Wendell Holmes' poem "Old Ironsides" aroused such strong popular sentiment in favor of the ship that funds were appropriated to rebuild her. Rebuilt again in 1905, 1913 and 1973 the ship has about 8% of her original timbers.

USS Constitution Museum (M). – *Open 9 AM to 5 PM (6 PM late June to early September); closed major holidays; $2.00, under 16, 1.00*. Exhibits in the granite building (designed by Alexander Parris) trace the history of Old Ironsides from 1794 to the present.

Berthed a short distance from the *USS Constitution* is the **USS Cassin Young** *(open 9:30 AM to 5 PM)*, a World War II destroyer similar to the type built here in the 1930s and 1940s. *For guided tours apply at the Visitor Information Center.*

BROOKLINE (BX: *p 88*) – Pop 53 302

This affluent suburb was the birthplace of **John Fitzgerald Kennedy**, the 35th President of the United States. Ever since 1870 Boston has made six attempts, unsuccessfully, to annex Brookline, one of the largest towns in Massachusetts and a pleasant residential community located only 4 miles from the center of the city's downtown area.

John F. Kennedy Birthplace National Historic Site (BV). – *83 Beals Street. Open 10 AM to 4:30 PM; closed major holidays; 1.00.*

Joseph and Rose Kennedy lived in this modest wooden house from 1914 to 1920, a period during which four of their children including John Fitzgerald Kennedy (1917-1963), the former president of the United States, were born. The house, restored to its 1917 appearance, contains family furnishings and personal mementoes.

WALTHAM (AV: *p 88*) – Pop 57 713

Located on Boston's peripheral Route 128, Waltham is an industrial center and a leading producer of electronic equipment.

Gore Place★. – *52 Gore Street. Guided tours (1 hour) April 15 to November 15 10 AM (2 PM Sunday) to 5 PM; closed Monday; $3.00.*

This brick Federal style country mansion completed in 1806, was the residence of lawyer-politician Christopher Gore. Mr. and Mrs. Gore decided to have the house built while they were in Europe, and it is believed that at that time they chose the French architect, Jacques Legrand, to draw up the plans for their new home. Oval-shaped rooms, delicate period furnishings, marble paved floors and a flying staircase grace the interior.

Brandeis University. – *415 South Street.*

Brandeis University, named for former Supreme Court Justice, Louis D. Brandeis, was the first Jewish sponsored nonsectarian university founded (1948) in the United States. A strong commitment to the liberal arts underlies the program of study at Brandeis where 3 400 students of all faiths from the United States and 40 foreign countries are enrolled in the 32 undergraduate and 21 graduate programs offered.

Architecturally the more than seventy modern buildings on the 300 acre campus are unified by a basic harmony of contemporary design. The three chapels (Jewish, Protestant, Catholic) designed by **Max Abramowitz** exemplify this influence. The **Rose Art Museum** contains exhibits of paintings and sculpture *(open 1 to 5 PM; closed Monday year round and Wednesday and Friday July and August)*. Plays and dance programs are presented in the attractive **Spingold Theatre**.

SAUGUS (CU: *p 89*) – Pop 25 313

The buildings of the Saugus Iron Works, which operated in this small town north of Boston in the 17C, were reconstructed in 1954 to appear as they did during the colonial period when they were one of New England's earliest pioneering industries.

Saugus Iron Works★. – *244 Central Street. From Boston take Rte 1 North to Main Street in Saugus, then continue to the rotary. A sign in front of the Town Hall indicates the direction to the ironworks. Open 9 AM to 5 PM (4 PM November through March); closed January 1, Thanksgiving Day and December 25; concerts Wednesday evenings July and August.*

In 1646, encouraged by the government's interest in developing the natural resources of the colonies, John Winthrop, Jr., the son of the governor of Massachusetts, established the first ironworks in America at Hammersmith (Saugus). Despite the advanced techniques used and the skill of the workers, the operation was a financial failure and within 30 years ceased to function. By this time, however, many workers had been trained and the ironworks at Saugus had provided the impetus for the development of the iron industry in America.

Museum. – Artifacts excavated at this site, including items turned out by the early ironworks and a 550 pound hammerhead used in the original forge, are on display.

Iron Works House. – This dwelling which served as the home and office of the manager of the ironworks, is a good example of 17C American Elizabethan architecture. Batten doors, steep gables, casement windows, and the second-story overhang decorated with pendants underscore the medieval character of this style.

Other buildings include the **Furnace** – where the ore was transformed into liquid and cast into bars; the **Forge**, with its fires and large waterwheels; the **Rolling and Slitting Mill** – where the iron bars were flattened and cut into nail rods; the **Iron House** – iron products were stored here before being shipped down the Saugus River to Boston or Lynn.

111

LINCOLN Michelin tourist map – fold 16 – Pop 7 464

Settled in the mid-17C, Lincoln – named for Lincoln, England – is a pretty residential town.

Gropius House. – *16 miles west of Boston at 68 Baker Bridge Road. From Rte 128 Exit 47 follow Trapelo Road west to Sandy Pond Road; take the left fork onto Baker Bridge Road. Guided tours (1 hour) June to October 15, Friday, Saturday and Sunday 12 noon to 5 PM; the rest of the year Saturday and Sunday only; $2.50.*

Designed by Walter Gropius (1883-1969) in collaboration with Marcel Breuer, this house was the home of Gropius, one of the originators of modern architecture. Gropius founded the **Bauhaus** school of art and architecture in Germany and later emigrated to America where he was named Director of the Harvard School of Architecture. His innovative style differing radically from that of the Beaux Arts school, influenced the design of buildings around the world.

The exterior of the house, severe and unadorned with its plain siding, ribbon windows, narrow staircase, glass bricks and protective canopy is simple and functional. The building materials used were all machine made – an important element of the Gropius aesthetic – and obtained through catalogs or supply houses. Inside, the relaxed flow of space in the living area conveys a sense of order and tranquility. Many of the furnishings are family pieces.

DeCordova Museum. – *15 miles west of Boston on Sandy Pond Road. From Rte 128 Exit 47 take Trapelo Road west to Lincoln Center, then continue 1 mile on Sandy Pond Road. Open 10 AM (12 noon Saturday and Sunday) to 5 PM (9 PM Friday); $2.00.*

Exhibits feature every style of art from traditional landscape and marine painting to Pop Art and superrealism. *Concerts in summer in the outdoor amphitheater.*

SHARON Michelin tourist map – fold 16 – Pop 14 197

This pleasing community is one of the more than ninety cities and towns that comprise the Boston Metropolitan Area.

Kendall Whaling Museum. – *27 Everett Street. 1 mile north of the village center. Open 10 AM to 5 PM, closed Sundays, Mondays and major holidays; $2.00.*

The museum is small, but its fascinating collection of artwork, artifacts and other whaling memorabilia make the trip worthwhile. International in flavor, it displays British, Dutch, American and Japanese **paintings★** that illustrate several centuries of whaling including the "factory ship" era of the 20C. Equally impressive is the extensive collection of **scrimshaw★**: note the scrimshandered violin. In addition to whaling implements and tools, ship models, Eskimo whaling gear and the museum's seal-hunting collection, there are small craft on exhibit: an Eskimo kayak; a whaleboat used aboard the *John R. Manta* (the last American sailing whaler).

SOUTH SUDBURY (AV: *p 88*) – Pop 13 993

20 miles west of Boston on the Old Post Road (Rte 20) is the **Wayside Inn,** made famous by Longfellow's *Tales of A Wayside Inn.* Overnight guests are welcome at the inn which also serves meals and allows visitors to tour *(8 AM to 10 PM; 50¢),* among other rooms, the Longfellow Parlor where the clock, etched panes of glass and other memorable objects described in the *Tales of A Wayside Inn* have been preserved.

OTHER ATTRACTIONS OUTSIDE OF BOSTON *see map pp 88-89*

Dedham (BX). – Pop 24 399. In the 1920s this quiet community became known nationwide when the controversial murder trial of Sacco and Vanzetti was held here.

Fairbanks House. – *511 East Street at Eastern Avenue. Guided tours (45 min) May through October 9 AM to 12 noon and 1 to 5 PM; closed Monday; $3.00.* This early wooden dwelling built in 1636, was enlarged on several occasions as the owner's family and good fortune increased.

Medford (BV). – Pop 57 343. This attractive Boston suburb is the home of **Tuft's University.**

Isaac Royall House. – *156 George Street. Guided tours (50 min) May through October 2 to 5 PM; closed Monday and Friday; $1.50.* This three-story mansion (1732) served as the headquarters of New Hampshire's General John Stark *(p 198)* before the evacuation of Boston in 1776, and in the 19C was acquired by the textile magnate Francis Cabot Lowell. Lovely woodwork and period furnishings are found throughout the house.

Weston On Rte 20 (AV). – Pop 10 908. Pleasant homes, attractively landscaped, line the streets of this growing Boston suburb.

Cardinal Spellman Philatelic Museum. – *235 Wellesly Street. Open Tuesday, Wednesday and Thursday 9 AM to 3:30 PM; Sunday 1 to 5 PM. Changing exhibits on the main floor.*

This brick building, on the Regis College campus, houses the Cardinal Spellman philatelic collection and the collection of Philadelphia's National Philatelic Museum and Library, representing a combined total of 500 000 postage stamps from around the world.

If you love natural beauty,
take care to pollute no stream, spoil no woodland,
and leave only your footprint behind.

CAMBRIDGE ★★★

Michelin tourist map - fold 17 – *Map of the Boston region p 88* (**BV**) – Pop 92 535

Located on the Charles River across from Boston, is the university city of Cambridge, home of Harvard University and the Massachusetts Institute of Technology. World renowned as the site of these two institutions, the city is a maze of university buildings, commercial streets and residential neighborhoods. Massachusetts Avenue travels the length of Cambridge from Harvard Bridge, past MIT and through **Harvard Square,** the center of Cambridge with its lively coffee shops, restaurants and theaters. Between Harvard Square and the Common lie quiet streets lined with colonial dwellings.

Tree-lined **Memorial Drive** borders the Charles River, affording views of central Boston.

HISTORICAL NOTES

From New Towne to Cambridge. – In 1630 New Towne, the small settlement across the river from Boston, was chosen as the capital of the Bay Colony. Fortifications were built to protect the town and six years later, when the Puritans voted to establish a college to train young men for the ministry, New Towne was selected as the site of the new institution. Leaders of the Bay Colony agreed to give the college a sum of money equal to the total colony tax, and in 1638, recognizing the close bond between the college and the colony, they changed the name of New Towne to Cambridge, after the English university town.

Later that year, a Charlestown pastor **John Harvard,** who had bequeathed half his estate and library to the college, died, and the school was named Harvard in his honor.

Literary Cambridge. – Cambridge developed as a publishing center in the 17C when the first printing press in the colonies was established here by the widow of an English pastor and her assistants, the Daye brothers. A Bible in an Indian language, an almanac and the *Bay Psalm Book* were among the first works printed.

As the seat of Harvard College, Cambridge became the home of many leading educators and scholars of the day. By the mid-19C the city had developed into a major center of enlightened and progressive thought, attracting a circle of prominent writers, reformers and intellectuals to live, study or teach in Cambridge. Among the more famous figures associated with Cambridge were Henry Wadsworth Longfellow, Oliver Wendell Holmes, Margaret Fuller and Dorothea Dix.

Cambridge and the Revolution. – Following the events at Lexington and Concord, the patriots established their military headquarters in Cambridge. Harvard buildings and private homes, abandoned by fleeing Tories, were transformed into hospitals and barracks. July 3, 1775 George Washington took command of the Continental Army on the Cambridge Common, and during the months that followed he lived in the Vassal House *(p 117)* closeby, on Tory Row (Brattle Street).

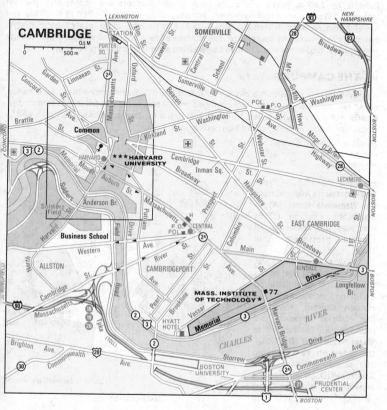

City of the Future. – The development of modern technologies by Harvard and MIT have made the city a vital center of research. A majority of the research programs on information centers and computers was carried out by scientists from around the world working in Cambridge. Research fosters industry, and since World War II research-and-development industries have flourished in Cambridge and have been a key factor in the growth of the industrial parks on Route 128.

■ HARVARD UNIVERSITY★★★ *time: 1 day*

Harvard College. – Harvard, the first college established in America, has been one of the nation's most prominent educational institutions since it was founded in 1636 to train young men for the ministry. The school's affiliation with Congregationalism declined as new and more liberal programs and policies were adopted, however, church and state control continued until 1865, when Harvard became a private institution.

Harvard University. – Harvard developed as a modern university in the 19C with Harvard College as its center. The school's physical plant expanded: the professional schools of Medicine (1782), Divinity (1816), Law (1817) and Arts and Sciences (1872) were founded, and teachers renowned for their learning: **James Russell Lowell, William James, Louis Agassiz, Henry Wadsworth Longfellow** introduced new fields of study into the curriculum. With an endowment of $22.5 million, Harvard continued to expand in the early 20C as new laboratories, lecture halls, museums and libraries were built. By the 1960s, 4 900 undergraduate and 2 900 graduate students were enrolled at Harvard.

Harvard's superior academic traditions, extensive course offerings, distinguished faculty, and devotion to research have made it one of the leading institutions of higher learning in the world. The university library, one of the finest in the world, has a total of more than 10.5 million volumes and the Fogg Art Museum *(p 116)* is a world leader among university art museums. Harvard is closely associated with research facilities such as the Astrophysical Observatory of the Smithsonian Institution and the Peabody Museum of Archaeology and Ethnology *(p 116)*. The university engages scholars to study and resolve problems relating to government, health, history and education on a global level.

Harvard's $3.5 billion endowment, the largest of any university in the world, is shared by the undergraduate college and ten graduate schools: Divinity, Law, Dental Medicine, Medical, Arts and Sciences, Business Administration, Education, Public Health, Design, and the John F. Kennedy School of Government. A majority of the undergraduate students continue with graduate study, the principal choices being business (18%), law (10%), medicine (13%), and the arts and sciences (21%). As a member of the **Ivy League,** Harvard does not award athletic scholarships or academic credit for physical education courses, but a wide range of sports is offered. The university's rowing teams, practicing on the Charles River, are a familiar sight to local residents.

Harvard Men and Harvard Women. – Some 6 600 students attend Harvard and **Radcliffe** *(p 116)* colleges and more than 17 300 students are enrolled in Harvard University. Women undergraduates are admitted through and enrolled in Radcliffe and thereby also enrolled in Harvard. Students live in Houses, often lovely Georgian style buildings that surround courtyards. The Houses allow students to enjoy a small college atmosphere, and at the same time to benefit from a modern university setting.

■ THE CAMPUS *Plan p 115*

Harvard is a city within a city with 400 buildings, including more than ten libraries, seven museums and dozens of laboratories on 380 acres of land primarily in Cambridge. A variety of architectural styles, from colonial to the modern creations of Gropius and Le Corbusier, trace the historic traditions of Harvard.

Begin at Holyoke Center, location of the Harvard Information Center.

Harvard Yard★★. – From Massachusetts Avenue, note the **Wadsworth House (A)**, a clapboard dwelling (1726) that was the residence of Harvard presidents until 1849.

Walk through the Yard. This is the oldest part of the University. Administration buildings, dormitories and Holden Chapel, Harvard's first official chapel, are found here. To the left is **Massachusetts Hall (B)** (1720), the oldest Harvard building still standing; opposite is **Harvard Hall (D)** (1766). Beyond Harvard Hall is **Holden Chapel (E)**, ornamented with the

(Courtesy Harvard University)

Massachusetts Hall.

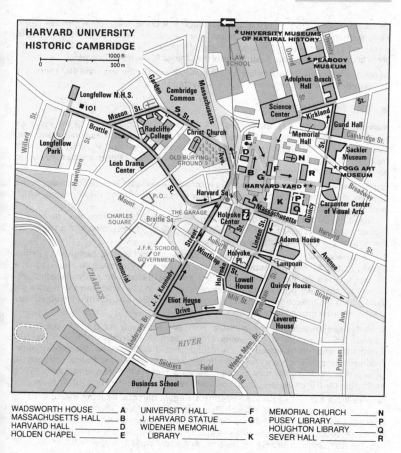

HARVARD UNIVERSITY HISTORIC CAMBRIDGE

WADSWORTH HOUSE	**A**	UNIVERSITY HALL	**F**	MEMORIAL CHURCH	**N**
MASSACHUSETTS HALL	**B**	J. HARVARD STATUE	**G**	PUSEY LIBRARY	**P**
HARVARD HALL	**D**	WIDENER MEMORIAL		HOUGHTON LIBRARY	**Q**
HOLDEN CHAPEL	**E**	LIBRARY	**K**	SEVER HALL	**R**

blue and white Holden coat of arms. On the other side of the Yard is **University Hall (F)** (1815), a granite building designed by Charles Bulfinch. Daniel Chester French's **statue of John Harvard (G)** stands in front of University Hall; because of the plaque on the statue that reads: "John Harvard, founder 1638" the statue is known as the "statue of the three lies", for the college was founded in 1636, John Harvard was a benefactor not a founder, and the figure is of a student who attended Harvard in the 1880s.

To the rear of University Hall stands **Memorial Church (N)**, dedicated to Harvard men killed in the World Wars. Opposite, rises the **Widener Memorial Library (K)** with its imposing stairway and columns. The library, the largest university library in the world, is named for a former Harvard student who lost his life when the Titanic sank.

Nearby is the modern **Pusey Library (P)** where the Harvard University archives are stored; the **Houghton Library (Q)** possesses the rare books and manuscripts of Harvard. Pass in front of the Romanesque facade of **Sever Hall (R)**, the work of H. H. Richardson, and leave the yard. *Turn left onto Quincy Street.*

The concrete and glass **Carpenter Center of Visual Arts**, triumphing over its small site, is the only structure in North America designed by Le Corbusier; nearby is the **Fogg Art Museum** *(p 116)* and just beyond is the **Sackler Museum** *(p 116)*, a contemporary L-shaped orange brick structure. Continue on to **Gund Hall** (the Graduate School of Design) with its modernistic glass-enclosed stairway. Across the way is **Memorial Hall**, a bulky Victorian building topped with a square tower and pyramidal roofs, housing the Sanders Theater. *Turn left onto Kirkland Street.*

Pass in front of the **Busch-Reisinger Museum** *(p 116)*, then the striking **Science Center**, completed in 1973. The modern Center is the work of Jackson, Sert and Associates. *Cross the Yard.*

■ THE HARVARD HOUSES

Many Harvard students live in the elegant Georgian "houses" (there are about ten on the campus) found between Massachusetts Avenue and the Charles River: **Adams House, Quincy House, Lowell House**. These houses – most of which are brick, share a similar design and have broad grassy courtyards – bring a small-college atmosphere to the sprawling university community. During the warmer months, students will be found in the yards preparing for class, studying for exams – or perhaps enjoying a game of frisbee.

*From Massachusetts Avenue (Holyoke Center) turn right onto Linden Street. You will pass Adams House, Quincy House, Leverett House. Cross Mount Auburn Street. From here a whimsical building that resembles a Flemish castle is visible; the building houses the offices of the **Lampoon**, a satirical magazine published by Harvard students. Continue* on Holyoke Place. Opposite rises the blue cupola of **Lowell House**; for a glimpse of the elegance that typifies the Harvard Houses glance into its Yard. *Continue on Holyoke Street, then cross the yard opposite. Arriving at Memorial Drive, turn right.* The buildings of the **Business School,** on the Boston side of the Charles River, come into view.

To return to Harvard Square follow J.F. Kennedy Street. On the way pass **Eliot House** and the "Garage," an exciting complex of youth-oriented shops.

■ THE MUSEUMS

Harvard University Art Museums★. – The museums described below serve as teaching facilities for Harvard's Department of Fine Arts and operate as public museums. *Open 10 AM (1 PM Sunday) to 5 PM (9 PM Thursday); closed Mondays and major holidays; $3.00, under 18, free. Saturday mornings free. Ticket entitles holder to admission to all the University art museums.*

Fogg Art Museum★. – *32 Quincy Street.* On entering the museum, before continuing to the galleries take a moment to view the two lower floors, surrounding the courtyard, which are a replica of a 16C canon's house.

Exhibits span all periods of Western art from the Middle Ages to the present and include notable examples of **Italian Renaissance** painting, impressionist and postimpressionist painting and sculpture, and classical art.

Sackler Museum. – *485 Broadway.* A dramatic contemporary building designed by James Stirling (1985) houses the Sackler Museum, a companion museum to the Fogg. The Sackler focuses on Ancient, Near Eastern and Far Eastern Art. Oriental sculpture, ceramics, Japanese prints, and a noteworthy group of Chinese **bronzes** and **jades** are highlights of the collection. In addition, temporary exhibitions on a variety of subjects are presented in the ground floor galleries.

Busch-Reisinger Museum. – The museum is known especially for its holdings in 20C German art, in particular the works of the German Expressionists such as Max Beckmann, and the members of the Bridge and the Blue Rider (Kandinsky, Klee, Feininger) groups. There are also works from the medieval, baroque and rococo periods. *During construction of a new museum building (scheduled completion early 1990s) works from the Busch-Reisinger collection will be exhibited at the Fogg Art Museum.*

Adolphus Busch Hall. – *29 Kirkland Street.* This elegant baroque building dating from the early 20C formerly housed the Busch-Reisinger Museum *(see above).* The garden and East Wing have been restored as gallery space for the museum's collection of medieval sculpture, architectural fragments and plaster casts of important German monuments from the Romanesque and Gothic periods. *At present closed; reopening date late 1988.*

Harvard University Museums of Natural History★. – *Entrances on Divinity Avenue and 24 Oxford Street. Open 9 AM (1 PM Sunday) to 4:30 PM; closed major holidays; $2.00, Mondays free.*

This building contains four distinct museums.

Peabody Museum of Archaeology and Ethnology★. – Founded in 1866 by George Peabody, the museum contains objects and works of art brought back from expeditions sponsored by Harvard University. On the ground floor, in the **Hall of American Indians★** *(closed for renovation),* a group of totem poles stands amidst a collection of North American Indian art that features artifacts gathered by Lewis and Clark. Dioramas present the habitats of different tribes. Second floor exhibits on the Indians of the southwest include Hopi musical instruments and Katchinas (dolls representing the ancestral spirits of the Hopi Indians). On the third floor are highlights of the **Mayan collection★★**: plaster casts of Mayan stone monuments and a stone head of the God of Mais. Displays on the fourth and fifth floors are related to the peoples of the Pacific and Africa, and prehistoric man.

Botanical Museum. – The museum houses the unique collection of **Blashka Glass Flowers★★**. Created in Germany by Leopold and Rudolph Blashka between 1877 and 1936 these flowers, hand blown glass models accurately representing more than 780 species of flowering plants, are scientifically and aesthetically a work of art.

Geological and Mineralogical Museum. – Exhibits of minerals, gemstones and meteorites. Of special interest are the giant gypsum crystals from a cave in Niaca, Mexico.

Museum of Comparative Zoology. – Among the rare finds on display are: the Harvard **Mastodon** (25 000 years old), found in New Jersey; a Paleosaurus, one of the oldest fossil dinosaurs (180 million years old); and a Kronosaurus (120 million years old), perhaps the largest marine reptile to have ever lived.

One of the museum's most exciting finds has been the **Coelacanth**, a prehistoric fish thought to have been extinct for 70 million years. Also of interest are a fossilized turtle shell, the largest ever found (5-6 million years old); the world's oldest egg (225 million years old), and a large diorama featuring prehistoric mammals. In the Thayer Hall of North American birds, every species that breeds north of Mexico is represented.

■ HISTORIC CAMBRIDGE★ *time 2 hours – plan p 115*

Cambridge Common. – The Common was the town center for more than three hundred years, and the scene from 1775 to 1776 of General Washington's main camp. According to tradition George Washington took command of the Continental Army under the "Washington Elm" that stood on the Common until the 1920s. The site is marked on the Garden Street side of the green by a plaque (**S**) and scion of the Washington Elm.

Christ Church. – *Zero Garden Street.* This grey wooden structure designed in 1760 by Peter Harrison, is notable for its lovely Georgian interior. Abandoned at the beginning of the Revolution, the church was later used as a barracks for American troops.

Radcliffe College. – Radcliffe, named for Ann Radcliffe, a Harvard benefactor, was established in 1879 to provide women with an education similar to that received by the men at Harvard. Despite the fears of Cantabrigians that groups of unescorted women walking to classes might be cause for scandal, Radcliffe students fared very well and in 1894 Radcliffe became officially associated with Harvard. Classes were conducted by professors from Harvard, and Radcliffe degrees were countersigned by Harvard.

Radcliffe's commitment to women's education over the years, has made it a distinguished leader in the field. The special relationship between Harvard and Radcliffe continues to steadily evolve. In 1975 the admissions offices of both colleges were joined, quotas for women were abolished and equal admission standards were established for men and women. Today, while Radcliffe remains a separate corporate institution, its students are also Harvard students with access to all of Harvard's resources.

In the **Yard** note: the Federal style of **Fay House**, the first structure acquired by Radcliffe; the **Gymnasium**, which now serves as a data and resource center on women's lives, and the dance center; and **Agassiz House,** part of the original yard. A building at the far end of the yard houses the **Schlesinger Library** which possesses the most extensive library of women's studies in the country and the **Bunting Institute,** a postdoctoral fellowship program for women scholars, artists and writers. Before exiting from the yard and turning onto Mason Street, observe the First Church (19C) surmounted by a gilded cock weathervane made in the 17C by Deacon Drowne.

Brattle Street. – Wealthy Tories built their homes along this street in the 18C, thus the name Tory Row. The residences now lining Brattle Street date primarily from the 19C: note Nos. **101** (Hastings House) and **113** and **115** (belonged to Longfellow's daughters).

Longfellow National Historic Site. – *105 Brattle Street. Guided tours (1/2 hour) 10 AM to 4:30 PM; closed January 1, Thanksgiving Day and December 25; $2.00.*

This Georgian dwelling built in 1759 by the Loyalist John Vassall, served as the headquarters of General Washington during the siege of Boston. In the 19C **Henry Wadsworth Longfellow** lived in the house between 1837 and 1882, the period during which he wrote his most memorable poems including *Hiawatha* and *Evangeline.* A chair made from the wood of the "spreading chestnut tree" will be seen on the ground floor. **Longfellow Park,** opposite the house, extends down to the river.

Returning to Harvard Square by Brattle Street, you will pass in front of the **Loeb Drama Center** (No. 64), Harvard's modern theater.

■ MASSACHUSETTS INSTITUTE OF TECHNOLOGY★ *city map p 113*

Founded during the 19C in Boston's Copley Square, the Massachusetts Institute of Technology was at first known as Boston Tech. By 1916 the school had outgrown its Copley Square site, and, accompanied by three days of parades, speeches and celebrations, Boston Tech moved to its new location in Cambridge.

The school was established as the Massachusetts Institute of Technology in 1861 by **William Barton Rogers,** a natural scientist, who stressed the practical application of knowledge as the institute's principal goal. Guided through its early years by Rogers, MIT continued to pursue its original goal in the 20C and is today at the vanguard of modern research and development, with schools of Engineering, Science, Architecture and Planning, Management, and Humanities and Social Science. The international character of the Institute is evidenced by its enrollment of almost 9 800 students, including 2 340 women, from 50 states and 98 foreign countries, who benefit from MIT's sophisticated teaching methods and modern equipment. Scientific works published by MIT are diffused to centers of learning and cities around the world.

East Campus. – *To the right of Massachusetts Avenue arriving from Harvard Bridge.* The Neo-Classical buildings along Massachusetts Avenue were designed by Welles Bosworth as part of the Institute's new campus in 1916. A low dome tops the **Rogers Building** (No. 77). The **Hart Nautical Collections** *(entrance: 77 Massachusetts Avenue – open 9 AM to 5 PM, Saturday 10 AM to 4 PM; closed Sunday)* has ship models, half models and engine models which demonstrate the evolution of shipbuilding.

Contemporary art exhibits are held in galleries at the **List Visual Arts Center** *(open 10 AM to 4 PM, Saturday and Sunday 1 to 5 PM; closed July and August)* on the main floor of the Wiesner Building. Between the Hayden Memorial Library and the Earth Sciences Center looms Alexander Calder's stabile *The Big Sail;* a black steel sculpture by Louise Nevelson *Transparent Horizon,* stands close by.

West Campus. – *To the left of Massachusetts Avenue arriving from Harvard Bridge.* The smooth surfaced, modern Student Center houses the Tech Coop, the student union and restaurants. The **Kresge Auditorium★** and the **MIT Chapel★** were designed by **Eero Saarinen** in 1956. Of special interest is the triangular shell roof of the auditorium which rests essentially on three points. The interfaith chapel, a cylindrical brick structure, is topped with an aluminum sculpture by Theodore Roszak, replacing the traditional bell tower. Inside the chapel, light enters from above, illuminating the mobile over the altar. Water in the exterior moat casts reflections on the interior walls, creating an interesting play of light and shadows.

Baker House, a dormitory designed in 1947 by the architect Alvar Aalto, is nearby.

CAPE ANN ★★

Michelin tourist map - fold 17

Salty sea air, exhilarating and clear, pervades the fishing villages, coastal estates and harbors of this rockbound peninsula north of Boston. The Cape was explored in 1604 by Champlain, then in 1614 by Captain John Smith who mapped and named the area in honor of the Queen. A small colony was established in 1623 at Gloucester, by a group of Englishmen who had come "to praise God and catch fish." Their descendants were the generations of

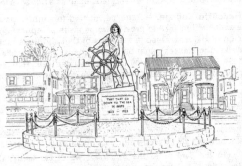

The Gloucester Fisherman.

Cape-born sailors who have made the region one of the world's major fishing centers.

Bostonians frequent the Cape on weekends and during the vacation period, seeking out its genuinely salty atmosphere, splendid art galleries and abundance of fine seafood restaurants. Browsing in the shops and enjoying the Cape's ruggedly beautiful scenery are among the popular pastimes. Camera buffs delight in the magnificent natural light, which strikes the rocky shores and transforms the landscape into a changing spectrum of color and shadows throughout the day.

TOUR OF CAPE ANN ★★

From Magnolia to Riverdale – *28 miles – 1/2 day – local map p 119*

The itinerary for the most part follows Routes 127 and 127A around Cape Ann, passing through quaint fishing villages and offering views of the coast and the ocean.

Magnolia. – This former fishing village developed into a summer resort in the 19C. Many of Magnolia's large comfortable dwellings, built as vacation homes during that era, are now year-round residences. Following Shore Road along the coast there are views of the modest harbor and, in the distance, the skyline of Boston's towers.

From Shore Road turn left onto Hesperus Avenue then right onto Lexington Avenue; turn right again onto Norman's Avenue which becomes Hesperus Avenue.

Hammond Castle Museum ★. – *Guided tours (45 min) 10 AM to 4 PM; closed major holidays. $3.50.* This stone castle, inspired by a castle of the Middle Ages, overlooks Gloucester Bay. Built 1926-29 by the inventor John Hays Hammond, Jr., the castle contains Mr. Hammond's collection of medieval furnishings, paintings and sculpture. During the summer organ recitals are performed in the Great Hall, on the impressive organ (8 600 pipes, 126 stops) he constructed over a period of 20 years. From the museum you can look down onto Norman's Woe, the treacherous rocks that are the setting of Longfellow's poem the *Wreck of the Hesperus.*

Return to Hesperus Avenue which leads into Rte 127 (Western Avenue). Drive by **Stage Fort Park**, site of the settlement established in 1623, then cross the drawbridge that links the Cape to the mainland. To the right is Leonard Craske's statue the **Gloucester Fisherman ★** (**A**), a tribute to the thousands of Gloucestermen who have died at sea.

Enter Gloucester by Main Street.

Gloucester. – Pop 28 092. Gloucester, the oldest seaport in the nation, is one of the world's leading fishing ports. Gloucester's fleet of schooners which once sailed between Virginia and Newfoundland in search of cod, halibut, mackerel was immortalized by Rudyard Kipling in his novel, *Captains Courageous.* Still a major provider of fish, with its fleet of about 250 boats, Gloucester is also a major distribution center for the industry. At the seafood processing plants near the waterfront, the catch of fishermen from Canada, Iceland, Greenland and Scandinavia – as well as New England – is cured, packaged and prepared for shipping to cities across the nation.

The fishermen, many of whom are of Portuguese or Italian descent, remain devoted to their traditions, and especially to the annual **Blessing of the Fleet** *(see Calendar of Events p 13)* which takes place the last weekend in June on the feast of St. Peter.

From Main Street turn left onto Pleasant Street.

Cape Ann Historical Association (**B**). – *27 Pleasant Street. Open 10 AM to 5 PM; closed Sundays, Mondays, holidays and the month of February; $2.00.*

The society owns a superb collection of **seascapes ★** by the 19C American marine painter **Fitz Hugh Lane**. His views of Gloucester Harbor and the harbor islands are admired for their warm, luminous colors, attention to detail and serene atmosphere.

Return to Main Street by Prospect Street. You will pass the Portuguese-inspired **Church of Our Lady of Good Voyage** (**D**), surmounted by two blue cupolas.

Follow Main Street, bearing right at the first fork, then right again at the second fork, onto East Main Street.

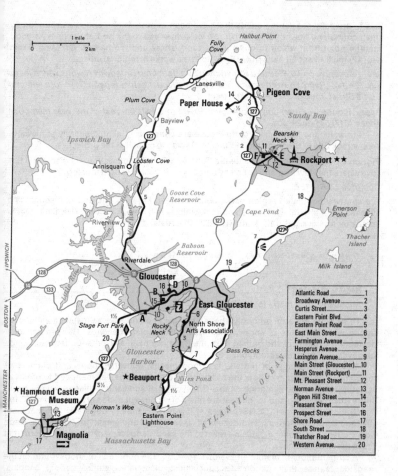

East Gloucester. – Among East Main Street's restaurants and art galleries is the **North Shore Arts Association** located in a red weather-beaten barn *(197 East Main; open June 14 to September 30, 10 AM – 2:30 PM Sunday – to 5:30 PM)*. The Association features the work of local artists. Opposite is **Rocky Neck,** the site of an artists' colony in the 19C.

Follow Eastern Point Road to Eastern Point (private). Visitors to Beauport may enter.

Beauport★. – *Guided tours (1 hour 15 min) mid-May to mid-October weekdays 10 AM to 4 PM; mid-September to mid-October Saturday and Sunday also 1 to 4 PM; closed holidays; $4.00.*

The diversity of period styles and decor found in Beauport, formerly the 40 room summer residence of architect-decorator Henry Davis Sleeper (1873-1934), was planned by Sleeper who wished to create, for each room, a different mood or character. Beneath the varied roofline of chimneys, turrets, spiral flues and towers, he assembled architectural elements and furnishings, and designed a series of rooms: the Paul Revere Room, Indian Room, Byron Room, China Trade Room that made him one of the most celebrated decorators of his day.

At the tip of Eastern Point is **Eastern Point Lighthouse,** dominating a long, granite breakwater at the entrance to Gloucester Harbor.

Return along Eastern Point Boulevard to the entrance of the private road, then turn right onto Farmington Avenue and left onto Atlantic Road.

The drive along Atlantic Road affords a good **view** of the coast, and opposite, the twin lights on Thacher Island. Return to Rte 127A (Thacher Road) which skirts beaches, occasional salt marshes and rocky, wooded areas. Thacher Road becomes South Street as you approach Rockport.

Rockport★★. – Pop 6 603. *During the tourist season it is difficult to park in the village. We suggest you leave your car in one of the lots outside town (parking: $4.00) and take the shuttle bus that operates every 15 minutes between the lots and the center of town (free).*

This tranquil fishing village that developed as an artists' colony in the 1920s, had its industrial heyday in the 19C, when granite quarried from its shores was shipped to ports as far away as South America. Rockport's main attractions are the numerous art galleries and shops found in the vicinity of Main Street, as well as the village's charming character and coastal setting.

The village is especially picturesque in the late afternoon when the setting sun illuminates the sea, the granite ledges, the boats anchored offshore and the red fishing shed **Motif No. 1★ (E),** named for the many paintings it has inspired. To the left, on **Bearskin**

Neck★, are salty old fishing sheds that have been converted into shops surrounded by small courts and flower gardens. Narrow walkways lead to the end of the neck, a good vantage point from which to observe the rocky shore and the harbor. On Main Street (No. 12) the **Rockport Art Association (F)** exhibits the works of regional artists.

Leave Rockport on Mt Pleasant Street, then turn right onto Broadway Avenue which leads into Rte 127 (Railroad Avenue and Granite Street). Just before Pigeon Cove turn left onto Curtis Street, then onto Pigeon Hill Street.

Paper House. – *Open July and August 10 AM to 5 PM; the rest of the year telephone ahead (617) 546-2629. 50¢.*

The walls and furnishings of the house are constructed almost entirely of newspapers. It took Elis F. Stenman and his family 20 years to complete the project.

Pigeon Cove. – Turning right, after the Cape Ann Tool Company, you will discover a tiny cove where the New England Lobster Company sells freshly caught lobster.

Continue on Rte 127.

The sparsely populated region of the coast between Pigeon Cove and Annisquam is a succession of charming villages and rocky inlets: **Folly Cove, Lanesville, Plum Cove, Lobster Cove.** After **Annisquam**, Rte 127 joins Rte 128 in Riverdale.

The key on p 34 explains the symbols used on the maps.

CAPE COD ★★★

Michelin tourist map - folds 17, 18, 23 and 24

This large bent arm, an oddly-shaped extension of the Massachusetts mainland, is fringed with 300 miles of sandy, often wild and desolate beaches. The product of a fascinating geological and human past, the Cape has been a favorite tourist resort since the development of the automobile.

Despite the strings of motels, fast food places, souvenir shops and clusters of condominiums found in or near the old fishing ports, the Cape has managed to preserve its natural beauty and seafaring charm. Small colonial and fishing villages dot the North Shore (the Bay Side), and to the east are miles of windswept dunes protected in the Cape Cod National Seashore (CCNS). Acres of low-lying cranberry bogs and salt marshes, pine and scrub oak forests, and dozens of lakes, ponds and small, grey-shingled "Cape Cod" houses *(p 27)* offer a pleasing relief to the sandy landscape of this peculiar arm that lies in the Atlantic Ocean.

A large number of craftsmen live on Cape Cod. The hundreds of shops found on the roadside feature their handmade specialties: glassware, leather goods, candles, wooden decoys, fabric, pottery.

A Glacial Past. – During the last Ice Age glaciers moved down across Canada and New England, reaching, with the Laurentide ice sheet, the present-day site of Long Island and the Cape Islands: Martha's Vineyard *(p 134)* and Nantucket *(p 136)*. The ice sheet deposited enormous mounds of earth and stone at its snout forming a frontal moraine. As temperatures rose, the ice melted, with a subsequent retreat of the ice sheet to the Cape Cod area – forming a second moraine. At the end of the Ice Age the sea level rose leading to a marine incursion which flooded the land around the upstanding morainic masses, now Cape Cod.

In addition, the wind and sea have played a part in shaping the Cape. Marine erosion created the tall cliffs of the Outer Cape, and ocean currents, carrying sand northward, are responsible for the formation of the sandy hook at the tip of Cape Cod – the Province Lands sector of Provincetown.

Cape of the Cod. – Cape Cod was named by the explorer **Bartholomew Gosnold** who landed here in 1602 and was impressed by the cod-filled waters that surrounded the Cape Eighteen years later, in 1620, the *Mayflower* en route to its original destination, Virginia anchored at the present site of Provincetown, and the Pilgrims spent five weeks exploring the region before continuing on to their landfall at Plymouth.

The earliest permanent settlements on the Cape were established around 1630 with fishing and farming as the mainstays. Shore whaling gave way to ocean whaling, and in the 18C whaling grew into a principal industry on the Cape as vessels sailed out of Barnstable, Truro, Wellfleet and Provincetown to hunt whales. Apart from the Cape Codders who engaged in fishing and farming, there were those who earned their livelihood from a less "traditional" means: mooncussing. Mooncussers caused ships to go aground on the shoals off the Cape, and grew rich by gathering the booty from the wrecks

The shoals, themselves rocky and treacherous, a challenge to even the most experienced seamen, posed a great danger to all shipping in these waters. Traces of a handful of the hundreds of vessels that went down off the Cape before the construction of the Canal *(p 125)*, are on occasion revealed for a brief time on the beach during low tide, then, as the tide rushes in, are once again hidden by the shifting sands.

The Cape Islands. – The Cape Islands are the islands to the south: **Martha's Vineyard** **Nantucket** and the **Elizabeth Islands.** Purchased by Thomas Mayhew, an Englishman, in 1642 the islands developed into whaling centers in the 18 and 19C and remained unspoiled by industry into the 20C. Bordered by magnificent beaches bathed by the warm waters of the Gulf Stream, the islands are today devoted primarily to tourism.

Moccasins or Moraine. – The two triangles located under the bent arm known as Cape Cod, have inspired a variety of legends and theories about how they came into being. A popular Indian legend tells of a giant whose bed was Cape Cod. One night, his moccasins were so full of sand that he became irritated and was unable to sleep. He bent down, removed the moccasins and threw them into the ocean, thus creating the two islands.

Then there is the more scientific explanation. Thousands of years ago glaciers that covered New England stopped at the present site of Cape Cod and the islands. The deposits of earth and stone left by the melting glaciers, were thickest and highest at the points where two glaciers met. Each of the islands corresponds to one of these areas of thick deposits which was not submerged beneath the sea when the melting glaciers caused the sea level to rise *(see p 120)*.

Cranberry Bogs. – Half of the nation's cranberries come from southern Massachusetts where natural conditions similar to those that prevail on the Cape: marshy areas and sandy bogs, lend themselves to the production of this small, red berry. Named for the likeness of its blossom to the crane, the cranberry is used to make juice, spreads, jellies to be served with turkey and is traditionally a part of the Thanksgiving feast.

Widespread cultivation of the berry was begun in the early 19C when a local man, Henry Hall, discovered that the berries thrive best when covered with a layer of sand. Each spring sand was spread over the plants, and the berries were harvested in the fall. The process remains basically unchanged, although it is now mechanized. Festivals are held each fall on the Cape (Truro, Harwich ...) and in nearby areas to celebrate the harvest of the cranberry crop from the region's bogs.

Cape Cod Beaches. – Most beaches are town-owned. A parking fee of $5.00-$6.00 is usually charged at beaches that welcome nonresidents. Waters on the Atlantic Ocean are cooler than the waters along the South Shore. The ocean beaches usually have surf *(beware of the undertow)*, in contrast to the calmer beaches on Cape Cod Bay.

Consult the owner of the establishment where you are staying regarding beach fees and regulations, as they vary from town to town. *CCNS beaches daily parking fee $3.00 (p 122).*

THE NORTH SHORE ★★

From Sagamore Bridge to Orleans – *34 miles – allow 1 day – local map pp 122-123*

Rte 6A follows the North Shore, known also as the **Bay Side** because it fronts Cape Cod Bay. The road passes through tiny villages that were prosperous ports in the 19C.

Pairpoint Glass Works. – *Glassblowing Monday through Friday 8 AM to 4:30 PM.*

Visitors may observe skilled glassblowers as they produce, then decorate pieces of Pairpoint crystal according to the methods traditionally employed in the production of handmade glassware through the 19C.

From Rte 6A turn right onto Rte 130, then turn right onto Pine Street for Heritage Plantation.

Heritage Plantation ★★. – *Description p 152.*

Sandwich ★. – *Description p 151.*

Cranberry bogs, then dunes and marshes are visible as Rte 6A continues to Barnstable. Beyond the dunes and salt marshes lies **Sandy Neck,** a 7 mile strip of land that protects Barnstable Harbor. At one time whalemen boiled down whale blubber in cauldrons that lined the shores of **Sandy Neck Beach,** today a favorite of swimmers during the summer.

Barnstable. – Pop 35 080. Pleasure craft have for the most part replaced the fishing and whaling boats that formerly filled Barnstable's harbor. A road on the left *(follow the sign Barnstable Harbor)* leads to the water's edge. The Custom House has been transformed into the **Donald G. Trayser Museum** *(open July and August 1:30 to 4:30 PM, closed Sunday and Monday)*, which contains memorabilia and artifacts related to Barnstable's maritime past.

Yarmouth Port. – Pop 19 690. The beautiful sea captains' homes on Main Street are reminiscent of Yarmouth's era as a busy port. The **Winslow-Crocker House** *(c. 1780)* fronting Route 6A may be visited *(open June to mid-October Tuesday, Thursday, Saturday and Sunday 12 noon to 5 PM; $2.50).*

Dennis. – Pop 13 545. Light comedies are presented at the **Cape Playhouse,** a well-known summer theater. From **Scargo Hill Tower** *(from Rte 6A turn right after the cemetery, then left into Scargo Hill Road)* there is a **view** that reaches from Plymouth to Provincetown.

Sealand of Cape Cod (A). – *Open late June to Labor Day 9:30 AM to 7:30 PM; the rest of the year 10 AM to 4 PM, closed Wednesdays and major holidays; $6.45, under 12, $4.15. Several shows daily feature the dolphins, seals and sea lions.*

The aquarium, set against a vast expanse of salt marshes, has otters, harbor seals, dolphins and a variety of local marine fauna.

Pydenstricker Glass Factory (B). – *Demonstrations Tuesday to Saturday 10 AM to 12 noon.*

The owner of this glassworks has developed an original technique in glassmaking: two sheets of glass are used to make each item; one of the sheets is decorated, then fused to the second according to the principles used in the enameling process. Tableware and other items are produced.

Drummer Boy Museum (D). – *Guided tours (50 min) May 15 to Columbus Day 9:30 AM to 5 PM; $2.95, children, 75¢.*

The museum presents an account of the major events of the American Revolution through the use of twenty-one life-size murals. Among this series of murals is a reproduction of Paul Revere's engraving of the Boston Massacre.

Stony Brook Mill (E). – *5 miles from Rte 6A. Take Stony Brook Road (on the right). Open July and August, Wednesday, Friday and Saturday 2 to 5 PM.*

The old grist mill still grinds corn into cornmeal. The stream that runs beside the mill is the scene of an exciting natural phenomenon April through mid-May: a herring run. During this period alewives (fish 10-13 inches long) swim upstream to freshwater ponds and lakes to spawn. They then return downstream with their newborn fingerlings, following an instinct that is in some way similar to that of the salmon.

New England Fire and History Museum (F). – *Open late May to mid-September 10 AM to 3 PM; Saturday and Sunday only mid-September to Columbus Day; $4.00, under 12, $2.50.*

Five buildings contain equipment and memorabilia that tell the story of the important role played by the firefighters and their volunteer companies throughout the nation's history. A diorama vividly illustrates the Great Chicago Fire of 1871. A Blacksmith shop and 19C Apothecary shop are among the buildings on the green.

Nickerson State Park. – *Open year round. Camping $6.00 per site per day.*

Camping and picnic grounds and a restaurant are located in the park, the former estate of pioneer railroad builder Roland Nickerson. Swimming is permitted in Flax and Cliff ponds.

Orleans. – *Pop 5 741.* Orleans is the first town on the Cape where you will see ocean beaches. **Nauset Beach,** about 10 miles long, protects Nauset Harbor, Pleasant Bay, Orleans and Chatham from the violent northeasters that pound this section of the coast.

CAPE COD NATIONAL SEASHORE★★★

In 1961 the eastern coast of Cape Cod, with its fragile dunes, cliffs, marshes and woodlands, became an area protected and administered by the National Park Service: the Cape Cod National Seashore. Since that time bicycle trails, nature trails and dune trails for over-sand vehicles have been created, allowing visitors to enjoy the magnificent landscape. An information center is located at each end of the 27 000 acre Seashore, and lifeguard services are available at the CCNS beaches *(parking fee $3.00):* **Coast Guard Beach, Nauset Light Beach, Marconi Beach, Head of the Meadow Beach, Race Point Beach** and **Herring Cove Beach.**

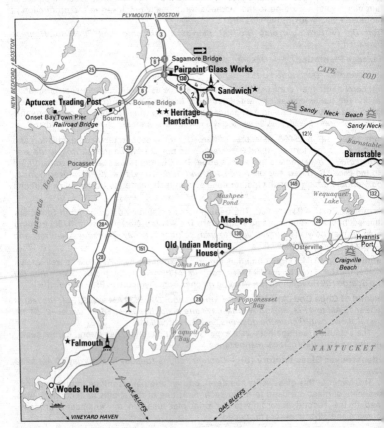

VISIT *time: allow 1 1/2 – 2 days*

Salt Pond Visitor Center★. – *Open 9 AM to 4:30 PM (8 PM late June to Labor Day); closed January and February. A film on the CCNS is shown.*

Rangers provide literature and information regarding Seashore regulations, trails, facilities and programs. A large room contains an exhibit on Cape Cod – its formation, history, Indians, animal and plant life, environment and architecture.

Nauset Marsh Trail. – *Trail: 1 mile (time: 1/2 hour). Access near the Information Center.*

Beautiful views of the pond and marshes.

Governor Prince Road ___ 1	Shore Road ___ 4
Pine Street ___ 2	Stony Brook Road ___ 5
Scargo Hill Road ___ 3	Trowbridge Road ___ 6

Fort Hill Trail. – *To reach the Fort Hill parking lot from Rte 6 take Governor Prince Road. Trail: 1 1/2 miles.*

The trail leaves from the Penniman House and leads through open fields that afford expansive views of the marshes.

Marconi Station. – The area was named for **Guglielmo Marconi,** the Italian physicist who established the transatlantic wireless station which operated here between 1901 and 1917. The first formal transmission from the station was a communication between President Theodore Roosevelt and King Edward VII, January 19, 1903. Scattered remnants of the station remain, the other sections having been destroyed by shore erosion. The effects of erosion on the cliffs and beach are especially evident here.

Atlantic White Cedar Swamp Trail★. – *Access: Marconi Station parking lot; length: 1 1/4 miles.*

The trail reveals various aspects of the vegetation on Cape Cod as it leads through a lowbush area where beach grasses prevent erosion, then passes into an area of scrub oaks and pitch pines. The trail continues through a white cedar swamp before opening out onto the road that formerly led to the wireless station.

Pilgrim Spring Trail. – *Length 1/2 mile. Access from the Interpretive Shelter near the Pilgrim Heights parking lot.*

The trail leads through a section of scrub pines and bush to the site of a spring where the Pilgrims are believed to have first found drinking water in 1620.

Province Lands Visitor Center. – *Open 9 AM to 4:30 PM (8 PM late June to Labor Day); closed December through March.*

From the observation deck, there is a good view of the dunes of Province Lands.

A trail for over-sand vehicles begins at Race Point Beach. *Vehicle inspection and permit are required. Vehicle use permitted April 15 to November 15. Information Race Point Ranger Station ☏ (617) 487-2100.*

Beech Forest Trail. – *Length: 1 1/2 miles; access from Beech Forest parking lot.*

The trail passes through a beech forest threatened at certain spots by the advancing dunes. A pond that is filling in and will one day be a swamp or a bog and eventually forestland, can be seen from the trail.

Provincetown★★. – *Description p 145.*

SOUTH SHORE – *local map pp 122-123*

Route 28 runs along the South Shore through the major shopping centers of the Cape: Hyannis, Dennis Port and Yarmouth. Extremely commercial and tourist oriented with its shops, motels and restaurants this section of the Cape also has a number of pretty villages such as Chatham, Harwich and Falmouth.

Chatham★. – Pop 6 401. Protected by the sandy offshore barrier, Nauset Beach, Chatham remains an active fishing port. Fishing boats depart daily from the **Fish Pier** *(off of Shore Road)* and return to the harbor in the late afternoon. Further on, Shore Road leads to **Chatham Lighthouse** which affords a good view of Pleasant Bay and Nauset Beach.

Chatham Railroad Museum. – *Depot Road. Open July to early September weekdays 1:30 to 4:30 PM; closed weekends and the rest of the year.*

Located in Chatham's former Victorian style railroad depot, the museum has schedules, posters, the original ticket office and other exhibits that evoke the history of railroading.

Monomoy Island. – *Access by boat only.* Because of the island's importance as a resting place for birds in the Atlantic Flyway, it has been established as a nature preserve: "Monomoy National Wildlife Refuge." *For information ☏ the Refuge April through September (617) 945-0594; other times (617) 465-5753.*

Harwich. – Pop 9 632. The white columned buildings in the center of Harwich include the **Brooks Free Library** and the local history museum, the **Harwich Community Museum at Brooks Academy** *(open late June to mid-September Monday, Wednesday and Friday 1 to 4 PM).* Harwich is a leading producer of cranberries.

Harwich Port. – Picturesque **Wychmere Harbor** is visible from Route 28.

Hyannis. – Pop 11 258. Situated midway on the South Shore, this town is the major shopping center for the Cape. Hyannis is also an important gateway to Cape Cod with its regularly scheduled airline and island ferry services *(pp 134 and 137).*

Hyannis Port. – This fashionable waterfront resort is the site of the Kennedy family's summer home. *The Kennedy home is not visible from the road nor is it open to the public.* The **John F. Kennedy Memorial,** a bronze medallion set in a fieldstone wall, is located on Ocean Street. **Craigville Beach** *(off of Rte 28)* is a pleasant place to swim and sunbathe.

Mashpee. – Pop 4 691. The Massipee Indians were already living on the Cape when the English settlers arrived. In the 17C, in response to an appeal made by the Reverend Richard Bourne who was devoted to the Indians, the Massachusetts legislature set aside hundreds of acres for the Massipees – Mashpee Plantation – and in the 19C this large parcel of land became the town of Mashpee. The **Old Indian Meeting House** *(Meetinghouse Road, off of Rte 28; open June through October, Saturday and Sunday 12 noon to 4 PM)* built in 1684 for Richard Bourne's praying Indians is the oldest meetinghouse on the Cape

Falmouth ★. – Pop 25 007. Despite its development as a tourist town, Falmouth has retained its quaint 19C atmosphere. Lovely old homes stand near the green.

Woods Hole. – This former whaling port is a world center for the study of oceanography and marine life. Three large organizations operate in Woods Hole:

National Marine Fisheries Service. – Foreign ships are often seen at Woods Hole because of the international scope of the studies that are carried on by the Service. The **Aquarium,** used by the Fisheries Service in its research, may be visited *(open late June to mid-September 10 AM to 4:30 PM; the rest of the year 9 AM to 4 PM weekdays only).*

Marine Biological Laboratory. – The approximately four hundred scientists working at the MBL are engaged in conducting research in the field of marine fauna and flora.

Woods Hole Oceanographic Institute. – Studies conducted by the Oceanographic Institute deal with ocean currents, marine life, topography of the ocean floor. The Institute has three laboratories and a fleet of ocean-going vessels, most famous of these vessels being *Alvin*, a small submarine that was used in locating the H-bomb off of Spain in 1966.

Martha's Vineyard and Nantucket. – *Steamship Wharf (for schedule and additional information see pp 134 and 137).*

■ THE CAPE COD CANAL

The Cape Cod Canal, dug between 1909 and 1914, made Cape Cod an island joined to the mainland by the Sagamore and Bourne bridges (for automobiles), and a railroad bridge, with pyramidal-topped towers, that resembles the Tower Bridge in London.

The 544 ft central span of the railroad bridge acts as a giant elevator that can be lowered in roughly 2 1/2 minutes to allow a train to cross the bay.

Cruises (time: 2 and 3 hours) operate on the Canal spring through fall; departures from Onset Bay Pier. For rates and schedule ☎ (617) 775-7185.

Aptucxet Trading Post. – *From the rotary on the Cape Cod side of Bourne Bridge, follow the sign for Mashpee, then Shore Road. Turn right onto Aptucxet Road and follow the signs. Open mid-April to mid-October 10 AM (1 PM Sunday) to 5 PM; closed Tuesday mid-April through June and September to mid-October; $1.50, Children 50¢.*

(From a photo by Peter H. Dreyer.)

The Bourne Railroad Bridge.

The Pilgrims established this trading post in 1627 to promote trade with the Dutch from New Amsterdam, and the Wampanoag Indians. Furs, sugar, tobacco and cloth were bought and sold here, with wampum made by the Indians from shells, serving as currency.

The present building was reconstructed in 1930 on the foundations of the former trading post. Inside there are examples of the goods bartered. An ancient Rune Stone found in Bourne bears an inscription that has been translated as: "God Gives us Light Abundantly." A saltworks similar to those used by early settlers on the Cape to evaporate salt from seawater, has been built near the canal.

CONCORD ★★

Michelin tourist map - fold 16 – 20 miles west of Boston – Pop 16 455

Quiet and refined, a colonial town with beautiful homes tucked amidst the rustic landscape, Concord is a very desirable place to live.

Named in the 17C for a "concord" of peace between the Indians and the settlers, this small town was the site 150 years later of a confrontation between American patriots and British soldiers that changed the course of American history forever. April 19, 1775 following a skirmish with the minutemen at Lexington, the British marched to Concord. At the **Old North Bridge** the untrained, poorly equipped farmers stood their ground against His Majesty's troops, triggering the "shot heard 'round the world" and the American Revolution. *(For an account of the events leading up to April 19 see p 131).*

Concord has had a distinguished literary past as well having been the home, in the 19C, of intellectuals and writers such as Ralph Waldo Emerson, Henry David Thoreau, Nathaniel Hawthorne and Bronson Alcott.

Transcendentalism. – **Ralph Waldo Emerson** (1803-1882), a native of Concord, popularized transcendentalism (a philosophical movement characterized by mystical pantheism) and expressed his philosophical ideas in his *Essays on Nature,* a series of lectures he delivered across the United States. Other writers and thinkers attracted by the liberal ideas and return to nature inherent to transcendentalism, came to Concord to live near Emerson. Among them was **Henry David Thoreau** (1817-1868) who built a cabin in the woods near Walden Lake where he lived from 1845 to 1847. Thoreau's *Walden* is an account of the author's personal experiences during this period.

Nathaniel Hawthorne, Margaret Fuller and other intellectuals founded Brook Farm, an experimental community that was envisioned as a retreat from Victorian society, and a return to a simple way of life. Amos Bronson Alcott, a philosopher of transcendental thought, established his School of Philosophy adjacent to Orchard House where his daughter, Louisa May Alcott, wrote an account of her childhood in *Little Women*.

Admirers come to Concord to tour the literary shrines associated with these writers: the Emerson House, the Wayside where Nathaniel lived for several years, the Orchard House and School of Philosophy, and to visit Sleepy Hollow Cemetery *(p 127)* where many of them have been laid to rest.

■ **SIGHTS** *time: 2 hours*

Minute Man National Historical Park★. – The Minute Man National Historical Park was established to commemorate the events that took place April 19, 1775 along the Battle Road *(Rte 2A between Lexington and Concord)* and in the towns of Lexington, Lincoln and Concord. Sections of the 750 acre park are located in each of the three towns.

The principal attractions in the park are:

Battle Road Visitor Center. – *Off of Rte 2A in Lexington. Open April through November 8:30 AM to 5 PM. Information on park programs is available.*

A movie and an electric map program relating to the events of April 19 are shown.

(From a re-engraving, Boston Athenaeum.)

The Engagement at the North Bridge in Concord.

North Bridge Unit★★. – A replica of the **Old North Bridge★** (A) marks the place where the farmers advanced on the British and the "shot heard 'round the world" was fired. Emerson immortalized the old "rude bridge" in his poem the *Concord Hymn. (Brief interpretive talks at the North Bridge April through November weather permitting.)* Daniel Chester French's famous statue of the **Minute Man** nearby, honors the patriots who resisted the British at Concord. The **North Bridge Visitor Center** (B) *(walk up the road from the North Bridge)* has exhibits and provides information regarding Ranger talks and other special programs (open 8:30 AM to 5 PM; closed January 1 and December 25).*

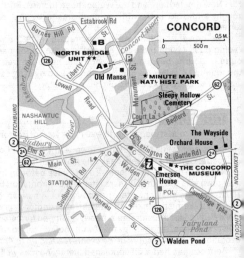

As you leave, on the right is the **Old Manse** *(guided tours – 30 min – June through October 10 AM (1 PM Sundays and holidays) to 4:30 PM,* closed Tuesday and Wednesday; mid-April through May Saturday and Sunday only $2.75)* where Ralph Waldo Emerson and later Nathaniel Hawthorne lived.

The Wayside. – *Guided tours (25 min) mid-April through October 9:30 AM to 5 PM; close Wednesday and Thursday; $1.00.*

The residence of Concord's muster master in 1775, the house was, in the ne century, the home of Nathaniel Hawthorne (who named the house), Margaret Sydney (at thoress of *Five Little Peppers and How They Grew*), and Bronson Alcott, who at one tim hoped to establish a community similar to Brook Farm *(see Transcendentalism p 12 here.*

The Concord Museum★. – *Lexington Rd and Cambridge Tpk. Guided tours (45 min) 10 AM (1 PM Sunday) to 4 PM; January and February 10 AM (1 PM Sunday) to 3 PM, closed Monday, Tuesday and Wednesday; $3.00.*

The museum's gracious setting and handsome brick exterior suggest its tastefully decorated interior. Admirers of early American furnishings will enjoy visiting the fifteen period rooms that reflect the style trends in America from the 17C to the 19C. One of the lanterns used to signal the riders April 18, 1775, a diorama of the battle at Old North Bridge, and the belongings used by Thoreau at Walden Pond *(see below)* are displayed.

Orchard House and School of Philosophy. – *399 Lexington Road. Guided tours (30 min) April to mid-September 10 AM (1 PM Sunday) to 4:30 PM; mid-September through October, 1 to 4:30 PM; $2.75.*

Orchard House was the home of the Alcott family from 1858 to 1877, the period during which Louisa May Alcott wrote her autobiographical novel *Little Women* (1868). The **School of Philosophy** built on the hillside, was operated by her father, Bronson Alcott, until the end of the 19C and is at present a center for the study of 19C American philosophy.

Ralph Waldo Emerson House. – *28 Cambridge Turnpike at Route 2A. Guided tours (30 min) mid-April to late October 10 AM (2 PM Sundays, 1 PM holidays) to 4:30 PM; closed Monday through Wednesday; $2.50.*

The house is furnished as it was during the years the New England writer philosopher-intellectual Ralph Waldo Emerson lived here (1835-1882).

Walden Pond Reservation. – *A road from the meadow leads to Walden Pond.* Thoreau *(p 125)* built his cabin on the shore of this lake. A cairn marking the site of the cabin can be reached from the parking lot by following trail signs to a granite post where the trail turns right before reaching the site *(time: 15 min).*

Sleepy Hollow Cemetery. – *From Concord center turn right onto Rte 62. Enter the cemetery through the second gate on the left. Follow signs for Author's Ridge. The road leads to a parking lot.* A short climb from the parking lot leads to **Author's Ridge** where the Alcotts, Nathaniel Hawthorne and Margaret Sydney are buried. A large boulder marks the grave of Ralph Waldo Emerson.

DEERFIELD ★★

Michelin tourist map - fold 15 – 33 miles north of Springfield – Pop 4 503

Deerfield's mile-long Main Street with its 18 and 19C dwellings and shops provides a picture of a wealthy early American farming community. A **church** (1824) and the administration building of **Deerfield Academy** stand on the grassy **common**, near the post office – a replica of a Puritan meetinghouse. A little further down the street is the **Deerfield Inn.**

A Frontier Town. – Deerfield was not always the tranquil town it appears to be today. Settled in 1669, Deerfield was abandoned in 1675 after the massacre at Bloody Brook and again in 1704 after the village was burned down. A Treaty of Peace signed in 1735 encouraged the settlers to return, and during the following century the village grew into one of the most prosperous agricultural centers in New England.

Architecture and Preservation. – The restoration of Deerfield's colonial and Federal structures, initiated in the 19C, was the first project of its kind in the United States. Painstakingly renovated and redecorated these large, substantial-looking structures have an air of well-being about them, reflecting the prosperity of their early owners. Many of the dwellings are topped with a gambrel roof, and adorned with richly carved entranceways characteristic of the style of the Connecticut Valley; within, the interiors are luxurious and elegant, evidence of the wealth of this early rural community.

■ HISTORIC DEERFIELD★★

Open 9:30 AM (11 AM Sunday) to 4:30 PM; closed major holidays. Guided tours 35 min per house; one day ticket $6.50. Tickets available in the Hall Tavern. A visitor orientation film is shown at the Hall Tavern.

Twelve buildings are open to the public. Special collections are displayed in the **Helen Geier Flynt Fabric Hall** (textiles), the **Parker and Russell Silver Shop** (silver) and the Hall Tavern (pewter).

Ashley House★★. – 1730. The house is typical of the dwellings that were built in the Connecticut Valley in the 18C. The interior has richly carved woodwork and beautiful furnishings. This house was the home of the Parson Jonathan Ashley, a devoted Tory who, despite threats from the townspeople to bar him from the church and deny him his salary, persisted in his loyalty to the Crown during the Revolution.

Wright House★. – 1824. The light and airy Federal dwelling has American paintings, porcelains and a very fine collection of Federal and Chippendale furniture.

Asa Stebbins House★. – 1810. The Stebbins House, recognized by its arched doorway, contains a splendid collection of wall coverings including 19C French wallpaper illustrating Captain Cook's voyages to the South Seas, and wall decorations executed by an itinerant artist.

Hall Tavern★. – 1760. The tavern has many rooms decorated with 17 and 18C New England furniture. The Ballroom is embellished with stenciled designs.

Frary House. – 1720. This early dwelling was later enlarged to serve as a tavern. There is a ballroom with fiddlers' gallery and rooms filled with country antiques.

Wells-Thorn House. – This house exemplifies the evolution that occurred in the architecture of 18C Deerfield. The kitchen (1717) retains its early primitive characteristics while the refined paneling, furnishings and the use of a variety of colors in the later section (1751) reflect the increased desire for elegance and comfort that accompanied the owner's good fortune.

Dwight Barnard House. – 1725. The facade is ornamented with a handsome, skillfully carved doorway, a feature typical of Connecticut Valley architecture.

Memorial Hall. – This brick building houses the museum of the **Pocumtuck Valley Memorial Association**, a memorial to the Pocumtuck Indians and the settlers of Deerfield. Among the exhibits is the door from the original Indian House, the only house not destroyed in the 1704 raid.

Door of the Dwight Barnard House.

FALL RIVER

Michelin tourist map - fold 23 – Pop 92 038

Warehouses and factories standing along the river are reminiscent of Fall River's heyday as a major 19 and 20C textile center. During the same period, luxurious steamships of the **Fall River Line** linked New York to Boston, and carried the wealthy to their summer cottages in Newport. Fall River was hard hit by the Depression, then by the migration of the textile mills to the South and the development of synthetics; however, textiles and clothing have remained among the city's most important products.

■ BATTLESHIP COVE★★

Access from 195, Exit 5. Open 9 AM to 5 PM (6 PM July and August); closed January 1, Thanksgiving Day and December 25; $6.00, under 14, $3.00.

In 1965 the battleship *USS Massachusetts* was sailed to Fall River to serve as a permanent memorial to the 13 000 Massachusetts men and women who gave their lives in service to their country during World War II. Since 1965 several other naval ships have joined the *Massachusetts* as exhibits at this outdoor museum.

PT Boat 796. – The ferocious shark painted on the hull of the boat symbolizes the threat these modest-sized boats were to the enemy. PT boat memorabilia is displayed.

Submarine Lionfish. – This World War II submarine carried 20 torpedoes and a crew of 75. The vessel's sophisticated operating equipment can be seen in the control room.

Destroyer USS Joseph P. Kennedy. – The ship was named for the eldest of the four Kennedy brothers who was killed on a volunteer mission in World War II. The *Kennedy*, a typical World War II destroyer, carried a crew of 275.

Battleship USS Massachusetts. – *Earphones are distributed at the entrance to the vessel for a detailed, taped visit of the ship (time: 2 hours).* Awesome for its enormous size and the large crew required for its operation (2 300 men), the *Massachusetts* logged 200 000 miles in wartime service between 1942 and 1945, and was the first to fire 16-inch shells against the enemy (off the coast of North Africa in 1942). On the upper deck observe the Japanese suicide sub, similar to those used by Kamikaze pilots against American ships. Below deck, sections of the ship have been set aside for an exhibit devoted to aviation and for the Memorial Room honoring the Massachusetts men and women killed in World War II. Narrow corridors lead visitors past the barbershop, laundry, shoe shop, and other service areas that were indispensable aboard such a large ship.

Fall River Heritage State Park Visitors Center. – *Take the pedestrian bridge at Battleship Cove. Open 9 AM to 4:30 PM (8 PM mid-May to mid-September), Thursday evening 9 PM; closed major holidays and Monday mid-September to mid-May. Slide show presented hourly late June to late fall; 10:30 AM, 2 PM and 3 PM the rest of the year.*

The red brick riverside Center has the appearance of a 19C New England mill. From the tower visitors are treated to a sweeping view of the entire Mt. Hope Bay region.

A slide show *(time: 1/2 hour)* relating the history of the city's textile industry is shown daily.

Marine Museum. – *70 Water Street. Open June through September 9 AM (10 AM Saturday and Sunday) weekdays only to 7 PM; the rest of the year 9 AM to 4:30 PM; $2.00.*

The museum's photographs, marine paintings, prints and ship models evoke memories of the region's maritime past and the Fall River Line. Accurately constructed ship models such as the 28 ft model of the *Titanic* and the 13 ft 9 inch model of the *Puritan*, and photographs of the plush Victorian interiors found on the Fall River steamers, suggest the luxury and comfort passengers riding on the Fall River liners enjoyed.

The times given after the distance for drives and excursions,
allow the traveler to see and enjoy the scenery.

FRUITLANDS MUSEUMS ★★

Michelin tourist map - fold 16 – 22 miles north of Worcester

The museum is located on Prospect Hill Road in Harvard. From Rte 2 take Rte 110 to Harvard, then Old Shirley Road. Follow the signs. Open May 15 to October 15, 10 AM to 5 PM, closed Monday; $4.00, under 16, $1.00.

In 1843 the philosopher of Concord **Bronson Alcott** *(p 126)*, together with the English reformer **Charles Lane** and a group of their followers, attempted to establish a Utopian community on the 18C farm known as Fruitlands. Idealistic, and reacting against the materialism of the times, they became vegetarians, wore only linen clothing and spent most of their time outdoors. Their return to nature lasted but a few months, as disillusioned or still "searching," one by one, members of the community left Fruitlands.

Fruitlands, the farm that was for a brief while their home, is on a hill that dominates the Nashua Valley. The farmhouse has been transformed into a museum of transcendentalism and other museums on the grounds treat varied aspects of early American culture. From the restaurant there is a **view** of the region and Mounts Monadnock and Wachusetts.

Fruitlands. – The museum of transcendentalism *(p 125)* is arranged in this 18C farmhouse. The museum has mementoes of the philosophers and writers of the period: Emerson, Thoreau, Alcott.

Shaker House. – 1794. This simple Shaker house was moved to Fruitlands after the Harvard Shaker Community, founded in the late 18C, was disbanded in 1919. The house contains exhibits of Shaker industries, products and furnishings.

American Indian Museum. – Two statues by Philip Sears: *The Dreamer* and *He Who Shoots the Stars* flank the entrance to the building, inviting visitors to enter and view the superb collection of North American Indian artifacts.

Picture Gallery. – The primitive portraits and landscape paintings hanging in this building are representative of America's 19C itinerant portraitists and the artists of the **Hudson River School** (Cole, Bierstadt, etc.).

*For your trip to Canada – use the **Michelin Green Guide Canada**.*

HANCOCK SHAKER VILLAGE ★★★

Michelin tourist map - fold 14 – *Local map p 85*

The Hancock Shaker Village, an active Shaker community between 1790 and 1960, is today a museum village that tells the story of this sect, which for more than two centuries has practiced a form of communal living that continues to interest outsiders.

Origin of the Shakers. – In the mid-18C a group of Quakers in Manchester, England were called the "Shaking Quakers" because of the dances they performed during their religious services. Later, they became known simply as the Shakers. In 1774 a member of the group, **Ann Lee**, who preached under the name "Ann the Word," emigrated from England to America to avoid persecution for her religious beliefs. Ann, known to the Shakers as Mother Ann, settled in New York where she and her followers dedicated themselves to preaching the beliefs of Shakerism. They attracted New Believers wherever they went, and by the mid-19C the Shaker movement had reached its peak, with a total of 19 communities in the United States. The number of Shaker communities has since steadily declined, although the Shaker experience in communal life never ceases to fascinate people from all walks of life.

The Shaker Community. – Life in the community was based on the principles of community property, equality of the sexes, celibacy, separation from the outside world and public confession of sin. Men and women lived in families of thirty to one hundred persons with responsibilities shared by the Elders and Eldresses (two men and women from the village). Duties in the field, shops and kitchen were divided equally among the members and all activities in the community were governed by a rigid time schedule. Because members lived a celibate life, converts or New Believers were important to the continued existence of the community. New Believers came to the community from the outside world and from the Shaker society as well, since orphans adopted by the Society often remained and became permanent members.

Shaker Industries. – Guided by the words of Mother Ann: "Do all your work as though you had 1 000 years to live, and as though you were going to die tomorrow," the Shakers became well-known for the products they made. Shaker products, invented for the use of Shakers only, were in time marketed across the country as the Shakers grew dependent on the outside world for certain goods. The garden and seed industry was their specialty; however, the Shaker label on the brooms, furniture ... they made, was a guarantee that these items, as well as the seeds and herbs, were of the highest quality.

Architecture. – Shaker architecture was a model of simplicity, purity and functionalism. Buildings were designed to serve a specific purpose and were constructed from materials that were best suited to that purpose. The order and peace that guided the religious life of the Shakers inspired the designs of their buildings: the Brick Dwelling – spacious, light and airy *(see p 130)* had 100 large doors, 245 cupboard doors, 369 drawers, and 95 windows with 3 194 panes of glass. Shaker innovations such as the pegboard, sliding cupboard and low-back chair reflect the functionalism of their products.

129

Visit. – *Open Memorial Day weekend through October, 9:30 AM to 5 PM; $6.50. A slide show orientation (20 min) to the Village and a documentary film (1 hour) on the Shakers are presented.* From the Visitors Center, pass the **herb garden,** then the **garden tool shed.**

Poultry House. – This former poultry house has exhibits of Shaker life, industry and religion.

Brick Dwelling ★★. – The community dining room, kitchens and retiring rooms were located in this structure. Several rooms now serve as workshops *(see Architecture p 129).*

(From an engraving, Collection of the Library of Congress.)

Shakers Worshipping.

The Shops. – In these shops the Brothers made tinware, brooms, oval boxes and clocks; and the Sisters dried herbs, wove cloth and made dairy products.

The Round Stone Barn ★★★. – Built in 1826, the barn is a masterpiece of Shaker architecture and functionalism. Wagons entered the third level and emptied their hay into the central haymow. On the middle level stables radiated out from the central manger, making it easy for one person to feed the entire herd. Manure pits were located on the lower level.

Nearby are the **Tan House,** which served as a blacksmith shop, cider room, tannery; the **Ice House** and the **Printing Office.**

Trustees Office and Store. – Official community business was conducted in this building. Items similar to those made by the Shakers are sold at the Shaker Fancy Goods Store.

On the other side of Route 20 are the Shaker **cemetery,** the **school** and **ministry shop.**

The Meeting House. – The Shakers met here every Sunday for their religious services. Neatness and symmetry characterize the overall design of the structure, and the meeting room, a large open hall, provided ample space for the dancing. The offices and living quarters of the community's spiritual leaders were on the second floor.

Laundry and Machine Shop. – The machines in this large building were at one time activated by a turbine, powered by water flowing from a mountain reservoir to the north of the village. A herb and seed room and the laundry are in other sections of this building.

HINGHAM

Michelin tourist map - fold 17 – *Map of the Boston region p 89* (DX) – 19 miles southeast of Boston – Pop 19 942

Hingham is a lovely old town on the South Shore. A suburb of Boston, this small coastal settlement has pretty, tree-shaded streets lined with 18 and 19C dwellings.

Old Ship Church ★. – *90 Main Street. Open July and August 12 noon to 4 PM; closed Monday.* Built by ship's carpenters in 1681, Old Ship Church is the last remaining Puritan meetinghouse in the United States. Inside, the beautifully crafted pulpit, galleries, columns, paneling and box pews remain unpainted and the interior glows with the rich tones of natural wood. The church probably received its popular name, Old Ship, because of the curved ceiling timbers which give the roof the appearance of a ship's hull turned upside down.

World's End ★. – *Follow Rte 3A to the Hingham Harbor rotary, then take Summer Street east 1/2 mile. Turn left onto Martin's Lane and continue 3/4 mile to sign for World's End. Open April through October 10 AM (8 AM Saturday and Sunday) to 5 PM; the rest of the year 11 AM to 4 PM; $2.50. Trail access: to the left of the parking lot. From the entrance bear left onto the wide gravel road; always take the left fork. (Time: 1 1/2 hours RT.)*

This "end of the world" is a quiet peninsula only 14 miles from Boston. Gentle hillsides are covered with grassy meadows, shaded paths and wildflowers. The trail leads past Pine Hill, Planters Hill and then over the Bar (a narrow neck of land) before arriving at the tip of the peninsula World's End. Views of Boston and Nantasket beach.

IPSWICH

Michelin tourist map - fold 17 – 26 miles northeast of Boston – Pop 11 566

This small colonial town bordered by white sandy beaches and woodlands attracts many artists and tourists. The popularity of Ipswich has given rise to the concentration of restaurants and shops in and near the center of town, and the gastronomically famous **Ipswich clam** is a regional favorite. Beautifully restored 17 and 18C dwellings line the streets of Ipswich, enhancing its centuries-old charm.

Whipple House. – *Near the green. Guided tours (30 min.) April 15 through October, 10 AM (1 PM Sunday) to 5 PM; closed Monday; $2.00.*

This handsome dwelling (1640) acquired by John Whipple in 1642 is evidence of the comfort and refinement that graced the lives of many early New Englanders. The house has spacious rooms, enormous fireplaces and period furnishings.

Richard T. Crane Beach Reservation★. – *From Rte 1 A, south of Ipswich (opposite the Whipple House) take Argilla Road 6 miles. Open 8 AM to one hour before sunset (6 PM Memorial Day to Labor Day). Parking: Memorial Day to Labor Day $10.00 ($6.50 weekdays); off season $3.75 ($3.50 weekdays).*

This sandy beach stretches for several miles along the coast. The dunes beyond the beach are covered with a pitch pine forest and red maple swamp. The best way to explore the area is by following the **Pine Hollow Trail** *(access to the right of the parking lot; time: 45 min).* During the summer concerts are presented at the mansion on **Castle Hill**, the former residence of the Crane family.

EXCURSION

Topsfield. – Pop 5 700. *7 miles from Ipswich by Topsfield Road. From the center of Ipswich take Market Street to Topsfield Road.* Topsfield was a prosperous farming village until the 19C, when it became a residential community.

Parson Capen House. – *1 Howlett Street, facing the green. Open mid-June to mid-September Wednesday, Friday and Sunday 1 to 4:30 PM; $1.00.*

The pitched roof, central chimney, overhanging stories and hanging pendants of this Elizabethan dwelling (1681) reflect the trend towards English building traditions in American colonial architecture.

LEXINGTON ★★

Michelin tourist map - fold 16 – Pop 29 033

This serene residential community has been historically inseparable in the minds of most Americans from the town of Concord since April 19, 1775 when British and colonial troops clashed at Lexington and at Concord, triggering the events that exploded into the American Revolution. The Revolutionary War sites and monuments related to that day 200 years ago have been preserved and allow visitors who come each year, to retrace step by step the incidents that occurred April 19, as the British marched from Boston to Lexington and on to Concord.

April 19, 1775. – Tensions between the colonists and the British increased steadily following the passage of the Stamp Act in 1765. In 1774 the colonists established their own legislative body, the Provincial Congress, with John Hancock as its president and within a year the Congress had created a militia and stockpiled arms in Concord for colonial troops. England reacted swiftly by dispatching troops to Boston and closing the city's port; and in an attempt to put an end to the rebels' activity, General Gage, the leader of the British troops in Boston, decided to march on Concord and seize the weapons hidden there. Forewarned of the General's plans, the colonists were ready. On the evening of April 18, as 700 British soldiers began to march from Boston to Concord, several riders, including Paul Revere, rode off to warn John Hancock, John Adams and the people of Lexington and nearby towns, of the British advance.

During the early hours of April 19, seventy-seven minutemen who had spent the night at **Buckman Tavern** in Lexington awaiting the enemy columns, moved toward the **Green** where their leader, Captain Parker, advised them: "Stand your ground, don't fire unless fired upon, but if they mean to have a war, let it begin here!" However, at about 5 AM as the British began to arrive and Parker realized his men were greatly outnumbered, he gave the order to disperse ... but it was too late: a shot rang out and during the skirmish that followed eight minutemen were killed and ten others lay wounded. The British commander ordered his men to regroup and they marched on to Concord.

In Concord, the minutemen who had arrived from nearby villages observed from a hilltop as British soldiers began to search for the supplies. Aware that fires were burning in the town below, and fearful that the British would burn Concord to the ground, the patriots descended to the **Old North Bridge**, where they found themselves confronted by the enemy. A shot was fired and a battle ensued until the British, weary and reduced in numbers, began their retreat to Boston along the Battle Road. Snipers firing from the woods added to the number of British casualties for the day, while yet another skirmish between the two forces took place before nightfall at **Meriam's Corner**.

Minute Man National Historical Park★. – To commemorate the events that took place April 18-19, 1775 a national park has been created along the Battle Road *(Route 2A)* between Lexington, Lincoln and Concord *(for historical details see Concord p 125).*

E. Am. 6

■ SIGHTS

The Lexington Green★★. – The first confrontation between the British soldiers and the minutemen on April 19 took place on this triangular green. Henry Kitson's statue of the **Minuteman (A)** represents the leader of the Lexington militia, Captain Parker. Seven of the minutemen killed here that day are buried beneath the **Revolutionary Monument (B)**.

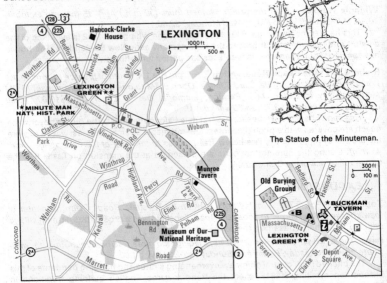

The Statue of the Minuteman.

Old Burying Ground. – In the old cemetery behind the church there are well-preserved examples of gravestone sculpture dating from the 17C *(see illustration p 32)*.

Hancock-Clarke House. – *36 Hancock Street. Guided tours (1/2 hour) mid-April through October 10 AM (1 PM Sunday) to 5 PM; $2.00, under 16, 50¢. Combination ticket ($4.50) valid for Hancock-Clarke House, Buckman Tavern and Munroe Tavern.*
   Samuel Adams and John Hancock were at this house (dating from 1698) the evening of April 18 when Paul Revere rode into Lexington to warn them to flee.

Buckman Tavern★. – *Guided tours (1/2 hour); same hours and admission as above.*
   The minutemen gathered here on the evening of April 18 to await the arrival of the British troops. Following the battle between the British and the militia on the green, the minutemen who had been wounded were carried to Buckman Tavern, where they were given medical care.
   Restored to its original 18C appearance, the tavern appears as it did then with its barroom, bedchambers, ballroom, separate rooms set aside for women, and attic where for a few pennies a night drovers were permitted to sleep.

Munroe Tavern. – *133 Massachusetts Avenue. Guided tours (1/2 hour); same hours and admission as the Hancock-Clarke House.*
   This 17C tavern served as headquarters and hospital for the British troops the afternoon of April 19 during their retreat from Concord to Boston.

Museum of Our National Heritage. – *Rte 2A and Massachusetts Avenue. Open 10 AM to 5 PM; Sunday 12 noon to 5 PM; closed major holidays.*
   This contemporary brick and glass building contains a museum and library of American history. Exhibits feature the growth and development of the nation from its founding to the present. Weekend programs include films, concerts and special events.

LOWELL
Michelin tourist map - fold 16 – Pop 93 473

   In the early 19C businessman-innovator **Francis Cabot Lowell** (1775-1817), who had developed the power loom for American use, selected this site where the Merrimack River drops 32 ft within the distance of a mile, as the location of the planned industrial community he intended to build. He died before his plans to develop the area were realized; however, within five years a group of Boston investors undertook the project. The result was a mill town of red brick factories, company-owned dwellings, warehouses, stores – even company-owned burial grounds. Incorporated as a town in 1826, Lowell quickly rose to prominence as a world leading producer of textiles. The city prospered until the crash of 1929; then the exodus of textile companies to the South led to a period of economic depression.
   Today, Lowell is once again a principal manufacturing center. Urban renewal, the efforts of preservationists, and the relocation of Wang Labs, a major employer, to Lowell in the late 1970s have been significant factors in the revitalization of the city's economy.

Sections of the city were declared a National Park in 1978, and since that time Lowell's 5 1/2 mile canal system and many of its 19C buildings have been restored. Pleasant park-like walkways border the **Merrimack Canal** in the heart of the downtown area.

Lowell National Historical Park. – Administered by the National Park Service, the Park was established to preserve and interpret Lowell's mills, canal system and other related structures and buildings. Rangers conduct tours *(free)* on the history, industrialization and growth of Lowell in the 19C *(year round; time: 1-2 hours)*. The **Mill and Canal Tour★** *(Memorial Day to Columbus Day only, 9 AM to 3:30 PM; time: 2 1/2 hours)* by trolley, canal barge and foot provides an insight into the workings of the canal system; short boat trips on the Northern Canal, Pawtucket Canal and Merrimack River are included. *Reservations required. Apply at the Visitor Center (see below).*

Visitor Center. – *246 Market Street. Open 8:30 AM to 5 PM year round.* ☎ *(617) 459-1000.*

The Center is located in a renovated turn-of-the-century mill complex which now houses artist's studios, shops and apartments. Exhibits and a multi-image slide presentation serve as an introduction to the city of Lowell from the 1820s to the present.

The **Lowell Heritage State Park Waterpower Exhibit** *(25 Shattuck Street, open 9 AM to 4:30 - 9 PM Thursday)* opposite the Visitor Center explores the uses of waterpower from early times to the generation of hydro-electricity.

EXCURSIONS

Andover. – *Pop 27 203. 11 miles from Lowell by Rte 495 North, then Rte 28.* This small colonial village is home to the select preparatory school, **Phillips Academy** (1778). The focal point of the village is the Academy's spacious green and attractively designed buildings: Bulfinch Hall, the Andover Inn, the Archaeological Museum and the Addison Gallery of American Art. The **Addison Gallery of American Art** has a noteworthy collection of American paintings and sculpture *(open 10 AM - 2 PM Sunday - to 5 PM; closed Mondays, August, and holidays)*.

North Andover. – *Pop 21 670. 11 miles from Lowell by Rte 495 North to Massachusetts Avenue Exit, turn right onto Massachusetts Avenue.*

As the production of cloth shifted from the home to the factory in the 18 and 19C, North Andover developed into an important textile center. At the **Museum of American Textile History** *(800 Massachusetts Avenue; open 10 AM (1 PM Saturday and Sunday) to 5 PM; closed Mondays and holidays; $2.00)* permanent exhibits of tools, charts, illustrations and machines trace the changes that occurred in the production of textiles, as machine-made processes replaced the traditional methods of making cloth.

MARBLEHEAD ★

Michelin tourist map - fold 17 – *Map of the Boston region p 89* (**DU**) – 18 miles northeast of Boston – Pop 19 755

Prior to the Revolution this small fishing port had grown into a flourishing center of trade. Marblehead vessels returned home with great wealth, and their owners and captains spent freely in building the colonial and Georgian homes that line the narrow, winding streets of Old Marblehead. Losses suffered during the war, competition from other ports and the gale of 1846, which destroyed ten Marblehead ships and killed 65 men, caused the inhabitants to turn to industry – shoe manufacturing – for a living.

The sea once more was the source of prosperity for Marblehead when, in the late 19 and early 20C, the town developed into a resort and boating center because of its magnificent harbor.

Marblehead continues to be one of the major yachting centers on the east coast. In season the sight of large numbers of sail and motor pleasure craft crowding the harbor is especially impressive viewed from **Fort Sewall** *(at the end of Front Street)*, **Crocker Park** *(off of Front Street)* or from the lighthouse on **Marblehead Neck**, a select residential area.

Jeremiah Lee Mansion. – *161 Washington Street. Guided tours (45 min) mid-May to mid-October 10 AM to 4 PM; closed Sunday; $2.25.*

The exterior of this dignified 16 room Georgian dwelling constructed in 1768 for the successful merchant Jeremiah Lee, has been painted and sanded to appear as if it were constructed of stone.

Inside, the immense entrance hall, with its grandiose proportions, highly polished mahogany woodwork and English mural papers, makes this house one of the most memorable of the period in New England. The house is furnished and decorated with objects brought back from around the world by Marblehead ships.

An upstairs room contains a group of brightly colored primitive paintings by the Marblehead artist John Frost, formerly a Grand Banks fisherman.

Abbot Hall. – *Town Hall. Open 8 AM (9 AM Saturday, 11 AM Sunday) to 9 PM (5 PM Monday and Friday, 6 PM Saturday and Sunday); closed weekends November to Memorial Day.*

The familiar patriotic painting, **The Spirit of '76**, painted by A. M. Willard to celebrate the nation's centennial, hangs in the Selectman's Room. The picture was given to the town by General John Devereux whose son was the model for the drummer boy.

Walkers, campers, smokers - fire is fatal to forest land.

MARTHA'S VINEYARD ★★

Michelin tourist map - fold 23 – Pop 9 540

In 1602 when Bartholomew Gosnold landed on this island he named it Martha's Vineyard for the abundance of wild grapes he found growing here, and in honor of his daughter, Martha. No longer covered with wild grapes, this triangular-shaped piece of land, 5 miles south of Cape Cod, has a landscape that resembles that of the Cape: wild, rolling heaths spotted with ponds and lakes give way to forests of oak and pine, seaside cliffs and broad sandy beaches.

The towns on the Vineyard are small fishing villages and summer resorts, each with its own blend of history and character.

Getting There. – By Ferry – The **Steamship Authority** offers daily service between Woods Hole and Vineyard Haven *(time: 45 min one way)*. Some ferries continue on to Oak Bluffs and Nantucket *(time: 2 hours one way)*.

For information on fares and schedules and reservations for automobiles write: Steamship Authority, PO Box 284, Woods Hole, MA 02543 ☎ (617) 540-2022. Toll free from Martha's Vineyard ☎ 693-9130.

By Plane. – Martha's Vineyard is serviced by *Provincetown-Boston Airline ☎ (617) 693-2070; ☎ toll free (800) 722-3597.*

Staying on Martha's Vineyard. – To get around on the island there are automobile, bicycle and moped rentals available at Vineyard Haven, Oak Bluffs and Edgartown *(auto and bicycle rentals only)*; or take the shuttle bus *(departs from the ferry dock)* that operates between these towns. Bus tours of the island *(time: 2 1/2 hours)* depart from the ferry wharf.

For assistance in obtaining **lodging** *inquire at the Chamber of Commerce, PO Box 1698, Vineyard Haven, MA 02568 ☎ (617) 693-0085.*

Beaches. – The island's white sandy beaches are major attractions. Because of the warming influence of the Gulf Stream, water temperatures of island beaches are mild.

Katama Beach on the south shore *(follow Katama Road to South Beach Road – 3 miles)*, is a favorite of surfers. There are also public beaches in the towns.

VISIT

Allow one day – local map below

Begin at Vineyard Haven.

Vineyard Haven. – Gift shops and coffee shops will be found along the Main Street.

Oak Bluffs★. – Pop 2 214. In the 1830s the Methodists of Edgartown began to meet regularly in an oak grove at the northern end of town. Each summer the group attracted an increasingly larger number of followers who spent the summer in a tent camp situated a short distance from the place where religious services were held.

By the 1850s more than 12 000 persons were attending the annual services at Cottage City (as the encampment came to be known) and, by the end of the 19C, Cottage City had been renamed Oak Bluffs for the oak grove where the first revival meetings were held. At about the same time, small wooden cottages were built to replace the family tents that stood near the Tabernacle, the center of religious worship.

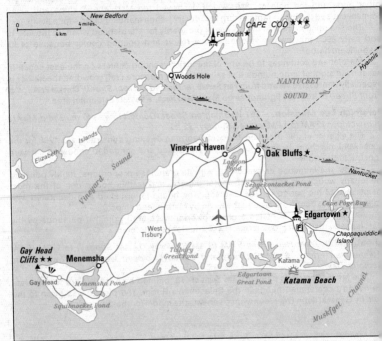

Gingerbread cottages.

Trinity Park and Gingerbread Cottages ★★. – *Leave the car near the harbor and follow Central Avenue to Cottage City.* Small ornate Victorian "gingerbread" houses, gaily painted and decorated with lacy wooden trim resembling the frosting on a cake, ring the Tabernacle, a beautiful example of ironwork architecture.

Edgartown ★. – Pop 2 633. Most of Edgartown's large, handsome dwellings were built in the 1820s and 1830s when the town was an important whaling center. A number of these homes line North Water Street and face Edgartown Harbor, once dominated by a fleet of whaling vessels and now filled with modern pleasure craft.

Opposite Edgartown is **Chappaquiddick Island** where private homes and unspoiled natural areas are sheltered by thick woodlands. The ferry *On Time*, so called because it has no regular schedule, provides service between Edgartown and Chappaquiddick.

Dukes County Historical Society. – *Open mid-June to mid-September 10 AM to 4:30 PM; closed Sundays, Mondays and holidays; the rest of the year Thursday and Friday 1 PM (10 AM Saturday) to 4 PM; $2.00.* The skill of the ship's carpenters who built the Thomas Cooke House (1765) is reflected in the fine interior wood paneling and trim. Artifacts related to whaling, including a picture of Captain Valentine Pease, master of the *Acushnet* (on which Herman Melville sailed) and model for Melville's Ahab in *Moby Dick,* offer glimpses of the era of whaling.

Katama Beach. – This sandy stretch of beach linking Edgartown to Chappaquiddick, extends the entire length of the south shore.

Drive across the island, east to west, through oak and pine forests. As the road approaches Gay Head, it begins to climb above Menemsha and Squibnocket Ponds where alewives spawn in the spring; from here there is a **view** of Menemsha.

Gay Head Cliffs ★★. – These 60 ft high cliffs composed of striated layers of clay are a rainbow of color: blue, tan, grey, red, white and orange. Dating back 100 million years, the cliffs contain fossils of prehistoric camels, wild horses and ancient whales. Erosion of the cliffs often causes the inshore waters to turn a reddish color. Gay Head's predominantly Indian population uses the clay to make the decorative pottery they offer for sale.

Menemsha. – With its picturesque lobster traps and weathered fishing sheds, this tiny waterfront village is a popular subject of photographs.

MOHAWK TRAIL ★★ _____

Michelin tourist map - fold 14

Route 2, a scenic stretch of highway from central Massachusetts to the Massachusetts-New York border, is known as the Mohawk Trail. Following an old Indian path that ran along the banks of the Deerfield and Cold Rivers, through the Connecticut valley and into the Berkshire Hills, the Trail passes through tiny mountaintop hamlets, sheer river gorges and penetrates thick forests. Views from the highway and off-road parking areas are especially spectacular during the foliage season.

From Greenfield to Williamstown – *67 miles – allow 3 hours*

Greenfield. – Pop 18 073. This small agricultural town at the eastern end of the Mohawk Trail is named for its fertile green valley.

Follow Rte 2. After 6 miles the road rises, affording views into the valley. Continue to the intersection with the road to Shelburne Falls (13 1/2 miles after Greenfield).

Shelburne Falls ★. – Pop 1 986. This quiet mountain village is located beside the falls of the Deerfield River. Glacial potholes, ground out of granite during the last Ice Age, can be seen on the riverbank near Salmon Falls *(Deerfield Avenue).*

Bridge of Flowers. – *On the south side of the bridge over the Deerfield River.* Originally used by trolleys, this bridge has been transformed into a 400 ft long path of flower beds above the Deerfield River.

Return to Rte 2. Two miles past Charlemont the road enters **Mohawk Trail State Forest**. At the entrance to the forest is the statue of an Indian brave, **Hail to the Sunrise**, created as a memorial to the Mohawk nation.

The road continues through a very mountainous and rugged section of Rte 2. Between Florida and North Adams there are good views from **Whitcomb Summit**: views of Mount Monadnock, Mount Greylock, the Green Mountains; **Western Summit**: view of the Hoosac Valley; and **Hairpin Curve**: expansive **views★★** of the Hoosac Valley, Berkshire Valley and Taconic Range.

Just before North Adams turn right onto Rte 8 North, then left after 1/2 mile.

Natural Bridge State Park★. – *Open mid-May to late October 10 AM to 6 PM (8 PM Saturdays, Sundays and holidays); $3.00 per car. Picnicking and walking trails.*

   The white marble natural bridge which gives the park its name rises 60 ft above the churning waters of a narrow 475 ft long chasm. Glaciers eroded, sculpted, and polished this marble which was formed primarily from deposits of seashells laid down about 550 million years ago.

(By permission of the
Mohawk Trail Association.)
Statue: Hail to the Sunrise.

North Adams. – Pop 17 387. North Adams's bulky red brick mill buildings are wistful reminders of the city's past as a leading industrial center in western Massachusetts. The mills attracted thousands of Canadians and Italians to settle in the area and in 1875, with the opening of the **Hoosac Tunnel** linking Massachusetts to the West, North Adams grew into a bustling railroad center as well. Manufacturing and light industry continue to support the economy today.

Western Gateway Heritage State Park. – *Rte 8 South.* Occupying the restored buildings of the city's old freight yard, this urban park preserves the history of North Adams's heyday as a manufacturing and railroad boom town. In the **Visitor Center** *(open June through October 10 AM to 6 PM – 9 PM Thursday, 8 PM Friday and Saturday; the rest of the year 10 AM to 4:30 PM – 9 PM Thursday)* displays tell the story of the Hoosac Tunnel, one of the major engineering feats of the 19C. Built over a period of 25 years (1851-1875), the 4.7 mile tunnel through the Hoosac Mountains marked the first use of nitroglycerin as a blasting agent, and was the longest tunnel in the nation when it was completed. Its glory has always been overshadowed, however, by the fact that almost 200 workers lost their lives during construction of the project.

Return to Rte 2 West, then 1 mile after North Adams center turn left onto Notch Road and follow the sign for Mount Greylock Reservation.

The road rises through wooded areas to the summit.

Mount Greylock★★★. – Located between the Taconic and Hoosac ranges, Mount Greylock (alt 3 491 ft) is the highest point in Massachusetts. The mountain was named for chief Grey Lock whose tribe once hunted on these lands. From the War Memorial Tower at the summit there is a magnificent **view★★★** of the entire region: the Berkshire Valley, the Taconics and nearby states.

Descend to North Adams and continue on Rte 2 West.

Williamstown★★. – *Description p 158.*

Business Hours – **Banks:** *9 AM to 3 PM.*
Shops: *10 AM to 5 PM (or 6 PM).*
Shopping Centers: *9 AM (or 10 AM) to 9 PM (or 10 PM).*
Post office: *8 AM to 5 PM (12 noon Saturday).*

NANTUCKET ★★★

Michelin tourist map - fold 24 - Pop 5 876

   Lying 30 miles south of the elbow of Cape Cod, Nantucket – an Indian name meaning "distant land" – is a triangular patch of land 14 miles long and 3 1/2 miles wide. The rather flat relief, sandy soil, rounded ponds and tree-studded moors are evidence of the island's glacial origins and underlying moraine *(p 120)*. Nantucket Island includes the village of the same name, situated on a magnificent harbor protected by a long, narrow barrier of sandy beach. The history of the island is interwoven with that of its famous port which was the world capital of the whaling industry in the early 19C.

   Nicknamed "the little grey lady in the sea" because of its picturesque, weathered grey cottages covered with pink roses in the summer, Nantucket was spared the industrialization of the 19C; and with its wharfside structures, comfortable old homes, salty wharfside structures and cobblestone streets is today one of the most charming, well-preserved towns on the East Coast.

Getting There. – Daily ferry service between **Woods Hole, Martha's Vineyard** and **Nantucket**. Contact: Steamship Authority. *Address: Box 284, Woods Hole, MA 02543 ☎ (617) 540-2022. Departures from Woods Hole, time: 3 hours. Departures from Hyannis: Pleasant Dock ☎ (617) 771-4000 (time: 2 hours 20 min). Fares and schedules subject to change. For information contact the Steamship Authority. For advance automobile reservations ☎ (617) 540-2022. Fare one way: passenger $8.50, automobile $66.50.*

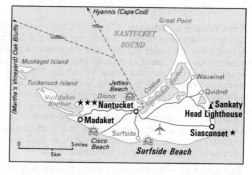

Staying on Nantucket. – The island is a wonderful place to stay, however, lodging may be difficult to find in season; reservations are advised. There is a wide range of accommodations including motels, inns and Bed and Breakfast establishments. For assistance contact the **Information Bureau**, *25 Federal Street ☎ (617) 228-0925;* or the **Nantucket Chamber of Commerce**, *Pacific Club Building, Main Street ☎ (617) 228-1700.*

Getting Around. – Since the island is small, the most pleasant way to get around is by bicycle *(rentals available near ferry dock).*

Automobile rentals and bus tours are also available; jeep rentals for those wishing to go to Great Point.

Beaches. – Nantucket is known for its fine beaches. Temperatures of the waters that bathe the shore are warmed by the Gulf Stream that passes close by.

Located near the center of town is **Jetties Beach;** on the harbor side of this beach are the shallow flats of **Children's Beach**, an ideal beach for youngsters. Surfers will prefer **Surfside** and **Cisco** beaches.

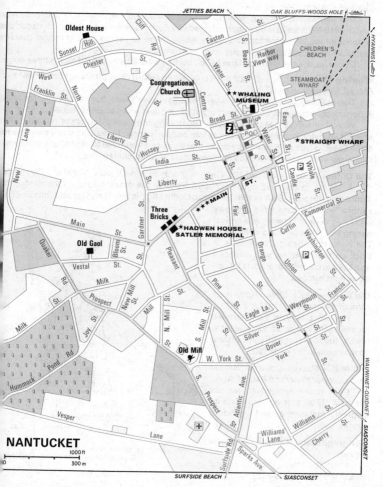

NANTUCKET

HISTORICAL NOTES

From Fishing to Whaling. – In the 17C the settlers learned from the Indians how to harpoon whales that passed close to shore. Once captured, the whales were dragged ashore where they were cut into, and the meat, oil and bone were divided among the hunters. As the number of inshore whales decreased, Nantucketers set out on long ocean voyages to hunt the whale. For almost 100 years, between 1740 and the 1830s, Nantucket reigned as the world capital of the whaling industry. Merchants and shipowners grew rich by selling thousands of barrels of oil in London and other major cities, and built the magnificent homes that stand on Main Street near the wharves. Then came the decline. Nantucket harbor, too shallow for the vessels that were being constructed, gave way in importance to the deepwater port of New Bedford *(p 139).* A great fire in 1846, the California Gold Rush, and the discovery of oil in Pennsylvania ultimately brought Nantucket's golden era to a close.

Nantucketers. – The difficult life led by seamen and their wives, and the Quaker religion many of them practiced, contributed to developing the simple, austere and strong character for which Nantucketers are known. **Peter Foulger,** the grandfather of Benjamin Franklin, and **Maria Mitchell,** the first American woman astronomer were Nantucketers. A less well known yet splendid example of the determination of Nantucketers was the wife of Captain Charles Grant, who, with her newborn baby in her arms, made a trip around the world in search of her husband when his ship was reported missing.

■ THE CENTER ★★★ *Allow 1 day*

The Nantucket Historical Association sells a special pass ($6.50) to the historic houses and museums it administers. The pass may be purchased at any of the sights.

Main Street ★★★. – Shaded by ancient elms, paved with cobblestones, and lined with captains' homes, shops and art galleries, Main Street has preserved its other-century atmosphere. During the summer it is a delightful place for a leisurely stroll.

Straight Wharf ★. – This wharf at the head of Main Street, and its old fishing sheds have been transformed into modern marinas and shops, art galleries and restaurants. Yachts and other pleasure craft tie up at the wharf in summer.

Hadwen House — Satler Memorial ★. – *Main and Pleasant Streets. Open mid-May to mid-October 10 AM to 5 PM. $1.50.*

This impressive dwelling, with its classically inspired pediment and columns, was built in 1845 for the whale oil merchant, Hadwen Satler. The house and its rich decor are evidence of the life of comfort and luxury led by its owner. Large, well-lit rooms contain beautiful furnishings and numerous other treasures.

Opposite, are the identical **Three Bricks,** built by a wealthy merchant for his three sons.

Whaling Museum ★★. – *Broad Street. Open mid-April through December 10 AM to 5 PM; $2.50, children $1.00.*

The building, once a factory where candles were made from whale oil, contains important collections of scrimshaw, harpoons, models and paintings related to whaling.

Workshops have been reproduced, illustrating the trades and crafts related to the whaling industry: blacksmith shop, sail loft, cooper's shop. There is an interesting model of the **Camel,** a type of "floating dry dock" that was used from 1840 to 1850 to assist the new and larger vessels in entering the shallow waters of Nantucket Harbor.

The Oldest House. – *Sunset Hill. Open mid-May to mid-October 10 AM to 5 PM; $1.50.*

A narrow, gravel road outside of town leads to the oldest house on the island, the Jethro Coffin House. Built in 1686 for Jethro Coffin and his wife Mary Gardner, this wooden saltbox with its casement windows and large central chimney is a typical example of 17C colonial architecture. The horseshoe design, fashioned in brick on the chimney, was intended as a special charm to protect its inhabitants from witches.

Old Gaol. – *Vestal Street. Open June through September 10 AM to 5 PM.*

The old pillory in the courtyard recalls the severity of early justice. Inside, the four stone prison cells are as they were in the early 19C.

Old Mill. – *Mill Hill. Open mid-May to mid-October 10 AM to 5 PM; $1.00.*

Corn is still ground at this old windmill (1746) that operates with its original machinery and grinding stones.

Congregational Church. – *Centre Street.*

From the tower, there is a good view of the town and island.

(From a photo by Samuel Chamberlain.
Courtesy of Hastings House, Publishers

Old Mill.

■ OTHER POINTS OF INTEREST ON THE ISLAND

Siasconset★. – Islanders call the village "Sconset." Fishermen who came here during the 17C to fish for cod, built the sheds that were later converted into the grey **cottages★** of Siasconset. Discovered at the end of the 19C by artists in search of unspoiled natural scenery, Sconset rapidly grew into a fashionable resort as handsome dwellings were built on the land surrounding the small shanties. Between 1881 and 1918 a railroad linked Siasconset to the center of Nantucket.

Sankaty Head Lighthouse. – The lighthouse is a short walking distance from the shore road. Views to one side of the ocean, and to the other of cranberry bogs and rolling moors.

The road between Quidnet and Nantucket is scenic and offers a succession of landscapes.

Surfside Beach. – A road *(Surfside Road)* and bicycle path lead to the south shore where there is surf bathing at Surfside Beach.

Madaket. – A paved road leads through the moors to the western end of the island and Madaket Beach. Madaket's white sandy stretches and clear surf enjoy the afternoon sun.

NEW BEDFORD ★

Michelin tourist map - fold 23 – Pop 97 738

New Bedford, the former whaling capital of the world made famous by the writings of Herman Melville, earns its living from fishing and manufacturing. A salty atmosphere pervades this old, New England port city. Cobblestone streets lead down to the waterfront where ship's supplies and antiques are sold, and the wharves – beside which tall whaling ships once anchored – are crowded with fishing craft. Follow one of these streets up from the waterfront to discover, on Johnny Cake Hill, memories of New Bedford's illustrious whaling days which are well-preserved in the Whaling Museum and the Seamen's Bethel, the mariner's chapel described in Melville's novel, *Moby Dick.*

The Golden Age. – New Bedford's era as world capital of the whaling industry began in 1765 when Joseph Rotch, a Nantucketer who had successfully established the whaling industry on Nantucket *(p 136)*, came to the fishing village of Bedford in Dartmouth. Rotch's efforts and past experiences formed the foundation of Dartmouth's whale fishery and within ten years about 50 ships were setting out from the small port to hunt whales. New Bedford grew rich from whaling and by the 1830s had surpassed Nantucket as the center of the industry. In 1840 Melville, describing the town, wrote:

"All these brave houses and flowery gardens came from the Atlantic, Pacific and Indian Oceans, one and all they were harpooned and dragged up hither from the bottom of the sea."

Whale oil and bone were the basis of the city's wealth. Factories worked day and night converting the oil into candles; and whalebone, destined to be transformed into corset stays, umbrellas and walking sticks, was set out along the piers to dry. This period of glory lasted about 30 years: between 1830 and 1860; then came the decline.

The Decline. – The whaling industry peaked in New Bedford in 1857 with 329 ships valued at $12 million, and more than 10 000 men involved in whaling.

The discovery of petroleum in Pennsylvania brought about a decline in the demand for whale oil, however, the fatal blow to New Bedford's whaling was also due, in large part, to the reduction in the size of its fleet: 37 vessels were lost in the Stone Fleet episode *(p 25)*, and an additional 32 ships were abandoned after they became icebound in the Arctic Ocean in 1861. Similar disasters diminished the size of the fleet even further until, by the end of the 19C, almost all New Bedford capital had been shifted away from whaling and to manufacturing.

■ SIGHTS *time: 3 hours*

New Bedford Whaling Museum★★. – 18 Johnny Cake Hill. From I-95 Exit 15, follow the signs to downtown New Bedford. Open 9 AM to 5 PM, Sunday 1 PM (11 AM July and August) to 5 PM; closed major holidays; $2.50, under 14, $1.50. A whaling film (time: 20 min) is shown daily in summer 10 AM and 1:30 PM. The museum's collections are among the finest in the world related to the history of whaling. On the ground floor, in the section reserved for **crimshaw** (p 32), note such pieces as the scrimshaw sleigh and scrimshaw birdcage.

(From a photo by the Whaling Museum, New Bedford.)

Hunting the Whale
from the Russell and Purrington Panorama.

A large hall contains the one-half scale model of the **Lagoda**★★, a typical whale ship. The *Lagoda* made 12 voyages out of New Bedford in the 1800s. Visitors may climb aboard the vessel to examine the elaborate rigging and the try works.

The museum collection of marine engravings, illustrations of the various stages of the whale hunt, oils and watercolors, also includes ship portraits and seascapes by the 19C artists Benjamin Russell and **William Bradford**, and a series of panels painted by Charles Raleigh in the 1870s. In a separate gallery, sections from the vast **Panorama**★ by **Benjamin Russell** and **Caleb Purrington**, depicting a whaling voyage around the world, are on display.

Logbooks, with their simple often humorous illustrations, tell about life on board a whale ship.

On the floor above, a cooperage, sail loft, rigging loft, have been reconstructed to demonstrate whaling related trades.

Seamen's Bethel. – *Open May to Columbus Day 10 AM (1 PM Sunday June to Columbus Day) to 4 PM (5 PM June to Labor Day); closed the rest of the year.*

This chapel was a necessary stop for the mariner who was about to embark on a whaling voyage. The pulpit is shaped to resemble the hull of a whaleboat.

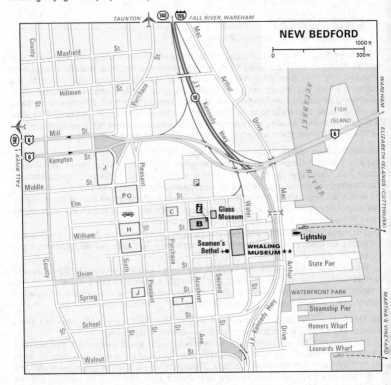

New Bedford Glass Museum. – *Second Street. Open 10 AM to 5 PM, Sunday 1 to 4 PM; closed January, February, Mondays in March and April, and major holidays. $2.00.*

Fine art glass was produced in New Bedford by the Mount Washington Glass Works between 1870 and 1894, and by the Pairpoint Corporation between 1894 and 1939. Glass made at these and other New England glasshouses is on display.

At the **New Bedford Glass Works (B)** *(47 N. Second Street; open 10 AM to 5 PM, Sunday 1 to 4 PM)*, opposite the museum, visitors may observe demonstrations of glassblowing by craftsmen who produce both traditional and contemporary art glass. *Advisable to call ahead for demonstration ☎ (617) 997-7928.*

Lightship New Bedford. – *The lightship is adjacent to and a part of the Coast Guard Exhibit at the State Pier. Open July and August 10 AM to 5 PM; 50¢.*

This vessel was one of the dozens of lightships that once guarded the waters where it was considered too dangerous to erect lighthouses.

Visit New York City with the Michelin Green Guide.

This guide provides the visitor with:

- *Practical information on visiting the Big Apple*
- *A description of the history, culture and economy of the metropolitan area*
- *Twenty-eight suggested walks in Manhattan*
- *A brief description of points of interest in the four other boroughs*
- *Excursions to points outside the city*
- *More than fifty color diagrams and maps including maps of the bus and subway systems.*

NEWBURYPORT ★

Michelin tourist map
fold 17 – 35 miles north
of Boston – Pop 16 545

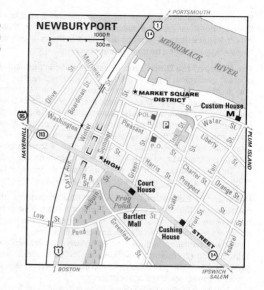

This small city at the mouth of the Merrimack River was the home of a large fleet of merchant vessels in the 18 and 19C. The dignified Federal mansions built on **High Street** by sea captains, and charming lanes reaching from Bartlett Square to the restored **Market Square District★** evoke the era when Newburyport was a bustling shipbuilding and coastal port, and trading center.

Down by the waterfront salty old buildings contain traces of the boatyards where some of the finest clippers ever sailed were constructed in the 19C.

High Street★. – Ornamented with carved porches, columns, etc., the houses on this street are representative of the major styles of 19C American architecture: late Georgian, Federal, Greek Revival. The **Frog Pond** and **Bartlett Mall**, fronting High Street, are the setting for the Bulfinch designed **Court House** (1800) which was remodeled in 1853.

Cushing House. – *At No. 98. Guided tours (1 hour) May through October 10 AM to 4 PM, Sunday 2 to 5 PM; closed Monday; $2.00.* This brick mansion was built in 1808 for Caleb Cushing, the first United States Ambassador to China. Furnishings brought back from the Orient by Mr. Cushing, a small group of early American paintings, and a collection of silver, clocks and needlework are among the exhibits.

Custom House. – *25 Water Street. Open April to late December 10 AM to 4:30 PM, Sunday 1 to 4 PM; the rest of the year 10 AM to 4 PM, closed Saturday and Sunday; $2.00.* Designed by Robert Mills, the architect of the Washington Monument (Washington, D.C.), this granite structure which welcomed mariners returning from long sea voyages is today of interest for its **Museum of the Maritime History of the Merrimack Valley (M)**. Exhibits are related to the past, and feature shipbuilding, the Coast Guard and foreign imports.

EXCURSIONS

Plum Island — Parker River National Wildlife Refuge★★. – *3 miles from Newburyport by Water Street then Plum Island Turnpike. Open dawn to dusk. Admission charged.*
The approximately six-mile long peninsula is a refuge for waterfowl in the Atlantic Flyway. Opportunities for bird watching are excellent (more than 270 species have been sighted), especially during the spring and fall migrations. The observation towers offer panoramic views of the island's 4 650 acres of dunes, marshlands and oceanfront beach.
Parking is available in the small parking lots off of the road that leads through the refuge. Certain lots provide access to the observation towers, trails and beach. The Hellcat Trail and Kettle Hole Trail offer views of the marshes. *The Refuge is closed when it reaches its total capacity (350 cars). Camping is prohibited.*

Haverhill. – Pop 47 715. Industry continues to be important to this community, a major center for the production of shoes in the 19C.

John Greenleaf Whittier Birthplace. – *305 Whittier Road. 13 miles from Newburyport by Rte 1 North, then Rte 110 West. Open 10 AM (1 PM Sunday) to 5 PM; closed Mondays and major holidays; $1.00.* The 19C Quaker, poet and abolitionist John Greenleaf Whittier was born in this rustic farmhouse. Whittier's gentle nature is reflected in the idyllic scenes he portrayed (as in *Snow-bound*) of the New England character, legends and countryside.

PIONEER VALLEY ★

Michelin tourist map-folds 14 and 15

The fertile Connecticut River valley, extending north-south through the center of Massachusetts, was one of the major axes along which settlements were established in the 17C, giving the region its name: Pioneer Valley. The valley remained the western frontier of New England until the 18C as the colonists did not dare risk the dangers involved in crossing the Berkshire Mountains and venturing into the Hudson Valley, the domain of the Dutch.

A Fertile Valley and its Unusual Relief. – The broad, gentle farmlands that reach from one end of the valley to the other, are framed against a backdrop of dramatic rocky ledges and **basalt ridges**. The craggy basalt ridges, of volcanic origin, rise abruptly from the valley floor, with sheer, steep slopes owing to the fact that basalt splits along the vertical.

Vantage points along these ridges command beautiful views of the valley and the Connecticut River *(see the descriptions of Mount Tom, Skinner State Park and Sugarloaf p 142)*. Vegetables and tobacco are raised in the valley's rich, fertile soil, with the tobacco fields easily identified by their netted coverings.

The Valley of the Dinosaurs. – Less dramatic in appearance than the basalt ridges, but of great geological interest, are the finer-grained sedimentary rocks which have yielded the tracks of dinosaurs which roamed the Connecticut Valley approximately 200 million years ago. These footprints, impressed in the mud on the valley floor and baked by the sun, were later covered over and preserved by layers of mud, then eventually transformed into sedimentary rocks: primarily sandstones and shales. Today these rocks reveal the story of the dinosaurs that once inhabited this region. These dinosaurs were small, about the size of a man, according to the size of the footprints they left. The giant dinosaurs did not attain their mammoth size until about 100 million years later.

Dinosaur tracks can be seen at the Pratt Museum at Amherst College, in their original formation in Rocky Hill *(p 43)* and at various other locations.

A Center of Education. – More than 60 000 students attend the numerous schools, colleges and the university in the Pioneer Valley. Five of these institutions have joined together in a consortium which encourages an exchange of professors and allows members to share a radio station and other facilities.

The consortium includes: – **At Amherst:** the **University of Massachusetts,** a sprawling campus with tall modern towers where 25 000 students attend classes; **Amherst College,** established in 1821; and the new and innovative **Hampshire College,** established in 1971 by the other members of the consortium.

– **At Northampton: Smith College,** founded in 1875 by Sophia Smith, and one of the most select colleges in the nation for women; **Mount Holyoke College,** across the river in South Hadley, was established in 1837 as the first college for women in the United States.

The poetess **Emily Dickinson** was a student at Mount Holyoke College before she settled in Amherst, where she lived the remainder of her life primarily as a recluse.

■ SIGHTS

Deerfield★★. – *Description p 127.*

Mount Sugarloaf State Reservation. – *Follow the signs from Rte 116.*
From the top of this basalt ridge there is an expansive **view★★** of the Connecticut River as it meanders through open farmlands. Small towns fleck the valley landscape.

Northampton. – Pop 29 215. Northampton has grown from a remote frontier town into a bustling commercial center. The **Smith College Museum of Art,** on Elm Street, owns a collection that is rich in works of the American and French schools of the 18 through 20C *(open July and August Tuesday through Saturday 1 to 4 PM; September through May, 12 noon (2 PM Sunday) to 5 PM; closed Mondays, holidays and June).*

Joseph Allen Skinner State Park. – *From Rte 47 follow the signs for the Summit House.* The old summit hotel, built on a basalt ridge, offers a **view★** of the valley. The towers of the University of Massachusetts in Amherst are visible in the distance.

Mount Tom Reservation. – *From Holyoke take Rte 141 North 3 miles.*
From the access road to the reservation Easthampton and Northampton can be seen in the valley below. The summit commands a view of the curved arm of the Connecticut River made famous by Thomas Cole's painting *The Oxbow* (Metropolitan Museum of Art), and Northampton and the Berkshire Hills beyond. There is skiing in the winter, and an alpine slide and water slide in the summer on the slopes of Mount Tom.

Quabbin Reservoir★. – *Access from Rte 9; 2 miles from Belchertown. Drive on Windsor Dam then follow the signs for Quabbin Hill Tower.* Construction of the immense reservoir (128 sq miles, storage capacity 412 billion gals) which serves the Boston region, was accomplished by damming the Swift River valley and flooding four of the valley towns. Quabbin's vast water reserves (*Quabbin* in Indian means: "a lot of water") and more than fifty islands, the hilltops of the submerged valley areas, create an island-studded landscape. The **view★★** can be admired from **Enfield Lookout;** the **Observation Tower** on Quabbin Hill also offers a **view★★.** The reservoir offers opportunities for fishing, hiking, picnicking and scenic shore drives *(swimming and hunting are prohibited).*

PLYMOUTH ★★
Michelin tourist map - fold 17 – 39 miles southwest of Boston – Pop 38 384

Americans come as Pilgrims to this place where, 350 years ago, the *Mayflower* made its landfall in the New World and the Plymouth Colony, the first permanent settlement in New England, was established. The long ocean voyage of the *Mayflower*, the hardships endured by the Pilgrims, and the eventual success of the Plymouth Colony are all part of the cherished story that is told by the historic monuments and sites in Plymouth.

The town itself, modern and attractive, is a residential and industrial community with hilly streets sloping down to the harbor. From **Burial Hill,** a hill on which there is an old cemetery with gravestones dating back to the Plymouth Colony, there are views that reach beyond the town and out to sea. The **Town Brook,** close to the place where the Pilgrims built their first homes, runs through a lovely public park, **Brewster Gardens.**

From Plymouth to Plymouth. – During the 16C a group of Puritans known as **Separatists** attempted to reform the Church of England. In 1607, to avoid persecution by the authorities, members of the group emigrated from Scrooby, England to Holland where they remained until, impressed by favorable accounts of the New World, they once again decided to emigrate – this time to America. Early in September 1620, 102 passengers, including 35 Separatists, boarded the *Mayflower* at Plymouth, England and set sail for the Virginia colony in North America.

Diverted north of their destination by a storm they landed two months later on the shores of Cape Cod *(p 145)*. They spent five weeks exploring the region, before again setting sail for Virginia. Detoured a second time by strong winds the Pilgrims headed for the bay that had been charted 6 years before by Captain John Smith and, on the shores of this bay, they established the Plymouth settlement.

The First Winter. – The harsh weather and a scarcity of food left almost half the colony dead by the end of the first winter. Burials were held at night on **Cole's Hill**, and graves were left unmarked to conceal the settlers' dwindling numbers from the Indians.

The spring brought hope and a group of Indians to the settlement, who befriended the Pilgrims and taught them how to raise crops, hunt and fish. In the fall, after the harvest, members of the Plymouth colony joined with the Indians in a three-day feast, the forerunner of the American **Thanksgiving celebration,** to give thanks for their blessings.

Pilgrim Progress. – Each Friday in August and on Thanksgiving Day men, women and children of Plymouth, dressed as Pilgrims, take part in a Sabbath procession up Leyden Street to Burial Hill, where a religious service similar to that conducted by the early Pilgrims is held.

■ **SIGHTS** *time: 1 day – plan p 144*

It is advisable to visit the historic district by walking since all the points of interest are concentrated within a small area. Begin at the Information Center.

Plymouth Rock★. – This boulder set at the harbor's edge has traditionally been regarded as the stepping stone used by the *Mayflower* passengers when they disembarked at Plymouth. The boulder is sheltered by a multi-columned granite structure. Opposite is **The Pilgrim Mother (A),** a fountain honoring the women of the *Mayflower.*

Mayflower II★★. – *Berthed at the State Pier. Open late March through November 9 AM to 5 PM (6:30 PM late June to Labor Day); $3.75; 5-12 years, $2.75.*

The *Mayflower II,* built in England (1955-1957), is a full-scale replica of the kind of ship which brought the Pilgrims to Plymouth in 1620. Nearby, on Water Street, are the **First House** and the **1627 House (B),** replicas of the type of cottages built by the Pilgrims.

Plymouth Wax Museum (M). – *16 Carver Street. Open March through November 9 AM to 5 PM; $3.50; children, $1.75.*

Located on **Cole's Hill** *(see above),* the museum contains 26 life-size dioramas which depict the Pilgrim story from the emigration of the Separatists from England to Holland in 1607, to the first Thanksgiving celebration in 1621. In front of the museum is a statue of **Massasoit (D),** chief of the Indians who helped the Pilgrims to survive that first spring.

Pilgrim Hall Museum★. – *75 Court Street. Open 9:30 AM to 4:30 PM; closed January 1 and December 25; $3.00.* Built as a memorial to the Pilgrims and the Plymouth Colony, this austere granite structure (1824) designed by Alexander Parris contains original Pilgrim furnishings and artifacts including chairs owned by Governors Bradford and Carver, the cradle of Peregine White, born on the *Mayflower,* John Alden's and Governor Bradford's Bibles and a sampler made by Lora Standish, daughter of Myles Standish.

Plimoth Plantation★★. – *3 miles south on Rte 3 from the center of Plymouth. Open late March through November 9 AM to 5 PM; $7.50; 5-12 years, $4.75; under 5 free. Orientation programs (films, exhibits) offered at the Visitor Center provide a good introduction to Plimoth Plantation and the period.*

The plantation is a reproduction of the Pilgrims' village as it appeared in 1627. Buildings, paths and gardens have been constructed to resemble those that stood originally on the site of modern Plymouth's business district.

Plimoth Plantation.

The **Fort Meetinghouse**, at the entrance to the plantation, is a good place from which to view the entire village with its neat rows of thatched-roof cottages similar to those lived in by the Aldens, Carvers, Bradfords, Standishes. Inside the houses there are recreations of the 17C English furnishings the Pilgrims would have owned. The village is animated with the activities of men and women in Pilgrim dress who are involved in gardening, cooking, harvesting crops according to the methods used in the early colony.

A path leads to the Wampanoag Summer Campsite where the culture of this native Indian group is interpreted by staff members engaged in raising crops, drying meat, weaving and other chores traditionally performed by the Wampanoag people. The campsite includes examples of the domed dwellings once built by the Wampanoags for shelter.

Mayflower Society Museum★ (E). – *4 Winslow Street. Guided tours (35 min) late May to mid-October 10 AM (12 noon Sunday) to 5 PM; closed Monday, Tuesday and Wednesday late May through June and mid-September to mid-October; $2.00.*

Built during the colonial period and enlarged in the 19C, the house is a graceful blend of colonial and Victorian architectural features. Attractive roof railings and the multi-paned cupola add harmonious relief to the white brick exterior.

Inside, a flying stairway joins the early and later sections of the house. Among the antiques found throughout the house is a rare set of biblical fireplace tiles in the drawing room.

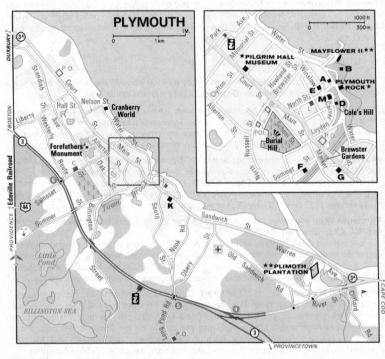

PILGRIM MOTHER STATUE **A**	MASSASOIT STATUE **D**	SPARROW HOUSE **F**
FIRST HOUSE - 1627 HOUSE **B**	MAYFLOWER	PILGRIM J. HOWLAND HOUSE **G**
PLYMOUTH WAX MUSEUM **M**	SOCIETY MUSEUM **E**	HARLOW OLD FORT HOUSE **K**

Historical Houses. – Other houses open to the public include:

The Richard Sparrow House (F). – *42 Summer Street. Open Memorial Day to Columbus Day weekend and Thanksgiving Day 10 AM to 5 PM; closed Wednesday.*

The oldest dwelling in Plymouth (1640); 18C furnishings, pottery demonstrations.

Pilgrim John Howland House (G). – *33 Sandwich Street. Open Memorial Day to October 12, 10 AM (12 noon Sunday) to 5 PM, Thanksgiving weekend 10 AM to 4 PM; $1.50.*

The only house remaining in Plymouth where Pilgrims are known to have lived.

Harlow Old Fort House (K). – *114 Sandwich Street. Open July to Labor Day 10 AM (12 noon Sunday) to 5 PM; weekends only Memorial Day through June; $2.50.*

The house is partially constructed from the timbers of a 17C fort that stood on Burial Hill.

National Forefathers' Monument. – *Allerton Street off Rte 44.* This large monument, a figure representing Faith (36 ft), is a tribute to the Pilgrims and their small colony.

Cranberry World Visitors Center. – *From Rte 3 take Rte 44 East 3/4 mile. Cross Rte 3A and continue on Rte 44 to the waterfront rotary, then bear left. Open April through November 9:30 AM to 5 PM (9 PM weekdays July and August).*

A leading producer of cranberries, Plymouth is headquarters to a nationwide cranberry cooperative, Ocean Spray. The Visitor Center has exhibits and miniature outdoor working bogs.

EXCURSIONS

Edaville Railroad. – *Rochester Road in So. Carver, 16 miles southwest of Plymouth. Leave Plymouth on Rte 44 West. Continue to Rte 58; turn left onto Rte 58 South, then after 6 miles turn right onto Rochester Road. Follow the signs. Open May weekends and holidays 12 noon to 5 PM; 1st Saturday in June to Labor Day 10 AM to 5:30 PM; day after Labor Day through October 10:30 AM to 3 PM (5:30 PM Saturdays, Sundays and holidays); mid-November to early January limited schedule. $7.50, children $5.00. ☎ (617) 866-4526.*

This narrow gauge railway acquired by Ellis D. Atwood in the 1940s to work his cranberry farm, is now a tourist attraction. The Railroad offers a 5 1/2 mile steam train ride through more than 200 acres of working cranberry bogs. The ideal time for this excursion is in the fall during the harvest period *(call ahead for harvest schedule). Diesel trains are used weekdays in the fall.*

The Railroad is part of a complex that includes a petting farm, picnic areas and a **museum**. Antique fire fighting equipment and automobiles, railroad memorabilia, toy trains and a display on the cranberry are among the museum exhibits.

Myles Standish Monument State Park. – *In Duxbury. 8 miles from Plymouth by Rte 3A to Crescent Street. Turn right, and enter gate on left.* The Standish monument, a gigantic figure of the Pilgrim leader Myles Standish, overlooks the bay and offers a **view★★** of Plymouth, Cape Cod Bay and Provincetown *(p 145).*

PROVINCETOWN ★★
Michelin tourist map - fold 18 – Pop 3 562

As the highway heads north through the Province Lands sector of the Cape Cod National Seashore, Provincetown Harbor is visible to the left, and in the distance a tall, solitary monument resembling an Italian bell tower appears on the horizon. Motels and bungalows stand sentry-like alongside the road, guarding the sandy stretches that lead into Provincetown, or P-town as the town is known. The town, an old fishing port that extends to the tip of Cape Cod, is a fishing village, artist's colony and resort town all in one.

During the summer the population of P-town climbs from 3 500 to 75 000 as tourists and vacationers arrive in droves. Crowds weave in and out of the shops, galleries and eating places that line the narrow streets, and **Commercial Street,** the main thoroughfare in town, becomes almost impassable. Visitors and townspeople alike find the beaches of the CCNS nearby (**Herring Cove Beach, Race Point Beach**) a refreshing contrast to the hustle and bustle that characterize the center of Provincetown during this time of year.

From the Mayflower to Whaling Port. – When the *Mayflower* was blown off course and arrived at this end of the Cape in November 1620, there were only stark, bleak stretches of sand for as far as the eye could see. The Pilgrims spent five weeks exploring the region, and aware that this area was not within the bounds of their charter, drew up the **Mayflower Compact** to serve as their instrument of government. Then they reset their sails for a voyage which ended a few days later at Plymouth *(p 142).*

By the 18C, less than 100 years after the landfall of the Pilgrims on the Cape, Provincetown had been established and grown into the third largest whaling center after Nantucket and New Bedford. In the mid-19C, seventy-five wharves could be counted along its shores, and the beaches were covered with fish flakes – racks for drying fish, and saltworks – wooden structures in which salt was obtained from seawater. Provincetown vessels recruited seamen in the Azores and Cape Verde Islands, which accounts for the town's large Portuguese population and the traditions they have preserved *(see below).*

Other Provincetowners found adventure and fortune closer to home. Smugglers and mooncussers (shipwreckers) took advantage of the isolated beaches and dangerous shoals to become rich. The place where they gathered was nicknamed "Helltown" and was cautiously avoided by the more respectable citizens of the village.

Provincetown of the Artists. – At the beginning of the 20C artists and writers were attracted to Provincetown by its wild natural beauty. In 1901 Charles W. Hawthorne founded the **Cape Cod School of Art** here, followed fifteen years later by the establishment of the **Provincetown Players,** a group of playwrights and actors rebelling against the rigid criteria of the Broadway stage. Eugene O'Neill's *(p 33)* career as a playwright was launched at Provincetown in 1916 with the production of his first play, *Bound East for Cardiff,* at the Wharf Theatre. At about the same time, P-Town became a prestigious artist's colony where writers and dramatists such as O'Neill, John Dos Passos, Sinclair Lewis and Tennessee Williams gathered. The cultural and artistic traditions so closely associated with the character of Provincetown are today carried on by the **Provincetown Art Association,** the **Provincetown Theater Company** and the **Provincetown Summer Theater.** Productions of the theater companies have been held in the Art Association and the Town Hall since the Playhouse-on-the-Wharf burned in 1977.

■ **SIGHTS** *time: 4 hours*

Mac Millan Wharf. – *Public parking lot on the wharf; April 15 to October 21 $1.00 per hour; off season free.*

Late in the afternoon fishing boats, announced by their procession of seagulls, return to the wharf where their fresh catches are unloaded and shipped to markets in Boston and New York. On the last Sunday in June the **Blessing of the Fleet,** a colorful and impressive Portuguese tradition, takes place in the harbor.

Pilgrim Memorial Monument and Provincetown Museum. – *Town Hill off Bradford Street. Open early April through November 9 AM to 5 PM; closed holidays. $2.00.*

The Pilgrim Monument, a tower inspired by the Italian architecture of the 14C, commemorates the landing of the *Mayflower* at Provincetown, and is a landmark for tourists approaching the lower Cape. There is a **view**★★ of the entire Cape from the observation deck.

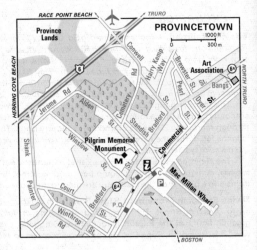

The **Provincetown Museum** (**M**), located near the base of the tower, has historical memorabilia related to Provincetown and Cape Cod: dioramas of the old saltworks and fish flakes, exhibits devoted to the Arctic expeditions of Admiral Donald Mac Millan, a rare group of 18C photographs, scrimshaw... . In the Pilgrims' Room a model of the *Mayflower* and life-size dioramas depict the arrival of the Pilgrims at Provincetown.

Dunes Tour★★. – Commercial operators, using over-sand vehicles, offer tours through the Provincetown Dunes of the CCNS. The tour is a magnificent way to explore the spectacular dune and ocean coastline that is constantly being shaped and reshaped by the winds. *Tours operate from the intersection of Commercial and Standish Streets April to mid-October. Time: 1 to 1 1/2 hours; $5.00. For additional information contact the Chamber of Commerce* (**i**), *PO Box 1017, 307 Commercial Street,* ☎ *(617) 487-3424.*

QUINCY

Michelin tourist map - fold 17 – *Map of the Boston region p 89* (CX) – Pop 83 682

Quincy, south of Boston, was prominent during its early days as the home of the Adams family, which gave to the nation its second and sixth presidents: **John Adams** and **John Quincy Adams**. In the 19C Quincy's granite quarries and shipyards attracted laborers from Finland, Greece, Ireland, Italy and eastern Europe and their descendents today form the basis of Quincy's ethnically diverse population. Quincy shipyards produced the only seven-masted schooner *(Thomas W. Lawson)* ever built, and the first atomic-powered surface ship in the 20C.

Today a hub of industrial and commercial activity and a suburb of Boston, Quincy is one of the region's major centers.

The Adams. – **John Adams** (1735-1826), a spokesman for the Revolutionary cause against England's colonial policies, was one of a group of men who drafted the Declaration of Independence. Beginning in 1778 his diplomatic posts took him to France, Scotland and England where he was instrumental in negotiating the Treaty of Paris (1783) to end the Revolution. He served as Vice President under George Washington, then as President from 1796 to 1801. After his defeat in 1801, John Adams retired to his home in Quincy. By incredible coincidence John Adams and Thomas Jefferson, who also served on the committee to draft the Declaration of Independence, died on the same day – July 4, 1826 – fifty years to the day the historic document was signed.

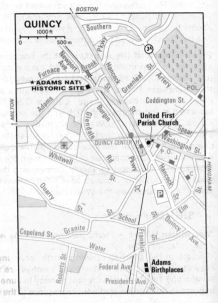

John Quincy Adams (1767-1848), who followed in the steps of his father, studied law then began a diplomatic career, serving at various times as Ambassador to Prussia, the Netherlands, Russia and Great Britain. In 1824 he was elected to the presidency of the United States, an office he held until 1829. Having lost the election in 1828, John Quincy Adams retired to Quincy. His election two years later to Congress was the start of a 17 year career in the legislature for the former president and devoted statesman.

■ **SIGHTS** *time: 2 hours*

John Adams and John Quincy Adams Birthplaces. – *133 and 141 Franklin Street. Guided tours (30 min) April 19 to October 15; closed the rest of the year; $2.00.*

These modest colonial **saltboxes** (p 27) where John Adams and John Quincy Adams were born, contain memorabilia and period furnishings.

Adams National Historic Site ★. – *135 Adams Street. Guided tours (45 min) April 19 to November 10, 9 AM to 5 PM; $2.00.*

John Adams and his wife Abigail bought this house, that was referred to by the Adams family as the "Old House," in 1787. The four successive generations of Adams that lived here each added its own mementoes and furnishings to the house, which explains the diversity of styles. Especially noteworthy is the study where John Adams died, the Panelled Room with its rich mahogany paneling, and the Long Room which is furnished with elegant French pieces. The Stone Library in the garden contains John Quincy Adams' library of 14 000 volumes.

United First Parish Church. – *1306 Hancock Street. Guided tours mid-May to Labor Day 10 AM to 4 PM, closed Sunday.*

This granite Greek Revival structure known as the "Church of the Presidents" is the final resting place of John Adams and John Quincy Adams and their wives.

SALEM ★★★

Michelin tourist map - fold 17 – *Plan p 146* – Pop 38 555

Salem, a town tormented in the 17C by its fear of witchcraft, and a port where, in the following centuries ships from around the world docked at the forty-odd wharves that lined the waterfront, is a bristling and pleasant city where historic districts adjoin industrial sites. The manufacture of electronics and the production of such familiar games as Monopoly are the city's principal businesses.

Renewal programs in the heart of the downtown area, around **Essex Street,** have transformed the shopping district into a colonial marketplace of brick walkways and shopping malls. Loft buildings renovated to house offices and shops, and the attractive Federal Style **Old Town Hall** front Derby Square, a center of activity in the summer.

HISTORICAL NOTES

A City of Peace. – Founded in 1626 by Roger Conant, Salem was named for the Hebrew word *Shalom,* meaning peace. However, it was intolerance and violence that dominated this Puritan city. Roger Williams, persecuted by the authorities, fled to Rhode Island in 1636, and thereafter zealous Salemites devoted their energies to driving the evil ones from the colony. With the intention of ridding the colony once and for all of evil doers, the notorious witch-hunts of Salem were unleashed in the early 1690s.

The Witchcraft Hysteria. – In 1692 several young girls whose imaginations had been stirred by tales of voodoo told to them by the West Indian slave, Tituba, began to have "visions" and convulsive fits. The doctor was called, and after examining the girls he declared that they were the victims of witchcraft. Impressionable and frightened, the youngsters accused Tituba and two other women of having bewitched them, and the women were immediately arrested and put into prison. From that point on, fear and panic spread through Salem, leaving no one free of suspicion. More than 200 persons were accused of witchcraft, 150 imprisoned and 19 found guilty and hanged, before the hysteria came to an end about a year later.

An Era of Maritime Glory. – Salem's sizable fleet of vessels, important to colonial trade in the 17C, won special recognition during the Revolution for when the ports of Boston and New York were occupied by the British, it was Salem ships that carried arms and supplies to the colonial troops. Operating as privateers, Salem ships also weakened the enemy by raiding and capturing about 400 British vessels before the war ended.

After the Revolution Salem's merchant vessels were prominent in worldwide trade. In 1786 the *Grand Turk* sailing out of Salem to China returned home to New England laden down with a cargo of luxury goods. To the many ships that followed the *Grand Turk,* the route to the Far East (p 25) became a familiar one, and the Chinese, who saw great numbers of vessels arriving in their ports and bearing the name Salem, imagined Salem was a vast and magnificent country.

Two years later, in 1788, trade between Salem and India was opened by another Salem ship, the *Peggy,* owned by Elias Hasket Derby. The China Trade brought such enormous wealth to Salem, that taxes paid in Salem on imported goods provided 8% of the nation's revenues. Salem merchants: the Derbys, Peabodys, Crowninshields were among the richest men in America, and their mansions were filled with treasures brought home, aboard their ships, from the Orient.

The decline of the port of Salem, due in part to the embargo enforced by President Jefferson, was hastened by the development of new and larger clipper ships which could only be outfitted in deepwater ports such as those of Boston and New York.

Two Famous Men of Salem. – Samuel McIntire (1757-1811) carpenter, wood carver, sculptor, builder and architect, influenced much of Salem's architecture. His solid, four-square wood and brick mansions, such as the Peirce-Nichols house (p 150), ornamented with handsome porches and balustrades, are among the finest examples of

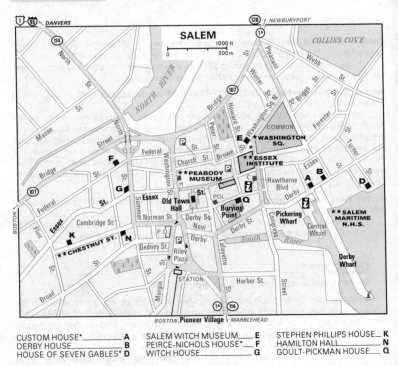

SALEM

CUSTOM HOUSE*	A	SALEM WITCH MUSEUM	E	STEPHEN PHILLIPS HOUSE	K
DERBY HOUSE	B	PEIRCE-NICHOLS HOUSE*	F	HAMILTON HALL	N
HOUSE OF SEVEN GABLES*	D	WITCH HOUSE	G	GOULT-PICKMAN HOUSE	Q

American Federal architecture. The masterfully carved doorways, ceilings, cornices and fireplaces for which he is especially known, are adorned with a variety of classical motifs (garlands, rosettes, baskets of fruits) that reflect his refined taste and attention to detail.

Nathaniel Hawthorne (1804-1864), a leading 19C American literary figure, was born in Salem, where he wrote his earliest stories. Salem's names and places familiar to Hawthorne were often the inspiration or setting for his works, such as the *House of the Seven Gables (p 148)*. Much of the atmosphere in his novel *The Scarlet Letter*, especially the descriptions of the Custom House *(p 148)*, was influenced by the years he spent as surveyor of the port.

■ SALEM AND THE SEA

After more than a century, Salem is once again alive with a vitality reminiscent of its days of maritime supremacy. **Pickering Wharf** has a concentration of specialty shops and restaurants; just beyond is the Salem Maritime National Historic Site.

The Historic district may be visited on foot; we suggest you begin at the Information Center on Central Wharf.

Salem Maritime National Historic Site★★. – Salem's historic waterfront site is administered by the National Park Service. At one time more than 40 wharves reached out into the harbor from Salem's shoreline. **Derby Wharf,** the longest (almost 2 000 ft), and for many years a busy mercantile center, still remains.

Visit. – *Open April through November 8 AM to 5 PM, the rest of the year 9 AM to 4:30 PM. Guided tours (25 min) of the National Historic Site structures are conducted by National Park Rangers June through September daily, the rest of the year weekends only. The Bonded Warehouse and the Derby House are included in the tour.*

Custom House★ (A). – *178 Derby Street.*

This Federal style building with its symbolic Eagle was constructed in 1819 to house the customs offices of Salem. Inside, several of the offices, including that used by Nathaniel Hawthorne when he was an officer of the port, have been restored.

To the rear of the Custom House, in the **Bonded Warehouse,** are samples of cargoes carried by Salem vessels, cargo handling equipment and weighing devices.

Derby House (B). – This brick mansion was built in 1761 for the wealthy merchant Elias Hasket Derby whose ships opened trade with India and the Orient, making him a very rich man. From its convenient waterfront location, the Derby ships could be seen as they docked at or near Derby wharf. Inside, the ship-type doors and wave motif ornamenting the stairway are interesting features.

House of the Seven Gables★ (D). – *54 Turner Street. Open July 1 to Labor Day 9:30 AM to 5:30 PM; the rest of the year 10 AM to 4:30 PM; closed major holidays and last two weeks in January. Guided tours (1 hour) include the main house and the Hawthorne birthplace; $4.00.*

The House of the Seven Gables, with its jagged peaks and steeply pitched roofs, was made famous by Hawthorne's novel of the same name. Built in 1668, the house was altered a number of times, however, it was completely restored in 1968

Inside, scenes from the novel come alive as visitors pass from Hepzibah's Cent Shop, to the parlor where the judge was found, to Clifford's room at the top of a secret stair-flcase.

Other buildings situated in the garden setting include Hawthorne's Birthplace (c. 1740), the Retire Becket House (1655), the Hooper-Hathaway House (1682) and a Counting House (c. 1840).

Peabody Museum of Salem★★. – *East India Square. Open 10 AM (1 PM Sundays and holidays) to 5 PM; closed major holidays; $3.00.*

(From a photo by Paula Phillips.)

House of the Seven Gables.

This museum pays tribute to Salem's maritime era and to the seamen who brought back the superb collection of art and artifacts from Asia and the Pacific Islands.

In 1799, a group of Salem ship captains organized the **Salem East India Marine Society** and later built the East India Hall, on Essex Street, to house a meeting hall, bank, insurance company and museum of "natural and artificial" curiosities from around the world. When the port declined leaving Salem with serious economic problems, the philanthropist, George Peabody, offered the Society financial assistance. The museum was renamed in his honor in the early 20C.

Two additions to the museum, an almost solid smooth-surfaced structure completed in 1976 and the Asian Export Wing dedicated in 1988, have greatly increased exhibition space.

The Peabody has four main departments:

Maritime Department★★★. – The collection of marine paintings includes works by major artists: Fitz Hugh Lane, Antoine Roux..., port scenes illustrating commerce with the Orient, and ships' portraits ordered by the owners of vessels.

A giant **diorama** depicts the port of Salem in 1820 at the peak of its splendor.

A room in the original building is reserved for nautical instruments, charts and maps. Other galleries contain souvenirs of Salem's trade with the Far East: Chinese port scenes, a splendidly carved elephant tusk, etc. At the entrance to the Port of Salem Room is "Lady with a Medallion", a ship's figurehead attributed to Samuel McIntire.

On the second floor are many ship models and figureheads from the museum's collection. Among the curiosities exhibited in East India Marine Hall note the miniature rosary bead containing more than 100 carved figures.

Department of Ethnology★★. – The collection of weapons, costumes, masks, pottery... from the Pacific Islands, Africa, Indonesia and the Americas includes a number of rare items: a gigantic wood carving of the Hawaiian War God **Kukailimoku**, a fern root carving, a war costume with gauntlets made of shark's teeth.

The **Japanese collection** was gathered under the direction of Edward Morse, who made several trips to Japan when that nation was first opened to the West. The holdings of clothing, weapons, ceramics, carvings is distinguished by its fine quality. A selection of artifacts from Korea, India, Burma and Tibet accompanies the Japanese collection.

Asian Export Art Department. – The outstanding collection of decorative and useful Asian Export Art includes beautiful porcelains, furniture, textiles and precious objects created by Chinese, Japanese and Indian artisans in the 19C for export to England and America. The laquer, ivory and mother-of-pearl work and items fashioned in gold and silver in particular are impressive for their refined style and detail, and suggest the high level of skill achieved by Asian craftsmen.

Department of Natural History. – The Emperor Penguin brought back from Antartica by Admiral Byrd, is displayed with a collection of birds (stuffed) of the Essex county region.

SALEM AND ARCHITECTURE *time: 1 day*

The architecture of Salem traces the evolution of more than two centuries of architecture in New England, from the primitive shelters of the first colonists to the magnificent Federal mansions built by Samuel McIntire for the town's merchant princes.

In chronological order the highlights are:

1630 Pioneer Village – Replicas of the crude shelters built by the early settlers
1636 Goult-Pickman House – Inspired by English Elizabethan architecture
1642 Witch House – American colonial architecture
1668 **House of the Seven Gables★** – American colonial architecture
1684 **John Ward House★** – American colonial architecture *(Essex Institute)*
1727 Crowninshield-Bentley House – Georgian style *(Essex Institute)*
1761 Derby House – First brick structure built in Salem *(Salem Maritime NHS)*
1782 **Peirce-Nichols House★** – Federal style – Samuel McIntire *(Essex Institute)*
1804 **Gardner-Pingree House★★** – Federal style – Samuel McIntire *(Essex Institute)*

Essex Institute★★. – *132 Essex Street.* Founded in 1821 to serve as the Essex County Historical Society, the Institute is comprised of a library, museum and seven period houses.

The Museum. – *Open 9 AM (1 PM Sundays and holidays) to 5 PM; closed Mondays November through May and major holidays; $2.00.*

The museum features the decorative arts, furnishings and historical memorabilia of the region. In the research library there is an interesting collection of rare manuscripts, log books, letters and diaries.

The Houses. – *Tickets may be purchased at the museum. Combination ticket for the museum and 3 houses $5.00; Peirce-Nichols House not included in this ticket.*

The houses are on the grounds or in the immediate vicinity of the museum. We suggest you visit the houses in their chronological order of construction in order to follow the evolution that occurred in architecture and furnishings in the region from the 17 to 19C.

John Ward House★. – *Guided tours (30 min) June 1 through October, 9:30 AM to 4 PM, Sundays and holidays 1 to 4:30 PM; $1.50.*

The Ward House (1684) is a good example of 17C American colonial architecture, with its steep gables, stained clapboards and small casement windows. The furnishings are of the same period. The lean-to contains an Apothecary Shop, weaving room and Cent Shop.

Crowninshield-Bentley House. – *Same hours and admission as the John Ward House.*

The hipped roof, symmetrically placed windows, and pedimented doorway of this dwelling built in 1727 are typical of 18C and pre-Federal architecture. The furnishings represent several style periods.

Peirce-Nichols House★ (F). – *Open by appointment only ☏ (617) 744-3390.*

In 1782 Jerathmiel Peirce, a wealthy China Trade merchant, asked Samuel McIntire to build him a home suitable for such a prosperous citizen as himself. McIntire was only 24 years old at the time. Inspired by the Georgian style, he created this formal mansion with its classical columns, delicate porch, and gateposts ornamented with urns.

Inside, it is interesting to compare McIntire's Georgian style room with the Adamesque room opposite, which he redecorated. The intricately carved rosettes, garlands and acanthus leaves were carved by McIntire.

Gardner-Pingree House★★. – *Guided tours (30 min) June through October 10 AM to 4 PM, Sunday 1 to 4:30 PM; $1.50.*

The solid four-square silhouette of this handsome brick mansion (1804) is lightened by its balustraded roof, many windows and curved porch supported by Corinthian columns.

Inside, the furnishings and decor create a mood of elegance and refinement. In the front entrance hall, wave and rope motifs ornament the flying staircase. In the sitting room, the walls are covered with panels of imported 19C wallpapers that represent the twelve months. Decorative motifs on the fireplaces and above the doorways: sheaves of wheat, baskets of fruit are the work of the master – Samuel McIntire.

(From a photo by Angelo Hornack.)

Interior of the Gardner-Pingree House.

The bedchambers reveal the same refinement of taste. Most of the furniture was made in Salem. The wallpaper murals on the second floor were executed by an Italian painter, Michel Felice Corne, and are original to the house.

Washington Square★. – In the 19C a number of Federal mansions were built bordering Washington Square, the common of colonial Salem. A notable group of these residences stands on Washington Square North.

Chestnut Street★★. – This broad street lined with Federal style mansions is evidence of the wealth of early 19C Salem. The dwellings that stand on Chestnut Street were built for the most part between 1800 and 1820 and are unrivaled for their size and richly adorned facades.

No. 9. – This structure, **Hamilton Hall (N)**, was designed by McIntire.

No. 17. – The **Stephen Phillips Memorial Trust House (K)**, *(Guided tours – 45 min – late May to mid-October 10 AM to 4:30 PM; closed Sunday; $1.50)* decorated with furnishings from around the world, allows visitors to view the interior of one of the homes on Chestnut Street.

Goult-Pickman House (Q). – *Charter Street. Not open to the public.*

This colonial dwelling (c. 1636) is adjacent to Salem's old cemetery, the **Burying Point,** where there are interesting examples of early tombstones.

Pioneer Village. – *Forest River Park, east of the Salem Teachers College, at the junction of Rtes 1A and 129. Open mid-June through October 9 AM to 4 PM; $2.00.*

Replicas of the diverse kinds of dwellings built by Salem's early settlers have been constructed at the village: thatched cottages, dugouts of mud and straw, wigwams that show the influence of the Indians on the first settlers.

■ SALEM AND THE WITCHES *time: 2 hours*

Several points of interest in or near Salem recreate, each in its own way, the tale of the witch-hunts and the story of its unfortunate victims.

Salem Witch Museum (E). – *19 1/2 Washington Square North. Guided tours (30 min) 10 AM to 5 PM (6:30 PM July and August); closed January 1, Thanksgiving Day and December 25; $3.00, under 14, $2.50.*

The museum presents a multimedia program of thirteen life-size scenes that trace the major events of the witchcraft hysteria from 1692 through its final days in 1693.

Across from the museum is Henry H. Kitson's statue of **Roger Conant,** the founder of Salem.

Witch House (G). – *310 1/2 Essex Street. Guided tours (1/2 hour) mid-March through November 10 AM to 4:30 PM (6 PM July to Labor Day); $2.50.*

This large dwelling (1642) was the home of Judge Corwin, one of the witch-trial judges. The interior appears much as it did in the late 17C when more than 200 persons accused of witchcraft were brought here, to the judge's chamber, for a preliminary hearing.

Rebecca Nurse House. – *In Danvers 4 miles from Salem at 149 Pine Street. Guided tours (1 hour) mid-June to mid-October, 1 (2 PM Sunday) to 4:30 PM; closed Mondays and holidays; $1.50.*

Rebecca Nurse, a victim of the Salem witch-hunts, lived in this old saltbox. Accused of being a witch, Rebecca was tried, convicted and hanged despite a petition in her favor that had been signed by the townspeople. An upstairs room overlooks the peaceful field where she is buried in an unmarked grave.

SANDWICH ★

Michelin tourist map - fold 17 – *Local map pp 122-123* – Pop 10 756

On the shores of Shawne Lake, tranquil and shaded by willow trees, are the Dexter Mill and the Hoxie House. Built in the 17C, the house and the mill, which is still in use, evoke the colonial charm of this village founded in 1637. Across from the green stands the Sandwich Glass Museum.

Boston and Sandwich Glass Company. – In 1825 **Deming Jarves** chose Sandwich as the site of the new Boston and Sandwich Glass Company because of the region's vast forests. An efficient administrator, Jarves brought skilled craftsmen from Europe to work in the factory, and built homes and company stores for them. Jarves reintroduced the use of the three-part mold that had been used centuries before by the Romans; and by exploring new methods, developed a process to mass produce clear, cut glass in a variety of shapes, forms and patterns. It was the delicate "lacy" pattern of cut glass that became known as Sandwich glass *(p 31)* and brought fame to the factory and the town of Sandwich. By 1850, 500 workers were employed at the factory; however, labor disputes in 1888 eventually forced the Sandwich Glass Company to shut its doors permanently.

■ SIGHTS *time: 3 hours*

Sandwich Glass Museum★. – *Open April through October 9:30 AM to 4:30 PM; November through February 9:30 AM to 4 PM, closed Monday, Tuesday and January; $2.50.*

Founded in 1907, the museum owns an extensive collection of the glass made in Sandwich between 1825 and 1888. Moderately priced when it was produced in the 19C, Sandwich glass is today highly valued by collectors.

Before visiting the general exhibit rooms, pause at the diorama that illustrates the Sandwich factory and its craftsmen at work. Various stages in the making of glass are portrayed; sand is mixed with potash, carbonate of soda, or lime, heated in the furnace (2 500° F) and then blown, molded or pressed.

Many items made in a wide range of patterns from Sandwich glass are on display: candlesticks, tableware, vases, furniture knobs and tiebacks. Examples of the early pressed lacy glass, the colorful (canaries, blues, greens, opalescents) mid-period pattern glass, and the less well-known blown, cut and engraved glassware are among the exhibits. Note in particular the collections of highly decorative Sandwich paperweights, the glassware engraved with scenes portraying the joys of childhood in the style of Mary Gregory (a former employee at the factory), and the one-of-a-kind presentation pieces made to commemorate special occasions or events.

Heritage Plantation of Sandwich★★. – *From the Sandwich green take Rte 130 to Pine Street then turn left. Open mid-May to mid-October 10 AM to 5 PM; $5.00. Changing art exhibits in the Old Barn Gallery. Transportation available between the buildings.*

The museum's collections of early American historical artifacts and folk art are arranged in several buildings that have been designed to harmonize with the 76 acre park-like setting. The Plantation, formerly the estate of horticulturist Charles Dexter who performed extensive research on rhododendrons in the 1920s and 1930s, is especially lovely mid-May through mid-June when the rhododendrons are in bloom.

Automobile Museum★★★. – This replica of the Round Stone Barn constructed by the Shakers at Hancock *(p 130)* contains antique automobiles dating from 1899 to the 1930s, and includes the 1931 Duesenberg owned by Gary Cooper. Restored to their original appearance, these mint-condition autos sparkle with their highly polished nickel and brass trim. Silent movies *(10 min)* of the early days of the automobile are shown.

Military Museum★★. – This reproduction of the Publick House, a recreation hall built by the Continental Army (1783) in New Windsor, New York, contains antique firearms (including a rifle owned by Buffalo Bill Cody), flags and military miniatures. The 2 000 hand painted miniatures represent American military units from 1621 to 1900.

Art Museum★★. – The superb collection of folk art is comprised of primitive portraits, wood carvings (trade signs and figures), metal work, glass, scrimshaw, birds carved by Elmer Crowell and approximately 150 Currier and Ives prints. A display of tools, covering prehistoric times through the 19C, includes examples of handmade antique tools decoratively carved by the craftsmen who used them.

Children will enjoy riding on the Carousel (1912) which has been restored.

SPRINGFIELD

Michelin tourist map-fold 15 – Pop 150 450

Established on the banks of the Connecticut River in 1636 as a trading post, Springfield grew into an industrial center by the 19C. For more than 200 years the city was known for the government arsenal (the **Springfield Armory**) located here, which turned out the first American musket (1795) and the weapons used by the northern troops in the Civil War. A rich industrial past has contributed toward making Springfield the hub of business, finance and industry in the Pioneer Valley and the third largest city in Massachusetts, with tools and plastics among its leading products. Each September, Springfield hosts the **Eastern States Exposition** *(p 154)*, the largest fair in the northeast.

The city is proud to be the place where basketball was first played in 1891.

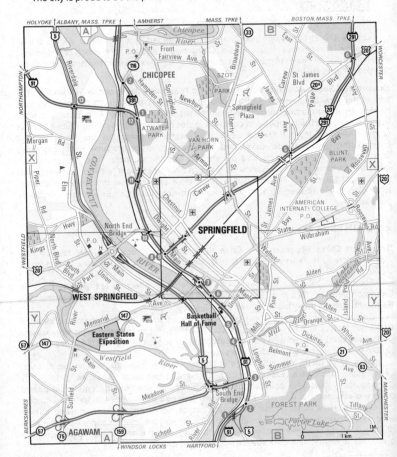

■ SIGHTS *time: 4 hours*

Court Square. – This pleasant park in the heart of downtown Springfield is bordered by buildings representing a variety of styles. Diagonally opposite the square rises the **Municipal Group*** (1913), a three-part complex consisting of a pair of classically inspired structures: City Hall and Symphony Hall with identical columned porticoes, and an Italian Renaissance bell tower. The **First Church of Christ** (1819) at the west end of the square, is a two-story wood frame meetinghouse surmounted by a gilded cock brought to America about 1750. Just beyond stands the **Hampden County Courthouse** (1871), a granite structure which has been substantially altered yet retains the late Gothic character of its original H. H. Richardson design.

Basketball Hall of Fame* (AY). – *1150 West Columbus Avenue. Open 9 AM to 5 PM; closed major holidays; $5.00, 8-15, $3.00.*

The Game. – Basketball was originated by Dr. James Naismith whose Springfield College team played the first game of basketball in 1891. Dr. Naismith developed the game to provide students with an exciting, competitive indoor activity that would be an alternative to the monotonous exercise program practiced in physical ed classes during the winter months. The equipment consisted of a ball and a peach basket, and each time a team scored someone had to climb a ladder to remove the ball from the basket. The game was adopted by the "Y" three years later and by 1936 had gained international recognition and acceptance as an Olympic sport.

The Exhibits. – Anyone who has ever played, coached or experienced the excitement of being a spectator at a basketball game, will enjoy reliving these moments at the Hall of Fame. Exhibits trace the development of the sport from amateur to professional and international status. Life-size action photos of such basketball greats as Wilt Chamberlain and Bob Cousy, video tapes of unforgettable coaches "in action" on the sidelines, film clips of the celebrated Harlem Globetrotters, and a selection of memorabilia (uniforms, equipment, etc.) comprise the displays. In the **Honors Court** outstanding players, coaches, and contributors to the sport are commemorated in a series of portrait medallions.

Before leaving visitors may test their skill at the Shoot Out on the ground floor.

The Quadrangle (Z). – *Open 12 noon to 5 PM; closed Mondays and holidays.*
The Museum of Fine Arts, Smith Art Museum, Connecticut Valley Historical Museum, Springfield Science Museum and city library are grouped together on the Quadrangle at Chestnut and State Streets.

Museum of Fine Arts. – The museum's holdings include a collection of European paintings of the 17C Dutch, 18C Italian, and 18 and 19C French schools. In the American section there are works by the 19C Primitive painters, canvases by Winslow Homer and John Singer Sargent, and the detailed *Historical Monument of the American Republic,* painted by Erastus Salisbury Field to commemorate the nation's centennial.

Smith Art Museum. – This building, designed to suggest an Italian Renaissance villa, contains the Smith collection of Oriental and American art and furnishings, and Classical casts. The collection includes American paintings, interesting examples of Japanese armor, exquisite carvings in jade, ivory, precious and semi-precious stones, and beautiful porcelains and Chinese *cloisonné.*

Connecticut Valley Historical Society Museum. – This building, recognized by its doorway similar to the type found in the Connecticut Valley, has period rooms and exhibits that feature the social and cultural development of the Connecticut Valley from the 17C.

Springfield Science Museum. – The museum has displays on plant and animal life and geology, and contains a collection of ethnological materials.

SPRINGFIELD

Springfield Armory National Historic Site (Z). – *1 Armory Square. Open 8:30 AM to 4:30 PM; closed major holidays.*
The main arsenal building of the deactivated Springfield Armory, home of the Springfield rifle, contains the **Benton Small Arms Museum** (M). The collection of small arms, edged weapons, and related military items dating from the 15C hand cannon to the present, includes examples of every gun manufactured here. Longfellow's poem *The Arsenal at Springfield* was inspired by the arsenal's Organ of Rifles on display.

EXCURSIONS

Eastern States Exposition (AY). – *2 miles from Springfield in West Springfield on Rte 147.*

New England's major fair, the Eastern States Exposition (the "Big E"), takes place at the 175 acre fairground in West Springfield during the month of September. Hundreds of exhibits, the Eastern States Horse Show and entertainment are presented. **Old Storrowtown Village,** a restored colonial village on the grounds, hosts tours.

The West Springfield fairground is also the site of the annual **American Crafts Council Fair** *(see Calendar of Events p 13)* formerly held in New York.

Stanley Park. – *400 Western Ave. 15 miles from Springfield in Westfield by Rte 20, then turn left onto Elm Street, left onto Court Street, and bear left onto Granville Road. Open mid-May to mid-October 8 AM to dusk. Carillon concerts in summer.*

A carillon and rose garden will be found among the many flower gardens in this 180 acre park. A covered bridge, old mill and blacksmith's shop are located in the pond area.

STOCKBRIDGE ★★

Michelin tourist map - fold 14 – *Local map p 85* – Pop 2 320

The grace and charm of this small town set in the heart of the Berkshires *(p 84)*, are evident as you stroll along Main Street, where inviting shops, the library, and the **Red Lion Inn** dating from colonial times, give way to white mansion-like clapboarded dwellings rimmed by broad, attractively landscaped lawns. In the summer, performances of classic American drama are presented by the Berkshire Theater Festival at the **Berkshire Playhouse,** designed by McKim, Mead and White in the late 19C as a casino.

Stockbridge has a history that is unique among most New England towns. In the early 18C the town was founded as an Indian mission. But the number of Indians steadily dwindled as the white population increased, and by the beginning of the 19C most of the **Stockbridge Indians** had migrated west to Wisconsin. The present-day population includes many artists and writers who have been drawn to the area by its natural beauty.

■ **SIGHTS** *time: 3 hours*

Mission House. – *Rte 102. Guided tours (35 min) Memorial Day to Columbus Day 10 AM to 5 PM, Sundays and holidays 11 AM to 3:30 PM; closed Monday; $3.00.*

John Sergeant, the first missionary sent to educate and Christianize the Stockbridge Indians, arrived in Stockbridge in 1734. This house which Sergeant had built as a wedding present for his wealthy wife Abigail five years later (1739), was extremely luxurious for its day. The elaborate front door made in the Connecticut Valley was hauled across the mountains in an oxcart to adorn the entranceway of the Mission House. A tour of the interior, in the semi-darkness due to the absence of electricity, suggests the conditions under which the pastor and his young bride lived in the early 18C. Most of the furnishings date from this period.

Norman Rockwell Museum at the Old Corner House★★. – *Main Street, next to the Stockbridge Library. Guided tours (1/2 hour) 10 AM to 4:30 PM; closed Tuesdays November through May, major holidays and the last two weeks in January; $3.00.*

The white Georgian style house contains a collection of almost 200 paintings and drawings by Norman Rockwell whose home was Stockbridge. Approximately 50 of the paintings are on view at one time.

An Illustrator of American Life. – Born in 1894 (d - 1978) in New York, Norman Rockwell began to draw as a child, and after high school studied at the Art Students League. At the age of 22 he sold to the *Saturday Evening Post* the first of the 300 covers he would design for this publication during the next fifty years.

Rockwell's paintings are a pictorial chronicle of changing times in America. His numerous scenes, most often depicting the routines of day-to-day living, were colored by a sense of humor, a spirit of joy and wonder

(From a drawing by Franklin Jones.)

Norman Rockwell.

and careful attention to detail; every wink of the eye, every ribbon, every gesture is important. His subjects were frequently children, modeled on persons he knew. In the 1960s contemporary personalities and social problems were increasingly the subjects of his works.

The Stockbridge Collection. – The Old Corner House collection includes some of Rockwell's best-known works: *The Peace Corps*, a triple *Self-Portrait*, his portrait of *John F. Kennedy*, his frequently reproduced winter scene of *Stockbridge Main Street at Christmas* and the *Four Freedoms*, which were responsible during World War II for selling a record $133 000 000 worth of government bonds, and include Rockwell's powerful expression of the *Freedom of Speech*.

Among the oils in the collection are *Looking Out to Sea:* an elderly man and his grandson observe wistfully as a ship clears the harbor; and the *Portrait of Ichabod Crane*, one of a series of illustrations created for *The Legend of Sleepy Hollow*. Rockwell's last works: the *New Kids in the Neighborhood, Busing*, and a portrait of *Robert Kennedy* reflect his treatment of such contemporary themes as integration and violence.

EXCURSIONS

Naumkeag. – *2 miles from Stockbridge center. From Main Street turn right onto Pine Street, then bear left at Shamrock Street and continue on Prospect Street. Open late June to Labor Day 10 AM to 5 PM; closed Monday. Memorial Day to late June and after Labor Day to Columbus Day Saturday and Sunday only. Guided tours (of the house) 45 min, last tour 4:15 PM. House and gardens $4.50.*

The Norman style mansion (designed by Stanford White) and its terraced hillside gardens were formerly the estate of Joseph Choate (1832-1917), United States Ambassador to England. The unusual design of the entrance to the Chinese garden was intended to prevent the devil from entering.

Chesterwood. – *3 miles west of Stockbridge. Take Rte 102 West to the intersection with Rte 183. Turn left onto Rte 183 and continue about 1/2 mile to a fork. There turn right onto the blacktop road, then turn left and continue 1/2 mile to Chesterwood. Open May through October 10 AM to 5 PM; $4.00.* This large estate, formerly a farm, was acquired in the late 19C by the American sculptor **Daniel Chester French** (1850-1931). French achieved his first major success at the age of 21 with his statue of the *Minute Man* at Concord *(p 126)*, but is probably best remembered for the impressive seated *Abraham Lincoln* he sculpted for the Lincoln Memorial in Washington, D.C. French executed more than 1 000 statues during his lifetime, most of which were for public monuments.

On the grounds of Chesterwood are:

– the **Barn Gallery,** where models and casts of French's works, including the *Alma Mater* sculpted for Columbia University will be found.

– the **House** a large Colonial Revival dwelling (designed by Henry Bacon) which replaced the farmhouse originally on the property. The house is furnished as it was when the artist lived here.

– the spacious, well-lit **Studio** (also designed by Henry Bacon) with its tall double doors and railroad tracks which allowed French to move large works such as the seated *Lincoln* outdoors where he could work in the natural light.

A nature trail *(20 min)* through the woods affords views of the hilly countryside.

STURBRIDGE ★★★

Michelin tourist map - fold 15 – 20 miles south of Worcester – Pop 6 565

Situated at the intersection of major north-south and east-west through routes, Sturbridge has been a stopping place for travelers since colonial days. Today, located at the junction of the Massachusetts Turnpike and Interstate-84, Sturbridge is more than ever a crossroads for travelers, and an ideal site for Old Sturbridge Village, one of New England's best-known attractions.

■ OLD STURBRIDGE VILLAGE★★★ *time: allow 1 day*

Old Sturbridge Village is a recreated farm village typical of the rural communities that dominated the New England countryside between 1790 and 1840. Remarkable for the beauty of its woodsy site and the authenticity of its buildings and atmosphere, the village is the result of an extensive amount of research. Guides wearing 19C dress farm the land, cook, make tools and implements according to traditional methods, creating for the visitor the illusion of having stepped back in time.

The village was the idea of Albert and J. Cheney Wells who wished to exhibit their collections of American antiques in a "living" museum. They began by acquiring farm buildings and shops of the early 19C, and by 1946 OSV was prepared to receive its first visitors.

OSV, an important research center for the years 1790-1840, publishes numerous works on daily life, customs and architecture of the period.

Visit. – *Open April through October 9 AM to 5 PM; the rest of the year 10 AM to 4 PM; closed January, December 25 and Monday December through March; $9.50, under 12, $4.00, under 6 free. Restaurants, cafeteria, shops on grounds.*

Visitor Center. – *Village maps and information are available.* Exhibits and a 15 minute film introduce the visitor to farm and community life in 19C New England.

Following the path to the Common, you will pass the **Quaker Meetinghouse** (1796); the simplicity of this small clapboard building seems to reflect the austere piety commonly associated with New England's Quakers.

The Common. – At one end of the Common is the white Greek Revival **Village Meetinghouse,** its spire rising gracefully above the other village structures. Daylight, streaming in through the large windows, illuminates the building's simple interior.

Houses on the Common reflect a diversity of styles. The **Fenno House** (1704), covered with wide rustic clapboards, is the oldest; inside the walls are covered with sheathing typical of the 18C; there are many American furnishings. The **Fitch House** (1737), in comparison, is more refined with its double-hung sash windows, stenciled floors and primitive portraits painted by itinerant artists. The **Richardson House Parsonage** (1740), a red and white "saltbox" *(p 27)*, is the home of the village parson.

(From a photo by Donald F. Eaton.)

Richardson Parsonage.

Inside, there are handwoven carpets and American country furnishings.

The **Tinsmith** next to the Richardson Parsonage turns out lanterns pierced with decorative designs. On the other side of the Parsonage is the tiny **Law Office** originally used by the Connecticut lawyer, John McClennan. Nearby is the well-stocked **Knight Store,** typical of the country store that was often the sole supplier of the farmer's needs and his only link with the outside world.

The Towne House. – 1796. Opposite the Village Meetinghouse and facing the Common this attractively proportioned Federal style house is similar to those dwellings built by well-to-do farmers, merchants and craftsmen. Unusually comfortable and luxurious for this early date, the house has period furnishings, delicately carved woodwork, Chinese porcelains and hand painted floor coverings. The large meeting-ballroom on the second floor is embellished with scenes painted directly on the plaster.

The Thompson Bank. – The Bank, a modest Greek Revival building, is similar to the banks that were established throughout New England in the 19C to meet the needs of the rapidly expanding economy. They were permitted to print their own notes until 1864 when the Federal currency system was established.

Isaiah Thomas Printing Office. – The grey wooden building beyond the bank is the printing office built in Worcester, Massachusetts for Isaiah Thomas, famed editor of the *Massachusetts Spy*, a newspaper which supported the Revolutionary cause. The activities carried on in a 19C printing establishment (production of tax forms, stock certificates, advertisements, broadsides) will be observed here.

Cross the Common and follow the road that leads to the Pliny Freeman farm. You will pass the **Animal Pound,** where stray animals were kept, the **School House** and **Pottery Shop.**

Pliny Freeman Farm. – The Freeman Farm, comprised of a gambrel roofed farmhouse and several outbuildings, is one of the liveliest areas in the village. Men and women in period dress cook, work in the fields, care for the animals as they did 150 years ago. Depending upon the season, the activities you will see may include maple sugaring, dyeing of cloth, sheep shearing, food preserving, fence building, cider making, etc.

A short distance down the road, in a stone building, is the **Blacksmith Shop;** further on are the **Carding Mill, Grist Mill** and **Saw Mill** located beside streams fed from the Mill Pond.

In the **Tavern** beyond the covered bridge buffet luncheons and fast food meals are served.

To reach the J. Cheney Wells Clock Gallery (adjacent to the visitor center) and the Formal Exhibits Area with its special displays, cross the Common and continue past the Printing Office.

Formal Exhibits. – In one area of the village small museums contain formal displays of traditional crafts and artifacts.

Glass Exhibit. – Glassmaking was an important industry in New England in the 19C *(p 31)*. The collection at OSV includes a selection of products in a wide variety of forms ranging from window glass to decorative paperweights. There is an interesting assortment of pictorial flasks featuring political, social and patriotic subjects as decorative motifs.

Firearms, Spinning and Weaving Exhibit. – Exhibits and demonstrations explain and show how spinning and weaving were done in the 19C. A fine collection of guns and military ware, accompanied by informative panels that present, in detail, the history of the militia in New England, is also displayed.

In the **Summerhouse** across the way there are changing exhibits on various subjects.

Lighting Exhibit. – The exhibit presents lighting devices from prehistoric times to the 19C, including examples of the **Argand lamp** which revolutionized the history of lighting. Developed in 1782 by Ami Argand, this lamp used a glass chimney, tubular wicks and air currents to produce a brilliant light never before achieved by earlier devices. Roman and Greek oil lamps, Betty Lamps (popular in early New England), Cape Cod lamps which burned whale oil, and kerosine lamps are among the interesting lighting devices

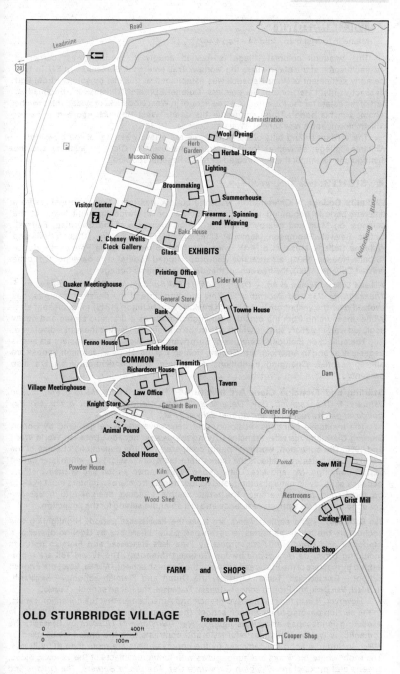

OLD STURBRIDGE VILLAGE

displayed. In a building nearby there is an exhibit related to the dyeing, culinary and medicinal uses of herbs. In the shop adjoining the herb garden brooms are made from broom corn.

J. Cheney Wells Clock Gallery. – The collection contains more than 100 American clocks – all in working order – produced between the late 18 and early 19C by New England clockmakers. Benjamin Cheney, Benjamin Willard, Seth Thomas, Eli Terry are represented, with the emphasis on Simon Willard and the clockmakers he influenced.

■ ADDITIONAL SIGHT

Sturbridge Auto Museum. – *Rte 20, 1 mile west of Old Sturbridge Village. Open mid-May through November 10:30 AM to 6 PM (9:30 PM late June to Labor Day); closed December to mid-May; $2.50.* The approximately 30 steam, gas and electric antique automobiles date from the late 19C through the 1930s. Historically interesting is the Metz Runabout (1897) built on two bicycle frames. In striking contrast to the simple Sears Highway Autobuggy (1908) which sold for $308, are the 1932 Rolls Royce, which sold for $23 000, and the 16 cylinder Cadillac limousine (1932), with its front grill, lights and horns to rival "a setting out of Tiffany's." There are two Pierce Arrows, the car that came with a free training course to familiarize the customer's chauffeur with the vehicle.

WILLIAMSTOWN ★★

Michelin tourist map - fold 14 – Pop 4 447

This beautiful colonial village is nestled snugly in the northwest corner of Massachusetts, at the place where the Mohawk Trail enters the Berkshires *(p 84)*. In 1753 the early settlement of West Hoosuck was established at this site by soldiers from Fort Massachusetts. Later, one of the soldiers, Colonel Ephraim Williams, Jr., bequeathed part of his estate for the founding of a free school in West Hoosuck, provided the town be renamed in his honor. Thus, soon after his death, West Hoosuck had a new name: Williamstown, and a new school: Williams College.

The verdant rolling hills of the Berkshires are a lovely setting for the buildings of Williams College, as well as for the Sterling and Francine Clark Art Institute and the distinguished summer theater directed by Nikos Psacharopoulos.

■ **SIGHTS:** *time 3 hours*

Williams College. – Chartered in 1793, the college has more than 50 buildings from different periods beginning in the late 18C. Set on the wide luxuriant lawns of the campus, on Main and nearby streets, are good examples of the Georgian, Federal, Gothic Revival (Thompson Memorial Chapel) and Greek Revival (Chapin Hall and Williams College Museum of Art) styles. On Main Street note the President's House (Sloane House – 1801), an attractive well-proportioned Federal style dwelling. Opposite is West College (1790), the free school that became Williams College.

Williams College Museum of Art. – *Open 10 AM (1 PM Sunday) to 5 PM; closed January 1, Thanksgiving Day and December 25*. This building, one of the finest on campus, has evolved over the years from a red brick Greek Revival octagon (1846) to its present size. While unassuming from the outside, the interior contains a dramatic atrium and neatly sculpted well-lit gallery spaces which add to the pleasure of viewing the works displayed.

The collection includes examples of European, non-Western and Ancient art and is especially strong in American art: Copley, Homer, Eakins, Hopper, Johnson, Inness are all represented. Changing exhibitions of modern and contemporary art are also presented.

Sterling and Francine Clark Art Institute ★★★. – *Open 10 AM to 5 PM; closed January 1, Thanksgiving Day, December 25 and Mondays, except major Monday holidays; guided tours July and August daily at 3 PM.*

The Institute's paintings, sculpture and decorative arts were gathered by Robert Sterling Clark and his wife, Francine, during the several decades between World War I and 1956. The collection, worthy of being compared with the collections of some of the world's finest museums, reflects the Clarks' early taste for classical art, which later turned to 19C paintings. Mr. and Mrs. Clark chose Williamstown as the site of their Institute because of its idyllic natural setting, and its location far from urban centers most likely to be threatened during wartime. The white marble building designed to house the collection suggests a private residence and is a splendid setting for the collection.

The Collections. – The earliest works are from the **Renaissance** period. Highlighting this section are the Italian paintings: a seven-part panel altarpiece by Ugolino di Nerio, a *Madonna and Child with Four Angels* by **Piero della Francesca;** and Flemish portraits including *David de Bourgogne* by Jan Gossaert (Mabuse). The **17 and 18C** are represented by masters of the European schools: the Spanish school – **Murillo, Goya;** the English school – **Gainsborough, Turner, Lawrence;** the Dutch and Flemish schools – **Rembrandt, Ruisdael, Van Dyck;** the French school – **Lorrain, Fragonard;** the Italian school – **Tiepolo.**

However, it is in the realm of 19C French and American art that the collection excels. In the section devoted to the French school, the group of **Corots** shows the artist's skill in executing landscapes as well as figures. *The Trumpeter of Hussars* by **Géricault**, the romantic, is typical of his masterful style and contrasts with the muted tones used by **Millet**. Included among the canvases by the impressionists are more than thirty **Renoirs**. The room where his works are hung, glows with luminous effects of the yellows, blues, greens and pinks of the *Sleeping Girl with a Cat, The Blond Bathers, The Onions* and others from his Impressionist period (1870 – 80s). **Degas'** treatment of his favorite subjects, dancers and horses, shows his extraordinary sense of movement. The **Monets**, shimmering with color, include one from his *Rouen Cathedral* series, and the *Cliffs at Etretat*. The postimpressionist **Toulouse-Lautrec** is represented by several works including his *Dr. Jules-Emile Péan*. Exhibited with the French school are portraits by **Mary Cassatt**, the American who lived in France and whose work shows the influence of the impressionists.

In the room reserved for her fellow countrymen Remington, Homer, and Sargent, it is interesting to note the different personalities of these three American artists who lived in the late 19C. **Frederic Remington** was the painter of the American West. During his lifetime he created several thousand paintings and pieces of sculpture that portrayed his favorite subjects: cowboys, Indians and the cavalry, and their heroic way of life. **Winslow Homer**, also a student of the American scene, chose to depict the rugged New England landscape in his paintings – the White Mountains of New Hampshire and the rocky Maine coast. **John Singer Sargent**, on the contrary, was a modern portraitist whose subjects, generally members of high society, were pictured with the artist's flair for sophistication. Sargent painted his famous *Fumée d'Ambre Gris* while on a voyage to Tangiers.

Displays of porcelain, furniture and silver accompany the paintings and sculpture. The Clark collection of American and European silver, one of the finest in the world, includes several dozen pieces made by the 18C English silversmith, **Paul de Lamerie.**

WORCESTER

Michelin tourist map - fold 16 – Pop 159 843

Worcester, the second largest city in New England, is a modern industrial center with more than 350 manufacturing plants. Playing an important role in the current rejuvenation of the downtown area are the Centrum, the new civic center offering facilities for trade shows and concerts; and preservation projects such as the renovation of **Mechanics Hall** (1857), a 19C architectural gem now a concert hall.

Between 1770 and 1776 the fiery anti-British newspaper, the *Massachusetts Spy*, was printed in Worcester by the patriot editor Isaiah Thomas. Following the Revolution Thomas was, in addition, influential in the establishment of the **American Antiquarian Society** (1812) which today owns an important collection of early American source material.

Educational institutions in the Worcester area include **Holy Cross College** and **Clark University.** The modernistic library on the Clark campus is named for the physicist **Dr. Robert Goddard** (1882-1942), a native of Worcester and professor at Clark, whose discoveries in the field of rocket propulsion led to the development of modern rocketry.

■ **SIGHTS** *time: 3 hours*

Worcester Art Museum★. – *55 Salisbury Street. Open 10 AM (1 PM Sunday) to 4 PM (5 PM Saturday and Sunday); closed Mondays and major holidays.*

The museum has collections of paintings, sculpture and the decorative arts which date from antiquity to the present. Displayed in a building inspired by the Italian Renaissance, the collections are arranged in galleries that surround a central court decorated with mosaics from Antioch (2-6C AD). The new 4-story addition to the museum, the Hiatt Wing (1983), provides gallery space for prints and drawings, 20C and contemporary art, changing exhibitions and an outdoor sculpture garden.

The **ground floor** is devoted to ancient art, Oriental art, and the art of the Middle Ages: note the 12C **Chapter House** formerly part of a Benedictine Priory in France, and the *Last Supper,* one of a group of 13C frescoes from Spoleto. In the central court is the large floor mosaic, *Hunting Scenes,* from the series excavated at Antioch.

On the **second floor,** the European schools of painting from the Middle Ages through the 20C are represented. Highlights include El Greco's intense *Repentant Magdalen, Saint Bartholomew* by Rembrandt, the *Rest on the Flight into Egypt* by the 16C Flemish

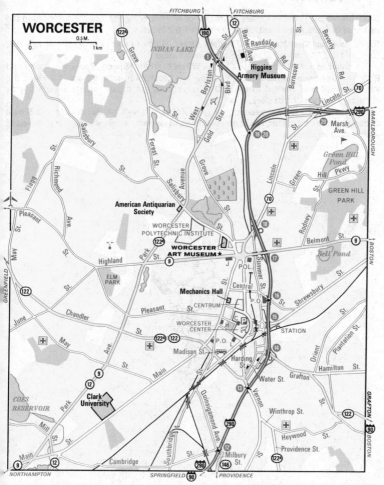

painter Quentin Massys, a portrait by Gainsborough of his daughters, Gauguin's *Brooding Woman,* and, in the Italian section, the dramatic *Calling of St. Matthew* by Strozzi.

The **third floor** features the American school of painting with works by John Copley, Worcester native Ralph Earl, James Whistler, Winslow Homer, John Singer Sargent, Mary Cassatt, Childe Hassam and the landscapists George Inness, Albert Ryder, Samuel Morse. The portrait of **Mrs. Freake and Baby Mary** *(illustration p 30)* by an anonymous 17C artist, is considered one of the finest portraits of the colonial period. An unusual feature of the self-portrait by Thomas Smith (c. 1680), is the naval battle scene which replaces the traditional landscape in the background. Another early work, by the Quaker Edward Hicks, is noteworthy for its simple, unsophisticated theme and treatment: *The Peaceable Kingdom. The Wave,* a more contemporary work, was painted by Marsden Hartley (1877-1943), an organizer of the New York Armory Show (1913) which introduced the American public to trends in modern European painting, and in particular cubism.

Worcester's sculpture collection includes an Egyptian female torso dating from the Fourth Dynasty and an eleven-headed Japanese Kwannon (9-10C AD).

Higgins Armory Museum. – *100 Barber Avenue. Open 9 AM (12 noon Saturdays, Sundays and holidays) to 4 PM; closed Mondays except July and August, and major holidays; $3.75. Demonstrations of arms and armor presented.*

This multi-storied steel and glass building constructed (1931) by John W. Higgins, formerly the president of Worcester Pressed Steel Company, houses a prize collection of armor as well as early tools and weapons that were gathered by Mr. Higgins during his travels abroad and across the United States.

The principal displays are arranged in an enormous exhibition gallery, modeled after the Great Hall of an 11C castle in Austria. Paintings, furnishings, banners and stained glass in the gallery add to the illusion of being in a medieval castle.

Along the walls there are more than 60 suits of parade, combat and jousting armor dating from the 14-16C. Produced by highly skilled craftsmen, there are suits which are truly works of art, such as the suit of Maximilian armor named for **Emperor Maximilian** whose preference was for fluted armor, and the **Franz von Teuffenbach** armor with its elaborate decorative etching. Tools and weapons of the Stone and Bronze Ages and a rare gladiator's helmet (3C BC) will be found among the other exhibits.

EXCURSION

Grafton. – Pop 11 850. *11 miles southeast of Worcester by Rte 122, then Rte 140 to the center of Grafton. From there follow the signs 1 1/2 miles.*

Willard House and Clock Museum. – *3 Willard Street. Guided tours (1 hour) 10 AM to 4 PM; Sunday 1 to 5 PM; closed Monday and major holidays; $2.00.*

A collection of 40 clocks made by the **Willard** brothers (Simon, Benjamin, Aaron and Ephraim) has been gathered in this house and clockshop (now a museum) where the Willards lived and worked in the 18C. Their clocks are today eagerly sought out by collectors and antique dealers.

Willard clocks were produced in a variety of styles: wall, shelf, tall case and Simon became famous for his improved timepiece the **banjo clock,** which was similar in shape to the musical instrument.

New Hampshire

Area : 9 304 sq miles
Population : 976 728
Capital : Concord
Nickname : The Granite State
State Flower : Purple lilac

In this triangle 168 miles long and 90 miles at its widest point, the mountainous relief of the Appalachian system to the west and north, contrasts with the hilly, low-lying region to the south which slopes gently down to the Atlantic Ocean.

The southern section of the state, benefiting in recent decades from the overflow of business firms of the Boston region, is heavily industrialized and populated. This is where New Hampshire's largest cities : **Concord, Manchester, Nashua, Keene,** and its only seaport : **Portsmouth** — at the end of the 18 mile coastline — are found.

Further north is the lakes region with its many Indian names : Ossipee, Squaw, Sunapee, Winnipesaukee. Hundreds of tiny islands pierce the surface of **Lake Winnipesaukee,** a vast inland body of water, rivaled in importance as a New Hampshire vacation area only by the **White Mountains,** New England's highest mountains. The White Mountains, great granite masses covered with forested slopes capped with rocky summits, and dominated by Mount Washington, are the domain of countless hikers who climb the scenic mountain trails while motorists drive through the rugged notches. Accustomed to receiving large numbers of visitors, the White Mountain region has a wide range of tourist accommodations and facilities.

History. – The colonization of New Hampshire proceeded slowly. The first settlement, established in 1623 on the coast, was followed by several other small settlements. New Hampshire was administered as a part of Massachusetts until 1679 when the region became a royal colony.

Its people, self-reliant, taciturn, industrious and independent were staunch supporters of the Revolution. The New Hampshire colony declared its independence from Great Britain seven months before the Declaration of Independence and set up its own government. The heroic words of Revolutionary War Colonel John Stark : "Live free or die," are today the state motto.

The character of New Hampshire's early population, primarily of Anglo-Saxon stock, was altered in the 19 and 20C by an influx of French Canadians and Europeans to the region, an ethnic mix which remains to this day.

Economy. – Despite its rural appearance – 80 % of the land is covered with forests – New Hampshire is essentially an industrial state. In the 19C factory complexes such as the **Amoskeag Mills** *(p 164),* at one time the largest textile manufactory in the world, were built on the banks of the Merrimack River. Textiles are still produced, but have been replaced as a major source of income by a variety of products : leather goods, machinery, electronic equipment, plastics and paper industries. Since the 1960s more than 250 Massachusetts firms have established branches in New Hampshire, attracted to the Granite State by its favorable tax structure and proximity to Boston.

Regarding its tax structure, New Hampshire is indeed unusual. Lacking a state income tax or sales tax, New Hampshire obtains revenues from alternate sources, notably the state-operated liquor monopoly, pari-mutuel betting, and taxes on business profits, meals and rooms.

Farming is oriented chiefly toward dairy and poultry products and the sale of Christmas trees.

Sand, gravel and feldspar are among New Hampshire's leading minerals and building granite is quarried on a limited scale. The introduction of concrete and steel construction has resulted in a decline of the formerly important granite industry which gave the state its nickname.

Recreation. – The White Mountains *(p 171)* are ideal for **hiking** and downhill and cross-country **skiing.** There are more than 30 ski areas in the state *(for the principal ski areas see the Michelin tourist map).*

Water sports are popular at the resort lakes : Sunapee, Newfound, Ossipee and especially Lake Winnipesaukee.

With its 1 300 lakes and ponds, and 1 500 miles of streams, New Hampshire offers the fisherman excellent opportunities for prize catches of brown and rainbow trout, salmon, bass, perch and pickerel.

Deer, bear, duck, pheasant and rabbit are among the animals that may be hunted in season. *For hunting and fishing regulations and information contact : New Hampshire Fish and Game Department, 34 Bridge Street, Concord, NH 03301.*

CANTERBURY CENTER ★
Michelin tourist map - folds 8 and 9 – 15 miles north of Concord – Pop 1 611

Attracted by the serene countryside and the gift of a very large tract of land in Canterbury, the Shakers established a community in the 18C near the small village of Canterbury Center. Several Shakers still live in the former Shaker community which is being restored as a museum of Shaker life.

Canterbury Shaker Village★ . – *Guided tours (1 1/2 hours) mid-May to mid-October hourly 10 AM to 5 PM; closed Sunday and Monday (except holiday weekends); $6.00. Tour includes a visit of the grounds and several restored buildings. Restaurant serving Shaker meals open 11:30 AM to 3:30 PM.*

The **Canterbury Shakers** farmed and made their own clothing, tools, furniture and machinery as did other Shaker communities. To obtain goods they were not able to produce, they specialized in the preparation of medicines and herbs which were sold throughout the United States and abroad.

The **Meeting House** (1792) where the Shakers gathered for their religious services, contains exhibits of their products: furniture, tools, wooden boxes, and examples of such Shaker inventions as the flat broom and the threshing machine. The simplicity of the meetinghouse is in contrast to the subtle ornamentation of the **Dwelling House** with its pedimented porch, urns and cupola. The well-equipped **Schoolhouse** reflects the commitment of the Shakers to educating the young people in their community.

CENTER SANDWICH ★
Michelin tourist map - fold 9 – 23 miles north of Laconia – Pop 978

Situated north of Lake Winnipesaukee and at the foot of the White Mountains, Center Sandwich is one of the prettiest villages in New England. The village is picture-perfect in the fall when its simple white clapboarded structures are framed by a tapestry of brilliant autumn color. On the green is the sales shop of the **Sandwich Home Industries**, the founding member of the state-wide guild of craftsmen: the League of New Hampshire Craftsmen.

Route 109 from Center Sandwich passes through **Sandwich**, a picturesque hamlet, with its old post office that still operates and houses the workshop of a silversmith.

CONCORD
Michelin tourist map - folds 8 and 9 – Pop 30 902

The capital of New Hampshire since 1808, Concord is the seat of the largest state legislature in the nation: 424 representatives. In the 19C Concord became known for its granite and the **Concord coaches** built here from 1813 to 1900 by Abbot-Downing Company. Offering increased riding comfort, the Concord coach encouraged passenger travel, and was later credited with "having settled the West."

Today, a center of government and commerce, the city is also a transportation hub of railway and road systems linking all corners of the state. The gilded dome of the State House dominates the cluster of office buildings that rises alongside the Merrimack River.

The State House. – *25 State Street. Open 8 AM to 4:30 PM; closed Saturdays, Sundays and holidays.* The New Hampshire State House is the oldest state capitol where the legislature still meets in its original chambers. Regimental colors are displayed in the Hall of Flags *(ground floor)*, and in the Senate Chamber *(second floor)* are the Barry Faulkner murals depicting scenes from the state's history.

Statues of the famous New Hampshire sons Colonel John Stark, Daniel Webster and Franklin Pierce stand on the grounds.

New Hampshire Historical Society and Library. – *30 Park Street. Open 9 AM to 4:30 PM (8 PM Wednesday); closed Sunday. Library admission $2.00; closed Saturday and Sunday.* The handsome marble and granite building contains a genealogical research library and museum galleries with changing exhibits of art, artifacts and manuscripts related to New Hampshire history. On the ground floor note the Concord coach made in the last century by Abbot-Downing Company.

League of New Hampshire Craftsmen. – *205 North Main Street. Open weekdays 10 AM to 4 PM; Sales Shop (36 North Main Street) 10 AM to 5 PM, closed Sunday.*

The League of New Hampshire Craftsmen maintains its headquarters and main sales shop in Concord. Handcrafted textiles, glass and silver are among the items sold.

EXCURSIONS

Hopkinton. – *8 miles west of Concord by Rte 9.* Pop 3 988. This appealing Concord suburb is well known to antique hunters. The town's wide main street is lined with attractive dwellings and shops, the Town Hall and St. Andrew's Church.

Henniker. – *15 miles west of Concord by Rte 9.* Pop 3 260. This lively college town is home to New England College. The Henniker covered bridge is visible from Route 114 between the college and the village center.

Hillsborough. – *22 miles west of Concord by Rte 9.* Pop 3 614. A small commercial center, Hillsborough has structures dating from the last century. From Route 9, a back road leads through **Hillsborough Center★** *(turn west at the blinking light onto School Street)* a country hamlet with white buildings and rambling stone walls tucked among the trees.

CONNECTICUT LAKES Region

Michelin tourist map - fold 3 – Route 3 from Pittsburg to the Canadian border

The narrow, northern section of New Hampshire is a densely wooded forest-and-lake region, a haven for hunters and fishermen because of its wide variety of animal life. South of the Canadian border, the **Third, Second** and **First** Connecticut Lakes give rise to the Connecticut River which continues southwest as the Vermont-New Hampshire border. From Route 3 there are glimpses of the lakes through the trees.

Lake Francis State Park. – *6 miles from Pittsburg by Rte 3; then turn right onto River Road. After 2 miles arrive at the entrance to the park after passing a covered bridge.*
The scenic shores of Lake Francis are an ideal spot to camp or picnic.

DIXVILLE NOTCH

Michelin tourist map - fold 3 – 41 miles north of Berlin

In northern New Hampshire Route 26, between Colebrook and Errol, passes through an area of rugged mountain cliffs and thick stands of evergreens: Dixville Notch. Here on the shores of Lake Gloriette, near the highest point in the notch, stands the grand and luxurious **Balsams Hotel** built in the 19C.

East of the hotel, there are two easy walks leading to waterfalls. For the first, begin at **Flume Brook Parking Area** on Route 26. The second, the **Cascades-Waterfalls Trail** to **Huntingdon Falls**, begins 1 mile east of Flume Brook Parking at the Dixville Notch State Wayside.

GRAFTON CENTER

Michelin tourist map - fold 8 – 37 miles west of Laconia – Pop 773

South of the White Mountains, several mountains have been exploited for their mineral resources. Among those no longer worked is the Ruggles Mine.

Ruggles Mine★. – *From the green at Grafton Center follow the signs 2 miles. Open mid-June to mid-October 9 AM to 5 PM (6 PM July and August); mid-May to mid-June weekends only; $4.95. Insect repellent advised especially following long periods of rain.*

The abandoned pegmatite mine on Isinglass Mountain is a curious and interesting place to explore with its arched stone tunnels, winding passageways, large open pits and mine dumps. The mine was owned and operated in the 19C by Sam Ruggles, a Yankee farmer who discovered mica deposits on the property. To prevent other landowners in the area from learning his secret, Sam worked the mine only at night and sold the mica in England – not in the United States! The Ruggles mine remained New Hampshire's first and only commercial mine until 1868.

Amateur rock hounds in particular may wish to rent equipment and dig for mica, feldspar or one of the other 150 minerals that have been found here.

(From a photo by Forwards Color Productions, Inc.)

Ruggles Mine.

HANOVER ★

Michelin tourist map - fold 8 – Pop 9 364

This pretty colonial town on the banks of the Connecticut River is the home of one of the nation's prominent Ivy League schools, Dartmouth College. Hanover is a college town, so much so that it is often difficult to separate its buildings and activities from those of Dartmouth. Despite the town's growth into a regional center, Hanover's early charm and pleasant tree-lined streets have remained essentially unspoiled.

DARTMOUTH COLLEGE★

Established in 1769 by the Reverend Eleazar Wheelock "for the education of Youth of the Indian Tribes" and "English Youth and any others," Dartmouth today offers its 600 students undergraduate programs in the Liberal Arts and Sciences, and graduate studies in medicine, engineering and business administration. Dartmouth's list of illustrious alumni includes the lawyer-orator Daniel Webster (1782-1852) and Nelson A. Rockefeller (1908-1979) the former governor of New York. The Dartmouth **winter carnival** featuring skiing, skating, art shows, ice sculpture contests and other special events is the social event of the winter season *(see Calendar of Events p 13).*

The Green ★. – The spacious green is bordered by the **Hanover Inn** and a number of the college buildings. The corner of Main Street and Wheelock Street is a good point from which to view Dartmouth Row; to its right is the modern Hopkins Center, to the left is Webster Hall, originally built as an auditorium; beyond Webster Hall is Baker Library.

Hopkins Center. – The fine arts center (1962), recognizable by its multistoried windows, houses art galleries, theaters and two concert halls. The Center provides the college and the entire Hanover region with a program of cultural events year round.

Hood Art Museum. – *Open 11 AM to 5 PM, closed Mondays and major holidays.*

(From a photo by Adrian Bouchard.)

Dartmouth Hall.

Tucked between the Romanesque Wilson Hall (1885) and the modern Hopkins Center, and connecting these stylistically very different buildings is the Hood, Dartmouth's art museum. The Hood galleries contain works from the permanent collection which covers many different periods and styles. American, European, Indian, African and Ancient art are featured, and the museum also hosts traveling shows. On the lower level a special area displays a group of 9C BC Assyrian reliefs; on the upper level contemporary art is shown in a spacious loft-type gallery.

Dartmouth Row. – This group of four colonial buildings includes, in the center, **Dartmouth Hall**, a replica of the original building constructed in 1784 and destroyed by fire in 1904.

Baker Memorial Library. – *North end of Green.* The building houses a series of **murals ★** painted by the Mexican artist José Clemente Orozco (1883-1949) in 1932-1934. Powerful, often brutal in their expression of the forces of good and evil which have shaped man, the murals are Orozco's interpretation of the 5 000 year history of the Americas. *Open 8 AM to midnight; during intersession 8 AM (9 AM Saturday, 1 PM Sunday) to 8 PM (6 PM Saturday); closed holidays.*

KEENE

Michelin tourist map - fold 8 – *Local map p 166* – Pop 21 572

This commercial and manufacturing center has grown rapidly during the past several decades owing to its location near the industrialized areas of Massachusetts which have spilled over the border into New Hampshire. Keene's pottery and glassworks, major New Hampshire industries in the 19 and early 20C, have been replaced in importance by the city's more than 50 factories that produce tools, shoes, machine parts and textiles.

Colony House Museum. – *104 West Street. Open May to October 12, 10 AM to 4:30 PM; closed Monday; $1.00.*

Glass and pottery made in Keene and the nearby village of Stoddard are featured in this Federal mansion (1820), the home of the city's first mayor, Horatio Colony. Among the many examples of locally made glass on display are the pictorial flasks embossed with patriotic themes, and one-of-a-kind pieces: walking sticks, miniatures, decorative panels. Glass inks, bottles and flasks produced in Keene are easily identified by their light green or aqua-green color. Stoddard glass is generally a deep shade of amber.

The attractively decorated earthenware vases, pitchers, tea sets and souvenir pieces were made at the Hampshire Pottery Works in Keene.

EXCURSION

Covered Bridges on the Ashuelot River. – Covered bridge enthusiasts will enjoy a side trip on Route 10 South to covered bridges Nos. 2, 4 and 5. *Roadside markers indicate direction to the bridges.*

MANCHESTER

Michelin tourist map - fold 9 – Pop 94 937

Manchester is the most important city and manufacturing center in New Hampshire. In the 19C the largest textile factory in the world, the **Amoskeag Mills,** was built here beside the Merrimack River. The mile-long stretch of red brick buildings still standing along the river, is an awesome sight. The factory was the major employer in Manchester and when the mills closed down permanently in 1935, the city was left financially destitute. The future appeared bleak until a group of investors, determined to revive the city, bought the mills with the idea of selling or leasing space to various businesses. Within ten years dozens of industries relocated in the mill complex and Manchester was on its way to economic recovery. Today Manchester's more than 200 companies make textiles, shoes, metal products, clothing and electronic equipment. The city's clothing and shoe outlets are major attractions in themselves, offering name brand items at discount prices.

The Currier Gallery of Art. – *192 Orange Street. Open 10 AM to 4 PM (10 PM Thursday); Sunday 2 to 5 PM; closed Mondays and holidays.*

A south entrance flanked by tall mosaic panels, and a north entry fronting a granite-paved courtyard provide access to this museum, known for its collection of paintings, sculpture and decorative arts.

In the central hall, hanging above the weathervane from the Amoskeag Mills, is the 15C Flemish tapestry referred to as *The Visit of the Gypsies:* the Lord and Lady are greeting the gypsies, but will they be allowed to enter the castle?

The first floor galleries contain the European collection: early Italian paintings, drawings by **Tiepolo**, the superb *Portrait of a Man* by Jan Gossaert called Mabuse (perhaps a self-portrait), and canvases from the French, Spanish, English and Dutch schools. In the west wing, 20C American paintings and sculpture is represented by **Andrew Wyeth**, O'Keefe, **Hopper**, Lachaise, Nevelson and others. Examples of American and European art glass are displayed in the east gallery.

The second floor is devoted to **American art** from the 17-19C, with the emphasis on New Hampshire pieces. Among the paintings are portraits by Copley and Trumbull and landscapes by Cole, Bierstadt and Church. Early portraits such as *Portrait of a Lady* attributed to Samuel and Ruth Shute never fail to charm the viewer by their simplicity.

EXCURSION

"America's Stonehenge". – *19 miles from Manchester by I-93 South to Exit 3 then follow Rte 111 East 5 miles; turn onto Island Pond Road to Haverhill Road. Open May through October daily, April and November Saturday and Sunday only, December through March weather permitting; spring and fall 10 AM to 4 PM, summer 9 AM to 5 PM; $5.00. ☎ (603) 893-8300.*

The large standing granite slabs of this stone complex give "America's Stonehenge" its name. There are many theories concerning the site, however, the astronomically aligned slabs have been among the factors leading to the speculation that this may be "America's Stonehenge," the remnant of a calendar site that was laid out 4 000 years ago by an advanced civilization with a knowledge of the movement of the stars, moon and sun. Carbon datings were conducted here in 1969 and 1970.

Visit. – The stone structures at "America's Stonehenge" are named to suggest their possible use: the Oracle Chamber, the Sacrificial Table, etc. It is especially interesting to follow the astronomical alignment trail (red arrow) on March 22, June 21, September 22 and December 21 to see the slabs that accurately indicate the summer and winter solstices and equinoxes.

The MOUNT MONADNOCK Region ★

Michelin tourist map - fold 8 – *Local map p 166*

Mount Monadnock, the isolated remnant of a mountain range formed eons ago, looms 3 165 ft above the tiny colonial villages, white steepled churches and farmland of southwestern New Hampshire. Its name **Monadnock** has entered into the vocabulary of geographers to designate the residual relief of a landscape that has passed through various stages of evolution. Hiking to the top of Mount Monadnock for its spectacular view became popular in the 19C and today Monadnock is one of the most frequently climbed mountains in the world: about 125 000 persons each year climb to its summit.

From Fitzwilliam to Hancock *33 miles – allow 1 day*

Fitzwilliam. – Pop 1 836. Large clapboarded structures, the old meetinghouse, inn and a Congregational Church surmounted by a "wedding cake" steeple face the green. **Rhododendron State Park** *(1 1/2 miles off of Rte 119)* has 16 acres of wild rhododendrons that are best viewed during June and July when they are in full bloom.

Take Rte 119 East, then after the intersection with Rte 202 turn left onto an unmarked road.

Cathedral of the Pines ★ . – *Open May to late October 9 AM to 4:30 PM.* Situated on the crest of a pine-clad hill, this outdoor cathedral, the work of a couple who lost their son in World War II, is a memorial to all Americans who gave their lives during wartime. Services are held at the **Altar of the Nation** which faces Mount Monadnock; stones set into the altar were received as tributes from U.S. presidents, military leaders, and the 50 states and 4 territories. The **Memorial Bell Tower**, rising in a clearing, is dedicated to American women war dead; the plaques above the tower arches were designed by Norman Rockwell. This place of worship welcomes persons of all faiths.

Turn left when leaving the Cathedral of the Pines, 1 1/2 miles further, at the fork, bear right to return to Rte 124.

New Ipswich. – *Pop 2 863. An additional 7 miles on Rte 124 East to Main Street.*

The **Barrett House** (1800), a handsome Federal mansion, and its sedate rustic surroundings have changed little over the years. Built by the wealthy mill owner, Charles Barrett, the house is furnished with Barrett family pieces *(guided tours – 50 min – June to October 15, Thursday, Friday, Saturday and Sunday 12 noon to 5 PM; $2.50).*

The itinerary follows Rte 124 West to Jaffrey.

Jaffrey. – Pop 4 520. Located at the foot of Mount Monadnock, Jaffrey provides easy access to Mount Monadnock State Park *(p. 166)*.

Follow Rte 124 West

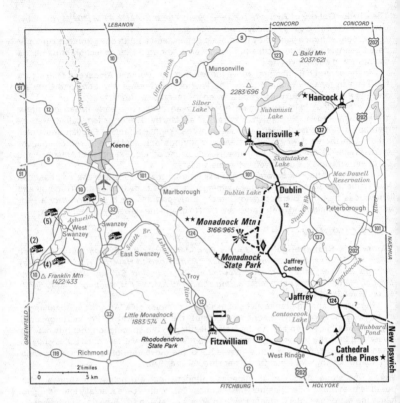

Jaffrey Center. – Pop 4 520. A series of lectures held at the old meetinghouse *(Rte 124)* each year honors **Amos Fortune,** a former slave who bequeathed a sum of money to the Jaffrey School when he died. The tombstones of Amos Fortune and his wife stand in the cemetery behind the meetinghouse. The inscription on Amos' tombstone reads:

> to the memory of Amos Fortune
> who was born free in
> Africa, a slave in America,
> he purchased liberty,
> professed Christianity,
> lived reputably, and
> died hopefully …

Continue on Rte 124 West. 2 miles after the meetinghouse turn right.

Monadnock State Park★. – *Open early April to Memorial Day weekends only and afte Memorial Day to mid-November daily for hiking, picnicking and camping; day use $1.00 camping $6.00 per night;* ☏ *(603) 532-8862. Skiing in the winter.* Trails to the summit o Mount Monadnock begin at the end of the tar road beyond the toll booth.

Mount Monadnock★★. – The trails most frequently taken are the **White Cross Trail** *(severa steep sections)* and the **White Dot Trail** *(time: 4 hours RT).* The **Cascade Link – Old Ski Path – Red Spot** and **Pumpelly Trail** *(time: 5 1/2 hours RT)* offers good views at lower elevations as well. The far reaching **view★★** from the summit on a clear day includes Mount Washingto to the north and the Boston skyline to the south.

Turn left as you leave the park, onto upper Jaffrey Road.

Dublin. – Pop 1 388. Such well-knowns as Mark Twain summered in this hillside hamlet, today the home of *Yankee Magazine* and *The Old Farmers Almanac.*

Continue north on upper Jaffrey Road.

Harrisville★. – Pop 971. The handsome ensemble of modest red brick buildings: mills, dwellings, the Congregational Church reflected in the village pond, is a pleasing example of an early rural mill village. Residents of

Harrisville.

Harrisville interested in preserving the character of their village, have restored these structures themselves, and in 1970, when the textile industry that had operated here for two centuries closed down, they were successful in attracting several small companies to relocate in Harrisville.

Follow the unmarked road along the lakes, then turn left onto Rte 137.

Hancock ★. – Pop 1 261.The tranquility of this colonial village is disturbed only once a year – on July 4th – when the bells of the meetinghouse peal from midnight to 1 AM to celebrate the anniversary of America's independence. The **John Hancock Inn** is in the center of the village, opposite the general store. In the old **cemetery** at the end of the street, there are good examples of the skill of the early stonecutter.

NASHUA

Michelin tourist map - fold 9 – Pop 72 458

Located close to the Boston region, Nashua has experienced a surge of industrial growth since the 1960s, which has made it the second largest city in New Hampshire.

EXCURSIONS

Anheuser-Busch Hamlet. – *7 miles from Nashua in Merrimack. Take Rte 3 to Exit 8, bear left, then turn right and continue to 1 000 Daniel Webster Highway. On the grounds of the Anheuser-Busch brewery. Open May through October daily 9:30 AM to 3:30 PM; the rest of the year Wednesday through Sunday 9:30 AM to 3:30 PM.*

Budweiser Clydesdales can be seen at the picturesque Hamlet where they are raised and trained. The white-stockinged Clydesdales, associated with Anheuser-Busch since 1933 when the company acquired its first team to celebrate the repeal of prohibition, tour the country, appearing in parades, at fairs and at other events.

Guided tours (1/2 hour) of the brewery, hours same as above. ☏ (603) 889-6631.

Playworld. – *8 miles east of Nashua in Hudson on Rte 111. Open Memorial Day to Labor Day 10 AM to 6 PM; May and after Labor Day to Columbus Day Saturday and Sunday only; $10.00.*

Mighty Mouse and other costumed characters are on hand to entertain visitors at this amusement park and zoo where there are rides, animal exhibits and live shows.

The NEW HAMPSHIRE Coast

Michelin tourist map - fold 9

Sandy beaches, rocky ledges and state parks alternate along New Hampshire's 18 mile coastline. The coastal Route 1A from Seabrook to Portsmouth winds past resort areas and elegant estates, affording views of the ocean.

Hampton Beach. – This lively amusement-resort center has a casino, and giant clusters of oceanfront hotels, motels and eating places, as well as a 3 1/2 mile sandy beach. The **New Hampshire Marine War Memorial**, a granite statue of a seated maiden looking out to sea, is located alongside Route 1A in the center of Hampton Beach. North of Hampton Beach the road skirts the waterfront estates of **Little Boars Head**.

Rye Harbor State Park. – This rocky headland is a good place to picnic and fish. *Open Memorial Day to Labor Day 8 AM to 8 PM (weekends only early May to before Memorial Day and after Labor Day to mid-October); $1.00.*

Wallis Sands State Park. – A gentle surf breaks onto the park's 1/4 mile long beach. *Open Memorial Day to Labor Day 8:30 AM to 6 PM; $4.00 per car. Bath house and snack bar.*

Odiorne Point. – This was the site of the first settlement in New Hampshire.

NEW LONDON ★

Michelin tourist map - fold 8 - Pop 2 858

New London's hilltop setting looks out onto neighboring and far reaching ridges and woodlands that are a flaming realm of color during Indian summer. On the main street, Route 114, there is a comfortable old inn, the campus of **Colby Sawyer College** (1837) and a meetinghouse: the Baptist Church. New London is one of those small, unspoiled New England villages where travelers are easily tempted to stop and spend a few days.

EXCURSION

Mount Sunapee State Park. – *13 miles from New London by Rte 11 South; after crossing Rte 89, turn left onto Rte 103A South, then turn onto Rte 103 West.* Lake Sunapee and the mountain of the same name are the center of a year-round vacation resort. Opposite the entrance to the park is the entrance to the mile-long **State Beach** *(weekends late May to mid-June 8 AM to 8 PM, daily mid-June to Labor Day; $2.00)* on the shores of Lake Sunapee. The League of New Hampshire Craftsmen holds its annual Craftsmen's Fair at the Park in early August *(see Calendar of Events p 13).*

The **gondola** to the summit of Mount Sunapee (alt 2 700 ft) operates during the summer and early fall, offering good **views ★** of the region *(Memorial Day to Columbus Day; for schedule and rates ☏ (603) 763-2356*

PLYMOUTH

Michelin tourist map - fold 8 – Pop 5 296

Lying just outside the White Mountain National Forest is Plymouth, a small resort town that is the site of Plymouth State College.

Polar Caves. – *Rte 25, 5 miles west of Plymouth center. Open mid-May to mid-October 9 AM to 4:30 PM; $5.50.*

The Polar caves are a series of caves and stone passageways that were formed during the last Ice Age, as freezing temperatures and ice caused gigantic boulders to break loose from the mountain. Eight conveniently placed stations with taped commentaries allow visitors to tour the caves at their own pace.

Wooden walkways lead to the first cave, the Ice Cave, named for the cool air that rises from within and fills the entire cave. The walkways continue over, around and through four more caves to the last, Smugglers Cave, which is entered by the narrow Lemon Squeezer passage or the more comfortable Orange Crush. In the Cave of Total Darkness there is an exhibit of flourescent minerals.

EXCURSION

Hebron★. – *14 miles from Plymouth by Rte 25 West, then Rte 3A.*

Hebron has all the elements of a New England village: an emerald green, the church with its pointed steeple, a general store, post office, and nearby, a handful of attractive dwellings. Together, they form a harmonious and charming ensemble.

Newfound Lake. – The tranquil setting of this spring fed lake nestled between two mountains, is best viewed from its western shore, south of Hebron. There is a beach in **Wellington State Park.**

Business Hours – *Banks: 9 AM to 3 PM*
Shops: 10 AM to 5 PM (or 6 PM)
Shopping Centers: 9 AM (or 10 AM) to 9 PM (or 10 PM)
Post Office: 8 AM to 5 PM (12 noon Saturday)

PORTSMOUTH ★★

Michelin tourist map - fold 9 – Pop 27 789.

New Hampshire's former capital and only seaport is a small low-keyed city on the banks of the Piscataqua River. Vintage Georgian mansions reminiscent of Portsmouth's past as a rich lumber and seafaring center, line the streets leading to the waterfront.

Since the 1950s renewal projects aimed at preserving Portsmouth's colonial structures and character have been carried out in the older sections of the city, the most interesting of these being the transformation of **Strawbery Banke,** the city's early waterfront community, into a museum. In the **Old Harbor District: Bow Street, Market Street, Ceres Street** restored and freshly painted restaurants, craft studios and antique shops, as well as the tug-boats tied up at the cove alongside Ceres Street, are reminders of a time when commerce was Portsmouth's main business.

The Waterfront.

Commerce is still one of Portsmouth's important industries, although the **Portsmouth Naval Shipyard** (located in Kittery, Maine) and the **Pease Air Force Base** (1956) have replaced shipping and trade as the area's leading employers.

Historical Notes. – In 1623 a group of English settlers arrived on the banks of the Piscataqua. Because the riverbanks were covered with wild strawberries they named their community "Strawbery Banke." Not until several decades later was the "port at the mouth of the river" renamed Portsmouth.

Fishing, shipbuilding, and the region's many saw mills that transformed New Hampshire's largest trees into timber for the British Navy, provided the settlers with their livelihood. After the Revolution maritime commerce brought increased prosperity to the city. Beginning in the 18C and continuing into the 19C, merchants and ship captains built dwellings which reflected their comfortable station in life and were among the finest Georgian and Federal dwellings in the country.

In 1800 Portsmouth gave its name to the new naval base constructed in Kittery, the Portsmouth Naval Base. The Treaty of Portsmouth which ended the Russo-Japanese War was signed at the base in 1905.

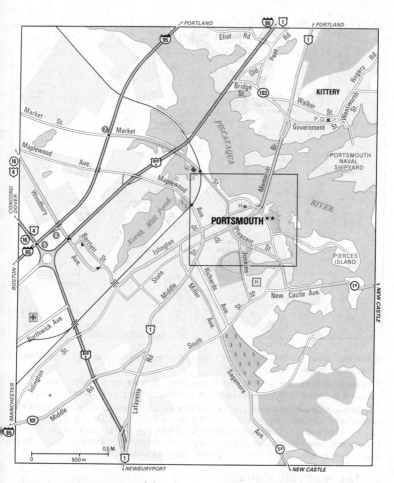

■ STRAWBERY BANKE★★

Open May through October, 10 AM to 5 PM; $6.00, under 17, $3.00; family rate $15.00.

A gift shop, several craft shops and a coffee shop are located on the grounds. A detailed map of Strawbery Banke is available at the entrance (Marcy Street). Guided tours offered on a variety of topics (included in museum admission); consult daily schedule distributed to ticket holders.

This 10 acre restoration project involving the **Puddle Dock area**, the site of Portsmouth's early Strawbery Banke settlement, is a living model of the techniques used and benefits to be derived from rehabilitating an entire district. The project has also been an example of what a group of determined citizens can achieve. Advised in the 1950s that the overall renewal plans for the city included demolition of the Puddle Dock neighborhood, citizens interested in preserving the area, urged, instead, that renewal funds be made available to restore and recycle the old shops and dwellings in the district. Their strong support of the project never waned and in 1957 the rehabilitation of Puddle Dock was begun.

Eighteen of the 35 structures at Strawbery Banke have been restored and are open to the public, while others currently under renovation allow visitors to view the various stages of the restoration process. Several craftsmen maintain workshops in Strawbery Banke and it is hoped that more tradesmen will find the district a desirable place to work and live.

Of the eighteen dwellings which have been restored, seven are furnished with period pieces.

Captain John Sherburne House. – c. 1695. This attractive 17C dwelling contains a detailed exhibit on the construction and restoration of the house.

Joshua Jackson House. – c. 1750. The house is an example of how a structure appears before it is restored. An exhibit traces the development of the Puddle Dock neighborhood.

Captain John Wheelwright House. – c. 1780. The house contains furnishings and some fine paneling from the Revolutionary War period.

Joshua Jones House. – c. 1790. An archeological lab and exhibits of artifacts excavated on "digs" at Strawbery Banke and elsewhere in Portsmouth will be seen here.

Stephen Chase House. – c. 1762. This handsome Georgian dwelling contains 18C wood carving believed to be the work of William Deering, a ship carver from Kittery, Maine.

Captain Keyran Walsh House. – c. 1796. Modest furnishings, a lovely staircase and notable examples of wood graining and marbleization are features of this typical 18C dwelling.

169

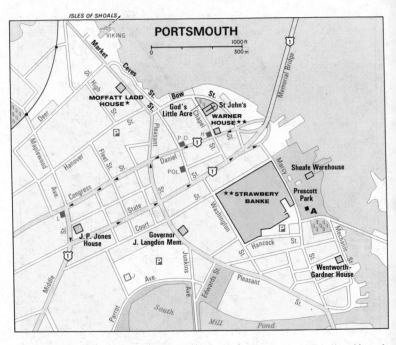

William Pitt Tavern. – (1766). The restored tavern now serves as a Masonic Lodge. Masonic museum on the second floor.

Governor Goodwin Mansion. – 1811. This is Strawbery Banke's most elegant dwelling. The interior is decorated with Victorian furniture, Goodwin family portraits and heirlooms.

Between Strawbery Banke and the river there is a large waterfront park, **Prescott Park**, planted with beautiful flower gardens during the summer *(see Calendar of Events p 13)*. Opposite the entrance to Strawbery Banke is a **Liberty Pole (A)**, similar to those raised by the patriots during Revolutionary days to signify their opposition to the Crown. In the old **Sheafe Warehouse**, located at the water's edge, there is a small collection of folk art.

■ THE HISTORIC HOUSES

The Warner House★★. – *15 Daniel Street. Guided tours (40 min) June 1 to October 15, 10 AM to 4:30 PM; closed Sunday and Monday; $2.00.*

This Georgian mansion, built in 1716 by the Scottish sea captain Archibald Mac Pheadris, is constructed of bricks that served as ballast aboard one of the Mac Pheadris ships. The house is decorated with European and New England-made furnishings and contains a group of portraits by Blackburn. Blackburn's elegant portrait of Polly Warner hangs in the parlor. The series of murals adorning the stairwell includes the life-size portraits of two Mohawk sachems, who journeyed to London with Peter Schuyler in the 18C. In back of the house is **St. John's Church** and the cemetery known as **God's Little Acre.**

The Moffatt-Ladd House★. – *154 Market Street. Guided tours (1 hour) June 15 to October 15, 10 AM to 4 PM, Sundays and holidays 2 to 5 PM; $2.00.*

Captain John Moffatt had this mansion built (1763) as a wedding present for his son Samuel who lived here only a short time. His descendants later occupied the house.

The grand scale of the entrance hall with its French wallpapers and elaborate wood paneling is an indication of the comfortable living style enjoyed by Portsmouth's mercantile class in the 18 and 19C. From the second floor, the owner was able to watch his ships arriving and departing from the harbor.

The Wentworth-Gardner House. – *Guided tours (1 hour) June to mid-October 2 to 4 PM; closed Monday; $2.00.*

The facade of this lovely Georgian mansion built in 1760 casts its reflection on the surface of the Piscataqua. The pineapple carved above the doorway was the symbol of hospitality *(p 187)*. Inside, the paneling, balusters and cornices are flawlessly carved.

The Governor John Langdon Memorial. – *143 Pleasant Street. Guided tours (1 hour) June 1 to October 15, 12 noon to 5 PM; closed Monday and Tuesday; $2.00.*

This handsome Georgian mansion (1784) is known primarily for its original owner, John Langdon, the first president of the United States Senate and a former governor of New Hampshire. A semi-circular portico adorns the exterior of this furnished dwelling.

The John Paul Jones House: the Portsmouth Historical Society. – *43 Middle Street. Guided tours (1 hour) mid-May to mid-October, 10 AM (12 noon Sunday) to 4 PM; $2.00.*

The American naval hero John Paul Jones stayed in this former boarding house on several occasions during the Revolution. Early furnishings, china, clothing and historical memorabilia owned by the Portsmouth Historical Society are on display.

EXCURSIONS

Isles of Shoals★. – *The M/V Thomas Laighton berthed at the Market Street dock offers daily service (2 1/2 hours RT) to the Isles of Shoals. Departures mid-June to Labor Day, 11 AM and 2 PM, additional departure 7:30 AM Monday to Saturday; the 11 AM cruise allows for a stopover at Star Island. Evening cruises and whale watching (May to November) trips also. For fares and fall schedule ☎ (603) 431-5500.*

The 10 mile boat trip to the islands follows the banks of the Piscataqua for 5 miles before heading out to sea. During the first part of the cruise there are good views of sights along the river: the dry docks of the **Portsmouth Naval Yard,** the former castle-like maximum security jail which once held 3 500 prisoners, **Fort McClary** (Kittery), **Fort Constitution** and the beautiful homes on the island-town of New Castle *(p 171).*

These nine islands discovered by Captain John Smith in 1614 were known briefly as Smythe's Isles until they were named by fishermen for the vast shoals (schools) of fish found in the offshore waters. In 1635 the islands were divided between Maine and New Hampshire when the boundary line was established between the two states. In the 19C the stark, picturesque quality of the Isles was popularized by writer Celia Thaxter and the other literary figures who gathered at her home on Appledore Island each summer.

The most important islands are: **Appledore** – site of the marine labs of New Hampshire and Cornell universities, **Smuttynose** – a private island linked to **Cedar** and **Star Islands** by a breakwater, **Star Island** – dominated by a rambling old hotel operated by the Unitarian and Congregational Churches as a summer religious conference center, and **White Island** – its solitary setting and lighthouse a favorite subject of photographers.

New Castle. – Pop 887. Built on an island linked to the mainland by bridge and causeway, New Castle is a residential town known for its large number of colonial dwellings. Along the waterfront rises the sprawling white clapboard **Wentworth-by-the-Sea,** a 19C hotel complex which continued to draw visitors for almost a century until it closed its doors in the 1970s. *Closed for renovation.*

The walls of **Fort Constitution** one of the oldest forts on the coast, overlook the point where the Piscataqua River enters the Atlantic Ocean.

Wentworth-Coolidge Mansion. – *Off of Rte 1A on Little Harbor Road. 1/4 mile after crossing the Portsmouth city line (sign says Welcome to Portsmouth) turn right just before the cemetery. Open June 20 to Labor Day 10 AM to 5 PM; Memorial Day to June 19 and Labor Day to Columbus Day Saturday and Sunday only; $2.00.*

This 18C mansion on the banks of the Piscataqua River was the home of Benning Wentworth, the son of New Hampshire's provincial governor John Wentworth. Unfurnished today, the house is, nevertheless, an elegant example of the sophisticated early American architecture of the Portsmouth region.

Exeter. – Pop 11 641. *13 miles southeast of Portsmouth.* The townspeople of Exeter were regarded as rebels against the Crown as early as 1734, when they stood their ground and prevented the King's agents from appropriating the tallest trees in the region for the British Navy. Exeter remained a patriot stronghold throughout the Revolution and served as the wartime capital of provincial New Hampshire in the 1770s.

Today, tranquil and reserved this colonial town is the home of **Phillips Exeter Academy** founded in 1781. The school's more than 100 buildings, many in the Georgian style, stand on the Academy's broad emerald-green campus. The Academy Building, a large Georgian structure set back on the lawn facing Front Street, is the main classroom building for the school's 980 students. The wide, pleasantly shaded streets and colonial dwellings are reminders that Exeter was one of New Hampshire's earliest settlements.

SAINT-GAUDENS National Historic Site

Michelin tourist map - fold 8 – 2 1/2 miles north of Windsor

Augustus Saint-Gaudens (1848-1907) was America's foremost sculptor in the 19C. Apprenticed to a cameo cutter as a boy, he later studied in Rome and at the Ecole des Beaux Arts in Paris before establishing himself in New York, where he quickly became famous. He is remembered for the monumental Civil War memorials he created such as the Shaw Memorial in Boston, and his portrait reliefs which brought him membership in the French Legion of Honor and the Royal Academy.

During the two decades he lived in Cornish, Saint-Gaudens produced about 150 sculptures. His home, studios and extensive gardens are maintained as a museum in his honor by the National Park Service.

Visit. – *Cross the Windsor-Cornish covered bridge, then turn left onto Rte 12A. Open late May through October, 8:30 AM to 4:30 PM; $1.00.*

The House. – The house (c. 1800), formerly a tavern before it was acquired and renovated by Saint-Gaudens, was named Aspet after his father's birthplace in France.

Studios and Galleries. – The Little Studio was Saint-Gaudens' workshop. A selection of his low relief portrait plaques, and the *Diana* he sculpted for the tower of the former Madison Square Garden are here. A copy of his statue *The Puritan* (Springfield, Mass.) stands among the other works in the Gallery.

A copy of the enigmatic **Adams Memorial** (commissioned by Henry Adams for his wife Marian's grave in 1885), generally regarded as an expression of the artist's interpretation of death, grief or divine peace, is located on the grounds.

The WHITE MOUNTAINS ★★★

Michelin tourist map - folds 8 and 9 – *Local map pp 174-175*

Spreading across northern New Hampshire and into Maine is the most mountainous region in New England, the White Mountains. Named for the blanket of snow that covers the area during most of the year, these mountains, dominated by Mount Washington, are characterized by their rounded summits, deep broad valleys, and U-shaped mountain passes known as **notches**.

Almost 80 of the White Mountains are included in the federally protected and administered White Mountain National Forest, known for its spectacular scenery, many natural attractions, picnic and camping grounds and more than 1 000 miles of foot trails. The region's long winter offers numerous opportunities for skiing in the White Mountain National Forest and in the valleys close by. Throughout the summer, hikers and motorists enjoy the cool woods and waterfalls and the views from the mountain summits; and in the fall, the season of "leaf watchers," the White Mountains explode into a sea of color as the blazing reds, golds and oranges of the maple and birch trees mix with the dark greens of the fir and spruce.

Practical Information. – Information can be obtained at centers in North Conway, Gorham and other villages, or by writing to: *The Supervisor, White Mountain National Forest, Box 638, Laconia, NH 03247.*

Lodging. – Hotels and motels will be found in Conway, North Conway, Jackson, Gorham, Twin Mountain, Franconia Village, Lincoln and North Woodstock.

Camping. – There are more than 800 campsites in the White Mountain National Forest. Reservations are not accepted. *For information contact White Mountain National Forest, PO Box 638, Laconia, NH 03247 ☎ (603) 524-6450.*

Relief and Climate. – The White Mountains are remnants of ancient primarily granite mountain ranges. During the last Ice Age, a mammoth glacier covered these mountains, grinding, carving and polishing summits until they were rounded. Several smaller valley glaciers moved through steep-walled valleys changing them to smooth U-shaped notches, while the swirling action of melting glacial water sculpted giant potholes, such as the Basin found in Franconia Notch *(p 176)*.

The subpolar climate that dominates the upper slopes of Mount Washington is exceptionally severe for mountains of this relatively low altitude. Mount Washington holds the world record for the strongest winds ever recorded: 231 mph. The severity of the climate is the factor responsible for the 4 000-5 000 ft timberline of the White Mountains which is regarded as considerably low when compared to the 8 000-9 000 ft timberline of the Colorado Rockies. At the summit regions the vegetation is similar to that growing in arctic regions, and includes species found nowhere else in the world.

Historical Notes. – Giovanni da Verrazano sighted the White Mountains from the coast in 1524 and as early as 1642 a settler climbed to the highest point, Mount Washington. The artists and writers who visited the region in the early 19C depicted the rugged beauty of the White Mountains in their paintings, novels, short stories and poetry, and during the same period New Hampshirites named Mount Washington and the other peaks in the Presidential Range after former United States presidents. It was soon after that the tourists began to arrive, and by the end of the century, with the construction of the railroad and the Victorian hotels that sprung up in the valley, tourism was established on a grand scale in the White Mountains. Many of the fine old hotels have since been destroyed by fire, to be replaced by clusters of motels and cottages.

The Trails. – There are 1 128 miles of trails in the White Mountain National Forest. **The Appalachian Mountain Club** (AMC) operates a system of huts and shelters in the forest, and a lodge on Route 16 at the base of Mount Washington. *For information contact the AMC Pinkham Notch Camp on Route 16: reservations ☎ (603) 466-2727; trails and weather ☎ (603) 466-2725.*

Forest trails vary in length and difficulty. Hikers should be prepared for the sudden changes in weather that can occur in the White Mountains. *For more information consult the Appalachian Mountain Club White Mountain Guide which may be obtained by writing to: Appalachian Mountain Club, 5 Joy Street, Boston, MA 02108.*

Wilderness areas (Great Gulf, Pemigewasset, Sandwich, Presidential Range – Dry River) have no roads and may be entered only by foot; motorized vehicles or equipment of any kind is prohibited.

MOUNT WASHINGTON ★★★

Mount Washington is the highest point in New England (alt 6 288 ft) and the principal peak in the Presidential Range, so called because of its peaks named for presidents of the United States: Mounts Adams, Clay, Jefferson, Madison, Monroe and the most recent to be named, Mount Eisenhower. A combination of bitter cold, wind and icing comparable to the subarctic climate of northern Labrador, governs the higher altitudes of this mountain, influencing the kind of plant and animal life that will grow and be capable of surviving near the summit. Tiny plants and dwarfed fir and spruce trees have adapted to this harsh environment and thrive in mountain crevices and amidst the chaotic jumble of boulders that lie in the region above the timberline. Mount Washington is known for the harsh climate that dominates its slopes and upper regions; the strongest winds ever recorded (231 mph) having swept across its summit on April 12, 1934.

Snow has fallen on Mount Washington during every month of the year and generally continues to fall until mid-June. Skiers who do not mind the climb to the top of **Tuckerman Ravine** *(there are no lifts)*, can ski in the ravine until late May or on occasion early June.

Fogbound at least 300 days of the year, the summit of Mount Washington, with its group of mountaintop buildings, is known as the City Among the Clouds.

To Reach the Summit. – The Mount Washington Cog Railway *(p 176)* and the Auto Road *(p 173)* are the quickest means of reaching the summit. Hikers in good condition will find one of the trails to the summit the most invigorating way to make the climb.

Summit Buildings. – Among the half dozen structures at the summit are the stone-walled Tip Top House (1853), radio and TV broadcasting facilities, and the new Summit Building. The summit and its facilities are a testing ground for items ranging from cold weather clothing, to equipment used in controlling icing on aircraft engines.

The **Sherman Adams Summit Building** *(open Memorial Day to third week in October 8 AM to 8 PM)*, a modern structure set into the mountain, houses a snack bar, gift and souvenir shops, the Mount Washington Weather Observatory, and a small museum *($1.00)*. Museum exhibits are related to the weather, geology and history of Mount Washington.

The rooftop deck of the Summit Building is a good place from which to see the view.

The View★★★. – The sweeping 50 mile vista from the summit of Mount Washington on a clear day stretches north to Montreal. The view presents an interesting picture of the entire region, capped by the barren, cone-like summits of the Presidential Range.

The Mount Washington Cog Railway★★. – *Hours and admission p 176.* This small steam train is almost as famous as the mountain itself. Built in 1869, the 3 1/2 mile railway was an outstanding technological achievement for its day, and still offers passengers a thrilling ride to the summit, especially as the train ascends **Jacobs Ladder,** the steepest grade on the trestle (37%).

During the leisurely 1 1/2 hour ride to the summit, it is interesting to note how the vegetation and landscape vary with changes in the altitude.

The Mount Washington Cog Railway.

PINKHAM NOTCH★★
From North Conway to Glen House (Route 16) – *25 miles – allow 1/2 day*

North Conway. – Pop 2 104. Situated on the edge of the White Mountain National Forest, North Conway is a major gateway to the White Mountains. The town offers many facilities for tourists and is a winter sports center, located within the vicinity of Attitash, Mount Cranmore, Tyrol, Black Mountain and Wildcat Mountain ski areas.

The Russian-inspired railroad station built in 1874, has been transformed into a museum and ticket office *(Rte 16)* for the **Conway Scenic Railroad,** which operates an 11 mile ride on an antique train through the Saco Valley. *Train departures mid-June to late October 11 AM, 1 PM, 2:30 PM, 4 PM (7 PM also Tuesday, Wednesday, Thursday and Saturday in July and August); weekends only early May to early June; $5.00.*

Cathedral Ledge. – *From the Scenic Railroad turn left opposite the White Mountain Bank and continue 1 1/2 miles to the sign for Cathedral Ledge then turn left.* Towering 1000 ft above the valley this ledge commands a good **view★** of Echo Lake and the surrounding forested and ruggedly beautiful Mount Washington Valley.

Continuing north on Rte 16 Mount Washington can be seen from the road.

Glen. – Located at the intersection of Routes 16 and 302 (Crawford Notch) Glen has two popular attractions: Story Land and Heritage-New Hampshire.

Story Land. – *Open Father's Day to Labor Day 9 AM to 6 PM; after Labor Day to Columbus Day weekends only 10 AM to 5 PM; $9.00, under 4 free accompanied by an adult.* This theme park featuring life-size characters and settings from children's stories and nursery rhymes, has rides, a picnic grove and snack bars.

Heritage - New Hampshire. – *Open Father's Day to Labor Day 9 AM to 6 PM; mid-May to mid-June and after Labor Day to late October 9 AM to 5 PM; $5.50, under 4 free accompanied by an adult.*

A maze of life-like scenes enhanced by special "involvarounding" techniques allow visitors to experience some of the most significant events in New Hampshire's past. Beyond the building's classic white exterior, you will discover the state's mountainous landscape, walk through the grim interior of the Amoskeag Mills in 19C Manchester, and see Daniel Webster age right before your eyes as he tells the story of his life. The visit concludes with a simulated train ride through Crawford Notch.

Continue north on Route 16 through the village of **Jackson.** Cross over the Jackson covered bridge to have a glimpse of the village's old resort hotels.

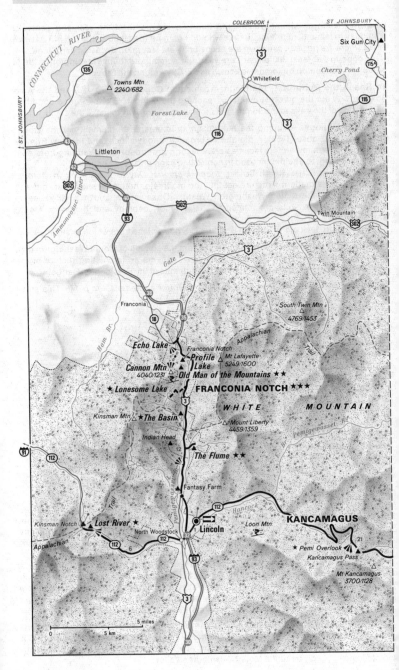

Pinkham Notch. – At this point between Mount Washington and Wildcat Mountain, the valley narrows.

Glen Ellis Falls ★ . – *Parking lot on left side of the road.* The falls and its pools, located on the east side of the road *(take the underpass),* are formed by the Ellis and Saco Rivers.

Wildcat Mountain. – *Parking area just off Rte 16.* Ski trails have been cut on the slopes of Wildcat Mountain that look across Pinkham Notch to Mount Washington. A gondola lift provides access to the summit which offers a **view★★** of Mount Washington and the northern peaks of the Presidential Range. *Gondola operates late May to Columbus Day weekends, 9:30 AM to 4:30 PM; mid-June to Labor Day daily 9 AM to 4:30 PM; $5.00.*

Glen House. – The 8 mile **Auto Road** to the summit of Mount Washington begins here. You can drive your own car or ride in one of the chauffeur driven vans that depart from Glen House. From the summit and scenic outlooks along the road there are spectacular views of the Great Gulf Wilderness Area and the Presidential Range.

Motorists planning to drive their own car to the summit, should be sure the car is in good condition before starting (check gas, brakes, water). The road is narrow, has steep curves and grades and is gravel most of the way. Only motorists accustomed to mountain driving should attempt this drive.

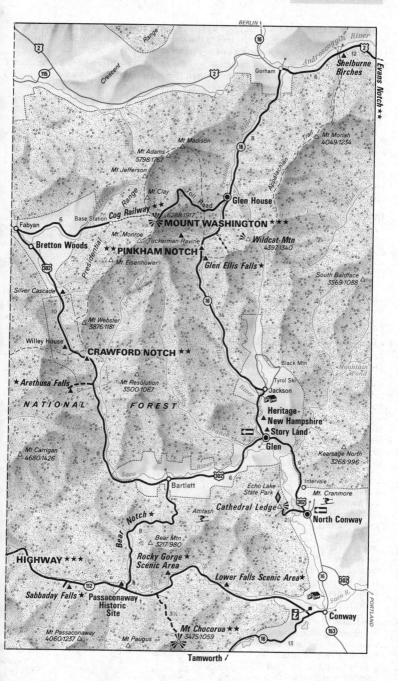

Chauffeur driven vans depart from Glen House mid-May to mid-October weather permitting 8:30 AM to 4:30 PM; time: 1 1/2 hours RT; $14.00, children $9.00. Auto Road open to private vehicles mid-May to mid-October 7:30 AM to 6 PM in summer, shorter hours early and late in the season; $10.00 car and driver, $4.00 each passenger.

The Shelburne Birches. – 14 miles from Glen House. Take Rte 16 then Rte 2 through Gorham. This is a picturesque roadside stand of slim, tall white birch trees.

Evans Notch★★. – 12 miles by Rte 2 from the Shelburne Birches. Description p 64.

CRAWFORD NOTCH★★

From Glen to Fabyan (Route 302) – 24 miles – allow 3 hours

Route 302 follows the Saco River through Crawford Notch, a broad valley in the heart of the White Mountains. The road passes **Attitash Ski Area** and continues to **Bartlett**. In Bartlett a road just past the library leads through Bear Notch.

Bear Notch★. – An additional 8 miles between Bartlett and the Kancamagus Highway. This drive is especially scenic during the foliage season. At the point where the road leaves Crawford Notch (3 1/2 miles after Bartlett) there is a beautiful **view** of the valley.

Crawford Notch★★. – This mountain pass was named for the Crawford family, White Mountain pioneers who cut the first trail to the summit of Mount Washington in the 19C and whose home in the notch served as a shelter for hikers.

Arethusa Falls★. – *Parking lot on the left side of the road. Cross the railroad tracks, then follow the path (right) into the woods.* The trail *(time: 2 hours RT)* follows a brook then crosses the brook just before reaching the falls, a refreshing picture in their forest setting.

Route 302 passes in front of the rustic **Willey House** (a snack bar) and **Mount Webster**, its slopes covered in places with the rocky debris of recent landslides. Further on you will pass the **Silver Cascade**, a roadside waterfall tumbling from a high ledge.

Bretton Woods. – The slopes of the Presidential Range form the backdrop for the **Mount Washington Hotel,** a sprawling hotel complex that is one of the few 19C hosteleries still in existence. In 1944 the hotel was the site of the United Nations Monetary and Financial Conference (Bretton Woods Conference) which established the American dollar as the medium of international exchange and developed plans to establish the World Bank.

After Bretton Woods, at Fabyan, turn right onto the road leading to the Cog Railway.

The Mount Washington Cog Railway★★. – *Departs from the Marshfield Base Station 6 miles east of Rte 302. Trains operate May to Columbus Day daily all day, last train departs 3 hours before darkness; $25.00, includes round trip railway ride and $2.00 general admission fee covering parking, shuttle from parking area to railway, and museum. Description p 173.*

FRANCONIA NOTCH★★★ (Route 3) *13 miles – time: 1/2 day*

Route 3, running along the floor of this scenic notch cradled between the Franconia and Kinsman ranges, offers easy access to many of the natural attractions.

Echo Lake. – *Rte 18.* Franconia Notch is reflected in the mirror-like surface of the lake.

Cannon Mountain. – Cannon Mountain is one of New Hampshire's finest ski areas. An aerial tramway operates to the summit which overlooks **Echo Lake** and affords a **view★★** of the notch. *Tramway operates mid-May to late October 9 AM to 4 PM; $6.00.*

Old Man of the Mountains★★ and **Profile Lake.** – The Old Man of the Mountains, a rocky formation that resembles the profile of a man (40 ft from chin to forehead), juts out from a mountainside above Profile Lake. The profile was discovered in 1805 by two men who compared it to a likeness of President Jefferson. Hawthorne described the profile in a short story *The Great Stone Face* and when P.T. Barnum *(p 36)* toured the notch almost twenty years later he was so impressed he wanted to buy the attraction for his circus. The Old Man of the Mountains is best viewed from a vantage point on the lake-shore.

Lonesome Lake★. – *Trail (time: 3 hours) leaves from the parking lot at Lafayette Campground. Follow the yellow markers.*

This lake is set in a clearing 1 000 ft above Franconia Notch. A trail around the lake leads to the Appalachian Mountain Club Hut, a shelter that accommodates hikers in the summer.

The Basin★. – The action of the churning waters rushing down from the falls above have formed this enormous granite pothole, a natural pool 30 ft in diameter.

The Flume★★. – *Open mid-May to late October 9 AM to 4 PM; $6.00. Films on Franconia Notch and the White Mountain National Forest are shown in the Visitor Center.* The Flume is a deep and narrow granite chasm through which the Flume Brook flows. A system of boardwalks and stairways guides visitors through the Flume and to **Ridge Path** *(1/2 mile)*. Ridge Path leads to Liberty Cascade and a little further on to the **Sentinal Pine Covered Bridge** which overlooks a clear natural pool.

(From a photo by Dick Smith.)

Pine Sentinel Bridge and Pool.

The **Wildwood Path** *(1/2 mile)* leads past mammoth boulders deposited here thousands of years ago by the glaciers, and returns to the entrance to the Flume.

Route 3 continues toward the village of Lincoln. Before arriving in Lincoln, you will notice a rocky formation to the right resembling a profile. The profile is known as **Indian Head.**

Lincoln. – Pop 1 283. Located at the southern entrance to Franconia Notch, Lincoln has a plentiful assortment of motels, restaurants, shops and commercial attractions.

Lost River★ . – *8 miles from Lincoln by Rte 112 West. Open June through August 9 AM to 6 PM; May, September and October 9 AM to 5:30 PM; last ticket sold 1 hour before closing. $5.00.* Located in Kinsman Notch, a pass between the Connecticut and Pemigewasset Valleys, Lost River Gorge is a steep-walled glacial ravine filled with enormous boulders that have been sculpted into potholes by the river. A system of boardwalks and staircases allows visitors to tour the caves, potholes and waterfalls in the gorge.

The KANCAMAGUS HIGHWAY★★★
From Lincoln to Conway – *33 miles – allow 3 hours*

This road through the White Mountain National Forest follows the **Hancock Branch** of the Pemigewasset River and the **Swift River,** cool, clear mountain streams with scattered sections of rapids. It is one of the most spectacular drives in New England during the foliage season, when the maples and birch trees take on their fall colors. Picnic and camping grounds along the streams are inviting places to stop. The mountains south of the highway have been named for some of New Hampshire's more famous Indians: Passaconaway, Kancamagus – a friend of the settlers – and Chocorua *(see below).*

The road passes in front of **Loon Mountain Recreation Area,** a ski and year-round resort, then begins to climb to Kancamagus Pass. During the ascent there is an exceptionally scenic **view★** from the **Pemi Overlook.** The road then descends into the Saco Valley.

Sabbaday Falls★ . – *Parking area on south side of the road. Take the Sabbaday Brook Trail (1/2 hour RT), an easy trail to follow.* The falls tumble over a series of ledges into a giant pothole, then into another pothole, then through a flume.

The Passaconaway Historic Site . – This is an information and nature center for the White Mountain National Forest. The short self-guided **Rail 'N River** trail begins here. The trail, nicknamed for the former railroad bed it follows, is an introduction to the trees and shrubs in this part of the forest. *The Center is open May to Labor Day 8:30 AM to 5 PM; weekends only late May to late June and early September to Columbus Day. Demonstrations of home crafts (candle making, baskets, etc.) by persons in period dress.*

The highway passes in front of the road (on the left) to Bear Notch (p 174).

Mount Chocorua★★ . – *5 hours RT hike to the summit, from the Champney Falls Trail parking area.* Follow the **Champney Falls Trail – Piper Trail** which climbs gently the first 1 1/2 miles and leads to a bypass *(on the left)* to Champney Falls. Return to the main trail which becomes moderately difficult as it begins to climb rapidly through various stages of forest vegetation to the rocky summit of Mount Chocorua. From the summit there are **views★★★** of the White Mountains on one side and Lake Chocorua to the other. Lake Chocorua and the mountain of that name honor the Indian chief Chocorua, who plunged to his death from the top of the mountain. According to legend, Chocorua avenged the death of his son by killing the family of the man suspected of accidentally poisoning the boy. A group of angry settlers pursued Chocorua to the upper ledge of the mountain that today bears his name. Cornered, the chief uttered a curse on all white men then jumped to his death. The settlers recalled the Indian's curse when an epidemic killed many of their cattle; however, the cause was eventually traced to the drinking water.

To return to the parking lot, carefully follow the signs for Champney Falls Trail; there are many trails on Mount Chocorua and it is easy to stray from the main trail.

Rocky Gorge Scenic Area★ . – The Swift River forms rapids at this point where the valley narrows.

Lower Falls Scenic Area★ . – The best view of the falls, rapids formed by the Swift River, is from the eastern end of the site.

Conway. – Conway is a major winter and summer resort. Ski shops, motels and restaurants will be found along Route 16 outside of town. The covered bridge spanning the Saco River can be seen from Route 16, about 1/2 mile north of Conway.

Chocorua and **Tamworth.** – *13 miles from Conway by Rte 16 South.* After 10 miles a picture-postcard **view★★** of Mount Chocorua, reflected in the lake of the same name appears. A little farther south pass through the tiny village of Chocorua. *Take 113 West.*

Tamworth. – This tranquil village with its white houses and cozy inn, is home to the **Barnstormers,** a theater group that performs in Tamworth during the summer.

OTHER SIGHTS IN OR NEAR THE WHITE MOUNTAINS

White Lake State Park. – *Rte 16 in West Ossipee.* There is camping *($9.00 per night),* fishing and swimming at a sandy beach in this park south of the White Mountains.

Mount Whittier. – *Rte 16/25 in West Ossipee.* From the summit of this mountain named for the poet John Greenleaf Whittier *(p 141)* who summered nearby, there is a view that includes the White Mountains and Mount Chocorua. Gondola rides summer and fall. ☎ *(603) 539-7740.*

Especially if you are traveling with children

Fantasy Farm. – *Rte 3 in Lincoln. Open late June to Labor Day 9 AM to 6 PM. Mid-May to mid-October 10 AM to closing; $6.00, under 4 free.*

Animals, birds and fish in an outdoor setting; also rides and picnic tables.

Santa's Village. – *Rte 2 in Jefferson. Open mid-June to Labor Day 9:30 AM to 7 PM; after Labor Day to Columbus Day 10 AM to 5 PM; $8.00, under 4 free.*

The village is the summer home of Santa Claus, his reindeer and helpers. The village's 40 gaily painted and decorated buildings are set in a grove of tall evergreens.

Six Gun City. – *Jct Rtes 2 and 115 in Jefferson. Open mid-June to Labor Day 9 AM to 6 PM; after Labor Day to Columbus Day weekends only 9 AM to 5 PM; $5.50.*

This replica of a small western town has a blockhouse, jail, saloon and fifteen other buildings. Activities include stage coach rides and log rides through a mill.

The LAKE WINNIPESAUKEE Region ★
Michelin tourist map - fold 9

This vast lake, the largest in New Hampshire, covers an area of 72 sq miles, has a shoreline of nearly 300 miles, and is dotted with more than 200 tiny tree-clad islands. The best way to view its shores and islands is by taking a ride on one of the sightseeing boats that operate on the lake. On a clear day the lake, with the White Mountains and Mount Washington as a backdrop, is a magnificent sight. The lake's Indian name: *Winnipesaukee,* meaning: "the smile of the Great Spirit," can be traced to the legend that tells of an Indian who, one night when he was canoeing on the lake, suddenly noticed the sky had become overcast and dark. When a brilliant ray of light shone through the clouds and onto the water, guiding his boat safely back to shore, the Indian interpreted this as a sign from the Great Spirit and named the lake, Winnipesaukee.

Lakeside Villages. – Each of the villages on the lake has its own character. **Laconia** is the industrial and commercial center of the region. The small charming village of **Wolfeboro** ★, with its large homes overlooking the lake, has been a summer resort for centuries. Unspoiled by industry, it is one of the prettiest communities on the shores of Lake Winnipesaukee. **Weirs Beach** with its amusement arcade, souvenir shops and lakefront Victorian dwellings is a lively resort; and **Center Harbor,** on a bay at the northern end of the lake, is an attractive resort which serves as the shopping center for the bungalow colonies and campgrounds nearby.

Activities. – Every summer thousands of vacationers enjoy boating on the waters of the lake. Public docks, marinas and launching ramps abound. Popular beaches include **Weirs Beach** and **Ellacoya State Beach.** For hikers there are walking trails in the hills encircling the area. During the winter **Gunstock Ski Area** and **Alpine Ridge Ski Area** are centers of activity. Ice fishing, snowmobiling, and the dog sled championships at Laconia *(see Calendar of Events p 13)* are added winter attractions.

EXCURSIONS

Sightseeing Cruises★★. – *Several excursion boats operate on the lake. For information on scenic cruises and moonlight cruises ☎ (603) 366-5531.*

The M/S Mount Washington ★★. – This boat offers the most popular cruise: a 3 1/4 hour *(RT)* excursion departing from Wolfeboro and Weirs Beach. *Operates late May to mid-October: departs from Weirs Beach 9 AM and 12:15 PM, from Wolfeboro 11 AM, with stops at Center Harbor (Monday, Wednesday and Friday) and Alton Bay (Tuesday, Thursday, Saturday and Sunday). Additional departures June 15 to Labor Day: from Weirs Beach 3:30 PM, from Wolfeboro 2:15 PM. $10.00.*

The M/V Doris E. – The 1 3/4 hour excursion on the *Doris E.* is suggested for those persons pressed for time. *Daily departures from Weirs Beach July 1 to Labor Day 10 AM, 12 noon, 2 PM, 4 PM and 6:30 PM, $6.00; from Meredith 10:30 AM, 12:30 PM and 2:30 PM; $6.50.*

The M/V Sophie C. – The *Sophie C.* is a mailboat that travels to the islands at the upper end of the lake. *Daily departures from Weirs Beach mid-June to mid-September 1 PM; additional cruise July 1 to Labor Day at 11 AM; $6.50.*

Castle in the Clouds ★. – *In Moultonborough, 18 miles north of Wolfeboro by Rte 109 then Rte 171. Open May to mid-October, 9 AM to 6 PM, weekends only May 1 to June 14; guided tours (40 min) of the Castle; $6.00.*

This 6 000 acre park-like estate was acquired in 1910 by the millionaire Thomas Plant, who made his fortune by developing machinery used in the shoe industry. The home Plant had built for himself high on the slopes of the Ossipee Mountains overlooks the forests and lakes below. From the terrace there is a **view**★★ of Lake Winnipesaukee with its myriad of tiny islands. There are miles of horse and foot trails on the property *(horses may be rented $9.00 per 1/2 hour).* A path beginning about 1 mile from the entrance gate leads to two waterfalls: the **Fall of Song** and **Bridal Veil Falls.**

Alpine Slide (Alpine Ridge Ski Area). – *7 miles northeast of Laconia by Rte 3 then Rte 11A East. Open late May to mid-June and after Labor Day to Columbus Day weekends only 10 AM to 5 PM; third week in June to Labor Day daily 10 AM to 6 PM; $4.50 per ride.*

This is an exciting mountain activity for all ages. Seated on a kind of sled, each person controls his own speed as he slides down the mountain along a track that descends to the base of the slope. A chairlift carries passengers to the starting point.

Rhode Island

Area : 1 214 sq miles
Population : 961 881
Capital : Providence
Nickname : Ocean State
State Flower : Violet

Little Rhody, as it is affectionately known, is the smallest state in the nation, the most densely populated, heavily industrialized, and has the longest name : the State of Rhode Island and Providence Plantations. Its name reflects the development of Rhode Island from a settlement on an island in Narragansett Bay, to a royal colony, when Rhode Island and the Providence Plantations were united by the Charter of 1644.

Narragansett Bay, the state's dominant natural feature, extends 28 miles inland dividing Rhode Island almost in half. The Providence metropolitan region, the only urban center in the state, sprawls inland from the head of the bay. Rhode Island's 400 mile coastline, bordered by sandy beaches and good harbors, is the domain of fishermen and yachtsmen, with Newport reigning as the sailing capital of the East.

A Land of Tolerance. — The earliest colonists came in search of the freedom and peace they could not find in Massachusetts. The first to arrive was the **Reverend Blackstone** (p 87), fleeing the invasion of his privacy on the Shawmut Peninsula by the Puritans (1630). He was followed by **Roger Williams** who founded Providence (1636) ; and the religious leader **Anne Hutchinson** who helped establish Portsmouth (1638). Then came the Quakers, Jews, Baptists..., and in the 19C, large numbers of Irish, Italian, Polish and Portuguese emigrated to this land of "Hope," the state's motto.

Relations between the colonists and the Indians remained friendly until 1675 when Philip, chief of the Wampanoags, united and led the Wampanoags, Narragansetts and Nimpucks in raids against the English settlements (**King Philip's War** 1675-1676). At the Great Swamp Fight (Mount Hope, R.I.) the Narragansetts, Rhode Island's most powerful tribe, suffered severe losses and by the end of the war, the Indian population had been greatly reduced due to wartime casualties and the emigration of the survivors to Canada and the West.

Economy. — Rhode Island's economy was at first based on the sea, with Newport and Providence among the nation's leading seaports. The great fortunes earned in trade provided the capital for the textile industry which had its beginnings at Pawtucket (p 188) in 1793, and by the mid-19C Rhode Island was the most heavily industrialized state in the country. The exodus of the textile factories to the South after World War II, led to an emphasis on diversified manufacturing, and today 28 % of its labor force is employed in manufacturing. The growth in the service and non-manufacturing sectors of the economy reflects the trend across the nation in the 1980s.

Recreation. — Some of the best fishing waters in the world lie off of Block Island. Beaches, quiet coves, and cool open spaces brushed with low-lying salt marshes are the main attractions of the resort-oriented southern counties, among which Newport is the undisputed leader.

BLOCK ISLAND ★

Michelin tourist map - fold 22 – Pop 519

This unspoiled island 10 miles south of the mainland is covered with cliffs, sand dunes and grassy moors. Probably discovered in the 16C by Verrazano, Block Island was named for **Adrian Block,** the Dutch navigator who explored the region in 1614. The first permanent colonists to settle here arrived at the end of the 17C. They were followed by smugglers, pirates, and most likely shipwreckers – as many of New England's shipping disasters occurred off the frequently fogbound coast of Block Island. In the late 19C the island developed into a summer resort with large, prim Victorian hotels such as those that front **Old Harbor.** Tourists were attracted by the mild sea breezes and the refreshing climate.

Quiet now, almost desolate, tourists enjoy the island for its good beaches, deep-sea fishing and boating. **New Harbor,** landlocked except for a narrow outlet to the sea, is a superb haven for boats and a playground for water sports.

Getting There By Plane. – Service on New England Airlines between Westerly and Block Island. *For information* ☎ *(401) 596-2460; toll free outside Rhode Island (800) 243-2460.*

Getting There By Ferry. – From Point Judith Galilee, State Pier: *summer 8 round-trips daily (9 trips weekends) from 8 AM to 8 PM; off season reduced daily service; time: 1 hour 10 min one way; $5.00 one way. Automobile $14.50 one way (reservations and deposit required). Interstate Navigation Company, Galilee State Pier, Point Judith, RI 02882* ☎ *(401) 789-3502.*

Summer only, daily service from New London, Conn. *(time: 3 hours one way), for information* ☎ *(203) 442-7891; from Providence (time: 4 hours one way) and Newport (time: 2 hours one way), for information* ☎ *(401) 789-3502.*

Getting around Block Island. – The ferry transports private vehicles *(see above).* Rental cars are available on the island. Because of the island's small size the most pleasant way of getting around is by bicycle. Bike rentals are available near the ferry dock.

■ SIGHTS *time: 4 hours*

Sandy Point★. – The northern end of the island has been set aside as a bird and wildlife preserve. The calls of sea gulls fill the air as you walk the sandy path to the old stone lighthouse. No longer in use, the old light with its 18 inch thick walls, has managed to withstand the force of the shifting sands and the powerful gales over the years.

Mohegan Bluffs★★. – The island's south shore is formed by a series of spectacular multicolored cliffs. Steep paths descend to the beach at the base of the cliffs.

Crescent Beach. – Life guards, dressing rooms and eating facilities are available at the state owned section (Block Island State Beach) of Crescent Beach. *Swimming is advised at guarded beaches only because of the strong undertow and rough surf at some of the island beaches.*

BRISTOL

Michelin tourist map - fold 22 – 15 miles southeast of Providence – Pop 19 756

Bristol survived the Revolution to become a leading seaport and shipbuilding center. Its citizens prospered from the triangular trade and trade with the Orient, and their mansions sprung up throughout the waterfront district. Note especially Linden Place *(No. 474 Hope Street)* designed by Russell Warren, and nearby *(Wardwell Street)* the Bristol Art Museum, formerly the ballroom for Linden Place.

The **Herreshoff** boatyards, operating in Bristol since 1863, have turned out steam and sailing yachts – seven of which were America's Cup *(p 182)* defenders.

A drive through **Colt State Park** *(off of Rte 114)* affords views of Narragansett Bay.

Blithewold Gardens and Arboretum. – *Rte 114. Grounds open year round 12 noon to 8 PM; $2.00. Guided tours (1 hour) of mansion and grounds mid-April through October; closed Monday; $4.00.*

Flower gardens *(in season)* and trees and shrubs from Europe and the Orient adorn the grounds of this former estate, built in 1907 for the coal magnate Augustus VanWinkle. Even during the off season this is a delightful place for a stroll, with its spacious surroundings, harborside setting and expansive water views. A rock garden and water garden are arranged in clearings a short distance from the water's edge and near the mansion rises an 80 ft tall giant sequoia.

The mansion, a stone and stucco residence in the style of an English manor house, is furnished with family possessions, for the most part objects and artifacts acquired by the VanWickles on their trips abroad. About ten of the 45 rooms in the house are open to the public.

Haffenreffer Museum of Anthropology. – *From Rte 136 take Tower Road east and follow the signs. Open June through August, 1 to 5 PM; closed Monday; the rest of the year Saturday and Sunday only 1 to 5 PM; closed January, February and holidays; $1.00.*

The small museum is part of Brown University's *(p 191)* Department of Anthropology. Exhibits are from the university's rich collection of artifacts related to the cultures of aboriginal peoples of Africa, the Pacific and the Americas. The museum owns a selection of Arctic items gathered by a recent university-sponsored expedition to Alaska.

NARRAGANSETT PIER

Michelin tourist map - fold 22 – 16 miles west of Newport – Pop 12 523

Narragansett Pier and the neighboring coastal region extending south to Point Judith, have some of the finest beaches in New England. **Scarborough's** lively atmosphere draws a young crowd, while surfers prefer **East Matunuck State Beach** (adjoining Jerusalem), and families with young children are drawn to the calm waters at **Galilee Beach.**

Narragansett Pier began to develop into a fashionable seaside resort in the 19C after Rhode Island governor William Sprague and his wife built their summer mansion in the area. All activity centered around the Pier (only the name survives), which extended from the southern end of Town Beach into the ocean. Beyond the beachfront Victorian hotels stood the vacation homes of American businessmen and political figures. The **Towers,** two stone towers joined by an arch extending across Ocean Road, are all that remain of the lavish Narragansett Casino designed by McKim, Mead and White in 1884. The main section of the casino and many of Narragansett's grand hotels were destroyed by fire in 1900.

The Coast from Narragansett Pier to Point Judith
6 miles – allow 1/2 hour

Drive south on Ocean Road *(Rte 1A)* which passes under the Towers and skirts shorefront mansions which overlook the pounding surf. About 2 miles after Scarborough Beach, you will enter Galilee.

Galilee. – This fishing village is the site annually of the **Rhode Island Tuna Tournament,** a major sporting event *(see Calendar of Events p 13).* The Point Judith ferry to Block Island leaves from the State Pier at Galilee year round *(see p 180).* On the opposite shore of Point Judith Pond is **Jerusalem,** another tiny fishing village.

Point Judith. – The rocky headland with its octagonal-shaped lighthouse is a familiar landmark to mariners who sail these waters.

NEWPORT ★★★

Michelin tourist map - fold 22 – Pop 29 571

An all encompassing view of the city's beautiful setting in the midst of Narragansett Bay, greets motorists arriving from the west by Newport Bridge. A resort once devoted exclusively to the wealthy, Newport, today the sailing capital of the world and the home of the Newport Music Festival, is fascinating for its history and architecture.
Newport Bridge: passenger vehicles $2.00 one way.

A Harbor of Refuge. – In 1524 the Italian navigator Verrazano sailed into Narragansett Bay and along the coast of the island known to the Indians as Aquidneck. Impressed by the brilliance and clarity of the natural light, he noted, also, the similarity in appearance between Aquidneck and the Greek isle of **Rhodes,** and after Newport was settled, Aquidneck was renamed Rhode Island. In the following century, in 1639, settlers fleeing the intolerance of the Massachusetts Bay Colony established Newport. Other religious minorities arrived: the Quakers, Jews from Holland and Portugal, Baptists. They were industrious and had a talent for commerce, and the colony rapidly developed.

Newport's Golden Age. – By 1761 Newport had grown into a bustling port center second only to Boston. The colony's prosperity was due largely to the **triangular trade.** Vessels sailed to Africa, carrying a full cargo of rum; there the rum was exchanged for slaves who were transported to the West Indies and traded for the molasses used to

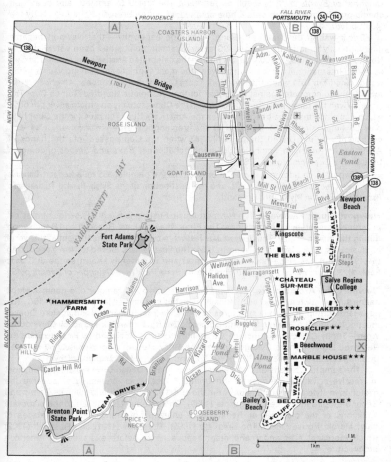

produce rum. The slave market represented an important source of income to Newport. An import tax levied on each slave brought into the colony, yielded sufficient revenue to build the roads and bridges needed to link the growing settlements. Rum was also exported to Europe where it was exchanged for goods not available in the colonies.

The Revolution. – These were Newport's darkest days. Marked by the British for destruction, Newport was occupied from 1776-1779. Inhabitants were forced to quarter English soldiers, and looting and burning were widespread. Following the British defeat the French troops, allies of the Americans, occupied Newport and it was here that the meetings between General Washington and Count Rochambeau took place.

By the end of the war Newport lay in ruins. Most of its merchants had fled to Providence (p 189), and the colony would never again regain its commercial splendor.

Summer Resort of the Wealthy. – During the years before the Revolution, planters from Georgia and the Carolinas escaped the heat of the southern summer by vacationing in Newport. In the mid-19C, with the introduction of steamboat travel between New York and Newport, an increasing number of visitors arrived each year. Following the Civil War, America's wealthiest families: the Astors, Belmonts, Vanderbilts began to summer here and Newport developed into a resort for the very rich. Impressed by the magnificence of the palaces and châteaux they had seen while making the "grand tour" of Europe, they commissioned America's finest architects to design the mansion "cottages" that are the pride of Ocean Drive and Bellevue Avenue.

In the summer Newport was the setting for a fabulous series of picnics, dinner parties and balls famed for their extravagances in luxury and taste. Presiding over these events were Mrs. William Astor, Mrs. O.H. Belmont, Mrs. Hermann Oelrichs and other matriarchs of high society. The search for unusual diversions led to such eccentricities as the champagne and caviar dinner given by Harry Lehr for his friends and their pets, during which masters and pets ate and drank at the same table; and the fleet of full-size make-believe ships made for Mrs. Oelrichs and placed on the ocean to convey the impression of a harbor.

Attracted by the latest fads and inventions, the affluent of Newport drove the first motor cars, built the first roads, filled the harbor with princely mahogany and brass trimmed yachts, and made boat racing an exciting part of life in this resort town.

Newport and Sports. – Several sports owe their development and popularity to Newport society whose favorite pastimes included tennis, golf and boating. In 1881 the first U.S. tennis championships were held on the courts of the Newport Casino, and annual tennis tournaments including the **International Tennis Hall of Fame Grass Court Championships** (see Calendar of Events p 13) are still played here. The first U.S. amateur and open golf championships took place on a 9 hole course laid out on Brenton Point in 1894 by the "400" (p 186).

But it was in the realm of sailing – yachting especially – that Newport became internationally famous. By the late 19C several yachting clubs had been established in Newport and from 1930 to 1983 the city hosted the celebrated **America's Cup** races. The Cup races, an international competition between the most sophisticated sailing yachts in the world, date from 1851 when the New York Yacht Club sent the schooner America across the Atlantic to compete against the British for the prestigious Hundred Guinea Cup. The America won the race and returned home with the Cup – actually an ornate silver pitcher – which has since that time been known as the America's Cup. The race for the Cup, held only 26 times since 1851 because of the tremendous expense involved, was won consistently by the United States until 1983 when the Cup passed into the hands of Australia. An American victory in 1987 by the challenger Stars and Stripes once again brought the Cup home to the U.S.

Newport is, in addition, the point of origin of the biennial 685 mile **Newport-Bermuda Race** (see Calendar of Events p 13), and the destination of the **Single-Handed Transatlantic Race** that begins at Plymouth, England.

Newport Music Festival. – The Newport Music Festival is a ten-day series of musical programs presented in the mansions: The Elms, The Breakers, Rosecliff and Beechwood during the month of July. The **Newport Jazz Festival**, a celebrated annual event in the world of music, first took place in Newport in 1954. The Festival was moved to New York during the 1970s, but has since returned to Newport and is currently known as the JVC Jazz Festival. Performances are held at Fort Adams State Park (see Calendar of Events p 13).

Newport and Architecture. – Newport is an architectural sampler of a number of the nation's most attractive and aesthetically pleasing building styles from the 17-19C. The city's large group of colonial structures vary in style from the simple and austere Quaker meetinghouse (The Friends Meeting House p 186), to a church inspired by Christopher Wren – Trinity Church; and include Georgian structures designed by **Peter Harrison**: the Redwood Library, Touro Synagogue and the Brick Market. Approximately 60 restored dwellings stand in the historic "Point" (p 187) and "Historic Hill" sections of town.

The sumptuous mansions on Bellevue Avenue and Ocean Drive are among the most impressive private residences in the United States. It is interesting to observe the evolution in style of these mansions from the mid-19C Victorian period with its Gothic and Second Empire influences: Kingscote (1839), Château-sur-Mer (1852); to the elaborate imitations of the classical or Renaissance châteaux of France and the palaces of Italy: Marble House (1892), The Breakers (1895), The Elms (1901) and Rosecliff (1902) which represent a splendor and magnificence never before expressed in American architecture.

■ THE MANSIONS★★★ *map p 181*

A number of the mansions can be seen by driving along **Bellevue Avenue★★★** and **Ocean Drive★★** *(10 miles).* Ocean Drive follows the coast to the southern end of the island and at sunset offers beautiful views, especially from **Brenton Point State Park.**

The **Cliff Walk★★** is a 3 mile coastal path that straddles the rocky shoreline which separates several estates: The Breakers, Rosecliff, Marble House and Salve Regina College, from the sea. In the 19C when fishermen protested against estate owners who attempted to close off the path, the state ruled in favor of the "toilers of the sea," and the walk has remained a public way ever since. The Cliff Walk extends from Memorial Boulevard (near Newport Beach) to Bailey's Beach *(private)* with an alternate access at the Forty Steps. *Sturdy, rubber-soled shoes are advised, especially after a rainstorm.*

Visit. – *Guided tours of the mansions April through October (Château-Sur-Mer and Kingscote weekends only in April) 10 AM to 5 PM. July to mid-September one mansion open each evening to 7 PM (see description of mansions below).*

Also, November through March guided tours of Marble House, The Elms and Château-Sur-Mer weekends only 10 AM to 4 PM; closed December 25.

Guided tours (1 hour each mansion) $4.00 per mansion; $4.50 The Breakers and Marble House; combination tickets available.

The Breakers★★★ (BX). – *Open Sunday, Tuesday, Wednesday and Thursday until 7 PM July to mid-September.*

In 1885 **Cornelius Vanderbilt II,** the grandson of the Commodore who had made his fortune in steamships and railroads, purchased the Ochre Point property and hired **Richard Morris Hunt** to design a summer residence for the site. Selecting a high Renaissance Italian palace as his model, Hunt created an opulent 70 room mansion: The Breakers. The palatial design with its elaborate use of French and Italian stone, marble and alabaster, reflected the great wealth of the Vanderbilts. The exterior, heavily ornamented with arcades, columns and cornices reveals an Italian influence. Within, The Breakers is a blend of rich marbles and wooden trim, gilded plaster, mosaics and ceiling painting.

(From a photo, the Preservation Society of Newport County.)

The Breakers — The Great Hall.

Interior. – The **Great Hall,** more than two stories high, is a spectacular array of columns and pilasters, marble plaques and ornate cornices. In the **Grand Salon** (Music Room) the coffered ceiling has a painting with figures representing Music, Harmony, Song and Melody. The **Morning Room** has four corner panels painted in oil on silver leaf representing the Muses; the room looks out onto the terrace where there is a beautiful Italian mosaic. Most impressive of all the rooms is the **Dining Room** where the Vanderbilts entertained their guests amidst a setting of warm red alabaster, bronze and gilt.

On the floor above is Mrs. Vanderbilt's spacious oval bedroom, one of a series of rooms on this floor decorated by Ogden Codman.

Marble House★★★ (BX). – *Open Friday until 7 PM July to mid-September.*

A gracefully curved, balustraded drive leads to the columned facade of Marble House, one of several Newport mansions designed by **Richard Morris Hunt.** Built for the millionaire-yachtsman **William K. Vanderbilt,** Marble House is thought to have been inspired by the White House in Washington, D.C., or by the Petit Trianon at Versailles.   Among the most lavish dinner parties and balls held at Marble House was the debut of Consuelo Vanderbilt, who after the celebration locked herself in her room to protest her upcoming marriage to the ninth Duke of Marlborough. The marriage nevertheless took place a short time later, in 1895, and the following year her parents were divorced. Her mother later married O.H.P. Belmont and moved to Belcourt *(p 185).*

Interior. – The interior is as elegant as the exterior suggests. The huge entrance hall faced with yellow Siena marble is decorated with Gobelin tapestries.

In the **Gold Ballroom,** the most ornate ballroom in Newport, gold gilt panels, pilasters, arches and doorways are reflected in the glittering crystal chandeliers and mirrors that capture every ray of light. In striking contrast to the Ballroom is the subdued mood of the **Gothic Room,** where the Vanderbilt collection of medieval art objects was displayed.

The luxuriant atmosphere of the **Dining Room** is created by the elaborate use of pink Numidian marble. The solid bronze Louis XIV chairs weighing about 60 lbs each made it necessary for the host to provide each guest with a servant who would move the chair for the guest when he wished to sit or leave the table.

The tour includes a visit to the spacious basement **Kitchen,** boasting an elegance all its own with its 25 ft long stove, built-in iceboxes and shiny monogrammed cookware.

The **Chinese Teahouse** *(May through October)* on the grounds, contains ten 8 ft wooden panels delicately painted with scenes inspired by a 15C Chinese court painter.

The Elms★★ (BX). – *Open Saturday until 7 PM July to mid-September.*

Edward Julius Berwind, the son of poor German immigrants, rose to prominence in the second half of the 19C as the King of America's coal industry. His coal fields in Pennsylvania, West Virginia and Kentucky supplied the major coal needs of the United States and other nations. In 1899, wealthy and powerful, he commissioned **Horace Trumbauer** to build him a residence to rival the "cottages" of Newport's established millionaires who regarded him as an outsider, a "nouveau riche."

Inspired by a French château, Trumbauer created The Elms, a reserved and dignified country-style residence on the outside, a grandiose mansion within. The house warming given by the Berwinds August, 1901 was the highlight of the season; countless varieties of exotic plants were used throughout the house and on the grounds, and the walls were covered with rose trees and flowering vines.

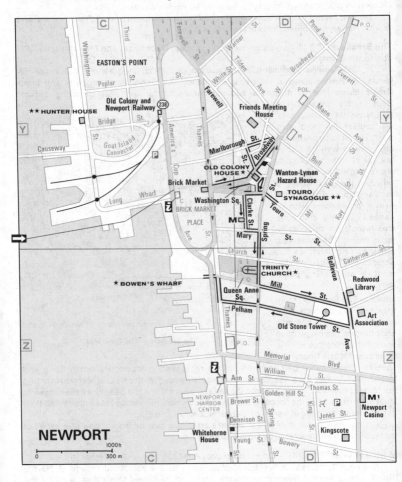

NEWPORT

Interior. – The large-scale proportions of the rooms, especially the entrance hall and **Ballroom** are awesome. In the **Ballroom,** smoothly curved corners, the restrained decoration, and an abundance of natural light create an inviting and pleasant atmosphere despite the enormous size of the room. The French classical style predominates: the **Conservatory** was inspired by the Hall of Mirrors at Versailles, the **Drawing Room** is in the Louis XVI style, the ballroom with its stucco reliefs and fine woodwork is in the Louis XV style. The four black and gold lacquer panels ornamenting the **Breakfast Room** date from the K'ang Hsi period (17C).

An upstairs hall contains an interesting set of 18C tapestries woven at the Imperial Russian Tapestry Manufactury in Leningrad. The tapestries represent paintings by Rembrandt, Van Dyck, Watteau and other masters.

Rosecliff★★ (BX). – *Open Monday until 7 PM July to mid-September.*

In 1891 **Mrs. Hermann Oelrichs,** the daughter of a wealthy Irish immigrant who had discovered the Comstock Lode in Nevada, and her husband moved to Newport. They purchased the Rosecliff estate, named for its many rosebeds, and finding the house or the property too modest for their taste engaged **Stanford White** to design a more elaborate residence. The result was a graceful imitation of the Grand Trianon at Versailles.

Outside, the off-white terra-cotta walls are finished in a technique that creates the impression of stone. Designed primarily for entertaining, Rosecliff has the largest ballroom (80 ft x 40 ft) in Newport. Windows open onto the terraces, allowing the outdoors to become an extension of the ballroom. Scenes from the *Great Gatsby* were filmed here.

Mrs. Oelrichs was one of society's most celebrated hostesses. The magnificent receptions she held at Rosecliff, including the official opening of the mansion in 1902, her famous Bal Blanc where everyone was dressed in white, and the "Mother Goose" ball were among the most spectacular events ever held in Newport.

A heart-shaped staircase leads upstairs to the sleeping quarters.

Château-sur-Mer ★ (BX).

In 1877 Château-sur-Mer was considered the most "substantial and expensive residence in Newport." Modeled after a French château, the property extended down to the sea, thus its name – "Castle by the Sea." Victorian in style, with a massive asymmetrical silhouette, the mansion was built in 1852 for **William S. Wetmore**, a China Trade merchant. Extremely spacious and luxurious for its day, Château-sur-Mer was later enlarged in 1872 by the architect **Richard Morris Hunt**.

Inside, several interesting decorative effects have been created: light streams into the heavily carved entrance hall through a colored glass ceiling panel 45 ft above the floor; the ballroom is embellished with decorative stucco mouldings and trim fashioned to resemble wood; the stairwell, illuminated by stained glass windows, is lined with canvas painted in the style of tapestry.

In the Turkish sitting room the blend of Oriental, European and American design elements and furnishings creates a style that is distinctly Victorian in character.

The library and dining room were decorated in the Renaissance style by the Florentine Luigi Frullini.

Kingscote (BX).

Designed in 1839 by **Richard Upjohn,** Kingscote was one of the earliest examples of a new style trend in American architecture: the adaptation of Greek Revival motifs and effects to private residences. Kingscote's irregular shape, expressed in wood rather than stone, and emphasized by gables, arches, eaves and varied roof lines, formed a striking contrast to the symmetrical, generally solid shape of earlier dwellings.

This mansion was built for the southern planter **George Noble Jones,** then sold in the 1860s to William H. King after whom it (King's Cottage) was named. The **interior** is extremely Victorian with its many Tiffany windows, heavy furniture and somber rooms. included among the furnishings is a prized collection of Oriental paintings, rugs, porcelain and furniture attributed to the Newport cabinetmakers, Goddard and Townsend.

Belcourt Castle ★ (BX).

Bellevue Avenue. Guided tours (1 hour) mid-June to mid-September 9 AM to 5 PM; spring and fall 10 AM to 5 PM; for winter hours ☎ (401) 846-0669; $4.50.

Richard Morris Hunt chose a hunting lodge of Louis XIII as his model for this castle (1896) designed for the 35 year old bachelor Oliver Hazard Perry **Belmont** who, in 1898, married Alva Smith Vanderbilt, formerly the wife of William K. Vanderbilt *(p 183)*. The castle, owned since 1959 by the Tinney family, contains an outstanding collection of European furnishings.

The interior is inspired by different periods of French, Italian and English design. The huge **Reception Room,** decorated with plush red upholsteries and stained glass windows, can accommodate 350 dinner guests comfortably. A pair of gigantic crystal chandeliers from a 17C Italian monastery dominates the room.

From the oval Family Dining Room on the second floor there is a view out to the ocean.

The spacious **French Gothic Ballroom,** also on this floor, has stained glass windows (13C), Oriental carpets, tapestries, and the enormous Castle-Fireplace designed to resemble a château of the Loire Valley.

Hammersmith Farm ★ (AX).

Ocean Drive. Guided tours (40 min) April to mid-November 10 AM to 5 PM (7 PM Memorial Day to Labor Day); weekends only mid to late March and mid to late November; closed the rest of the year; $4.50.

This estate was formerly owned by Mrs. Hugh Auchincloss whose daughter Jacqueline and John F. Kennedy were married in Newport and celebrated their marriage here in 1953. The Kennedys returned to Hammersmith on numerous occasions after their marriage, and following John Kennedy's election as President of the United States, the farm served (1961-1963) as the summer White House.

The mansion (1887) takes its name from the farm which has been operating on the property since 1640. The modest exterior, covered uniformly with wooden shingles, is a good example of the "shingle style" which was popular during the last several decades of the 19C. The bayside setting, enhanced by gardens designed by **Frederick Law Olmsted,** is especially scenic.

The interior is very simple, yet comfortably furnished. Highlights of the tour include Hammersmith's many mementoes and associations related to the years Jacqueline spent here as a young girl, then with her husband and children.

Beechwood.

Guided tours (50 min) mid-May through October 10 AM to 5 PM; $4.50.

A tour of this Mediterranean-style villa acquired in 1880 by William and Caroline Astor is unlike that offered by its palatial neighbors. From the moment visitors are greeted at the door by the "butler", they are transported back to the 1890s by "servants" and "house guests" (portrayed by members of a theater group) who accompany callers throughout the house.

Mrs. Astor's Beechwood. – Named for the beech trees on the grounds, Beechwood was originally built by Calvert Vaux for the merchant Daniel Parish. Destroyed by fire in 1855, the mansion was rebuilt by Andrew Jackson Downing for Parish, and later under the ownership of the Astors, redecorated and refurnished. The ballroom added at that time by **Richard Morris Hunt** was the largest in Newport when it was completed.

Beechwood is famous as the home of Caroline Astor – *The* Mrs. Astor as she insisted upon being known – whose husband was the grandson of John Jacob Astor. Mrs. Astor, the grande dame of New York and Newport society, compiled the list of society's elite "400", 400 being the number of persons her ballroom could accommodate.

A copy of Duran's portrait of Mrs. Astor is in the entrance hall. Among the public rooms on this floor is the light-filled **Ballroom**, ornamented with gilt and gesso relief and containing more than 450 mirrors. On the floor above, Mrs. Astor's Victorian bedroom has views of the ocean. It is said that Mrs. Astor ordered the window that formerly opened on to Rosecliff sealed off, after she learned the mansion had been built with a ballroom larger than Beechwood's.

■ COLONIAL NEWPORT★★ *walking tour: 4 hours – plan p 184*

Newport's extraordinarily large group of colonial structures is one of the nation's great architectural treasures. The itinerary below represents a selection of these dwellings and public buildings. Begin at the **Information Center** near the Brick Market.

Brick Market (CY). – Designed in 1761 by **Peter Harrison**, this handsome building is a fine example of the influence of the formality of the style of Palladio on Georgian architecture. The market was the commercial center of Newport; open market stalls were located on the ground floor, while the upper floors were reserved for offices and storage.

Washington Square (DY). – This was the crossroads of colonial Newport, at one end of the square was the Old Colony House, at the other end the marketplace. The homes, shops and warehouses of Newport's merchants stood nearby.

The Old Colony House★ (DY). – *Open June to Labor Day 10 AM (12 noon Saturday and Sunday) to 4 PM; closed Monday and Tuesday.*

This building designed by **Richard Munday** was the seat of Rhode Island's government from the colonial period through the early 19C. In 1781 General George Washington and Count Rochambeau, the leader of the French troops, met here to discuss plans for the battle of Yorktown.

Furniture made by Goddard and Townsend and one of Gilbert Stuart's full-length portraits of George Washington will be found inside.

Friends Meeting House (DY). – *Marlborough Street. Guided tours (40 min) mid-June through August 10 AM to 5 PM; closed Sunday and Monday; $2.00.*

By the end of the 17C Newport had a large population of Quakers. This meeting-house, constructed by the Society of Friends in 1699 and enlarged as the Society grew, was the regional center for New England's Quakers. The building is architecturally interesting for its pulley-operated walls, large stone supports, which prevent the lower floor from resting directly on the ground, and "ship" type ceiling construction.

Wanton-Lyman-Hazard House (DY). – *17 Broadway. Guided tours (40 min) mid-June through August 10 AM to 5 PM; closed Sunday and Monday; $2.00.*

Prior to the Revolution this was the home of Martin Howard, a tax collector whose official duties made him one of the most unpopular persons in town. During the Stamp Act riots, while the patriots ransacked his house, Howard fled to Canada. Considering himself fortunate to have escaped, the unpopular tax man never returned to Newport.

Touro Synagogue★★ (DY). – *85 Touro Street. Guided tours (25 min) late June to Labor Day 10 AM to 5 PM; closed Saturday.*

The earliest members of Newport's Jewish community arrived from Lisbon and Amsterdam in 1650, however, it was not until a century later (1759), under the guidance of their leader Isaac de Touro that a synagogue was built. This was the first synagogue constructed in the United States.

The building, designed by architect **Peter Harrison**, is a successful adaptation of the Georgian style to Sephardic Jewish tradition. Situated on a quiet street and set on a diagonal with the east wall facing in the direction of Jerusalem, the synagogue is plain, almost stark in appearance on the outside. Within, the interior is richly adorned with hand carved paneling, balustrades, columns; twelve columns support the galleries, twelve columns support the ceiling; twelve – symbolic of the twelve tribes of Israel. The Scrolls of the Law, the Torah, are preciously guarded in the Holy Ark.

Armory of the Artillery Company of Newport (DY M). – *23 Clarke Street. Open by appointment only; $1.00.*

The Newport Artillery Company participated in every major American military campaign from the colonial period through World War I. This granite-walled Greek Revival style building constructed in 1836 to serve as the company's armory, is now a museum of American and foreign military weapons, uniforms and flags. Personal mementoes of well-known military figures are on display.

Trinity Church★ (DZ). – This white clapboard church (1725-1726) rising above Queen Anne Square was designed by **Richard Munday** and is a contemporary of Boston's Old North Church *(p 97)* which was built only a few years earlier. Both Trinity Church and Old North were influenced by the designs of Christopher Wren.

Trinity's arcaded belfry surmounted by a tall colonial spire, is a landmark visible for miles around. Inside, the box pews and three-tiered pulpit are original to the church. The colonial dwellings bordering the square were moved to this location by the **Newport Restoration Foundation,** an organization established in 1968 to preserve and restore the early architecture of Newport.

The Old Stone Tower (DZ). – Known also as the Mystery Tower – because of the various legends surrounding its origin – this stone structure has been attributed to the Vikings, the Portuguese, the Indians and the Irish. Less romantic, but perhaps a bit more realistic is the theory that the Tower is the remnant of a mill which was constructed in the 17C.

Redwood Library (DZ). – **Peter Harrison** selected a Roman temple as his inspiration for the library, his first important architectural achievement. The building's classical design which includes a columned entranceway seems out of proportion to its modest size, and the wooden exterior painted and sanded to imitate stone appears artificial; however, in its day, the library – the first structure in the United States to employ a free-standing portico – was an impressive innovation in American architecture.

Newport Art Association (DZ). – Designed by **Richard Morris Hunt,** this is a good example of the "stick style": sticks expressing the framing elements are used as exterior decoration. *Temporary exhibits.*

Follow Pelham Street, lined with colonial dwellings, to the waterfront.

Bowen's Wharf★ (CZ). – Salty old dockside structures on the wharf have been transformed into in- and outdoor eating places; together with the neighboring craft shops and boutiques they form the heart of this waterfront square.

■ ADDITIONAL SIGHTS

Easton's Point (CY). – The large number of restored homes in this quiet residential neighborhood date from the 18C when the Point was a prosperous mercantile community. Quakers who lived in the area named the streets for trees and numbers to avoid "man-worship." Washington Street was later renamed for George Washington.

Hunter House★★ (CY). – *54 Washington Street. Guided tours (45 min) May through October 10 AM to 5 PM; April Saturday and Sunday only; $4.00.*

This elegant dwelling built in 1748 by a prosperous triangular trade merchant, was purchased by an ambassador, William Hunter, and subsequently served as the home of two governors and the headquarters of the commander of the French fleet during the Revolution.

The house is a beautiful example of the colonial style of the 18C. The carved pineapple ornamenting the doorway, is a symbol of hospitality that dates from the period when a sea captain, returning home from a voyage, placed a pineapple outside his home to announce his safe arrival and to invite everyone to share the refreshments that were waiting inside.

(From a photo, the Preservation Society of Newport County.)

Door of the Hunter House.

The interior contains an exceptional collection of furniture made by the famous cabinetmakers **Goddard and Townsend,** and skillfully carved woodwork.

Samuel Whitehorne House (CZ). – *416 Thames Street. Guided tours (1 hour) May through October Mondays, Saturdays, Sundays and holidays 10 AM to 4 PM, Fridays 1 to 4 PM; $3.50.*

The four-square brick Federal dwelling topped by a square cupola was built (1811) for Samuel Whitehorne, Sr., a sea captain whose shipping losses forced him to sell the house at auction in the 1840s. Subdivided into apartments, the building eventually deteriorated until the Newport Restoration Foundation acquired and restored the house.

The house is refurbished with a **collection**★ of 18C furniture, many pieces of which were turned out in the workshops of Goddard and Townsend.

Newport Casino (DZ). – Facing Bellevue Avenue, the Casino gives the impression of a commercial block, with its ground floor shops. The Casino was the most exclusive country club in the East when it was built in 1880 during the height of Newport's "gilded age." Pass through the deeply arched entranceway to discover the casino's tennis courts and the "shingle style" buildings designed by **McKim, Mead and White.** The casino's grassy courts were the site of the first Men's United States Lawn Tennis Association tournaments held between 1881 and 1914, after which the tournament moved to Forest Hills. Tournaments are still held here in July and August *(see Calendar of Events p 13).*

International Tennis Hall of Fame (M1). – *In the Casino. Open May through October 10 AM to 5 PM; the rest of the year 11 AM to 4 PM closed January 1 and December 25; $4.00.* Exhibits focus on the Davis Cup, tennis art and memorabilia related to the development of tennis as an international sport. On display is the sterling silver punch bowl awarded to Bostonian Richard Sears, the first U.S. men's singles champion in lawn tennis.

Fort Adams State Park (AX). – *Open 6 AM to 11 PM; $1.00 per car.*

Fort Adams, its walls constructed of granite hauled from Maine by schooner, was originally built to guard the entrance to Narragansett Bay. The fort ultimately developed into the command post for the coastal batteries in the northeast, and until 1945 was the center of a system of defenses to protect the bay and Long Island Sound.

Today the Fort is a state park and the site, each summer, of the JVC Jazz Festival *(see Calendar of Events p 13)*. From the perimeter walk there is a sweeping **view★★** of the harbor, Newport Bridge and Newport, including the downtown area.

Old Colony and Newport Railway (CY). – *America's Cup Avenue. Departures early July to Labor Day 1:30 PM; $4.00. The rest of the year for schedule ☏ (401) 624-6951.*

Chartered in the 19C the railway had its busiest year in 1913 when 24 trains daily, including the Boston "Dandy Express," arrived and departed from Newport.

Today the railway operates along the eastern shore of Narragansett Bay between Newport and Portsmouth. Round-trip excursions from Newport *(time: 2 hours)* stop at the Navy Base, the Bend Boat Basin at Melville, and Portsmouth. At Portsmouth a 40 minute stopover allows passengers to visit the Green Animals *(sea below)*.

EXCURSIONS

Middletown. – Pop 17 503. *North of Newport by Memorial Boulevard.* This small community is a blend of long sandy beaches and rural countryside. **Second Beach** and **Third Beach.**

Portsmouth. – Pop 14 993. *North of Newport by Rte 114.* Settlers from Portsmouth moved south and founded Newport in 1639. Today this hilly township is a summer resort.

Green Animals Topiary Gardens. – *From Rte 114 turn left onto Cory's Lane. Open May through September 10 AM to 5 PM; weekends and holidays only in October; $4.00.*

Colorful flowerbeds are arranged among this group of 80 green tree and shrub sculptures which include representations of a giraffe, lion, donkey and other animals.

■ PAWTUCKET

Michelin tourist map - fold 16 – Pop 72 803

Pawtucket, a busy city just north of Providence, is credited with being the birthplace of American industrialization. For it was here at the falls of the Blackstone River in 1793 that the **Slater Mill,** the first water-powered textile mill in the United States to produce cotton yarn successfully, was constructed.

The construction of the mill was the result of an association between **Samuel Slater,** who had been employed in a textile factory in England, and **Moses Brown,** a wealthy Providence Quaker *(p 189)*. Combining their resources: Slater's technical knowledge and the Brown family capital, the two men laid the groundwork for the major transition from handcraft to machine production. The mill they built pioneered the way for this change as well as for the diffusion of the textile industry throughout New England.

Several years later, in 1810, another factory: the Wilkinson Mill, specializing in the production of machine parts and tools, was built nearby. The two factories and a dwelling of the same period have been restored and are a part of the 5 acre Slater Mill Historic Site devoted to the origins of the industrial age in America.

(From a drawing by P.D. Malone. By permission of Slater Mill Historic Site.)

Slater Mill.

Slater Mill Historic Site★. – *From I-95 South take exit 29, Downtown Pawtucket; turn right on Fountain Street, then right on Exchange Street and left on Roosevelt Avenue. Guided tours (1 1/2 hours) with demonstrations of machines June 1 to Labor Day 10 AM (1 PM Sunday) to 5 PM; after Labor Day through May Saturday and Sunday only 1 to 5 PM, closed Monday and late December through February; $2.50.*

Slater Mill. – 1793. Here, operating textile machines: carding machine, spinning frame and mule, power looms, knitting and braiding machines are used to illustrate the processes in transforming cotton from the raw fibers to finished goods.

Wilkinson Mill. – 1810. This mill contains a 19C machine shop with belt-driven machine tools: a jigsaw, lathes, drill pressers, planers, shaper. An 8-ton breast wheel has been reconstructed in the basement. Water from the Blackstone River is admitted to the wheel through restored raceways, and the wheel drives the machine tools on the floor above. The mill originally housed a machine shop where textile machinery was built and repaired. Cotton and woolen thread were produced on the floor above.

Sylvanus Brown House. – 1758. This dwelling, furnished as it was in the early 1800s, was the home of a millwright and pattern maker. Demonstrations of hand spinning and weaving illustrate the tasks performed by household members.

PROVIDENCE ★★

Michelin tourist map - fold 16 – Pop 154 148

The capital of Rhode Island, a center of business and industry, and the third largest city in New England, Providence is the hub of a metropolitan region that has more than 900,000 inhabitants.

The city's location on a natural harbor at the head of Narragansett Bay, offered special advantages for the shipping and commercial activity which allowed Providence to prosper and expand. A result of this expansion was the development of the College Hill district with its lovely 18 and 19C structures. Today this tree-shaded residential neighborhood on College Hill is the home of Brown University, the Rhode Island School of Design and their students. On the hill across from College Hill is the Capitol building, its majestic white mass rising above the growing business area below.

HISTORICAL NOTES

Providence Plantations. – After **Roger Williams** was banished from the Massachusetts Bay Colony, he traveled south with a group of his followers until June 1636, when they arrived on the banks of the Moshassuck (later the Providence) River. Having decided to settle here, they bought the land from the Narragansett Indians and named it Providence, in honor of God's Providence which had led them to this place. Roger Williams declared that the new colony would be a safe and sure refuge for all persons seeking freedom of worship.

In 1644 he journeyed to England to obtain a charter for Providence and the Rhode Island (Newport) colony. The charter united the two colonies as "Rhode Island and Providence Plantations," but was declared void in 1660 following the restoration of the monarchy to the throne. Three years later a royal charter was issued by Charles II granting to all inhabitants "full liberty in religious concernments."

The Development of Providence. – Originally a farming settlement, Providence rapidly developed into a commercial center as its inhabitants turned to shipping and trade. By the mid-18C Providence vessels were engaged in the triangular trade, and in 1772 when Parliament passed legislation that threatened to limit American shipping, citizens were quick to react. They forced the British revenue schooner *Gaspee* aground at Warwick one evening in June, burned the vessel and captured its crew. Despite a generous reward offered by the Crown, the culprits were never captured.

During the Revolution, Providence was a privateering and supply depot and following the war the city emerged as Rhode Island's leading port. In 1787 **John Brown** sent his first ship to China. Other merchants followed his lead and amassed great fortunes in the China Trade. Then, as maritime trade declined capital investment shifted toward industry. Providence developed into a major center for the manufacture of textiles, tools, files and steam engines, attracting thousands of immigrants to work at its many factories. The city underwent an economic crisis after World War II when a number of factories moved to the South; however, as a producer of a variety of products including jewelry and silverware, Providence is today once again enjoying an active business life.

The Brown Brothers. – The Brown name, closely associated with the industrial, cultural, political and commercial growth of Providence, is the name of one of the city's oldest, most illustrious families. At the end of the 18C the four Brown brothers were prominent among the leaders of Providence. **John,** bold and adventurous, a leader of the attack on the *Gaspee*, was a prosperous merchant. His was the first ship from this port to reach China. **Joseph** was an architect: the Market House, First Baptist Church and John Brown House are only a few of the buildings he designed. **Moses,** a Quaker, was responsible for establishing the Providence Bank, and was the first to finance the development of the textile industry in the United States *(p 188)*. Finally, there was **Nicholas,** a successful businessman whose mercantile enterprise was known around the world.

COLLEGE HILL ★★ *time: 1/2 day – plan p 190*

In the early 18C the main thoroughfare – present-day North and **South Main Street** – through Providence, bordered the waterfront and was crowded with warehouses, wharves and shops. To relieve the congestion, a dirt path that ran along the crest of the hill that rose in back of the main street, was widened for the "common benefit of all" – thus **Benefit Street** *(p 190)*. Wealthy merchants built their homes on Benefit Street, high above the waterfront and by the beginning of the 19C the hill had developed into a fashionable residential enclave. Chosen as the site of Rhode Island College (Brown University) in 1770, the district came to be known as College Hill.

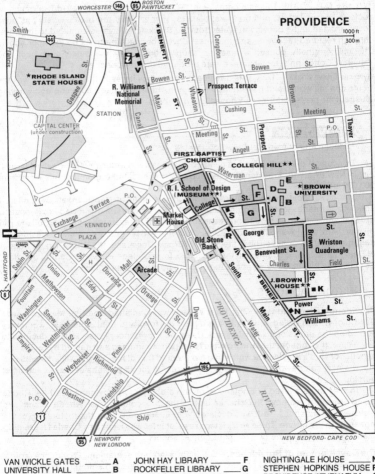

PROVIDENCE

VAN WICKLE GATES	A	JOHN HAY LIBRARY	F	NIGHTINGALE HOUSE	N
UNIVERSITY HALL	B	ROCKFELLER LIBRARY	G	STEPHEN HOPKINS HOUSE	R
MANNING HALL	D	POYNTON IVES HOUSE	K	PROVIDENCE ATHENAEUM	S
HOPE COLLEGE	E	CARRINGTON HOUSE	L	ROGER WILLIAMS SPRING	V

The Hill's charming, tree-shaded streets lined with architecture ranging from colonial, to Italianate and Greek Revival, represents one of the most beautifully preserved historic districts in the nation. High on the hill is **Thayer Street,** the shopping center of the youthful college-university community, with its bookstores, coffee shops, restaurants and many stores. Former warehouses and shops, at the south end of the main street below the hill, have been converted into boutiques, craft shops and restaurants, adding to the aura of the past that pervades this section of the city.

Market House. – This was the commercial center of early Providence. Located beside the river, boats could easily load and unload their cargoes here. The building is now a part of the Rhode Island School of Design (p 190).

First Baptist Church★. – *75 North Main Street. Open 10 AM to 3 PM (12 noon Saturday). Tours also Sunday 12:15 PM (following morning worship service).*
The Baptist Church, founded in Providence by Roger Williams, dates back to 1638. The first house of worship built by the Baptists in America stood on North Main Street, a short distance from the site of the present wooden clapboard church (1775) designed by Joseph Brown. Inside, the paneling, scrolled pediments, lighted urns and arches are painted in soft tones of green and white. Enormous columns support the galleries and roof, leading the eye upward to the carved ceiling. The handsome steeple is 185 ft tall.

Benefit Street★. – At Benefit Street pause to admire the graceful profile of restored dwellings to the right and to the left. More than one hundred homes ranging from colonial to Victorian in style line the narrow streets and brick walks leading to the Rhode Island School of Design and Brown University.

Rhode Island School of Design. – *2 College Street.* Established in the 19C to train artisans for industry, the RISD has earned a reputation as a teaching institution for design, architecture and visual art. Facilities available to the school's 1 800 students include sculpture, wood and metal labs, apparel design and textile workshops.

Museum of Art, Rhode Island School of Design★★. – *224 Benefit Street. Open September 1 to June 15 Tuesday, Wednesday, Friday and Saturday 10:30 AM to 5 PM; Thursday 12 noon to 5 PM, Sunday 2 to 5 PM; the rest of the year Wednesday through Saturday only 11 AM to 4 PM; $1.00. Saturday free.*

The museum presents, in an engaging manner, collections of art from various periods and civilizations: Egyptian, Greek, Roman, Oriental, European, African and American. Exhibits are arranged generally in chronological order, but often cross period boundaries to illustrate a common trend in contemporary sculpture, painting and textiles.

The **entrance floor** is devoted to Western art. Note the medieval carvings, 19C American and French paintings and Greek bronzes. On the **second floor** is the Oriental, Eastern, aboriginal and Egyptian art. The **Dainichi Buddha** (10C Japan), a wooden temple figure discovered in 1933 in the attic of a farmhouse, dominates one of the galleries. A bronze **Dancing Siva** (11C) with its arc and frames representing the universe is in a gallery nearby.

Before leaving the museum, visit the **lower level** where 20C art is displayed.

Pendleton House★. – Adjoining and a part of the museum is the Pendleton House, built in 1904 to house the **Charles Pendleton collection★★** of 18C American furnishings and decorative arts. The interior is extremely elegant with its rich mahogany woodwork, large central hall and luxurious rooms.

In the museum courtyard are several contemporary sculptures including works by George Rickey and Clement Meadmore.

Brown University★. – The seventh college established in the United States (1764), this **Ivy League** *(p 114)* school was founded at Warren as Rhode Island College and renamed in 1804 for its principal benefactor, Nicholas Brown II.

Approximately 5 580 undergraduate and 1 330 graduate students are enrolled at Brown's 133 acre College Hill campus which is comprised of about 150 buildings: large "halls" which house classrooms and administrative offices, student and faculty residences, five libraries and a sports complex that includes a 20 400 seat football stadium. The university libraries: the John Hay Library, Rockefeller Library, John Carter Brown Library, Annmary Brown Memorial, Science Library – contain more than 4 000 000 volumes and related items, including distinguished collections of early printed matter prior to 1500 and source material related to colonial America. **Pembroke College** (1891), founded by the university as a separate division for women, merged with Brown in 1971.

At the main entrance to Brown University, on Prospect Street are the **Van Wickle Gates** (**A**); the gates are opened twice each year: inward on the first day of classes, and outward on commencement day. From the Van Wickle Gates, Brown's oldest buildings are visible: **University Hall** (**B**) (1770), a stately red brick building known as the "College Edifice," was the sole university structure until 1822; the building with the four granite columns is **Manning Hall** (**D**) (1835) – the University Chapel is located in this Greek Revival Building; **Hope College** (**E**) (1822) serves as a dormitory.

On the west side of Prospect Street, opposite the Gates, are the **John Hay Library** (**F**) (1910) and the **Rockefeller Library** (**G**) (1964): the "Rock" houses the university's general collection in the humanities and social sciences. On Brown Street pass **Wriston Quadrangle** (1952), the campus residence of approximately 1 000 students.

Power Street. – At the corner of Brown and Power Streets stands a classic example of Federal architecture, the **Poynton Ives House** (No. 66) (**K**).

John Brown House★★. – *52 Power Street. Guided tours (1/2 hour) 11 AM (1 PM Sunday) to 4 PM; closed Mondays, holidays, and January and February; $2.50.*

The 3 story brick mansion (1786) designed for John Brown by his brother Joseph *(p 189)* impressed everyone who came to see it. John Quincy Adams who visited the house called it: " ... the most magnificent mansion I have ever seen on this continent."

Inside, the carved doorways, columns, fireplaces, cornices, highly polished natural wood trim, and lavish plaster ornamented ceilings provide an ideal setting for the treasured collection of Rhode Island furnishings, most of which are Brown family pieces. The nine-shell **blockfront secretary** attributed to Rhode Island cabinetmaker John Goddard, is one of the finest examples of American colonial furniture existent.

Williams Street. – At No. 66 stands another Federal mansion, the **Carrington House** (**L**).

Returning along Benefit Street note at No. 357 an attractive Federal dwelling, the **Nightingale House** (**N**); Just beyond Benevolent Street there is a good view of the gilded ribbed dome of the **Old Stone Bank**. A little further, on the left, is the 18C red clapboard dwelling: the **Stephen Hopkins House** (No. 43) (**R**), formerly the home of Quaker governor Stephen Hopkins, signer of the Declaration of Independence and ten-time governor of Rhode Island. The Greek Revival style is represented by the **Providence Athenaeum** (**S**) (designed by William Strickland) where, according to legend, Edgar Allen Poe courted Sarah Whitman, a resident of Benefit Street.

■ ADDITIONAL SIGHTS

Rhode Island State House★. – *Smith Street. Open 8:30 AM to 4:30 PM; closed weekends and holidays.*

From its position on Smith Hill, the Capitol building (designed by McKim, Mead and White – 1901) has a commanding view of downtown Providence. On a clear day the white marble exterior is especially impressive set against the deep blue sky.

The central section of the building is topped with the second largest free-standing dome in the world (after that of Saint Peter's in Rome) and surmounted by a statue of the **Independent Man**, a symbol of Rhode Island's spirit of liberty and tolerance.

From the **first floor** there is a good view of the dome mural portraying the history of Rhode Island and the Latin inscription on the inside of the dome: "Rare felicity of times when it is possible to think as you like and to say what you think."

On the **second floor** are the legislative chambers and the governor's office. A full-length portrait of George Washington, painted by Gilbert Stuart, hangs in the Governor's Reception Room. The royal Charter of 1663 is among the historical documents on display.

Prospect Terrace. – From this small park on Congdon Street high on the slopes of College Hill there is a **view**★ across the city to the State House.

Providence Arcade. – Extending from Weybosset Street through to Westminster Street, this Greek Revival "temple of trade" designed by Russell Warren and James Bucklin in 1828, is one of the few surviving 19C shopping malls in the United States.

Roger Williams National Memorial. – *N. Main Street, between Smith and Meeting Streets. Visitor Information Center (282 N. Main Street) open April through October 9 AM to 5 PM; the rest of the year Monday through Friday only 8 AM to 4:30 PM.*

A 4.5 acre landscaped memorial park surrounds the site of the spring (**V**) around which, according to tradition, Roger Williams founded the Providence colony. The place where the spring once flowed to the surface is marked by a stone well curb.

SAUNDERSTOWN

Michelin tourist map - fold 22 – 20 miles south of Providence

The celebrated early American portraitist, Gilbert Stuart, was born in this rural corner of North Kingstown.

Gilbert Stuart Birthplace. – *From Rte 1A, exit onto Gilbert Stuart Road and continue 1 1/2 miles. Guided tours (1/2 hour) 11 AM to 4:30 PM; closed Fridays, major holidays and mid-November through March; $1.25.* Born in the American colonies in 1755, Gilbert Stuart later studied in London and Dublin before he returned to the United States, where he painted his most famous portraits *(p 30)*. Stuart is best known for his portraits of George Washington: the two full-length portraits now hanging in the Rhode Island State House and the Old Colony House (Newport), and the Athenaeum Portrait *(see illustration p 106)*, a likeness of which appears on the one dollar bill.

Gilbert Stuart lived in this small frame dwelling until he was six years old. Located in a woodsy setting, the house contains period furnishings and an old snuff mill formerly worked by the artist's father.

WICKFORD

Michelin tourist map - fold 22 – 17 miles south of Providence

This colonial village on the shores of Narragansett Bay developed in the 18C as an important center for goods shipped from the plantations on the mainland to Newport. Fishing and shipbuilding became major activities after the Revolution as Wickford grew into a bustling, prosperous shipping port. The large concentration of 18 and 19C white clapboard dwellings for which Wickford is today appreciated, date from this period.

Smith's Castle. – *1 1/2 miles north of Wickford by Rte 1. Open April 15 to October 15 Thursday through Sunday 10 AM (1 PM Sunday) to 5 PM; $1.50.* In 1640 a garrison was built on this site, a short distance from a trading post established by Roger Williams. The garrison was destroyed by the Indians during King Philip's War and two years later, in 1678, a small dwelling, later enlarged to its present 2 1/2 story size, was constructed. The house contains 18 and 19C furnishings.

OTHER PLACES OF INTEREST

JAMESTOWN. – Michelin tourist map - fold 22 – 3 miles west of Newport – Pop 4 563.
Jamestown lies on Conanicut Island in the middle of Narragansett Bay.

Points of interest are clustered at the southern tip of the island. From **Beaver Tail Lighthouse** *(at the end of Beaver Tail Road)* there is a view along the south shore. An expansive vista across the bay to Newport can be admired from **Fort Wetherhill** *(off of Rte 138 and Walcott Avenue).* The fort's ramparts are built on granite cliffs that rise up to 100 ft tall. The shores of picturesque **Mackeral Cove** are flecked with summer homes.

LITTLE COMPTON. – Michelin tourist map - fold 23 – 15 miles south of Fall River – Pop 3 253
Located in the southeastern portion of the state known for its production of chickens : the "Rhode Island Red," Little Compton is one of Rhode Island's prettiest villages with its green, white Congregational Church and old cemetery. In the burial ground stands a monument honoring Benjamin Church, the Indian fighter who took part in the Great Swamp Fight and the capture and execution of King Philip *(p 179).*

Narrow roads (such as Route 77) winding through the rural countryside and down to the coast, are fringed with marshes and swampland.

WATCH HILL. – Michelin tourist map - fold 22.
Located at the southwesternmost point in Rhode Island, Watch Hill is a fashionable seaside community with elegant summer homes. Swimming, boating, golf and browsing in the fine shops are popular pastimes. From the **Watch Hill Lighthouse** *(south on Watch Hill Road)* Fishers Island, a private island off the coast of Connecticut, is visible. A short distance from Watch Hill is the mile-long **Misquamicut State Beach.**

Vermont

Area : 9 609 sq miles
Population : 530 032
Capital : Montpelier
Nickname : Green Mountain State
State Flower : Red Clover

"Les verts monts," exclaimed Samuel de Champlain describing the forested mountains he saw extending southwards from the lake that now bears his name. More than a century later his description of these mountains – *les verts monts* (the green mountains) – was adopted as the official name of the region : Vermont.

Vermont is a state of far-reaching hill-and-dale landscapes. Pastoral and uncluttered, it has no large cities or industrial centers (the largest city is Burlington with 38 000 inhabitants). Miles of backroads, often unpaved, skirt rocky streams and cross the wooden covered bridges found throughout the open countryside. In the north the fertile, rather flat terrain bordering Lake Champlain is covered with farms, easily sighted from a distance by their red barns and tall silvery-metallic silos.

The landscape varies with the seasons : dormant under a heavy cover of glistening white snow in winter, the region is a palette of rich greens in the spring and summer when the mountain streams run fastest, and aflame with color in autumn.

An Independent State. – After many other parts of New England had been settled, Vermont still remained virtually uninhabited and a battleground between the English and the French and the Indians. Not until the defeat of the French at Quebec by the British in 1759 did the colonists begin to arrive in large numbers.

Prior to the outbreak of the Revolution, **Ethan Allen** and the Green Mountain Boys *(p 198)* – the "Bennington Mob" – together with Benedict Arnold and his men captured Fort Ticonderoga from the British. The cannon and supplies seized by the Green Mountain Boys at Fort Ti were used by the Continental Army the following spring in the siege of Boston *(p 90)*.

In 1777 Vermont declared itself independent and a constitution was drawn up outlawing slavery and eliminating property ownership and personal wealth as voting requirements. Denied admission to the union because of land claims by New York, Vermont remained independent for 14 years, coining its own money, operating its own post office, and conducting negotiations with "foreign" powers. In 1791, the dispute with New York settled, Vermont joined the union as the 14th state.

For generations Vermonters have guarded their spirit of independence and the principle of strong local government. At one time heavily Republican, Vermont is today dominated by the Democrats, and remains a vigorous supporter of states' rights.

Economy. – In the 19C many Vermonters abandoned their land for the western plains. The forests have reclaimed about 80 % of the land, however, agriculture, represented primarily by dairy farming, still dominates the economy. Vermont's dairy farms supply milk and milk products to the Boston region and southern New England and, in addition, make the famous Vermont **cheddar cheese. Maple syrup** is the state's other important product. In early spring, when the snow is still on the ground, steam begins to rise from the small wooden sugarhouses where farmers use evaporators to boil down the sap from the maple trees, into syrup.

A major share of Vermont's wealth comes from the **granite** quarried in Barre and from the **marble** quarried on the slopes of the Green Mountains (Proctor). Industrially, Vermont is a producer of tools, computer components, furniture and paper. In this state where four-season tourism is an important source of income (skiing alone generates $230 million annually), outdoor advertising is prohibited by law. A system of modest, uniform signs is used to indicate lodging and other visitor services.

Recreation. – The **Green Mountains,** extending through the center of the state and including the Green Mountain National Forest (325 534 acres) is the main recreation area. Vermont is the **ski capital** of the East with year-round resorts such as Stowe, Killington, Bromley, Stratton and Sugarbush Valley among its approximately 35 ski areas. In the milder seasons **bicycle touring,** especially popular in Vermont because of the miles of scenic backroads, hiking on the **Long Trail** (a 262 mile footpath from Massachusetts to Canada...), horseback riding, soaring, windsurfing and sailboarding are among the many opportunities for the activity-minded who enjoy the exhilaration of the outdoors.

Fish are plentiful in the brooks and streams. Although lacking a coastline, Vermont borders Lake Champlain which is a playground for water sports.

ITINERARIES

To discover Vermont, you should leave the highway and drive on the backroads through the small villages with their white steepled churches, peaceful commons and country stores. Several itineraries are presented below. However, do not hesitate to plan your own itinerary by choosing from the selection of scenic roads *(some unpaved)* and villages presented on the tourist map accompanying the guide.

Driving the Backroads. – Speeds in excess of 30 mph are generally unsafe since many backroads are unpaved and have sharp curves, steep grades and uneven surfaces. Special caution is advised during the spring thaw or after a rainfall as unpaved roads will be muddy. Distances may be long between gas stations: begin with a full tank of gas.

(From a photo by Nathan Benn.)

A Vermont Village – Strafford.

THE VILLAGES OF SOUTHERN VERMONT★★
Circle tour from Manchester – *88 miles – 1 day*

This drive leads to a selection of pretty villages and ski areas in the Green Mountains.

Leave Manchester (p 201) by Rte 7, then at Manchester Center take Rte 30 East. Continue on Rte 11.

Bromley Mountain. – The Bromley ski area has become popular during the summer season because of its **Alpine Slide** *(p 178)*. Bromley's summit, accessible by chairlift *(May to October 12, 9:30 AM to 5 PM (6 PM July 4 to early August; $3.75)* or hiking trails, offers views of the Green Mountains.

2 miles after Bromley take the road on the left through the tiny hamlet of **Peru**. At the fork bear left and continue through **North Landgrove**, turning left in front of the Town Hall. After passing the cemetery and the Village Inn, bear right at the fork and continue to Weston.

Weston★. – Pop 653. With its attractive green and several craft shops and general stores, Weston is a popular tourist stop on Route 100. Flanking the green and facing the gazebo is the **Farrar-Mansur House** *(guided tours June to Columbus Day; $2.00)*, a former tavern that serves as the local history museum. Nearby is the **Weston Playhouse**, modeled after the earlier church-theater which burned in 1963. *Summer theater is presented at the Playhouse.*

From Weston follow Rte 100 past the green, then bear right at the sign for Chester (Rte 11 East – unmarked).

Chester. – Pop 2 900. The very wide main street of this small community is lined with lodging places and shops. Chester is the home of the **National Survey**, a major cartographic institution in New England.

From Chester take Rte 35 to Grafton.

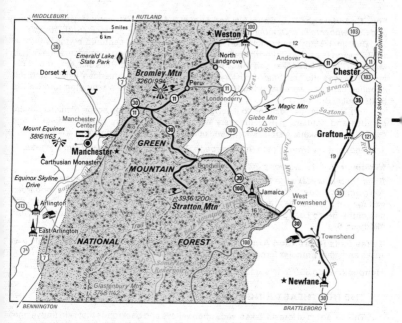

Grafton. – Pop 650. In the past this village was prosperous, owing to the woolen mills that operated here and the soapstone quarried from local mines. Grafton's restored inn and Greek Revival dwellings date from this early period.

At Grafton turn right, cross the bridge, and after 350 yds turn left before the tavern. Follow this road to Rte 35 which leads to Townshend, then take Rte 30 South to Newfane.

Newfane★. – Pop 1 213. This pretty village deep in the Green Mountains has grown little since the 18C when it was selected as the Windham county seat. During the fall Newfane's tree-shaded green with its white Congregational Church, the **Windham County Courthouse** and two old inns – the Newfane Inn and the Four Columns Inn – is a blaze of color as the leaves change from green to varying shades of red, gold, orange and rust.

(From a photo, Vermont Travel Division.)

Newfane – Windham County Courthouse.

Take Rte 30 back through Townshend. Between Townshend and West Townshend you will pass a covered bridge on the left. Continue through **Jamaica** into Bondville where a road leads to Stratton Mountain Ski Area.

Stratton Mountain. – This is one of Vermont's major ski areas. The Stratton Arts Festival featuring the work of Vermont artists and craftsmen is held at the base lodge the second week in September to Columbus Day *(9:30 AM to 5 PM; $2.50). Return to Manchester by Rte 30.*

BRANDON AND MIDDLEBURY GAPS★
From Rochester to Hancock – *75 miles – 1 day*

Broad panoramas unfold as you follow this itinerary through mountain gaps and past open farmlands of the Lake Champlain Valley.

From Rte 100 in Rochester take Rte 73 through Brandon Gap.

Rte 73 passes open farms and meadows, then enters the Green Mountain National Forest and skirts the base of **Mount Horrid** with its rocky face (alt 700 ft), before reaching the highest point in **Brandon Gap★**. From this point there is a **view★** into the Lake Champlain Valley with the Adirondacks as a backdrop. Descending west through the gap the road continues on to the villages of **Brandon** and **Orwell**, with their classic greens, bandstands and white houses. After Brandon there are vistas of rock-studded pasturelands, dairy farms with large barns and silos, and the Adirondack Mountains.

The ferry from **Larrabee's Point** crosses Lake Champlain, which is very narrow at this point, and provides access to Fort Ticonderoga in New York *(time: 6 min) (p 200).*

Fort Ticonderoga★★. – *Open July and August 9 AM to 6 PM; early May through June and September to mid-October 9 AM to 5 PM; $5.00, children, $3.00.* ☏ *(518) 585-2821.*

Built in 1755 by the French, Fort Ticonderoga was later captured by the British in 1759. The fort is especially known for the surprise attack launched here against the British May 10, 1775 by **Ethan Allen** and the Green Mountain Boys and Benedict Arnold and his men. This was the first time in history that the fort fell into American hands, and the supplies captured were used the following spring by General Washington to drive the British out of Boston.

Fort Ticonderoga, restored to its original appearance, is the scene of military drills, parades and soldiers in Revolutionary War dress. The **Military Museum** houses a fine collection of muskets, pistols, swords and colonial and Revolutionary War artifacts.

Take the ferry to Vermont, then Rte 74 through Shoreham, West Cornwall and Cornwall.

Middlebury. – *Description p 202.*

From Middlebury take Rte 125, named the Robert Frost Memorial Drive for the well-known New England poet. In Ripton you will pass the pert yellow and green clapboarded cottages of a former 19C resort, today the mountain campus of Middlebury College and site of the Bread Loaf Summer School of English. The road then continues on through **Middlebury Gap.**

Texas Falls Recreation Area. – A short trail leads to a series of falls that tumble over rocks and giant potholes formed by the glaciers, creating a delightful setting.

Hancock. – Pop 367. In this small tranquil village return to Rte 100.

THE NORTHEAST KINGDOM★★

This kingdom of forests, lakes, wide open valleys and backroads that skirt tiny villages includes the three northeastern counties that surround **St. Johnsbury** *(p 204)* and extend to the Canadian and New Hampshire borders. The region is busiest in the fall, when the countryside is a symphony of color: bright and dark greens mixed with shades of orange, yellow and gold, and everywhere the varied reds of the maple trees. During this period harvest suppers, bazaars, flea markets and auctions are held in many villages.

Six villages in the region: **Barnet, Cabot, Groton, Peacham, Plainfield** and **Walden** participate in the week-long **Northeast Kingdom Foliage Festival** *(see Calendar of Events p 13)*, during which a different village, each day, hosts activities ranging from church breakfasts to house tours and craft shows. *Reservations are necessary if you plan to travel in the Northeast kingdom in the fall.*

Two other interesting villages are **Craftsbury Common**, with its immense hilltop green which appears to meet the sky along the horizon; and **Danville** *(see below)*, the site of the annual meeting of the American Society of Dowsers.

The Burkes and Lake Willoughby

43 miles – circle tour north of St. Johnsbury – time: allow 4 hours

From St. Johnsbury take Rte 5 through Lyndonville to Rte 114, and continue north on Rte 114 to East Burke. There follow an unmarked road to Burke Hollow and West Burke.

The Burkes. – **East Burke, Burke Hollow** and **West Burke** are tiny hamlets at the base of Burke Mountain, a ski area. The gentle mountain landscape is especially scenic viewed from the road that leads to the summit of Burke Mountain (note Lake Willoughby to the northwest through the gap). *Access to the Burke Mountain auto road is from Route 114 in East Burke.*

From West Burke take Rte 5A to Lake Willoughby.

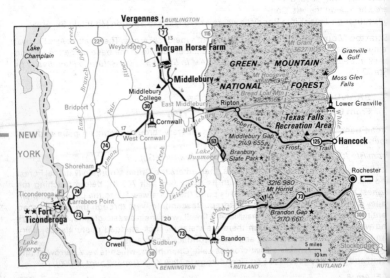

Lake Willoughby★. – Two mountains rising abruptly opposite each other in a formation resembling the entrance to a mountain pass, signal the location of Lake Willoughby. The taller mountain, towering above the southeastern end of the lake is **Mount Pisgah** (alt 2 751 ft). *There is swimming at the lake in the summer.*

Peacham - Barnet Center★

30 miles – circle tour south of St. Johnsbury – time: allow 2 hours

From St. Johnsbury take Rte 2 West.

Danville. – Pop 1 743. Because of its high elevation this rural agricultural-residential community enjoys refreshing breezes and clear air even on hot summer days. The village is the home of the **American Society of Dowsers**. The society's annual 4 day convention, held in Danville in September, attracts dowsers (dowsers employ a special method in searching for underground water and minerals) from across the nation.

From Danville take the unmarked road south in the direction of Peacham (through Harvey and Ewell Mills).

Peacham★. – Pop 581. Surrounded by a breathtaking hill-and-dale setting, Peacham is probably the most photographed of all Vermont's villages during the foliage season. Lovely white dwellings stand near the church, the general store and Peacham Academy.

Continue to Barnet Center (through South Peacham, turning left to West Barnet). At Barnet Center turn left before the church and continue up the hill.

Barnet Center. – Pop 1 331. From a vantage point beyond the church, near the top of the hill, you can look down on a beautiful pastoral setting: a large barn with its silo, and opposite, a **view**★★ of the countryside which reaches almost endlessly into the distance.

Return to the foot of the hill and turn left in the direction of Barnet. There take Rte 5 to return to St. Johnsbury.

Welcome to Peacham.

BARRE

Michelin tourist map - fold 8 – Pop 9 898

Situated on the hilly, eastern flank of the Green Mountains, Barre is the center of the largest granite industry in the nation. For over 150 years Barre's exceptionally high quality granite has been shipped to states across America; formerly to be used in the construction of public buildings, and today to serve primarily in the production of memorials and tombstones. Dozens of quarries have been worked here since 1812, and in 1833 the capitol in Montpelier *(p 202)* was the first public building in the United States to be constructed of Barre granite.

Four quarries on Millstone Hill are still active. These quarries and the manufacturing plant nearby are operated by the **Rock of Ages Company**.

Rock of Ages Quarry★. – *4 miles from the Barre Visitor Information Center (Main Street) by Rte 14 South; turn left after 2 miles onto Middle Road and follow the signs for the Rock of Ages Tourist Center and Quarries (located in Graniteville). Guided tours of the quarry by train (25 min) June to mid-October 9 AM to 5 PM; $1.95.*

The Quarries. – From the edge of the quarry, the view 350 ft down to the bottom of the mine is awesome. Enormous derricks capable of hauling stone blocks weighing up to 100 tons, are used to lift the granite slabs out of the quarry. Despite the use of the most modern machinery: jet-channeling flame machines, pneumatic drills, the work remains dangerous especially during the winter, when freezing temperatures cause ice to form on the stone.

Craftsmen Center. – *Open weekdays year round 8:30 AM to 3:30 PM.* Visitors may observe the workers at this manufacturing plant as they skillfully cut, polish and carve the granite, transforming it from rough stone into finished monuments and sculpture.

Hope Cemetery★. – *On Rte 14 north of Barre center. Open 7 AM to 4 PM, closed Saturdays, Sundays and holidays.*

The cemetery has come to be regarded by many as an outdoor museum of granite memorial sculpture. Gravestones carved and sculpted by craftsmen for departed members of their families impress by their artistry and uniqueness. Notice, in particular, the memorials adorned with scenes depicting the rural countryside.

EXCURSION

Brookfield. – Pop 100. *15 miles south of Barre by Rte 14, then Rte 65 West.*

Lying off the beaten path, this tiny picturesque community on the shores of Sunset Lake is sought out primarily for its inn, lakeside restaurant – formerly a pitchfork factory – and **floating bridge** which carries traffic across the lake. The bridge is buoyed by a network of 380 barrels that rise and fall with the water level. The present bridge, opened in 1936, is the latest replacement for the original floating structure completed in 1832.

BENNINGTON ★★

Michelin tourist map - fold 7 - Pop 16 323

This southern Vermont community surrounded by the Taconics and the Green Mountains includes commercial North Bennington, Old Bennington – an historic district with a rich ensemble of early American architecture, and **Bennington College**, distinguished for its progressive ideas and programs.

During the early days of the nation, Bennington was the home of Revolutionary War hero Ethan Allen and his Green Mountain Boys who, together with Benedict Arnold and his troops, were responsible for capturing Fort Ticonderoga from the British in 1775.

The Battle of Bennington. – Bennington was an important rallying point and supply depot for colonial troops even before the outbreak of the Revolution. May 1775, Ethan Allen and the Green Mountain Boys gathered here before they marched north to attack Fort Ticonderoga *(p 196)*.

Two years later, in August 1777, Bennington was once again to be associated with an important military victory for the patriots: the Battle of Bennington. On August 11, desperately in need of supplies for his army, the British General Burgoyne dispatched Lt. Colonel Friederich Baum and his troops to Bennington to seize the arms and munitions stored there. Forewarned of the British plan, New Hampshire's **General John Stark** led the colonial militia from Vermont into New York to head off the enemy. They encountered Baum and his men at the present-day site of Wallomsac Heights (N.Y.), and with a shout from General Stark: "There are the Red Coats and they are ours, or Molly Stark sleeps a widow tonight!" the militia attacked. The battle was a disaster for the British who lost many men and failed to obtain the much needed supplies. As for the Americans, the Battle of Bennington was an important military victory, and served as a prelude to the defeat of General Burgoyne's army at the Battle of Saratoga (October 17, 1777) later that same year.

■ OLD BENNINGTON★★
time: allow 3 hours – plan p 199

From the junction of Rtes 9 and 7 follow Rte 9 West then turn south onto Monument Avenue.

Old First Church★. – *Monument Avenue.* 1805. The white clapboarded church with its graceful lines and three-tiered steeple has been the subject of numerous photographs and paintings. The interior, with its box pews and six tall columns, each fashioned from a single pine tree, has been restored to its 19C appearance. The old cemetery in the back of the church is the resting place of Revolutionary War soldiers and early founders of Vermont. One of the white marble tombstones marks the grave of poet **Robert Frost** (1874-1963) *(p 33)* who wrote his own epitaph: "I had a lover's quarrel with the world."

Bennington Battle Monument. – *From Rte 9 West turn right onto Monument Avenue. Open April through October 9 AM to 5 PM; 50¢.*

This 306 ft obelisk was erected in 1891 to commemorate the Battle of Bennington *(above)*. The **view★★** from the observation deck (elevator) includes the Berkshires, the Green Mountains and New York State.

Old First Church and Burying Ground.

Seen from Route 9 west of Bennington, the monument, set against a backdrop of green mountains, is a picturesque sight.

Bennington Museum★. – *1 mile west of the center of Bennington on Rte 9. Open March through November 9 AM to 5 PM; closed major holidays; $4.00.*

The museum's diverse collections are related to Vermont history and life. Highlights include choice examples of fine American glassware, 19C Bennington pottery and porcelain, and the Bennington Flag, one of the oldest Stars and Stripes in existence. A large group of paintings by Grandma Moses hangs in a gallery on the ground floor.

Grandma Moses Schoolhouse. – *Adjacent to and part of the Bennington Museum.*

The story of Anna Mary Robertson Moses' *(p 30)* career as a painter is as memorable as her paintings; for Grandma Moses – as she became known – lacked formal training and did not begin to paint until the age of 70. Her simple scenes of the rural countryside and farm life had great appeal and her first show, in 1940, won her immediate fame. Grandma Moses was received by President Truman when she was 90, and continued to paint until her death at the age of 101. Her works have been shown throughout the United States and Europe and are familiar subjects of prints and greeting cards.

Several paintings by Grandma Moses and memorabilia of her life are exhibited in this schoolhouse she attended as a young girl.

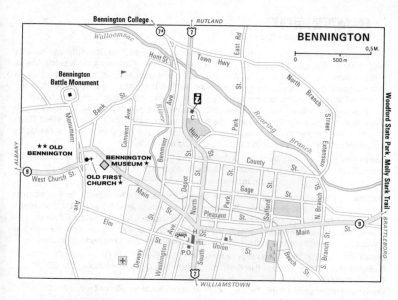

EXCURSIONS

Molly Stark Trail. – Route 9 between Bennington and Brattleboro (46 miles) is named for the wife of General John Stark *(p 198)*. From Hogback Mountain there are views into Massachusetts, and east to Mount Monadnock in New Hampshire.

Woodford State Park. – *11 miles east of Bennington on Rte 9. Open Memorial Day to Columbus Day; $1.00 per person day use.*

The 400 acre park hugs the shores of Adams Reservoir, a peaceful site encircled by trees. More than 100 campsites, a small bathing beach, a picnic area overlooking the lake, and boating are available for recreational use.

BRATTLEBORO

Michelin tourist map - fold 8 – Pop 12 081

Located at the southeastern tip of Vermont beside the Connecticut River, Brattleboro is a commercial and industrial center with a number of motels and restaurants. Brattleboro was the site of the first permanent settlement in Vermont (1724) and during the following century, the town grew owing to industry and tourism. Handsome 19C brick structures form the nucleus of the town center and preserve the atmosphere of that period when Brattleboro was evolving from a country village into an urban community. The third most heavily populated city in the state, Brattleboro is today home to wood and paper plants and is a producer of furniture, leather goods and precision tools.

Brattleboro Museum and Art Center. – *I-91 to Exit 1. Continue 1 mile into Brattleboro. The museum is off to the right (east) in the old Union Railroad Station. Open May to October 1, 12 noon (1 PM weekends) to 4 PM; closed Mondays and holidays.*

Changing exhibits related to art and history are held in this former railroad station.

BURLINGTON

Michelin tourist map - fold 7 – Pop 37 817

Located on Lake Champlain, Burlington is the urban and industrial center of Vermont. Approximately 38 000 people live here, making Burlington the most heavily populated city in a state where no other community has more than 20 000 inhabitants.

Burlington's successful past as an industrial center and commercial port in the 19C, is evidenced in the lovely residences remaining from this period. With the establishment of facilities by I.B.M., Digital Equipment Corporation and General Electric in the area, the city's industrial sector has been revitalized.

Culturally, Burlington is the site each year of the Champlain Shakespeare Festival and the Vermont Mozart Festival *(see Calendar of Events p 13)*, and benefits from the programs of art, music and theater presented by the University of Vermont.

Battery Park and **Ethan Allen Park** *(North Avenue to Ethan Allen Parkway)*, and a ride on the ferry that operates between Burlington and New York, offer good opportunities for viewing Lake Champlain.

The Ferry: Burlington — Port Kent. – *From mid-May to mid-October; time: 1 hour one way; car and driver $21.00 RT; for schedule information ☎ (802) 864-9804.*

EXCURSION

Shelburne★★★. – *Description p 204.*

Lake CHAMPLAIN

Michelin tourist map - folds 1 and 7

This immense lake (125 miles long) discovered by Samuel de Champlain in 1609, is the largest lake in the United States after the Great Lakes. Following the last Ice Age, a vast saltwater sea (Champlain Sea) invaded the Champlain Lowland, separating northern New England from the rest of the continent. As the land began to rise, free from the weight of the glaciers, the sea gradually receded, leaving the lake that one sees today.

Cradled in a broad valley between the Adirondacks and the Green Mountains, the lake's beautiful surroundings have made it a major recreation and vacation area. Three islands at the northern end of Lake Champlain: Grand Isle, North Hero and Isle la Motte are joined to Vermont by bridges, and afford views of the lake.

Isle la Motte. – A shrine honoring Saint Anne marks the site of **Fort Saint Anne** (1666), built by the French as a defense against the Mohawk Indians. The **statue of Champlain** (12 ft) was sculpted by a Vermonter, Ferdinand Weber, for the Montreal Expo (1967).

Ferries. – Ferry services operating on Lake Champlain offer scenic lake crossings between Vermont and New York. *For rates and schedule ℡ (802) 864-9804; Larrabee's Point – Fort Ticonderoga Ferry ℡ (802) 897-7999. Rates quoted, below are RT for car and driver, except for Larrabee's Point – Fort Ticonderoga Ferry (car and passengers included). Winter service conditions permitting.* Connecting points north to south are:

Grand Isle *(off of Rte 314)* – **Plattsburg:** *year round – 12 minutes; $10.00.*
Burlington *(King Street Dock)* – **Port Kent:** *mid-May to late October – 1 hour; $21.00.* The most scenic crossing.
Charlotte *(3 miles west of off of F5)* – **Essex:** *April to early January – 20 minutes; $10.00.*
Larrabee's Point *(Rte 74)* – **Fort Ticonderoga:** *May to late October – 6 minutes; $6.00.*

JAY PEAK

Michelin tourist map - fold 2

Jay Peak, located 8 miles from the border crossing at North Troy, is the prime ski area in northeastern Vermont and attracts many Canadians during the winter. An aerial tram lifts passengers to the summit *(late June to mid-October 10 AM to 4:30 PM; weekends only second and third week in September; $4.00)* from where there are **views★★** of Lake Champlain, the Adirondacks, the White Mountains, and north into Canada.

Several drives in the area are especially picturesque during Indian summer; in particular **Route 242** from Montgomery Center to Route 101, and **Route 58** from Lowell to Irasburg, which offers views of northern Vermont with the White Mountains as a backdrop.

MAD RIVER VALLEY ★

Michelin tourist map - fold 7

Remote, rural, and set in the midst of broad expanses of rolling mountainous terrain, the Mad River Valley is a premier four season resort famed for its three major ski areas: **Sugarbush, Sugarbush North** (formerly Glen Ellen) and **Mad River Glen.** The metamorphosis of this once quiet and secluded farm community into a sophisticated weekend-vacation place followed swiftly on the opening of Mad River Glen in 1947; Sugarbush began operating in the late 1950s, and in the mid-1960s came Sugarbush North. The valley's picturesque setting, abundance of accommodations from lodges to luxury trail-side condominiums, and wide range of amenities which include some of the best downhill and cross-country skiing in the East, have contributed to its great success.

Driving north on Route 100 from **Granville Gulf,** or along Route 17 through the **Appalachian Gap** (alt 2 356 ft) **views★★** of the region's unspoiled beauty unfold. An especially scenic drive is afforded by the East Warren Road from Warren to Waitsfield.

From Warren to Waitsfield★ 10 miles – allow 1 hour

The drive along the East Warren Road parallels Route 100 and the Green Mountains to the west.

From Rte 100 turn east onto the road to Warren.

Warren. – Pop 988. This tiny village has a couple of crafts shops and a country store frequented for its fresh baked goods and salads. The Warren covered bridge, reflected in the Mad River below, is a picture-perfect sight.

Leave the village to the east and drive north on the East Warren Road. After 5 miles you will pass the **Round Barn** (1908-1909), one of several which were built in the valley, and the only one still standing. *The road continues straight ahead over the Waitsfield covered bridge (1833) and into Waitsfield.*

Waitsfield. – Pop 1 440. The town has been a commercial center since the 19C when the daily stage coach from Waitsfield linked the valley with the railroad in nearby Middlesex. Two shopping centers today provide the inhabitants and guests in the area with a variety of stores and services.

Farming continues to be a principal activity in Waitsfield despite the influx of professionals and artists in recent years.

MANCHESTER *

Michelin tourist map - fold 7 – Pop 3 404

Favored as a summer resort and cultural center for more than a century, Manchester has become popular during the winter as well, with the development of **Bromley, Stratton** and **Magic Mountain** ski areas.

Manchester Center is a busy place year round with its rows of shops and restaurants, while further south off of Route 7 countrified estates are tucked among the foothills of the Taconics. In Manchester Village the **Equinox Hotel,** a stately 19C hostelry which catered to an elite clientele including Presidents Harrison, Grant, Theodore Roosevelt and Taft, has been renovated to combine modern comforts with the traditions and gracious service reminiscent of an earlier era.

To the fisherman Manchester is the home of the **Orvis Company,** producers of fishing tackle and equipment, and one of the oldest surviving fishing tackle manufacturers in the United States.

Hildene★. – *Rte 7, 2 miles south of the junction of Rtes 7 and 11/30. Guided tours (1 1/2 hours) mid-May to late October 9:30 AM to 5:30 PM; $5.00. ☎ (802) 362-1788.*

This 412 acre "hill and valley" estate was the home of Robert Todd Lincoln (1843-1926), the eldest of four children of Abraham and Mary Lincoln. The Lincoln family had vacationed in Manchester during Robert's college years. Later, when as president, then chairman of the board of the Pullman Company he sought a country retreat he chose this place, nestled between the Taconic and Green Mountains, as the site of his new home. Hildene was occupied by succeeding generations of Lincolns until the 1970s.

In the main house, a 24 room Georgian Revival mansion, an elegant staircase leads from the entrance hall to the floor above; to the left of the entrance, in the dining room, the unusual layered wall covering gives a collage effect; to the right, in the library, the dark, mahogany stained paneling conveys a subdued atmosphere. The furnishings are family pieces.

From the gardens there are panoramic views of the mountains and the valley below.

American Museum of Fly Fishing. *Rte 7. Open 10 AM to 4 PM; closed Saturday and Sunday November trough March, and major holidays; $2.00.*

Novice and serious anglers alike will be interested in this museum devoted to the history and lore of fly fishing. Early books on the subject, an extensive array of multicolored artificial flies, and the fly fishing tackle of Daniel Webster, Andrew Carnegie, Ernest Hemingway and other well-known Americans are among the artifacts in the collection.

Southern Vermont Art Center. – *From the village green, take West Road 2 miles north. Open June to mid-October 10 AM (12 noon Sunday) to 5 PM, closed Monday; the rest of the year 10 AM to 4 PM, closed Saturday and Sunday.*

Changing exhibitions of paintings, sculpture, prints and photography are held in the Georgian mansion on this mountainside estate. *Music and films are presented in July and August.*

EXCURSIONS

The Villages of Southern Vermont★★. – *Description p 194.*

Equinox Skyline Drive. – *5 miles south of Manchester by Rte 7. Open May through October 8 AM to 10 PM; $5.00 per car.*

The 5 1/2 mile drive leads to the top of Mount Equinox (alt 3 816 ft), the highest point in the Taconic Mountains. From the road the Carthusian monastery *(private)* completed in 1970 is visible in the distance.

At the summit there is a Communications Center and an inn. The **view★** reaches from the Hudson River valley deep into the Green Mountains.

Dorset★. – Pop 1 733. *6 miles north of Manchester by Rte 30.* The abandoned **quarry** on the right, 4 1/2 miles north of Manchester, was one of the first commercially exploited marble quarries in Vermont.

Dorset is an artists' colony of painters and writers attracted by the charm of the village's mountain setting. Summer theater is presented at the Dorset Playhouse.

Arlington. – Pop 2 290. *8 miles south of Manchester by Rte 7.* This tranquil village and its residents served as models for the illustrator **Norman Rockwell** *(p 30)* who at one time lived here. The **Batten Kill River** provides Arlington with some of the best trout fishing grounds in New England. From Route 7 you can admire the St. James Episcopal Church and gravestones and monuments in the old churchyard.

MIDDLEBURY ★

Michelin tourist map - fold 7 – local map p 196 – Pop 7 806

Set amidst gently sloping hills and rolling countryside, Middlebury is a very pleasant town with its pristine Congregational Church and Victorian style buildings converted into stores, restaurants and craft shops. Middlebury College, chartered in 1800, is renowned for its summer school of foreign languages and Bread Loaf School of English, which convenes at the foot of Bread Loaf Mountain in Ripton (p 196). Just outside town note the Fletcher Field House (1974), one of the most recent additions to the main campus.

■ SIGHTS

Sheldon Museum. – One Park Street. Guided tours (1 hour) June 1 to October 31, 10 AM to 5 PM, closed Sundays and holidays; the rest of the year Tuesday and Friday only 1 to 4 PM; $2.00.

In 1882 Henry Sheldon moved into this brick house with his pianos, old clocks, books and other bric-a-brac and hung out a sign that read: "Sheldon Art Museum Archaeological and Historical Society." His museum, the first of the many local museums and historical societies that have since sprung up throughout New England, today includes a country store and blacksmith shop.

Vermont State Craft Center at Frog Hollow. – Open 9:30 AM (12 noon Sunday) to 5 PM; closed Saturday and Sunday November through June.

Located in a renovated mill beside Otter Creek, the Center displays and sells fine quality blown glass, metalwork, jewelry, woodenware and handwoven fabrics made by leading Vermont craftspeople.

EXCURSIONS

Morgan Horse Farm. – In Weybridge, 1 1/2 miles northwest from Middlebury. Take Rte 123/23 West from the center of Middlebury. At the traffic circle bear right onto College Street (Rte 125), then turn right onto Rte 23 (Weybridge Street). Follow the signs to the Farm, bearing left at the fork with the covered bridge. Open May through October 9 AM to 5 PM; the rest of the year 9 AM to 4 PM; $2.00.

Little did the Vermont schoolmaster **Justin Morgan** suspect, when he obtained a colt in payment for a debt in the 1780s, that the colt would sire the first American breed of horse: the Morgan horse. Strong, thick muscled and fast the stallion was capable of outpulling draft horses in clearing logs and could outrun some of the best thoroughbreds. His descendants have been bred, raised and trained in Vermont ever since the 1790s. A major U.S. export in the 19C, the Morgan was named Vermont's official state animal in 1961.

The Morgan Horse Farm was established in the last century to carry on experimentation and development of the Morgan breed. The farm, owned since 1951 by the University of Vermont (UVM), operates exclusively as a breeding and training ground for the Morgan horse, and for educational purposes. Visitors are permitted to tour the large 19C barn where present-day descendants of the original Justin Morgan are trained and housed.

Branbury State Park ★. – In Branford, 10 miles southwest of Middlebury by Rte 7 South, then Rte 53.

This popular warm-weather destination has wooded picnic areas, a large sandy beach on lake Dunmore, and hiking trails: **Falls of Llana** (1.1 miles RT, 3/4 hour) – some difficult sections; **Silver Lake** (3 miles RT, 1 1/2 hours).

Vergennes. – Pop 2 517. 13 miles northwest of Middlebury by Rte 7 North. Vergennes, covering 1.8 sq miles and with a population of 2 500 inhabitants, is hailed as the smallest incorporated city in the United States.

Button Bay State Park, 6 miles from the town center (West Main Street to Panton Road, turn right onto Basin Harbor Road, then left on unmarked road) is named for the unusual geological formations, resembling buttons, found in the clay banks. The nature center displays "buttons" of different sizes and has exhibits on local geology. Campsites, picnic areas, foot trails, views of Lake Champlain and the Adirondacks.

MONTPELIER

Michelin tourist map - fold 8 – Pop 8 167

This small city, the capital of Vermont since 1805, is nestled among wooded hillsides that rise above the Winooski River. The golden dome of the State House, ablaze in the afternoon sun, dominates the city and is a magnificent sight when the trees are changing color in the autumn. The granite industry, which enabled the city to grow, has been supplanted in importance by state government and the insurance business.

■ SIGHTS time: 1 hour

The State House (Capitol Building). – State Street. Open weekdays 8 AM to 4 PM closed Saturdays, Sundays and holidays.

The present State House is the third erected on this site, the first (1808) and second (1836) having been destroyed by fire. The Doric columns and portico of the second State House are incorporated into the present structure, which was modeled after the Temple of Theseus in Greece. A 14 ft statue of Ceres, the goddess of Agriculture, rises from the pinnacle of the golden dome.

The legislative chambers may be visited.

Vermont Museum★. – *109 State Street; in the Pavilion Office Building. Open weekdays 8 AM to 4:30 PM year round, and Saturday and Sunday in July and August 10 AM to 4 PM.*

The Victorian facade of this building was modeled after the **Pavilion Hotel** which stood on the site between 1876 and 1965. Inside, the 19C lobby has been reconstructed. Beyond are the

The State House.

rooms occupied by the Vermont Historical Society. Displays relate to the history, economy and traditions of Vermont. A telephone switchboard dating from 1919, and a catamount that was the last panther shot in Vermont (1881), are among the exhibits.

PLYMOUTH ★
Michelin tourist map - fold 8 – Pop 414

This tiny hamlet nestled among the hills of the Green Mountains, was the birthplace of **Calvin Coolidge** (1872-1933), the 30th president of the United States. It was here, on August 3, 1923 that Vice President Coolidge, upon receiving the news of the death of President Warren Harding, was sworn into office by his father, John Coolidge, a notary public. This was the only occasion in the history of the nation, on which a president was administered the oath of office by his father.

Several buildings in the Plymouth Historic District on Route 100A *(in the village of Plymouth Notch)* are related to the life of Calvin Coolidge, and may be visited *(open mid-May to mid-October 9:30 AM to 5:30 PM; $2.00).*

The Coolidge Birthplace. – Calvin Coolidge was born in this small, modest dwelling. The house is attached to the country store once owned by his parents.

Coolidge Homestead. – Vice President Coolidge was sworn into the presidency in 1923 in this house where the family had lived from the time Calvin was a youngster.

Also in the historic district are the 19C cheese factory which is still in operation and a Barn transformed into a museum of early American tools, both of which welcome visitors.

PROCTOR ★
Michelin tourist map - fold 7 – Pop 1 967

With its string of quarries from Dorset to Lake Champlain, Vermont is the nation's leading producer of marble. The majority of the state's quarries are operated by the Vermont Marble Company in Proctor, and while it is not possible to visit the quarries being worked, others that lie abandoned may be seen near the roadside (p 201).

Marble Exhibit★. – *61 Main Street. Open late May through October 9 AM to 5:30 PM; the rest of the year weekdays only 9 AM to 4 PM; $2.50.* The exhibit, located at the Vermont Marble Company plant in Proctor, presents the origin, quarrying and finishing of marble. Polished marble slabs from Vermont and around the world are used to illustrate the rich diversity of colors and graining characteristic of this stone. Visitors may observe a sculptor at work, traditional and contemporary sculpture, and from a balcony overlook, the finishing factory. Marble bas-relief portraits of the Presidents of the United States are arranged in a special gallery.

Wilson Castle. – *West Proctor Road, south of Proctor. Guided tours (45 min) mid-May to late October 9 AM (8 AM September and October) to 6 PM; $4.00.* This massive brick mansion (1864) built by a Vermont doctor offers a glimpse of the opulence that characterized the private homes of 19C America's upper classes. Luxurious furnishings and art pieces are enhanced by the surrounding heavily carved woodwork, stained glass windows, and hand painted and polychromed ceilings. Note the Louis XVI Crown Jewel case.

RUTLAND
Michelin tourist map - fold 7 – Pop 17 809

Situated at the junction of Otter and East creeks Rutland, settled in the 1770s, is today Vermont's second largest city. The town developed into a railroad center in the 19C and marble quarrying flourished, giving Rutland the nickname "the marble city." Many small industries now thrive, producing a variety of goods.

Rutland's picturesque mountain and lake surroundings make the region a winter and summer playground. Killington – one of the largest ski resorts in the East – and Pico are among the recreation areas close by.

Norman Rockwell Museum. – *Rte 4, east of Rte 7. Open 9 AM to 5 PM, closed major holidays; $2.00.*

The museum contains hundreds of examples of the work of Norman Rockwell *(p 154)*, illustrator, humorist, and chronicler of more than half a century of American life. The series of 300 magazine covers Rockwell created for the *Saturday Evening Post* and for which he is probably best remembered, is displayed together with other magazine covers, movie and war posters, advertising work, calendars, and greeting cards which also brought him fame.

EXCURSIONS

Proctor★. – *6 miles from Rutland by Rte 4 West, then Rte 3 North. Description p 203.*

Hubbardton Battle Site. – *18 miles northwest of Rutland in East Hubbardton. Take Rte 4 West to Exit 5. Follow the signs north.* A monument and visitors center commemorate the Revolutionary War battle which occurred at Hubbardton in 1777.

Early July 1777 American troops, which had held Fort Ticonderoga since 1775, were forced by the British to surrender control of the fort. Pursued by the British, the Americans retreated into Vermont until July 7, when the two armies clashed on a hillside in East Hubbardton. The battle left both sides with hundreds of casualties, and when it was over, neither side could claim victory. However, the British decided to halt their pursuit of the colonists and to return to the fort, and for the Americans, tired and reduced in number, this was victory enough as they withdrew deeper into Vermont.

Visitors' Center. – *Open mid-May to mid-October 9:30 AM to 5:30 PM; closed Monday and Tuesday.* A small museum and a diorama of the battle are in the visitors' center.

Killington. – *10 miles east of Rutland on Rte 4; gondola station 15 miles east of Rutland on Rte 4.* Killington, with 100 trails cut on six interconnecting mountains, is one of New England's major ski resorts. The Killington gondola is the longest ski lift *(3 1/2 miles)* in the world. A ride on the gondola affords views★★ of the Green Mountains. *In the summer and fall the gondola operates 10 AM to 4 PM; late June to September 2, weekends only; late September to mid-October daily; $9.00, under 12 $6.00.*

Lake St. Catherine State Park. – *On Rte 30 in Poultney, 22 miles southwest of Rutland. Take Rte 4 to Exit 4, then Rte 30 South. Open Memorial Day weekend to Columbus Day weekend; $1.00 per person day use.*

Cool gentle breezes sweep over the surface of Lake St. Catherine, making this a good site for sailboarding. Facilities include two small swimming beaches, campsites, boat launch and nature trails; there is good fishing for trout and northern pike.

ST. JOHNSBURY
Michelin tourist map - fold 8 – Pop 7 844

This small city began to prosper in the 1830s when a grocer named **Thaddeus Fairbanks** invented and began to manufacture the platform scale here. Fairbanks scales have been produced and shipped around the world ever since. The **St. Johnsbury Athenaeum** (a library and art gallery) and the **Fairbanks Museum of Natural Science and Planetarium**, both in the downtown area, were established by the Fairbanks family, devoted patrons of their hometown.

Trucking and the production of maple syrup are major occupations in St. Johnsbury.

Maple Grove Museum. – *On Rte 2 east of the city center. Open late May through October 8 AM to 4 PM; 50¢.*

Exhibits and brief films illustrate how maple syrup is harvested and produced. The tour introduces visitors to the step-by-step procedures involved in transforming maple syrup into Maple Grove candies.

Northeast Kingdom★★. – *Description p 196.*

SHELBURNE ★★★
Michelin tourist map - fold 7 – Pop 5 421

Shelburne town comprises Shelburne Village, Shelburne Falls and Shelburne Harbor, sedate pastoral communities on Lake Champlain with sweeping vistas of the Adirondacks and the Green Mountains. During the glory days of steamboat travel a shipyard on Shelburne Bay turned out vessels that carried passengers and freight on the lake. The SS *Ticonderoga (see p 206)* the last of these steamers, was launched from a local pier in 1906.

A lakeshore resort for many years, Shelburne's fame today rests primarily on the Shelburne Museum, a museum of Americana which preserves the early spirit of the nation.

■ **SHELBURNE MUSEUM**★★★ *time: allow 1 day - plan p 205*

The Shelburne Museum is more than a museum, it is a collection of collections. homecrafts, folk arts, trade tools, transportation, fine arts, furnishings and architecture representing three centuries of American life, history and art. The collections are displayed in the museum's thirty-five buildings spread across 45 acres near the banks of Lake Champlain.

The museum was established in 1947 by **Electra Havemeyer Webb** and her husband **J. Watson Webb,** a wealthy Vermonter. An avid collector of art, especially American crafts and folk art, Mrs. Webb assembled varied collections of Americana over the years, then purchased a number of old barns, dwellings and other structures and had them moved to Shelburne to house the collections. Within ten years, Shelburne had its own church, school, jail, barns, houses, a general store, even a lighthouse, railway depot and steamboat. Meticulously restored and filled with the treasures gathered by Mrs. Webb, each of these buildings and exhibits has its own story to tell of America's past.

VISIT

Open mid-May to mid-October 9 AM to 5 PM; $9.50, under 17, $4.00. Cafeteria on the grounds. The museum's principal buildings and collections are described below.

Round Barn★★. – Built in 1901, this is one of the few remaining round wooden barns in Vermont. The labor-saving design of the circular three-story barn became popular around the turn of the century, prior to the developments of modern technology. Hay was loaded into the huge central silo from the upper level and the animals, held in stalls surrounding the silo on the middle level, could be easily fed by one person.

The barn contains agricultural exhibits and equipment.

Circus Parade Building★. – The semicircular building houses a 525 ft model circus parade, carousel horses and hundreds of circus posters. The circus parade is remarkable for its accuracy of detail.

Beach Gallery and Beach Hunting Lodge. – Nature and hunting are the themes of these collections. Paintings, trophies and Indian artifacts are shown.

Shelburne Railroad Station★★. – This is a classic example of the Victorian style railroad stations that were built across America in the 19C. The private car Grand Isle (outside the station) was owned by former Vermont governor William C. Smith.

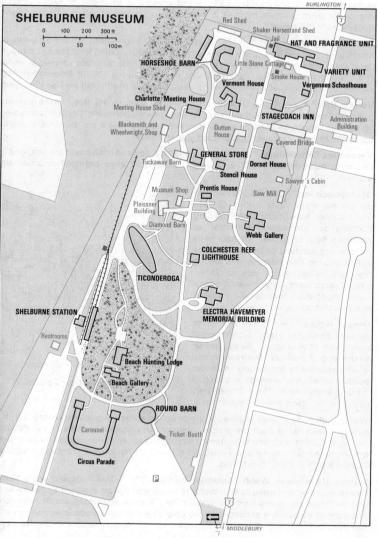

SS Ticonderoga★★. – After steaming along on Lake Champlain for almost fifty years hauling passengers, freight and other tourist traffic, this side-wheeler was saved from the scrap heap in the 1950s by Shelburne Museum. A specially constructed dike allowed workers to transfer the *Ti* out of water to a series of tracks which extended several miles overland to Shelburne; a film shown on the *Ticonderoga* illustrates this feat. Inside, exhibits and the plush decor recall the *Ti's* past as a luxurious steamship.

Colchester Reef Lighthouse★★. – 1871. Located at one time in the waters off of Colchester Point in Lake Champlain, the lighthouse was moved to Shelburne where it now serves as a gallery of marine art. Paintings, photos, figureheads, scrimshaw and lithographs depict whaling and the great days of sail.

Prentis House. – 1733. This 18C house is impeccably furnished with antiques.

Stencil House★. – 1790. The interior contains splendid examples of decorative wall stenciling.

Tuckaway General Store★★. – 1840. This brick building which originally stood in Shelburne houses a general store, post office, barbershop, dentist's and doctor's office and apothecary shop. On the first floor every item imaginable necessary for daily living on a farm will be found on the shelves, hanging from the ceiling or tacked onto the timbered posts of the store.

Upstairs in the doctor's and dentist's offices, are displays of their instruments. The apothecary shop contains remedies guaranteed to cure almost any ailment.

Charlotte Meeting House. – 1840. The simple brick meetinghouse has been refurbished with new wooden pews and *trompe l'œil* wall panels.

Vermont House. – 1790. Furnished like the home of a New England sea captain, this dwelling contains colorful wallpapers illustrating port scenes.

Horseshoe Barn★★★. – 1949. This barn, in the shape of an enormous horseshoe, houses more than 140 horse-drawn carriages and sleighs. Among the phaetons and buggies on the second floor is a calèche and a luxurious **Berlin** with an exquisite satin interior. Concord coaches, buggies, a conestoga wagon and brightly painted peddlers' wagons are in the Annex.

Hat and Fragrance Unit★★. – 1800. Among the varied collections is a superb group of American quilts: appliqué, pieced work, reverse appliqué, dating from the 17C through the present. With their intricate pattern and needlework these quilts are admired as works of art. Victorian dollhouses, Parisian gowns designed in the 19C for America's richest women, hooked rugs, lace samplers and an assortment of needlecraft are also displayed.

Variety Unit★★. – c. 1835. This is the only building that originally stood on the museum grounds. The unit houses numerous examples of pewter, porcelain, clocks and amusing figure jugs known as Toby mugs. On the second floor there are all kinds of dolls: porcelain, bisque, wax, dried apple, wood, paper mâché.

Vergennes Schoolhouse★. – The books, charts, maps and chalkboard are arranged in this brick schoolhouse (1830) as though the children were expected to arrive any moment.

Stagecoach Inn★★. – 1783. Formerly an inn on the stage route linking Canada and southern New England, the building contains an outstanding collection of American folk sculpture. An enormous wooden eagle carved for the Marine Base at Portsmouth, New Hampshire is among the many other eagles, weather vanes, ships figureheads, sternboards, trade signs, cigar store Indians and carousel figures found throughout the Inn.

Dorset House★. – c. 1840. The house contains Shelburne's famous collection of more than 1 000 decoys: ducks, geese, swans and shorebirds. The realism and artistry attained by the carvers of decoys benefited the hunter, while decoys such as those executed by A. Elmer Crowell were intended for decorative purposes only.

(From a photo by Forwards Color Productions Inc.

Shelburne Museum – Cigar Store Figures.

Webb Gallery★. – Three hundred years of American painting are represented in th gallery. Works range from the simple, anonymous primitive portraits of the colonia period, through the classic seascapes (Fitz Hugh Lane) and landscapes (Hudson Rive school) of the 19C and include a selection of canvases by contemporary artists such a Andrew Wyeth and Grandma Moses.

Electra Havemeyer Webb Memorial Building★★. – This imposing white Gree Revival mansion dedicated to Mrs. Webb contains works of art acquired by her parents and six complete rooms from the Webb's Park Avenue apartment. Inside, the war understated elegance is enhanced by the English paneling, European furnishings an paintings by Rembrandt, Corot, Manet, Degas, Monet... hung in the rooms and hallway

■ ADDITIONAL SIGHT

Shelburne Farms. – *Follow Harbor Road east from Shelburne Center. Guided tours (1 1/2 hour) June to mid-October 9:30 and 11 AM and 12:30, 2 and 3 PM; $5.00. Visitor Center open year round 9 AM to 5 PM.*

This agricultural estate in the grand style of the 19C was the country home of the wealthy businessman **William Seward Webb** and his wife, **Lila Vanderbilt Webb**, granddaughter of the "Commodore." The Webbs had been attracted to the area by its beautiful setting on the shore of Lake Champlain and after acquiring the 30-odd farms which originally stood on the property, they turned to the architect Robert Robertson, the landscape designer Frederick Law Olmsted *(p 91)*, and Gifford Pinchot, one of the nation's first conservationists, to plan and build Shelburne Farms. The terrain was leveled, buildings razed and in their place was created a new park-like landscape of undulating knolls and forests studded with Queen Anne structures. At its peak the Webb estate, encompassing 3 800 acres of fields, pasture and woodlands, was the family residence as well as a "model" farm known for its advanced methods and experimentation in crop raising and animal husbandry.

Reduced in size over the years to about 1 000 acres, Shelburne Farms continues to operate as a working experimental farm and learning center. The **Farm Barn** (1888) – an enormous turreted structure enclosing a two acre courtyard – and the **Coach Barn** (1901), two of the principal buildings on the property, serve as centers for programs in conservation and rural land use.

Shelburne House (1899), a 110 room mansion with **views**★★ of Lake Champlain and the Adirondacks, is the setting for educational and cultural events and summer lawn concerts to which the public is invited.

EXCURSION

Vermont Wildflower Farm. – *On Rte 7 in Charlotte 5 miles south of Shelburne. Open May through October 10 AM to 5 PM; $2.00. An audio-visual presentation (15 min) on New England wildflowers and foliage is included in the admission.*

The many species of wildflowers growing in the farm's field and woodland habitats transform the landscape into a wonderful display of changing color spring through fall. The familiar Jack-in-the-pulpit, black-eyed Susan, aster, Devil's paintbrush are here in abundance together with dozens of other lesser-known varieties. Descriptive panels accompany the plants, providing interesting facts and anecdotes (*daisy* is from "day's eye," the comparison referring to the golden center believed by the ancients to represent the sun) regarding the history, legends, and uses of some of the flowers.

STOWE ★
Michelin tourist map - folds 8 and 2 – Pop 3 167

As Route 108 winds north into this small village situated in a valley at the foot of Mount Mansfield, Stowe's distinctive landmark, the slim white spire of Christ Community Church, is visible to the right. The valley's exceptionally long snow season, thus the expression – "There is always snow at Stowe" – coupled with an abundance of picturesque Swiss style chalets, and motels, lodges and restaurants lining the main road *(Rte 108)*, have made Stowe a principal northeast ski resort. In season up to 8 000 skiers ranging from beginners to expert use the trail systems on the slopes of Stowe's two interconnected mountains: **Mount Mansfield,** Vermont's highest peak (alt 4 393 ft), and **Spruce Peak** (alt 3 320 ft).

A summer resort as well, Stowe has horseback riding, hiking, swimming, mountain climbing, summer theater and concerts to offer vacationers.

■ SIGHTS
time: 3 hours

Trapp Family Lodge. – *Follow Rte 108 North 2 miles, then turn left at the Trapp Family sign in front of the white church.*

The Trapp family of *Sound of Music* fame chose this setting as the site for their home because it reminded them of their native Austria.

The main Lodge (1983) replaces and was inspired by the original lodge, a Tyrolian chalet which burned in 1980. Open year round it is a major resort and ski touring center with 60 miles of trails.

Mount Mansfield ★★. – From the summit of Mount Mansfield, the highest point in Vermont, there is a sweeping **view** ★★ of the entire region: Lake Champlain and the Adirondacks west, Jay Peak and on a clear day Montreal north; and east to the White Mountains.

During the 1930s when a skier had to climb the mountain he was going to ski down, Mount Mansfield's unplowed Toll Road was the only ski trail on the mountain. Today a network of well-groomed ski and hiking trails lace the slopes of the mountain.

Mount Mansfield Auto Road. – *Rte 108 North 7 miles from Stowe. Open late May to mid-October (weather permitting) 9:30 AM to 5 PM; $6.00 per car.*

The Auto Road *(toll)* is a 4 1/2 mile gravel road that leads to a point near the summit. From there it is a 1 1/2 mile hike to the top.

Mount Mansfield Gondola. – *Rte 108 North 8 miles from Stowe. Operates late June to mid-October (weather permitting) 9:30 AM to 5 PM; $6.00 RT.*
 The gondola lift provides access to a point near the summit; the summit can be reached by a short, very steep trail.

Alpine Slide. – *Spruce Peak Ski Area Rte 108, 8 1/4 miles north of Stowe. Operates late June to Labor Day 9:30 AM to 5 PM; late May to late June and after Labor Day through foliage season Saturday and Sunday only 9:30 AM to 5 PM; $4.00, children $3.00.*
 This is one of the numerous ski areas in New England where an alpine slide *(p 178)* will be found operating on mountain slopes during the milder seasons.

Bingham Falls. – *1/2 mile north of the Auto Road there is a path (difficult to find) to the right that leads through the woods to the falls.*
 A series of waterfalls is formed by the West River as it tumbles through a ravine.

Smugglers Notch★★. – *Rte 108, 8 miles north of Stowe (closed in the winter).*
 The road linking Stowe and Jeffersonville is extremely narrow and climbs rapidly as it twists through the rugged scenic notch (alt 2 162 ft) between Mount Mansfield and Spruce Peak. The forest allows little light to enter the area even on a bright day. Caution should be exerted while proceeding between the large roadside boulders that have split from the walls of the notch. During the War of 1812 cattle, liquor, slaves and other contraband were smuggled from the U.S. into Canada through this pass, giving it its name.

WINDSOR
Michelin tourist map - fold 8 – Pop 4 004

 This historic town on the banks of the Connecticut River was the birthplace of Vermont in 1777. Representatives meeting here that year agreed upon the official name – "Vermont;" declared Vermont an independent republic; and drew up its first constitution, the first constitution in the nation to prohibit slavery and grant the right to vote without regard to property ownership or individual wealth.
 In the 19C several inventions including the hydraulic pump and the coffee percolator were developed in Windsor. The town is a center of the machine tool industry as illustrated by the **American Precision Museum** *(196 Main Street).*

Constitution House. – *16 North Main Street. Open mid-May to mid-October 10 AM to 5 PM.* Delegates meeting in this old tavern July 1777 drew up Vermont's first constitution. Historical memorabilia and examples of early Vermont crafts and industries are arranged in the Old Taproom, Sitting Room, kitchen and other tavern rooms.

Vermont State Craft Center in Windsor. – *Main Street. Open 9 AM (12 noon Sunday) to 5 PM; closed Sundays January through April, July 4, Thanksgiving Day, December 25 and January 1.* Located in Windsor House, a restored 19C Greek Revival hotel, the Center features the work of Vermont's finest crafts people. Pottery, weavings, jewelry, leather goods, glassware, stuffed and wooden toys are among the hundreds of original items displayed in the retail gallery on the first and second floors.

Windsor-Cornish Covered Bridge. – *South of the Constitution House, after two sets of lights turn left.* Spanning the Connecticut River between New Hampshire and Vermont, this is the longest covered bridge (460 ft) in New England.

WOODSTOCK ★★
Michelin tourist map - fold 8 – Pop 3 315

 A touch of urban elegance and sophistication has characterized this pretty village since the 18C when it was selected as the Windsor County seat. Businessmen, lawyers, doctors and teachers settled here during the next two centuries, building frame, brick and stone dwellings and shops which reflected the wealth and good taste of the community. A lack of industrial development in the 19C and the devotion of the town's affluent families to preserving Woodstock's early architectural ensemble, have allowed the gracious 18 and 19C structures bordering the green and lining Elm, Pleasant and Central Streets to remain basically unchanged over the years.

HISTORICAL NOTES

 Established in 1761 by settlers from Massachusetts, Woodstock developed quickly after it was selected as the county seat. Mills were built on the outskirts of town and tradesmen, working in shops surrounding the green, provided most of the goods needed for daily living. Woodstock was self-sufficient and prosperous. During the heyday of the 19C "water cures" the village became a fashionable summer vacation spot.
 In 1934 skiers experimenting with a Model T motor and a piece of cable on a hill near Mount Tom (outside of Woodstock) developed the nation's first ski tow. Twenty years later a poma lift, then more modern lifts: chairs, aerial trams were adopted by Vermont' burgeoning ski industry. While the ski tow devised 50 years ago near Mount Tom is still remembered for the role it played in the history of skiing in the United States, today the most modern equipment is used at **Suicide Six**, a ski area nearby.
 The **Woodstock Inn**, facing the green, was opened in 1969. The hotel's 120 rooms and diversified facilities have increased Woodstock's ability to accommodate conventions and seminars.

■ **SIGHTS** *time: 2 hours*

To enjoy Woodstock you should stroll along **Elm** and **Pleasant Streets**, browse in the emporia and galleries that line **Central Street**, and walk across the covered bridge (in the middle of town) that spans the Ottauquechee River. The Town Crier bulletin board near the corner of Elm and Central Streets has notices regarding auctions, flea markets and other events.

The Green★. – The oval-shaped green is fringed with buildings of different styles: Federal mansions, the **Windsor County Courthouse** (Greek Revival) and the **Norman Williams Library** (Romanesque).

Woodstock Historical Society★. – *26 Elm Street. Guided tours (1 hour) May through October 10 AM (2 PM Sunday) to 5 PM; $2.50.*

Constructed in 1807 by the merchant Charles Dana the house contains furnishings, clocks, dolls and clothing formerly owned by Woodstock families.

Billings Farm and Museum★. – *River Road. Follow Elm Street, cross the bridge, then .2 mile on River Road. Open early May to third week in October 10 AM to 4 PM; $4.00. The slide show (8 min) is an introduction to the farm and life in rural Vermont in the late 19C.*

The Billings Farm is both an operating modern-day dairy farm and a museum depicting life on a Vermont farm in 1890. The farm was established in 1871 by lawyer-businessman **Frederick Billings** whose interest in animal husbandry and conservation led him to stock the farm with pure breed Jersey cattle, and to plant thousands of trees in the area to replace the woodlands which had been exhausted by lumbering. The Billing's herd, a prize winner over the years, continues to be a blue ribbon winner to this day.

The exhibits are housed in several restored barns. Life-size displays illustrate the daily and seasonal activities performed by a 19C Vermont family: there are the tasks still performed – preparing the land, planting, threshing, sugaring; and those which are no longer common – ice harvesting, butter-making, cheese-making. Examples of the tools, implements and equipment used are shown and described.

The rural community, in many cases the family's only contact with the outside world, is presented through a series of scenes which recreate the interior of a church, school and country store.

EXCURSIONS

Plymouth★. – *15 miles southwest of Woodstock by Rte 4 West, then Rte 100A. Description p 203*

Quechee Gorge. – *6 miles east of Woodstock on Rte 4.*

Quechee Gorge, formed during thousands of years by the erosive action of the Ottauquechee River, is spanned by the Route 4 highway bridge. The sheer walls of the gorge rise approximately 165 ft from the river below. Best seen from the bridge on Route 4.

A trail, steep in sections, leads to the bottom of the gorge: *1.2 miles RT, time: 3/4 hr. Insect repellent advised during the bug season.*

Silver Lake State Park. – *In Barnard. 10 miles north of Woodstock by Rte 12.*

The park, within walking distance of Barnard village, has a small beach on the lake, a picnic area, and campsites set in a pine grove. There is a country store on the grounds.

BOOKS TO READ

Art — Economy — Geography — History

How New England Happened by Christina Tree *(Little, Brown and Company, Boston, 1976)*.

The New England States by Neal R. Peirce *(W.W. Norton and Company, Inc., New York, 1976)*.

New England Wilds by Ogden Tanner and the Editors of Time-Life Books *(Time-Life Books, New York, 1986)*.

A Guide to New England's Landscape by Neil Jorgensen *(Barre Publishing Co., Inc., Barre, Massachusetts, 1980)*.

The Flowering of American Folk Art by Jean Lipman and Alice Winchester *(Penguin Books, New York, 1980)*.

Young America, A Folk-Art History by Jean Lipman, Elizabeth V. Warren and Robert Bishop *(Hudson Hills Press, Inc., New York, New York, 1986)*.

The Boston Globe Historic Walks in Old Boston by John Harris *(The Globe Pequot Press, Chester, Connecticut, 1984)*.

Nature — Trail Guides

Summer and Fall Wildflowers by Marilyn S. Dwelley *(Downeast Enterprise, Inc., Camden, Maine, 1986)*.

Connecticut Walk Book *(Connecticut Forest and Park Association, Inc., East Hartford, Connecticut, 1984)*.

Collection Fifty Hikes (series presented by state) *(Back Country Publications, Woodstock, Vermont, 1983)*.

Guides published by the Appalachian Mountain Club *(5 Joy Street, Boston, Massachusetts, 02108)*.

Guide to Baxter State Park and Katahdin by Stephen Clark *(Thorndike Press, Thorndike, Maine, 1986)*.

Guide Book of the Long Trail *(Green Mountain Club, Inc., Rutland, Vermont, 1985)*.

Inns — Bed and Breakfast

Bed and Breakfast in New England by Bernice Chesler *(Globe Pequot Press, Inc., Chester, Connecticut, 1987)*.

Country Inns and Back Roads *(Berkshire Traveller Press, Stockbridge, Massachusetts, 1987)*.

A Guide to the Recommended Country Inns of New England by Suzy Chapin and Elizabeth Squier *(Globe Pequot Press, Inc., Chester, Connecticut, 1987)*.

Literature *(p 33)*

The works mentioned below can be obtained through public libraries.

Moby Dick by Herman Melville

The Scarlet Letter by Nathaniel Hawthorne

The Bostonians by Henry James

The Country of the Pointed Firs by Sara Orne Jewett

The Late George Apley by John P. Marquand

The Last Puritan by George Santayana

Two Years Before the Mast by Richard Henry Dana

The Outermost House by Henry Beston

INDEX

Boston (Mass.) . . . .   Major towns, cities, points of interest and tourist regions.

North Landgrove (Vt.) . . . .   Other towns, cities and points of interest referred to.

Gardner, Isabella Stewart   Historical events, persons and particular terms appearing in the text.

Sharon (Conn.) . . . . fold 13   Location on Michelin tourist map of picturesque villages and ski areas not described in the guide.

MANUFACTURE FRANÇAISE DES PNEUMATIQUES MICHELIN
Société en commandite par actions au capital de 700 000 000 de francs
place des Carmes-Déchaux - 63 Clermont-Ferrand (France)
R.C.S. Clermont-Fd B 855 200 507

© Michelin et Cie, Propriétaires-Éditeurs 1987
Dépôt légal 12-87 - ISBN 2 06 015 693 - 9 - ISSN 0763-1383

Printed in France - 12-87-28
Photocomposition : IOTA, Nanterre - Impression : AUBIN IMPRIMEUR à Ligugé-Poitiers, nº P 28969

YANKEE INGENUITY, MICHELIN INNOVATION... PIONEERS FOR PROGRESS!

When the first colonists arrived in New England they immediately set about the business of exploring the resources of this vast new nation, America. These pioneers carved their way through the wilderness, spanned a continent, and laid the groundwork for countless future technological advancements.

This same pioneering spirit is what has made Michelin the leader in radial tire technology. When we introduced the radial tire in 1948, we knew it was only a matter of time before America would recognize the need for radials. Our constant research and innovation in tire excellence continues in order to serve America's growing need for high quality radial tires.

SEE NEW ENGLAND ON MICHELIN!

Colonial New England offers the tourist and native alike a variety of things to do and see for all ages, every season. See historic monuments, faithfully-restored colonial villages, covered bridges and quaint lighthouses. Taste a delicious lobster dinner or sample maple syrup right from the tree. Ski down the slopes or swim in the blue-green Atlantic.

New England has it all!

If you travel by car, Michelin suggests that you check the condition of your tires. Be sure that they are properly inflated and inspect them for signs of wear. If your tires are worn and need replacing, your authorized Michelin dealer has a wide selection of quality Michelin 'X' radials in stock at a price you can afford.

Wherever you travel, there's only one name to remember when you need tires … Michelin … we put America on radials!